# THE FUTURE OF INTERNATIONAL LAW

The world is changing rapidly, and there are increasing calls for international legal responses. There is and will be increasing social change in areas such as globalization, development, demography, democratization, and technology. Because of this change, international relations does and will occupy an expanding proportion of the concerns of citizens and the responsibilities of states. This will drive greater production of international law and organizational structures. The resulting denser body of law and organizations will take on more prominent governmental functions. It is in this sense that the future of international law is global government. This book draws together the theoretical and practical aspects of international-cooperation needs and legal responses in critical areas of international concern. On this basis, the book predicts that a more extensive, powerful, and varied international legal system will be needed to cope with future opportunities and challenges.

Joel P. Trachtman is Professor of International Law at The Fletcher School of Law and Diplomacy at Tufts University. The author of more than eighty scholarly publications, Professor Trachtman has written books including *The International Law of Economic Migration: Toward the Fourth Freedom* (2009); *Ruling the World: Constitutionalism, International Law, and Global Governance* (2009); *Developing Countries in the WTO Legal System* (2009); *The Economic Structure of International Law* (2008); and *International Law and International Politics* (2008). He has consulted for the United Nations, the Organization for Economic Cooperation and Development, the Asia-Pacific Economic Cooperation organization, the World Bank, the Organization of American States, and the U.S. Agency for International Development. He has served as a member of the boards of the *American Journal of International Law*, the *European Journal of International Law*, the *Journal of International Economic Law*, the *Cambridge Review of International Affairs*, and the *Singapore Yearbook of International Law*.

ASIL Studies in International Legal Theory

Series Editors

Elizabeth Andersen (ASIL)
Mortimer Sellers (University of Baltimore)

Editorial Board

Samantha Besson (Université de Fribourg)
Allen Buchanan (Duke University)
David Kennedy (Harvard University)
Jan Klabbers (University of Helsinki)
David Luban (Georgetown University)
Larry May (Vanderbilt University)
Mary Ellen O'Connell (University of Notre Dame)
Onuma Yasuaki (Meiji University)
Helen Stacy (Stanford University)
John Tasioulas (University College London)
Fernando Tesón (Florida State University)

The purpose of the ASIL Studies in International Legal Theory series is to clarify and improve the theoretical foundations of international law. Too often the progressive development and implementation of international law has foundered on confusion about first principles. This series raises the level of public and scholarly discussion about the structure and purposes of the world legal order and how best to achieve global justice through law.

This series grows out of the International Legal Theory project of the American Society of International Law. The ASIL Studies in International Legal Theory series deepens this conversation by publishing scholarly monographs and edited volumes of essays considering subjects in international legal theory.

Volumes in the Series

**International Criminal Law and Philosophy** edited by Larry May and Zachary Hoskins (2010)
**Customary International Law: A New Theory with Practical Applications** by Brian D. Lepard (2010)
**The New Global Law** by Rafael Domingo (2010)
**The Role of Ethics in International Law** edited by Donald Earl Childress III (2011)
**Global Justice and International Economic Law: Opportunities and Prospects** edited by Chios Carmody, Frank J. Garcia, and John Linarelli (2011)
**Parochialism, Cosmopolitanism, and the Foundations of International Law** edited by Mortimer Sellers (2012)
**Morality, Jus Post Bellum, and International Law** edited by Larry May and Andrew T. Forcehimes (2012)

# The Future of International Law
## Global Government

JOEL P. TRACHTMAN
Tufts University, The Fletcher School

CAMBRIDGE
UNIVERSITY PRESS

32 Avenue of the Americas, New York NY 10013-2473, USA

Cambridge University Press is part of the University of Cambridge.

It furthers the University's mission by disseminating knowledge in the pursuit of education, learning and research at the highest international levels of excellence.

www.cambridge.org
Information on this title: www.cambridge.org/9781107435858

© Joel P. Trachtman 2013

This publication is in copyright. Subject to statutory exception
and to the provisions of relevant collective licensing agreements,
no reproduction of any part may take place without the written
permission of Cambridge University Press.

First published 2013
First paperback edition 2014

*A catalogue record for this publication is available from the British Library*

*Library of Congress Cataloguing in Publication data*

Trachtman, Joel P.
The future of international law : global government / Joel P. Trachtman, Tufts University, The Fletcher School.
　　pages cm. – (ASIL studies in international legal theory)
Includes bibliographical references and index.
ISBN 978-1-107-03589-8 (hardback)
1. International law.　2. International organization.　I. Title.
KZ3410.T728　　2013
341–dc23　　　2012037612

ISBN　978-1-107-03589-8　Hardback
ISBN　978-1-107-43585-8　Paperback

Cambridge University Press has no responsibility for the persistence or accuracy of URLs for external or third-party internet websites referred to in this publication, and does not guarantee that any content on such websites is, or will remain, accurate or appropriate.

## 2013

Are we speaking of hollistic soft instead of lex montoria   → re βεαιναςι ίου ου βυτζη

*To my students – past, present, and future.*

— Will International remain the same?
  NO holistic
— Will the need of "international" increase?
  YES and the need of reg-lation
— Will international law have the same shape?
— Will the regulation have the same form?
  NO   net not pyramid
— Will the actors be the same?

the most evolutive form in the cosmos is spider <ιστος

# Contents

| | | |
|---|---|---|
| Preface | | page xi |
| Acknowledgments | | xiii |
| 1 | Introduction: The Crisis in International Law | 1 |
| 2 | Reasons for International Law and Organization | 22 |
| 3 | International Law and Organization as a System for Transnational Political Linkage | 41 |
| 4 | The Futurology of International Law | 66 |
| 5 | Cyberspace and Cybersecurity | 85 |
| 6 | Human Rights | 118 |
| 7 | Environmental Protection and Public Health | 146 |
| 8 | Global Regulation of Finance | 168 |
| 9 | Economic Liberalization: Trade, Intellectual Property, Migration, and Investment | 193 |
| 10 | Fragmentation, Synergy, Coherence, and Institutional Choice | 217 |
| 11 | International Legal Constitutionalization | 253 |
| 12 | Conclusion: Functionalism Revisited | 288 |
| Index | | 299 |

# Preface

As I finalize this book in the summer of 2012, it is not difficult to see some of its concerns raised in current newspaper headlines. The Euro zone will either collapse or be fortified by stronger centralization of fiscal and monetary authority. The recently discovered "Flame" virus has prompted calls by Russia for a cyberweapon ban. The financial crisis continues to reverberate with new banking scandals. The international community is unable to craft a meaningful response to Syrian despotism. Unusual weather patterns cause avalanches and other natural disasters.

The world is changing rapidly, and there are increasing calls for international legal responses. Although the world changes in diverse ways, occasioning diverse challenges, there are important commonalities among the changes, challenges, and responses available to us. Getting ahead of these challenges will require us to think about the future, and to use the international legal tools available to us more creatively and without the artificial constraints of sovereigntist biases. The challenges to society increasingly transcend national borders, and this book argues that governmental functions, too, will sometimes be required to transcend national borders. International law is the main formal mechanism by which governmental functions can transcend national borders.

This book is an attempt to draw together some of the theoretical and practical aspects of international-cooperation needs and legal responses in some of the critical areas of international public policy. International policy professionals, among them international lawyers, tend to examine only their particular functional areas, such as trade, human rights, finance, environment, or security. This specialization is perfectly appropriate and responsible, but occasionally it is useful for each of us to climb out of our individual silo and survey the similarities, differences, conflicts, and synergies among the different functional areas.

# Acknowledgments

This book has benefited greatly from its exposure to and responses from my graduate students at The Fletcher School of Law and Diplomacy. All of the chapters have formed the basis for lectures, and most have been imposed on students as readings at one time or another. I have also benefited from helpful suggestions from colleagues, both at The Fletcher School and elsewhere. I have presented portions of this book at the American Law Institute, the American Society of International Law, Case Western, Columbia, the European Society of International Law, European University Institute, George Mason, Georgia, Hamburg, Harvard, Hong Kong, Meiji, NYU, Temple, UCLA, Virginia, Warwick, and Yale, and have benefited from discussions with and received helpful comments on various portions of this work from many kind colleagues. These include Anne van Aaken, William Alford, Diane Marie Amann, Douglas Arner, Gabriella Blum, Anu Bradford, Rachel Brewster, Howard Chang, Antonia Chayes, Harlan Cohen, Juscelino Colares, Cosette Creamer, Lori Fisler Damrosch, Jeff Dunoff, Caroline Gideon, Michael Glennon, Gene Grossman, Hurst Hannum, Ian Johnstone, Neil Komesar, Nico Krisch, Matthias Kumm, Chin Leng Lim, Miguel Maduro, Petros Mavroidis, Timothy Meyer, Andrew Moravcsik, Junji Nakagawa, Gerard Neuman, Jide Nzelibe, Kal Raustiala, Peter Bowman Rutledge, Jeswald Salacuse, Greg Shaffer, Beth Simmons, Paul Stephan, Christian Turner, Joseph Weiler, and Peer Zumbansen. I could not have completed this work without research assistance from Sanhita Ambast, Anusha Jayatilake, Jeremy Leong, and Filippo Ravalico.

# 1   Introduction: The Crisis in International Law

> In international law it is today of both theoretical and practical importance to distinguish between the international law of "coexistence," governing essentially diplomatic inter-state relations, and the international law of co-operation, expressed in the growing structure of international organization and the *pursuit* of common human interests.
> Wolfgang Friedmann, *The Changing Structure of International Law* (1964)

International law is the precursor of international government, and international government is nothing more than an intensification of international law. Similar to international society, international law has constantly evolved from its inception. There is no reason to believe that its evolution has ceased. Similar to natural evolution, the evolution of international law responds to changing conditions. This book thus claims that international law evolves functionally: it changes as its constituents determine new uses. The new uses evolve with factors such as globalization, development, demography, technology, and democratization, as well as with our understanding of our situation.

Indeed, international law may grow in a way similar to municipal law: establishing basic property rights and rules of security first and turning to creation of public goods and regulatory purposes later. As Wolfgang Friedmann explained, early international law only needed to be concerned with the right to territory, the commencement and conduct of war, and the treatment of emissaries. These were the requirements in a world where there were few externalities or public goods worth addressing, and in which most cooperation problems could be addressed through ad hoc and informal diplomacy. Under more interdependence, greater international law becomes functionally useful. It is clear that a static vision of the structure and function of the international legal system would be ignorant of this dynamism. Moreover, as the needs addressed by international law grow and its functions broaden, structural changes become appropriate.

The main argument of this book has five principal threads. First, expected changes in globalization, economic development, demography, technology, and democracy suggest greater need for international law in a number of areas of cooperation. These needs can be understood as a broadening of the domain of international law, but in addition, some of these needs will necessitate fortification of the power of international law. As greater issues are addressed among asymmetric states over longer periods of time, a stronger version of international law will be required. No longer will we be able to accept the concept that, to be effective, individual international legal rules must take the form of self-enforcing contracts.

Second, because domestic politics is increasingly insufficient to address important areas of public policy alone, international law's principal function is to serve as a mechanism by which the domestic politics of different states can be linked, in order to construct a formal mechanism of international politics. Within domestic politics, this international political linkage allows for the formation of domestic political coalitions that could not be formed in autarky. International law is thus a mechanism by which the costs or benefits to other states can be brought to bear on national decision making.

Third, although there are many ways in which international cooperation can take place within narrow fields, there are also many linkages, natural and constructed, between different narrow fields. Natural linkages are the types of issues that we generally consider under the heading "fragmentation," where a rule in a particular area has effects on the achievement of policy goals in another area. Natural linkages grow as more areas of international law are developed in greater depth, and these natural linkages are already pervasive. As the volume of international law grows, more natural linkages arise, precipitating the need to determine how different areas of law relate to one another. Constructed linkages may be devised in order to induce agreements that might not otherwise occur.

Fourth, as linkages occur naturally or are constructed, and as the aggregate volume of international law increases, these linkages make it more likely that states will comply with international law. This enhancement of potential enforceability actually increases the utility of international law and therefore induces states to make more international law. It is worth noting that there will still be many instances in which states choose not to establish international law with maximal enforcement power.

Fifth, as more international law is needed in more fields, and as stronger international law is required in some fields, there will be circumstances in which more highly articulated constitutional or organizational structures – including executive, legislative, and judicial functions – will be useful.

The growth of constitutional or organizational structures will benefit from economies of scale and scope and network externalities, and will therefore tend to expand until these economies are exhausted.

In summary, because of social change, international relations will be an increasing proportion of the concerns of citizens and the responsibilities of states. This will drive increasing production of international law and of organizational structures. This increasingly dense body of law and organizations will be seen to perform governmental functions. It is in this sense that the future of international law is global government.

Just a century ago, none of the categories of international law described in the functionally focused chapters of this book – addressing cyberspace, human rights, environment and health, finance and trade, intellectual property, migration, and investment – were very significant. There were good reasons – functional reasons – why they were not. There simply were few international concerns raised by these types of issues.

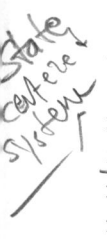

As Wolfgang Friedmann explained in his classic 1964 work, *The Changing Structure of International Law*, "The principal preoccupation of the classical international law, as formulated by Grotius and the other founders, was the formalization, and the establishment of generally acceptable rules of conduct in international diplomacy."[1] Note that these were formal rules designed to facilitate informal interaction. They formalized the process of diplomacy, not the substance of international cooperation. That is, this international law simply formed the preconditions for informal and ad hoc diplomatic action, rather than the contractual structure of formal cooperation over international regulatory issues. This was the international law of coexistence. It also included the regulation of war. War was the first area in which cooperation became desirable.

## A) CHANGING DEMANDS

As Friedmann explained, the changing demands of international society produced a demand for additional types of international law. In order to know what types of international law and institutions will be required in the future,

---

[1] Wolfgang Friedmann, *The Changing Structure of International Law* 5 (1964). See also Douglas M. Johnston, *Consent and Commitment in the World Community: The Classification and Analysis of International Instruments* (1997). Johnston suggests that the period until World War I was a period of "classical" international law, focusing on constraining the use of force, communication, and settlement of disputes. The subsequent "neo-classical" period until the mid-1960s extended this project to intergovernmental organization, codification, and human rights. For Johnston, the current "post-classical" period is concerned with the establishment of cooperative regimes and the transformation of international society to a world community.

we must ask ourselves how the issues we see today as international concerns, and the issues that we have not yet identified as international concerns, will develop. We must next ask what requirements for cooperation – in terms of both rules and organizations – they will occasion. Of course, we cannot anticipate everything, but we should not ignore the issues that can be anticipated by extrapolation from what we know.

Change has occurred along several major dimensions. First, with industrialization and the development of modern economies, including technological change and urbanization, the state has found it useful to intervene domestically in a variety of regulatory contexts. By the beginning of the twentieth century, we see the rise of the regulatory state in response to externalities, information problems, public goods, and other market failures. Second, with globalization, these interventions and the circumstances to which they respond often cross borders or affect the conditions of cross-border competition. Furthermore, globalization has included greater industrialization of developing countries, increasingly involving poor countries in these concerns. Third, technological change, apart from its contribution to industrialization and globalization, has increased the need for international law to regulate technologies in order to limit adverse consequences. Fourth, demographic change, including shifting population densities contributing to urbanization, will have important effects on the demand for international law.

## B) LIBERAL GOVERNMENT AND INTERNATIONAL LAW

Another type of change that will have great effects on the demand for international law is increasing democratization or accountability of governments. As governments become more accountable, their citizens will more effectively demand efficiency in the provision of governmental services. The state is less and less the society of the sovereign, served by the people, and increasingly the society of the trustee government, servant of the people. As such, the trustee government will be forced to admit that in order to serve the people best, there will be situations in which it must give up authority.

In accordance with the principle of subsidiarity, which is a principle of efficacy and efficiency, the state must sometimes give up authority to subnational units; non-territorial but local social units such as professional associations, churches, or schools; global non-territorial and non–state-based social units; and multilateral, regional, or bilateral organizations of states. It gives up authority on behalf of its citizens, in the exercise of subsidiarity driven by accountability, to allocate authority to the social organization best suited to exercise authority in the particular context. As discussed later in the book, this

## Introduction

search for efficacy and efficiency takes place even assuming that government officials are not purely interested in public welfare.

Illiberal governments would have fewer reasons to cooperate than liberal governments, simply because they are characterized by unaccountability. Illiberal governments have self-interested rulers, whose goal is to maintain complete sovereignty, or autarchy, in order to maintain their ability to better themselves at the expense of the population. The recent governments of North Korea and Myanmar are examples. However, self-interested rulers who see themselves in a strong position might be interested in increasing the size of the pie by engaging in welfare-enhancing governmental practices, including international cooperation. But an illiberal government would be expected to satisfice rather than maximize regarding the size of the pie, in order to maximize its chance to stay in power. Tyrants may be compared to monopolists, providing the minimum consumer welfare and maximizing producer welfare. Purely illiberal governments also conform to the political science "realist" model of the security-maximizing government, insofar as they maximize relative gains versus domestic and international opposition, rather than absolute gains.

Observing the Arab Spring of 2011, increasing accountability of authoritarian regimes around the world, and a contagion of decreasing tolerance of authoritarian regimes by their citizens, one might be forgiven for developing an optimistic anticipation of the reduction of authoritarianism, or at least of the most unaccountable authoritarianism. Liberal governments would more often have reasons to cooperate. By cooperating in appropriate circumstances, they enable themselves to deliver more of the goods that their citizens desire, even if they compromise their own autonomy to do so. "It is curiously true that after trouncing the claim to 'divine right' of the absolute monarchs, political theory allowed it to be transferred to the absolute State, and we have suffered it to persist to our own day, though our culture rejects the absolute and our outlook discounts the divine in politics."[2]

In his recent book, *The Globalization Paradox: Democracy and the Future of the World Economy*, Dani Rodrik argues that there is a policy trilemma among local autonomy, democracy, and globalization.[3] He argues that globalization requires some constraint over national measures. He assumes that domestic autonomy, combined with democracy, will produce unconstrained national measures inconsistent with globalization. He concedes that it would

---

[2] David Mitrany, *The Progress of International Government* 71 (1933).
[3] Dani Rodrik, *The Globalization Paradox: Democracy and the Future of the World Economy* (2011).

be possible to have globalization with democracy, but only with global government as opposed to national autonomy. However, he views it as unlikely that we will soon move toward the type of global government that would include democratic accountability. Furthermore, among the three, he would preserve local autonomy and democracy at the expense of globalization.

Rodrik seems to discount the possibility that domestic governments, in the exercise of sovereignty or "autonomy," may recognize that they could achieve greater results in terms of national welfare or political support by accepting constraint over national measures. International lawyers recognize that local autonomy is not an all-or-nothing game, but a selective exercise in which international law is the tool for selectively compromising local autonomy. There is much potential nuance in international commitments, which might require a certain result, but leave it to local autonomy to achieve that result. International legal rules can permit a wide variety of mechanisms for customization or conditional constraint. This incomplete contracting function of international law and organization, allowing international law to apply selectively under particular contingencies, is discussed in greater detail in Chapter 9.

Furthermore, Rodrik seems to assume that democratic accountability can only operate at the level of either the state or international law, but not at both levels. However, the growth of the role of the European Parliament has shown that international democratic accountability may coexist with national democratic accountability, so there is no necessary trade-off between globalization and democracy.

The most characteristic idea of the liberal democratic philosophy leaves the individual free to enter into a variety of relationships – religious, political, professional, social, and cultural – some of them of international scope.[4] Liberalism requires both vertical and horizontal subsidiarity.

Liberal society requires compromise. In a liberal framework, social groups decide to take certain collective actions; these actions benefit some members of the group more than others, or even harm some members of the group. These compromises are accepted as the price of society. Indeed, liberal society would be highly unstable – and would eventually fail – if, first, the aggregate benefit from collective actions did not exceed the aggregate detriment and, second, the aggregate detriment to a significant subset of members substantially exceeded the aggregate benefit to those members. To be sustainable, liberal society must, as a whole, be collectively and individually rational. It is possible to have an illiberal society in which coercion may maintain stability even where society is collectively or individually irrational. Indeed, the development of enlightened

[4] David Mitrany, *Retrospect and Prospect* (1975).

societies and the move away from feudalism may be measured in terms of the movement from illiberal government to liberal government, from coercion to choice, and from government as ruler to government as servant.

Within the modern liberal state, we increasingly take this liberal rationality for granted. Constitutions are structured – both formally and informally – to ensure a process that makes decisions that are collectively beneficial and, on a prospective risk-adjusted basis, individually beneficial. Compromise may involve logrolling or even more diffuse structures for reciprocity over long horizons – to provide for satisfactory anticipated distributive outcomes that meet the requirements of collective and individual rationality.

This domestic process is complex and delicate, but we must also make the same kind of analytical move that economists made when they moved from closed-economy analysis to open-economy analysis: we must consider the effects on domestic society of many types of actions by foreign persons. These actions might include security threats, industrial policy, pollution, financial recklessness, and many others. Additionally, we must consider that inaction by foreign persons might have effects on domestic society: the failure to regulate or join in the production of global public goods might have adverse effects.

If national government did not exist, it would have to be invented. In the words of longtime Massachusetts Congressman Barney Frank, "Government is the name we give to the things we choose to do together."[5] Modern liberal government functions to improve people's lives: providing public goods, and regulating in order to achieve collective and individual improvement. The *public choice* critique of government views government as an instrument of redistribution – redistributing from the weak to the powerful. Although this critique has power, it is not a complete critique. Rather, all governments contain facets that promote efficiency, and thus welfare, and facets that promote redistribution. Terry Moe observes as follows:

> Political institutions serve two very different purposes. On the one hand, they help mitigate collective action-problems, particularly the commitment and enforcement problems debilitating to political exchange, and thus allow the various actors in politics to cooperate in the realization of gains from trade. On the other hand, political institutions are also weapons of coercion and redistribution. They are the structural means by which political winners pursue their own interests, often at the great expense of political losers. If we

---

[5] As quoted in Jim Geraghty, "The Things We Choose to Do Together," *National Review*, August 27, 2008. Retrieved from http://www.nationalreview.com/campaign-spot/8984/things-we-choose-do-together. Of course, Frank's statement is somewhat overbroad: we sometimes do things together informally, or through social organizations, rather than through government.

are to understand where political institutions come from and why they take the specific forms they do, we have to pay serious attention to both sides of their theoretical story.⁶

An argument that redistribution, or the political, dominates efficiency would be analogous to arguing that the irrationality that forms the focus of behavioral economics dominates the preference orientation of welfare economics. Both public choice and behavioral economics have explanatory power, but they both leave room for *welfarist* analysis. The scope of relative power of these analytical approaches can only be assessed empirically.

Furthermore, the redistributive component may be seen as benevolent – in the form of transfers to the needy, for example – or as pernicious. The main point, however, is that even if the redistributive component is pernicious, it is not necessarily dominant in relation to the efficiency-promoting component. Throughout this book, I assume that government has both purposes: efficiency and redistribution.

## C) INTERNATIONAL GOVERNMENT

National government is constantly reinventing itself as technological, social, and other changes drive demand for different public goods and regulation. This change can be more specific, in the form of specific rules or structures, or more general, in the form of decision-making processes or structures. The more general types of processes or structures can often be understood as constitutional in nature. However, there is a bias toward the existing institutional structures, privileging these structures in our discourse. This bias sometimes appears to play a role in resistance to new international law or organizations. We can also observe, however, that given the modern demands of society, if international government did not exist, it would have to be invented. Broadly speaking, government is the name we give to the things we choose to do together through formal rules and organizations, even in the international arena.

I avoid the vague term "governance" in favor of the more concrete term "government." By referring to government instead of governance, I wish to focus on formal rules and organizations, on law. There are international public goods and regulatory needs that can provide collective and individual improvement. There is a domain for informal action, and for so-called soft law, as well as a substantial domain for hard international law. By using the term government

---

⁶ Terry M. Moe, "Political Institutions: The Neglected Side of the Story," 6 *Journal of Law, Economics, and Organization* 213 (1990).

# Introduction

I also reject the idea that a certain institutional intensity or scale is required in order for a mechanism to be considered governmental. Rather, in this book I see government as infinitely scalable, with each rule of international law an element of international government. The interesting question is whether we have the right kind and amount of government.

On this basis, it is easy to say that international government exists. The existing structures of international law and organization comprise a kind of rudimentary government. It has a set of rules that is limited in volume compared to an advanced domestic system. Its legislative system is largely dependent on unanimity, it has little capacity for mandatory adjudication, and it has little executive or enforcement capacity. The description of the international legal system as a rudimentary form of government is only by reference to existing liberal national governments. This comparison is largely inapt, however, because the functions demanded of the international legal system are generally different from those demanded of national governments.

Will international law become a less rudimentary, more elaborate, form of government? The question asked by this book is what changes in international law seem suggested by existing international cooperation opportunities, and what changes are likely to be suggested in the future. So, this book is about the future of international law. Given the understanding of international government described previously, it is about the future of international government. We might hypothesize that in an efficient government system all law that is efficient has already been created. To borrow from a classic joke about economists: there are no $20 bills waiting on the sidewalk to be found, because if they existed they would already have been found. However, no market is perfectly efficient, and the market for institutions depends on imagination and evaluation – we will not reach efficient institutions unless we engage in an analytical process. Furthermore, a lack of institutional imagination, artificially limiting the possibility for international government, may blind us to the existence of many $20 bills available to us if we simply had the imagination and evaluative capacity to see them.

Another important respect in which the present international legal system is rudimentary is that it tends to make and administer rules in separate functional categories, often without a clear and effective system for integrating the resulting rules. This is the issue that has come to be known as *fragmentation*. Although fragmentation is not necessarily a problem, there are important ways in which greater integration might be desirable in particular circumstances.

First, there are some natural overlaps between policy measures. Some policy pairs that serve as examples include industrial policy and environmental policy, human rights and security, or financial services regulation and monetary policy. Second, integration might allow for broader and longer-term reciprocity when making agreements. For example, including intellectual property rights as a topic for negotiation in the Uruguay Round of trade negotiations broadened reciprocity, allowing more complex barter arrangements. These types of complex barter may also serve to promote compliance with international legal rules, providing greater capacity for retaliation in the event of violation. Third, in an embedded liberalism sense, one type of instrument might serve to balance out the distributive effects of another type of instrument. Thus, trade liberalization might be combined with more extensive aid for development. Fourth, there may be economies of scale or scope in the development of institutions. It may not be efficient to create an institutional structure for dispute settlement in connection with disputes regarding division of the international tax base, but if an institutional structure has already been created to deal with foreign investment disputes or trade disputes, adding to the jurisdiction of these structures might be more attractive.

## D) INSTITUTIONAL CHANGE

This book is an exercise in institutional imagination, but not in institutional speculation, and not, I hope, in idealism. The goal is to challenge a state-dominated understanding of global society, but not to ignore the continuing importance of the state as the central structure of government for many years to come. Moreover, the goal is to examine real international issues, and realistically evaluate the actual and incipient needs for international law and organization, rather than to speculate about those needs. Finally, this book gives politics its due, by recognizing that, although increased welfare is an important vector in determining international cooperation, most international cooperation must be mediated through national political systems.

Whereas many have criticized the concept or principle of state sovereignty, often with good reason, it does not advance debate, or understanding, to simply reject a concept. Although others have posited state sovereignty as an immutable law of nature, we know that sovereignty was constructed, and is constantly being reconstructed, by real-world social events and international law. Rather than adopt one of these incompletely considered hate or love relationships with sovereignty, it is incumbent on us to look backward and forward, in order to pragmatically evaluate the types of government structures that we need, and to recognize that the state, and its sovereignty, are contingent. As the social context that produced them has changed, so must our evaluation of their utility.

The state itself has been, and remains, a highly malleable and variable form of association. As Wolfgang Friedmann observed, "From the sixteenth to the early twentieth century, the national state, in many cases coalescing from the older and smaller entities of dukedoms, principalities, and city republics, became the sole source of legal power and the exclusive focus of political allegiance."[7] By recognizing the historical evolution and contingency of the state, we are able to recognize also that the evolution of forms of human association did not begin or end when the state was invented.[8]

Throughout history, man has shown some degree of institutional conservatism: "When the surrounding environment changes and new challenges arise, there is often a disjunction between existing institutions and present needs."[9] So, if to a man with a hammer every object is a nail, perhaps to men and women with a state every object of human cooperation is a matter for the state. We know, however, that many things should be addressed by civil society or substate entities, in accordance with the principle of subsidiarity, and it seems increasingly possible that a wider range of supra-state tools might be useful. I hasten to add that as the tool of international organization is developed, it will only be useful for a specific range of activities; subsidiarity remains the operative principle. Furthermore, there will always be a gulf between what is best and what is politically feasible – the purpose of this work is to narrow that gulf by assisting the analysis of what is best, in order to inform the political process.

This book by no means advocates or even predicts a world state. The more modest goal of this book is to examine the utility of supra-state forms of formal cooperation. The supra-state forms of cooperation that are useful may now be thin, but they may grow more extensive over time; however, they would only be selected according to the principle of subsidiarity, which in fact is simply a principle of practicality, efficacy, and efficiency. Whereas the supra-state forms of cooperation that will be necessitated will not equate to a world state, a clear-eyed view must recognize that they are a form of government. This is no different than saying that the European Union (EU) is a form of government, or that the U.S. federal government was in 1776 and 1787, and is today, a form of government. Government, indeed, may exist at multiple levels simultaneously. This is the core of the federal insight, and a corollary of the principle of subsidiarity. It is also evident in historical experience:

---

[7] Friedmann, *supra* note 1, at 21.
[8] *See* Francis Fukuyama, *The Origins of Political Order: From Prehuman Times to the French Revolution* (2011).
[9] *Id.* at 7.

When tribal-level societies were succeeded by state-level societies, tribalism did not simply disappear. In China, India, the Middle East, and pre-Columbian America, state institutions were merely layered on top of tribal institutions and existed in an uneasy balance with them for long periods of time. One of the great mistakes of early modernization theory, beyond the error in thinking that politics, economics, and culture had to be congruent with one another, was to think that transitions between the "stages" of history were clean and irreversible.[10]

In fact, the jus gentium, understood as the Roman predecessor of modern international law, originated as a distillation of the customs of the early Italian tribes, or *gentes*, for use in adjudicating disputes between Romans and foreigners or two foreigners.[11] This is an early example of the coexistence of tribal, imperial, and even international law.

The range of tools that we are able to use depends on two main parameters. First, it depends on what our needs are, and what tool would actually address those needs the best. Second, it depends on our ideas about our needs and about the available tools. It is at least worth entertaining the possibility that new tools beyond the state might be helpful, and that our institutional imagination has not been sufficiently active to recognize the availability of tools beyond the state. The purpose of this book is to test the bounds of our institutional imagination.

Although not all tools for human cooperation beyond the state must be legal in nature, many of these tools will take the form of international legal rules or formal international organizations. As we develop these tools, we will revise or redefine international law. Indeed, it would be striking if, given expected technological, economic, political, and social changes, there were no change in the forms of international law useful to respond to these changes.

Our loyalty to states may well be valuable, but it need not be exclusive, and we must recognize its contingency. Whereas the future of international law is not likely to be a world state, following the form of a national state, we already have a modest set of global government structures. To paraphrase a somewhat bawdy joke attributed to Winston Churchill, we've already established that we need global government; we are just negotiating the extent. This book will show that the extent of our need for global government will change with technological, economic, social, and ideational change. This is no different than saying that the scope of the responsibilities of the U.S. federal government vis-à-vis the states has changed since the founding of the republic, or that the

---

[10] Id. at 77–78.   [11] Henry Maine, *Ancient Law* 47 (1861).

# Introduction

scope of responsibilities of the EU vis-à-vis its member states has changed since 1957, due to these same types of factors.

## E) FUNCTIONALISM, NEW INSTITUTIONAL ECONOMICS, AND CONSTITUTIONAL ECONOMICS: A SOCIAL SCIENCE FUNCTIONALIST PERSPECTIVE

In this section, I explain the intellectual history of the approach taken in this book. The approach of this book is based, most broadly, on *new institutional economics*.[12] New institutional economics addresses the reasons for formation of institutions, and for particular institutional structures. This book utilizes the methods of new institutional economics, including price theory, transaction costs economics, and game theory. New institutional economics includes a subfield known as *constitutional economics*, which examines the social scientific causes and effects of constitutional structures. I discuss constitutional economics in Chapter 11.

I argue below that an appropriate evolution of the functionalist and neo-functionalist approaches to international integration – to the development of international government – would approach integration from the standpoint of the new institutional economics. Whereas functionalism, and its neo-functionalist enhancement, has evolved to be compatible in most dimensions with the new institutional economics, this compatibility has not been generally accepted.[13] By developing this compatibility, I am able to link functionalism to modern social scientific ideas about why people, and states, form institutions, including international law and international organizations.

The functionalist perspective was introduced in David Mitrany's 1933 work, *The Progress of International Government*. Mitrany posited that if international administrative capacity were developed in order to address specific technical problems, there would be a "spillover" effect, pursuant to which increasing functions would be assigned to international administration, and eventually individuals would transfer their loyalty to these organizations.

---

[12] *See* Douglass C. North, *Institutions, Institutional Change, and Economic Performance* (1990); Oliver Williamson, *The Economic Institutions of Capitalism* (1985); *The New Institutionalism in Organizational Analysis* (Walter W. Powell & Paul J. DiMaggio, eds. 1992); Joel P. Trachtman, "The Theory of the Firm and the Theory of the International Economic Organization: Toward Comparative Institutional Analysis," 17 *Northw. J. Int'l L. & Bus.* 470 (1997).

[13] *But see*, Wayne Sandholtz & Alec Stone Sweet, "Law, Politics, and International Governance," in *The Politics of International Law* (Christian Reus-Smit, ed., 2004) (referring to the new institutional economics literature).

Neo-functionalism, as first developed by Ernst Haas,[14] focused on regional integration. It sought to explain "the migration of rule-making authority from national governments to the European Union."[15] Haas argued:

> Integration would occur *to the extent that* (a) transnational activity and economic interdependence proceeds, revealing both potential to reap joint gains and to deal with the negative externalities created by transnational activity; (b) European elites (private actors, firms, and public officials) are led to seek regional – rather than national – solutions to shared problems; and (c) supranational organs of governance supply rules (law, procedures for the ongoing production of rules and dispute resolution) that satisfied these needs.[16]

Functionalism and neo-functionalism made the mistake of moving directly from cooperation problems to organizational solutions. They elided a critical intermediate, and perhaps final, step: the utility of international law separate from the establishment of additional international organizational structures. It is important to explain the need for international legal rules, and then separately to explain the need for international legal structures to make, interpret, enforce, and administer the rules.

Functionalism and neo-functionalism were often teleological: positing a certain direction in which history would move. They suggested that the formation of secretariats would have unintended spillover effects, providing a supply of integrative machinery that would stimulate demand. Their main causal mechanism was an agency problem, by virtue of which central institutions acquired additional powers: "In its most basic form, spillover occurs when actors realize that the objectives of initial supranational policies cannot be achieved without extending supranational policy-making to additional, functionally related domains. The inherent dynamism of supranational institutions, explored by Haas, remains at the heart of Neo-functionalism and fundamentally distinguishes it from competing approaches."[17]

This dynamic would cause political actors "to shift their national loyalties, expectations, and political activities to a new and larger center."[18] These spillover effects were never fully theorized, nor empirically validated, and the

---

[14] Ernst Haas, "Regional Integration: The Joys and Anguish of Pre-Theorising," 24 *Int'l. Org.* 697 (1970); and "Turbulent Fields and the Theory of Regional Integration," 30 *Int'l. Org.* 173 (1976).
[15] Sandholtz & Stone Sweet, *supra* note 13.    [16] *Id.* (emphasis in original).
[17] *Id.*
[18] Ernst Haas, "International Integration: The European and the Universal Process," 15 *Int'l. Org.* 366, 367 (1961).

teleology of integration posited by the neo-functionalists could not survive observations of reversals of integration.

Furthermore, functionalism has been criticized for assuming that institutions are merely responses to needs, rather than mechanisms of distributive contention. Of course, as Terry Moe suggests in the passage quoted earlier in this chapter, they are both. Because distributive contention is focused not on relative gains, but on absolute gains, the contenders would be expected to accept rules that increase the size of the pie even when diminishing their relative share of the pie, as long as their absolute share of the pie increases.

This book may be understood as an extension, and in modest respects a rectification, of the functionalist project. This book should not be understood as advocacy for integration, or, like functionalism, as assuming a telos of integration, but as an attempt to develop a methodology for the analysis of integration that includes the possibility of both integration and disintegration. Although there is no abstract telos of integration, it is possible to examine changing social, technological, military, environmental, and economic trends and anticipate resulting institutional needs. Real social change will drive integration. Also, whereas neo-functionalism was seen by some as confined to the European or regional integration context, the theory articulated in this book extends beyond the regional context, to a variety of contexts including the multilateral.

Mitrany himself rejected social scientific approaches, relying instead on judgment.[19] This may be understood as dissatisfaction with the then-current state of social science. Regardless, modern analytical sensibilities would find judgment inadequate where social scientific theory and methods possess greater analytical leverage.

However, the functionalist idea can be accommodated comfortably within established social science, including especially, but by no means limited to, new institutional economics. A social scientific perspective on functionalism simply asks the costs and benefits of legal rules and organizations. This normative social scientific functionalist theory is agnostic regarding the types of rules or organizations that will be selected, but theorizes that rules and organizations serve the function of allowing cooperation that provides benefits greater than its costs. A positive social scientific functionalist theory would seek to link certain causes to the establishment of rules or organizations, in order to predict the circumstances under which particular rules or institutions might arise.

---

[19] David Mitrany, "A Political Theory for the New Society," in *Functionalism* 26 (A. J. Groom & P. Taylor, eds., 1975).

Functionalism can be rehabilitated and operationalized by redefining its roots in new institutional economics, which includes constitutional economics. By showing the logic of integration, and of disintegration, in terms of the analytical techniques of new institutional economics, including price theory, transaction costs economizing, game theory, contract theory, and other social scientific techniques, it is possible to explain why we would observe integration, stasis, or disintegration under specific circumstances.

The basic methodology bringing these techniques together is comparative institutional cost-benefit analysis. The first step will necessarily be a ground-up analysis of specific cooperation problems. Second, we must evaluate alternative institutional solutions to each of these cooperation problems, including the status quo. Third, we must evaluate the possibility of horizontal overlaps and institutional synergies that make it useful to establish institutions that are linked with one another or that perform multiple functions. This, in short, is a social scientific reinterpretation of functionalism; we might call it "social science functionalism."

Mitrany's model began with national preferences: the need to cooperate with other states in order to achieve those preferences efficiently. This approach is consistent with a social scientific approach. Mitrany's second step was to posit that international organizations would be formed in response to these needs. This second step skipped over the possibility of the establishment of international law without a specific organization. We might say that establishment of international law without a specific organization relies on the default international legal system as its organization.

Third, Mitrany posited that once an international organization is established, bureaucratic imperatives would result in an expanded set of powers for the international organization. This third step seems least plausible, as it assumes a kind of error, or failure to anticipate, on the part of the constitutive states. An alternative explanation involves a revelatory role for international organizations, discovering further opportunities for beneficial cooperation that would not be discovered otherwise. Mitrany also thought in terms of a unique "seat of authority," with transfer of authority over time after national sovereignty died a death of a thousand cuts. Mitrany put it as follows: "By entrusting an authority with a certain task, carrying with it command over requisite powers and means, a slice of sovereignty is transferred from the old authority to the new, and the accumulation of such partial transfers in time brings about a translation of the seat of authority."[20] This approach seems historically incorrect and inconsistent with a federalist approach that would accept multiple

---

[20] David Mitrany, *The Functional Theory of Politics* 128 (1975).

loci of authority, or constitutional pluralism. It also seems inconsistent with a social scientific or subsidiarity-based approach, which would accept that different types of problems are best addressed at varying levels of authority. Finally, it seems to assume that delegations of authority to international organizations would be systematically overbroad.

Indeed, Mitrany was no world federalist. Rather, he found a federal system "by its nature both rigid and limiting."[21] Mitrany saw the functional method of change as both more gradual and more socially immanent. Mitrany explained that the function would determine its appropriate organs.[22] Mitrany's functionalism is based on the idea that "activities would be selected specifically and organized separately – each according to its nature..."[23] The current work seeks to explain how different functions would require specific organs. The recognition that different functions require different rules and organizational responses indicates that no one type of rule or international organization would be appropriate in response to multiple cooperation problems. However, within domestic government, we tend to aggregate functions at a single or small number of levels.

Thus, Mitrany's approach envisioned and validated what today we call "fragmentation." Although this approach did not fully evaluate the possibility of functional overlaps – overlaps between different activities – and synergies that might arise from combining functions within a single institution, Mitrany anticipated that some functions would intersect. Coordination among functions would, according to Mitrany, come about functionally. Neo-functionalism saw overlaps as an important engine of expansion of international organization responsibility.

The approach of this book is welfarist, in the sense that I have tried to specify the circumstances under which citizens, generally operating through states or perhaps regional organizations, would determine to utilize international legal cooperation in order to improve their welfare. There are, of course, other mechanisms. A *public choice theorist* would focus on political welfare instead of actual welfare. A *constructivist* would examine the ways in which individuals, as citizens or as government officials, establish their beliefs and identities. A *behavioralist* would similarly examine how individuals might develop loyalties separately from their welfare interests. I have no reason to exclude these mechanisms, and I have not performed the empirical research that would be necessary to show that the welfarist mechanism has greater explanatory power than these other mechanisms. In many other circumstances, however, welfare

---

[21] David Mitrany, A Working Peace System 32 (1966).
[22] Id. at 72.  [23] Id. at 70.

has great explanatory power, and so it presents a useful theory from which testable hypotheses might be derived, and, more speculatively, from which policy may be made under uncertainty.

## F) THE CHALLENGE TO THE WESTPHALIAN PARADIGM

Observers of international law have criticized the Westphalian paradigm, and its centerpiece, untrammeled sovereignty, for nearly a century. Over the long sweep of history, these criticisms have become more forceful. The Westphalian paradigm has become less useful, both as a general way to order the world, and as a general way to understand the world. Functional adaptation has already begun to reorder the world differently from the Westphalian paradigm. The EU is only the most obvious example. Less obvious examples can be found in areas such as international economic integration, international responses to environmental and public health problems, international responses to financial disorder, and international human rights, which evidence a growing set of commitments that transcend the state. However, this reordering has been impeded by the continued use of the Westphalian paradigm to understand the world. One of the goals of this book is to suggest a functionalist paradigm that understands the sovereignty of states in utilitarian, and contingent, terms.

Indeed, the exceptions to the Westphalian paradigm have been multiplying for the past 100 years, and the movement toward an international law of cooperation that Friedmann documented in 1964 has accelerated and intensified the exceptions to the Westphalian paradigm so much that it no longer satisfies the parsimony requirement of Occam's Razor. This is the central crisis in international law. A simpler paradigm, one admitting far fewer exceptions, is the *social science functionalist paradigm*, which accepts that the state is contingent, and that international law tends to constrain – indeed, to mold – the state on the basis of functional efficiency. Amartya Sen suggests that "there is something of a tyranny of ideas in seeing the political divisions of states (primarily, national states) as being, in some way, fundamental, and in seeing them not only as practical constraints to be addressed, but as divisions of basic significance in ethics and political philosophy."[24]

Nevertheless, the state's continuing centrality is supported by three forces: (i) its continuing ability to respond to many cooperation problems that fit well within its borders; (ii) path dependence, which makes it difficult to move to other systems of order given the existing Westphalian paradigm; and (iii) network externalities which similarly support isomorphism among states.

---

[24] Amartya Sen, *The Idea of Justice* 143 (2009).

Of course, the first is the most powerful force, but it has been growing weaker. Path dependence and network externalities are subsidiary forces. The slow erosion in the utility of the state to respond to certain types of cooperation problems can be expected to reach a point where it entirely demeans the force of path dependence and network externalities. This point will be something of a tipping point, where the availability of multiple institutional structures will deprive path dependence and network externalities of most of their power. At that tipping point, the Westphalian paradigm will cease to have significant power and will be replaced by the social science functionalist paradigm.

## G) THE STRUCTURE OF THE REMAINDER OF THIS BOOK

Chapter 2 examines the reasons for international law. Its perspective is functional in the sense described above, recognizing that international law arises from real-world cooperation problems that vary over time, and that in the broadest sweep have increased over time. Cooperation problems arise in international society because the actions or inactions of one state have effects on the ability of other states to achieve their goals. Chapter 3 explains that these goals are generally formulated within domestic politics, and so we must look to domestic politics to understand why international law is made and why states comply with it.[25] International law is the formal mechanism by which the decisions of states take into account the concerns of other states. Chapter 4 examines a set of predictions about future developments in globalization, economic development, demography, technology, and democracy, and how these developments may affect the role of international law.

Chapters 5 through 9 examine more specifically the cooperation problems, and how they may develop in the future in connection with several functional areas: cyberspace (Chapter 5); human rights (Chapter 6); international environmental and health regulation (Chapter 7); international finance (Chapter 8); and trade, intellectual property protection, migration, and investment (Chapter 9).

Each type of cooperation problem is different, and each calls for a specific type of international legal response. However, each international cooperation problem involves common themes, and each can be described to varying degrees in terms of all of the reasons for international law developed in Chapter 2. The functional Chapters (5–9) serve three purposes. First, they represent many of the major areas of international cooperation and serve to

---

[25] As international civil society becomes more influential, it may be that some goals will be developed transnationally, rather than just within particular states.

develop and illustrate the current and future needs for international law. Second, they serve to provide more intensive and concrete examples of the reasons for international law developed in Chapter 2, and the linkage to domestic politics explained in Chapter 3. Third, they provide the basis for the discussions of fragmentation and constitutionalization contained in Chapters 10 and 11. Of course, a number of other topics could be addressed, including international criminal law, the responsibility to protect, taxation, peacekeeping, refugees, and a host of others. I am not able to justify my choice other than to say that the topics I chose seemed broadly representative as areas in which international cooperation seems important, and seemed to provide appropriate examples with which to illustrate the analytical methodologies I judged most salient.

Chapter 5's discussion of the challenges of cyberspace introduces some of the jurisdictional problems raised by modern technology, and shows how these problems may be analyzed using some of the concepts of the new institutional economics. The rise of cyberspace increases the value of international cooperation, and also affects the costs of international cooperation.

Chapter 6, on human rights, highlights issues of asymmetry in international legal commitments and compliance, describing these issues in terms of the supply and demand concerns of price theory. It shows the potential power of combining diverse commitments in order to form and enforce international law. Chapter 6 also briefly describes the international law of human rights as a public goods problem.

In Chapter 7, I explore international externalities and global public goods problems in connection with international environmental protection and international public health in greater depth. In connection with climate change, I develop an asset specificity analysis of international contracting, suggesting that a resolution to the climate change problem will require greater certainty of enforceability of long-term international exchanges of value. Limits on trade in high carbon goods are an important way to improve cooperation in connection with climate change.

The discussion of international finance in Chapter 8 focuses on issues of externalities and regulatory competition, but also addresses the problem of asset specificity in connection with the related issue of monetary regulation. Chapter 8 explores the links between international finance regulation and international trade in services.

Finally, Chapter 9 explains problems of trade, intellectual property, migration, and investment using the concept of terms of trade externalities, as well as political support externalities and volume of trade public goods, and develops an incomplete contracting approach to some of these problems. This incomplete contracting approach helps explain the use of adjudication in connection

# Introduction

with some of these problems. This adjudication, determining which national measures are acceptable because either they do not impose policy externalities or because the policy externalities are appropriately justified, provides an important example of a device by which states agree to a case-based dynamic formula for subsidiarity.

Each of these chapters is intended to sketch a plausible understanding of the cooperation problem in the functional area that it addresses, and to suggest possible international legal and organizational responses. When viewed together, these chapters provide an image of extensive and varied cooperation, and extensive needs for greater international legal cooperation in order to cope with future opportunities and challenges.

As discussed in Chapter 10, there will be overlaps and conflicts between different areas of policy cooperation, and economies of scale and synergies in dealing with them. Chapter 11 examines a particular type of synergy: the extent to which broad constitutional rules are appropriate to facilitate or constrain the production of international law in specific areas. At each stage of the analysis, it is important to examine functional needs and international legal responses. In Chapter 12, I make some concluding observations.

## 2 Reasons for International Law and Organization

> The "international law" phase of such movements is a necessary intermediate stage between the traditional separateness of national legal and political systems, and an eventual integration in the form of a federal state. International law thus lies halfway between national laws and federation.
>
> Wolfgang Friedmann (1964)[26]

Why does international law exist, and how does it differ from nonlegal international cooperation? Although each rule of international law exists for a different factual reason than every other rule, and each state participant has its own set of reasons for entry into each rule, this chapter develops a taxonomy of the types of circumstances that give rise to cooperation, and the types of cooperation that seem better addressed through international law, as opposed to nonlegal, or informal, cooperation.[27]

Chapter 3 looks inside the state, to suggest how the same cooperation issues addressed in this chapter may be understood, and usefully analyzed, as linkages between states' domestic political structures. Chapter 4 examines future changes, and suggests how they may affect the demand for international law. Chapters 5–9 examine particular functional areas of international law, suggesting how the reasons for international law developed in this chapter apply to these specific functional areas. Chapter 10 shows that these functional areas may be linked synergetically, or may conflict with one another in ways that have important implications for the structure of international law and government.

As discussed in Chapter 1, the reasons for international law addressed here, and used as a guide to the future of international law, are not idealistic reasons. Instead, they are based on welfarism, and the assumption that individuals make

---

[26] Friedmann, *supra* note 1, at 18.
[27] For a more sustained articulation of the economic reasons for international law, and for its structure, *see* Joel P. Trachtman, *The Economic Structure of International Law* (2008).

# Reasons for International Law and Organization

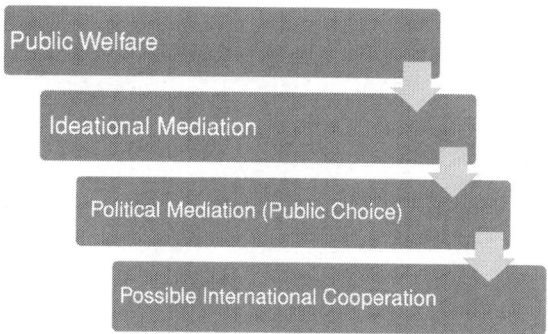

Figure 2–1. Welfare and International Cooperation

international law through states in order to better their lot. This is a liberal, methodologically individualist, and preference-based approach. Having said that, there is room for ideational or constructivist reasons for international law. Indeed, one purpose of this book is to illuminate the utility of international law now and in the future in order to influence perceptions of the need for international law. This is because institutional change is always mediated through perception and ideas.

On the other hand, I assume that international cooperation will generally not take place, or will not be sustainable, where it does not provide increased welfare. So, my assumption – difficult to prove, obviously – is that the growth of international cooperation is largely driven by opportunities to enhance welfare. Of course, a welfarist anarchist would argue the opposite: government, including international government, is driven by opportunities to increase government official welfare, without regard to public welfare.

Thus, an alternative assumption focuses not on public welfare, but on political welfare – the welfare of government officials. This public-choice approach has important descriptive power, but it must either incorporate a measure of public welfare, or concede incompleteness. Conversely, a public-welfare approach must incorporate a measure of political mediation, and distortion, of public welfare. Indeed, it might be said that public welfare is mediated through ideas, and that our ideas about public policy are largely mediated – are given effect – through national political systems. This trickle-through relationship is depicted in Figure 2–1 above.

As noted previously, a model that included in the determinants of national policy only public welfare would be deficient, as would a model that included in the determinants of national policy only political official welfare. Rather, national policy will be determined by a combination of the welfare of political actors and their constituents. Public-choice models that include public welfare as a determinant of political welfare are sufficient to do so. So are public-welfare models that recognize the mediating effect of politics. Whatever model is chosen, there will be circumstances in which a greater aggregate of public and political welfare may be achieved by international cooperation. To the extent that public welfare is a vector in national decision making, national governments will tend to seek international cooperation that enhances public welfare. Therefore, throughout much of this book, I analyze demands for cooperation in terms of public welfare, rather than public choice. In Chapter 3, where I focus on the domestic politics of adherence to and compliance with international law, I use a public-choice model that includes as one of its vectors public welfare. In accordance with that model, I believe that the public-welfare vector will at least be influential, and may in many circumstances dominate the public-choice vector. To the extent that public welfare is influential, whereas the public-choice vector may at times prevent the realization of arrangements for greater public welfare, international law arrangements will tend toward increased public welfare.

## A) REASONS FOR COOPERATION

This section articulates a set of reasons why states might move toward cooperation. The next section articulates why international law might be used as a tool of cooperation, as opposed to nonlegal, or informal methods for cooperation.

### i) Subsidiarity and Efficiency

As discussed in Chapter 1, it is clear that the welfarist role of international law and organization should be determined in accordance with the principle of subsidiarity. The principle of *subsidiarity* may be understood as a demand for efficiency: delegation from the state to international law or institutions would only take place where it enhances welfare compared to the alternative. Indeed, the welfarist, or normative individualist, model of the state understands its own powers as delegated from individuals.

There are four general types of reasons why international cooperation might enhance welfare. First, there may be external effects of national policies that are not sufficiently taken into account by the acting state. International law can serve as the mechanism to cause these effects to be taken into account. The following three types of reasons can also be considered in terms of external effects, but have special structures. Second, there may be economies of scale, economies of scope, or network externalities, causing joint action or harmonized action to be efficient. Third, international problems may have the nature of an international public good, where the non-excludible and inexhaustible nature of the benefits make international cooperation useful to induce states to act to achieve efficient international public goods. Fourth, there may be inefficient regulatory competition, by virtue of which states unconstrained by international law may tend to move to an inefficiently low or high level of regulation.

These types of structures are by no means arguments that international law is appropriate to be utilized for all or even many social purposes. Rather, they are analytical templates that allow us to structure our assessment of particular facts in order to evaluate whether cooperation may be efficient from a welfare perspective. They also allow us to begin to evaluate the distributive aspects of cooperation.

### ii) Externalities

According to the subsidiarity principle, states should have no concern with the activities of other states, unless those activities cause external effects. Broadly speaking, there should be no international law without external effects, including the effects entailed by public goods, economies of scale, and regulatory competition. These external effects may be physical, market based (pecuniary), moral, or aesthetic. They may be beneficial or harmful.

Thus, for example, the financial regulation (or deficiencies therein) in one state may be associated with adverse or beneficial effects (negative or positive externalities) in other states. Externalities may be addressed through rules of jurisdiction that accord the affected state control over the injurious behavior.

Domestic regulation may also cause adverse effects in other states by being too strict with respect to the entry of foreign producers into the national market, or too lax with respect to domestic producers, resulting in competitiveness effects (pecuniary externalities). Externalization through regulation that fails to protect foreign interests (or that implicitly subsidizes some local interests by failing to protect other local interests); pecuniary externalization through strict regulation that has protectionist effects or through lax regulation that may be viewed as a subsidy; and direct subsidization itself may all be viewed as questions of prescriptive jurisdiction. Which state – or international body – will have power to regulate which actions? International law is largely concerned with jurisdiction: the allocation of authority among states and to international organizations.

The externalization problem is accentuated by the diversity, or asymmetry, of states' positions. Some states may be regulatory havens that provide lax regulation because the adverse effects of the lax regulation will be felt largely externally, whereas the positive effects in terms of tax revenues and employment can be enjoyed by the regulatory haven. Certain jurisdictional rules, such as rules of regulatory recognition, might allow such externalization. On the other hand, jurisdictional rules of national treatment, or of managed recognition,[28] can reduce the possibility for such negative externalization.

Furthermore, one state's strict regulation might provide positive externalities to other states. Because this is a positive externality, the first state may require some incentive – in terms of some type of narrow or diffuse reciprocity – as compensation. International cooperation can set the terms of such reciprocity.

Importantly, Ronald Coase showed that it is not efficient for all externalities to be internalized through law. He showed that under zero transaction costs, any allocation of gain and loss would be efficient (although not necessarily satisfactory from a distributive standpoint), because winners and losers would contract to an arrangement that will maximize their joint gains. Of course, the real world always has positive transaction costs, so efficiency may be enhanced or diminished by the initial allocation of gain and loss, through property rights or regulation, or in the international setting, through rules of international law.

Thus, there will be circumstances in which international cooperation is useful in order to cause states to internalize externalities: to establish congruence between decision-making authority and the effects of the exercise of authority. In an increasingly interdependent world, we would expect increasing instances in which the national exercise of authority has consequences for people outside the national political community. Thus, the Coasean function of international law is to bring the international effects of national decisions to bear on the decisions of national authorities.

### iii) Economies of Scale and Scope and Network Externalities

Additional potential sources of gains from cooperation may arise from economies of scale and economies of scope, as well as network externalities. These are simply special types of externalities, in which the action of one state has effects on another. Economies of scale may give rise to circumstances in which coordinated action is beneficial, and conversely, failure to coordinate reduces welfare.

---

[28] See Kalypso Nicolaïdis & Joel P. Trachtman, "From Policed Regulation to Managed Recognition: Mapping the Boundary in GATS," in GATS 241 (Pierre Sauvé & Robert Stern, eds., 2000).

Given the increasingly global nature of society, and of problems such as global warming, the international financial crisis, or infectious disease, it seems likely that there would be economies of scale, under some circumstances, in the regulation of these matters.[29] There may be institutional economies of scale and scope: development of institutions may make it more likely that more issues will be addressed by those institutions. This is part of the functionalist insight. Network externalities may increase benefits with increases in the number of states party to an institution or rule.

Economies of scale have a number of components. First, states may enjoy economies of scale in contexts where they regulate transnational actors. For example, there may be efficiencies gained through coordinated rulemaking, surveillance, and enforcement activities. In the absence of these transactions, states may face heightened risks of evasion, detrimental regulatory competition (which can be driven by externalization), and unnecessary regulatory disharmony, all resulting in inefficiencies.[30] Second, there may be technological economies of scale, relating to equipment, acquisition of specialized skills, or organization. Certainly, as governmental activity has become more complex, there may be greater economies of scale in developing the necessary regulatory capacities. Economies of scale may provide a motivation for integration in order to capture these economies, in the sense that the economies of scale tilt the cost-benefit analysis in favor of integration.

Economies of scope are reductions in cost resulting from centralized production of a group of products, especially where the products share a common component.[31] International organizations may share analytical, negotiation, secretariat, or dispute settlement functions among a group of subject areas. Furthermore, it is possible that the ability to include multiple subject matters in a way that enhances negotiation and enforcement of any single commitment, such as the inclusion of intellectual property in the World Trade Organization (WTO) in the Uruguay Round, may provide economies. Thus, for example, the existence of the WTO may provide economies of scope that would facilitate coverage of additional areas in the WTO.

Network externalities include efficiencies that may arise simply from the adoption by different states of the same rule or technology. Harmonization of

---

[29] Of course, the fact that it is efficient to regulate activity from a global perspective does not mean that only one regulator should exist; rather, it is a problem of contracting and establishing the most efficient institutional structure in response to technical or contextual factors. A similar caveat applies with respect to economies of scope.

[30] *See* Joel P. Trachtman, "International Regulatory Competition, Externalization and Jurisdiction," 34 *Harv. Int'l L.J.* 47 (1993).

[31] *See* John C. Panzar & Robert D. Willig, "Economies of Scope," 71 *Am. Econ. Rev.* 268 (1981).

law can give rise to network externalities. Concentration of international legal transactions in a single institution can also give rise to network externalities.

Finally, economies of scale and scope and network externalities may arise from increased frequency of transactions, or from longer duration of transactions. Given greater numbers of transactions in international relations, one would expect greater economies of scale. In addition, learning-curve effects may, over time, give rise to economies of experience.[32]

### iv) International Public Goods, Club Goods and Common Pool Resources

Another type of cooperation problem in international society arises from circumstances in which international public goods exist.[33] Public goods problems are also a type of externality, insofar as the action of one state affects the welfare of another. *Public goods* are goods that are non-excludable and non-rival in consumption. As depicted in Table 2–1,[34] *private goods* are both rivalrous and excludable; *club goods* are non-rivalrous but excludable, such as a toll bridge. *Common pool resources* are rivalrous but non-excludable, such as a transboundary underwater oil deposit. At the international level, all except private goods provide a potential rationale for international cooperation, sometimes in the form of international law.

TABLE 2–1. Public goods

|  | Non-excludable | Excludable |
| --- | --- | --- |
| **Non-rivalrous** | Public good | Club good |
| **Rivalrous** | Common pool resource | Private good |

Public goods result in the problem of underinvestment. If a particular good is a public good, then because those who invest in its production may not capture all of the benefits, a collective action problem may arise and the public good may be under-produced. This is a problem of a positive externality that would be efficient to be provided, if the incentives were appropriate. On the other hand, a public bad involves adverse effects that are non-excludable and inexhaustible. Those who produce public bads may not internalize all of the

[32] See Kenneth Arrow, "Economic Welfare and the Allocation of Research for Invention," in *The Rate and Direction of Inventive Activity: Economic and Social Factors* 609 (1962). All of these economies may be related to the phenomenon of spillover often considered in connection with neo-functional approaches to international integration, as discussed in Chapter 1.
[33] See Scott Barrett, *Why Cooperate? The Incentive to Supply Global Public Goods* (2007); *Providing Global Public Goods: Managing Globalization* (Inge Kaul et al., eds., 2003).
[34] See Elinor Ostrom, *Rules, Games, and Common Pool Resources* (1994).

detriments, and the public bad may be overproduced. This is a type of negative externality.

States affected by public bads, or that observe the possibility of underproduced international public goods, may thus determine to seek to alter other states' activities, through their own regulation or by seeking changes in the first state's regulation. There are two main ways to do so: informal and formal. Informal methods involve nonlegal reciprocity, perhaps institutionalized through comity or soft law, or perhaps simply effected by one-off exchanges. Reciprocity may be more narrow or diffuse.[35] Formal means include the establishment of law and possibly international organizations to administer the law.

Not all public goods or club goods have the same structure. Some public goods may only produce benefits if all states contribute. These are known as *weakest link* public goods. Interestingly, for some of these types of public goods, such as control of weapons technologies, the greatest problem is coordination and assurance that others will contribute. Other public goods may have the characteristic that any contribution benefits all, without the ability to exclude others from benefit. Under these circumstances there are free rider problems, and international law or other institutional mechanisms would be necessary in order to induce each state to contribute its share. The negotiation of the appropriate share for each state – of the distributive arrangements – may be a barrier to agreement, as in the case of global warming. Because club goods benefit from excludability, it is easier to induce contribution by withholding the benefits of creation of the club good; thus, the free rider problem is easily addressed.

## v) Regulatory Competition

To the extent that we continue to operate under uncertainty regarding the appropriate structure of regulation, diversity may allow us to learn from further experience. On the other hand, where we believe that diversity is driven more by externalization or protectionism than by good faith regulatory views, there can be no assurance that diversity will be beneficial.

The utility of regulatory competition is recognized as dependent on the question of regulatory jurisdiction, in the form of questions of positive and negative externalities that may limit the utility and domain of the Tiebout model.[36] The Tiebout model's prediction of efficient regulatory competition depends on a number of assumptions, including the absence of externalities,

---

[35] *See* Robert O. Keohane, "Reciprocity in International Relations," 40 *Int'l Org.* 1 (1986).
[36] *See e.g.*, Robert P. Inman & Daniel L. Rubinfeld, "The Political Economy of Federalism," *in Perspectives on Public Choice: A Handbook* 73, 85 (Dennis C. Mueller, ed., 1997). After stating that current empirical evidence is suggestive that competitive local governments can provide

so in order to assess its applicability, we must evaluate the match between regulatory jurisdiction and effects.

In the regulatory context, proponents of greater competition in some areas, notably securities regulation, argue that there is a joint jurisdictional decision made by producers and consumers. Thus, analysis must examine the degree to which consumers are able to make an informed choice. The economic theory of regulation would suggest that at least some regulation is motivated by the inability of consumers to protect themselves by making an informed choice. It is difficult to imagine that consumers who are unable to make an informed choice regarding the regulated subject matter would be able to make an informed choice regarding the choice of regulatory law governing this subject matter. Given that it is probably more difficult to grapple with issues of applicable law than direct issues of policy, it is unrealistic to say that consumer choice of mandatory regulation will be informed enough to make regulatory competition beneficial.

Furthermore, there are substantial concerns as to whether the Tiebout model can result in a stable equilibrium.[37] The stability of intergovernmental competition is separate from its efficiency: an unstable market for regulation might be characterized by "price wars" or a race to the bottom.[38] Externalities can be a source of instability.[39] Breton points out that centralization may not be the best way to provide stability, but the existence (without necessarily the assertion) of central authority appears necessary to address problems of instability.[40] The central government may set minimum standards of regulation, as has been done in the EU's essential harmonization technique.

Breton concludes, "In the area of international competition, it would be impossible to prevent an unstable competitive process from degenerating, unless, in the language of international relations 'realists,' a hegemonic power

---

an efficient level of congestible (local) public goods, Inman and Rubinfeld offer the following caveat:

> What is not assured is the efficient allocation of public goods with significant spillovers. In this case, a subsidy is needed to internalize the externalities. But any such policy to control interjurisdictional spillovers would require the agreement of the competitive city-states. For such agreements we must look to more encompassing political institutions. In Madison's compound republic this is the representative central government. *Id.*, at 86.

[37] Edward M. Gramlich, "Cooperation and Competition in Public Welfare Policies," 6 J. *Policy Analysis & Mgt.* 417 (1987). *See also* Albert Breton, "The Existence and Stability of Interjurisdictional Competition," in *Competition among States and Local Governments* 46 (Daphne A. Kenyon & John Kincaid, eds., 1991).
[38] Breton, *supra* note 37, at 43.   [39] *Id.* at 51.
[40] *Id.* at 49.

undertook to prevent the debacle."[41] There appears to be no reason in theory why the hegemonic power in this type of context must be a state; we have seen the EU emerge as just such a power in Europe, and it might be argued that the Basle Committee on Bank Supervision, the WTO, or another functional organization may also play such a role. Alternatively, perhaps the United States or EU exercises, or shares, hegemony through these organizations.

A dynamic governance structure along the lines of cooperative federalism or managed mutual recognition may provide a kind of contingent hegemony or centralization that can maintain stability. Within the U.S. federal system, stability is provided by the ability of the federal government to intervene. This is an important distinction between regulatory competition in the U.S. domestic context and regulatory competition in the international context, and may be an important distinction between corporate law – where the federal government has generally not intervened – and securities law or banking law – where it has chosen to intervene.

### B) LAW VERSUS ORDER; HARD LAW VERSUS SOFT LAW

As suggested above, not all cooperation takes legal form. In fact, social scientists have not yet developed an agreed behavioral rationale for law, as opposed to other forms of reciprocal order. Of course, the development of this rationale is not so urgent in domestic systems, where existing states exercise a level of coercive force that significantly distinguishes law from social norms. On the other hand, jurisprudential analysis has searched with little consensus for a distinction between totalitarian law, or immoral law, and ordinary law. The same elusive welfarist explanation of the distinct character of law can also distinguish law from the mere exercise of coercive force, so these two questions are linked.

Economists speak in terms of self-enforcing contracts, and the same characteristics that result in stable contracts – absent external coercive enforcement – can also support national constitutions and international law.[42] International law generally lacks centralized coercive enforcement, although I will argue that it is unnecessary for each individual international legal rule or treaty to be self-enforcing.

Putting this aside, why are some self-enforcing contracts labeled international law while others are informal? One answer is behavioral, or constructivist:

---

[41] Id. at 51–52 (emphasis added).
[42] For an effort to compare national constitutions and international law in these terms, see Jack Goldsmith & Daryl Levinson, "Law for States: International Law, Constitutional Law and Public Law," 122 Harv. L. Rev. 1791 (2009).

rules that are cast as international law instead of as informal rules may be seen by citizens, and perhaps by governments, as meriting greater respect.[43] Is there a reason for these beliefs, and is there also a rationalist reason for distinguishing between law and non-law? In other words, under what circumstances will future international rules be made in the form of law, as opposed to in the form of non-law, sometimes referred to as "soft law"?

As its proponents concede, the term soft law itself is not without some confusion. Perhaps the best way to characterize the rules that are studied under this heading is that they are: (i) non-binding under formal international law, although they may in some cases form the basis for legislation of binding national law; (ii) prepared in contexts similar to those in which binding international law is prepared; (iii) prepared in a form similar to that in which binding international law is prepared; and (iv) expected to affect state behavior. I will use soft law to refer to rules with these four characteristics. Obviously, these characteristics are chosen arbitrarily, but I believe that they capture the essence of the literature on soft law.

First, as Andrew Guzman and Timothy Meyer[44] have explained, there is no reason to believe that soft law could not be a satisfactory, indeed an optimal, method of cooperation in particular cases. This is clear in theory, and the fact that states make soft law suggests that it serves some cooperation purposes. Some scholars have recently argued that in particular contexts, such as international finance[45] or carbon reduction,[46] soft law is superior to hard law.

Second, it is also true that soft law would not be a satisfactory method of cooperation in all cases. This is also clear in theory, and the fact that states make hard international law suggests that it is superior to soft law in some cases. The binding nature of hard law, the default rules that hard law implicates, the

---

[43] A Chicago Council on Foreign Relations survey showed that 43 percent of Americans consider "strengthening international law" a "very important" foreign policy goal, whereas another 43 percent rate it as "somewhat" important, and only 10 percent say it is not important. Chicago Council on Foreign Relations, American Public Opinion and Foreign Policy 33 (2002). Retrieved from http://www.thechicagocouncil.org/UserFiles/File/POS_Topline%20Reports/POS%202002/2002_US_Report.pdf. See also Michael Tomz, Reputation and the Effect of International Law (Working Paper, February 2008). Retrieved from http://www.stanford.edu/~tomz/working/Tomz-IntlLaw-2008-02-11a.pdf (finding that "Individuals are far more likely to oppose policies that would violate international law than to oppose *otherwise identical* policies that would not trammel upon the law").

[44] Andrew Guzman & Timothy Meyer, "International Soft Law," 2 (1) J. Legal Analysis (2011).

[45] See Chris Brummer, "Why Soft Law Dominates International Finance, and Not Trade," 13 (3) J. Int'l Econ L. 623 (2010).

[46] See Alexander Thompson, Efficiency, Distribution, and the Soft Law Future of the Climate Regime (unpublished manuscript, prepared for presentation at the International Policymaking and Agreements Conference, Yale University, April 8–9, 2011). Retrieved from http://www.yale.edu/leitner/resources/IEPA-papers/Thompson_Climate_Yale.pdf.

possible linkage to other hard law rules, and other features of hard law would be expected to be valuable in certain cases.

As Guzman and Meyer point out, where the only goal is coordination, soft law may serve well. However, where a state may gain by its violation, as in cases of externalities or public goods, cooperation as opposed to coordination is needed. Soft law can support cooperation, provided that the incentives for compliance are sufficient. However, there will be circumstances in which hard law will provide a stronger basis for cooperation, whereas soft law will fall short.

Guzman and Meyer are also concerned about the problem of costly punishments, and believe that soft law may have benefits by virtue of the fact that it avoids the use of costly punishments – it would be expected to be used where the cost of using punishments exceeds the benefits of compliance. However, there is no reason to believe that where punishment is needed, the soft law variety of punishments would be less costly than the possible hard law punishments that could be devised. Indeed, there is no reason why states could not specify in a hard law instrument the exact punishments they would use in a soft law context.

Guzman and Meyer posit that punishments are always costly, but this is not the case. They assume that the punishment will be in reputational terms, where the loss to the violator does not redound to the benefit of the injured party. However, first, not all punishments are reputational – some may involve cash payments or valuable permission to retaliate. Second, the violator's loss of reputation does not necessarily fail to benefit the injured party. In an information model of reputation, the knowledge of what type the violator is benefits the injured party and other potential injured parties. So costly punishment is unlikely to be a rationale for using soft law.

Rather than being a mere label for rational cooperation, international law is a special type of cooperation that has particular features. In a sense, all law is social order, labeled law. This jurisprudential observation can be made about the domestic legal system also: law is a special case of social order. Although it is true that the basic model of cooperation is generic, there are some distinctive and important aspects of international law that do not apply to general international cooperation.

First, international law rules may serve as equilibrium-selection devices that provide a greater possibility for a stable equilibrium. Second, a rule's designation as law brings into play a substantial set of default rules within the international legal system, thereby filling in a large portion of the incomplete contract regarding states' obligations and expectations under that rule, including the scope of remedies for violation. Third, it may be that designation as law serves to link compliance/noncompliance with any particular legal rule to other rules, thereby extending the possible scope of retaliation to fields that might not otherwise be considered "fair game." With regard to this last point, we might say that designation as law increases the returns to compliance by placing the general sense of international legality at stake. That is, if state A can be a scofflaw in one sector, what prevents state B from being a scofflaw in an area that injures state A? In this sense, there is a possibility for implicit multilateral retaliation, even if formal international law doctrine does not permit multilateral retaliation.

Thus, by including a particular rule in international law, states are accepting that the rest of the legal system is now open to being compromised or weakened by noncompliance with that rule. That is, by violating one legal rule, a state may undercut the entire legal system. This connectedness adds strong incentives for compliance.

So, designation as law certainly has meaning, and social effects. We might assume that legal rules are chosen over other types of rules – rules are designated law – when the legal method of cooperation is superior to the other methods. States may be expected to move from non-international law equilibrium behavior to international law, where the latter either makes equilibrium possible that would not otherwise be possible, or enables that equilibrium to be achieved more efficiently than through other means. Institutions are chosen for cost and benefit reasons. All institutions are social constructs, and all depend for their power on acceptance, either implicit or explicit.

Gillian Hadfield and Barry Weingast have developed a model that seeks to explain the distinctive characteristics of law, such as its generality, abstract reasoning, uniqueness, and reliance on open and public processes, on the basis of law's function to coordinate an equilibrium on the basis of decentralized enforcement of rules.47 They assume a system that lacks a sovereign to hold a monopoly on coercive force, and argue that "law has its distinctive structure in order to serve as an ambiguity-reducing institution that coordinates beliefs among diverse individuals and thus to improve the efficacy of the extra-legal rule enforcement mechanisms that cause behavior to align with rules."48 They show that the distinctive characteristics mentioned above can contribute to this function. Thus, for example, in their model, generality derives from the equilibrium requirement that harmed persons articulate their claim with a logic that attracts third parties to participate in a coordinated boycott triggered by the application of that logic.

---

47 Gillian Hadfield & Barry Weingast, "What is Law: A Coordination Model of the Characteristics of Legal Order" (U.S.C. Law Legal Studies Paper 10–20, March 1, 2011). Retrieved from http://papers.ssrn.com/sol3/papers.cfm?abstract_id=1707083.
48 Id. at 4.

A more general explanation of the use of law utilizes transaction costs and comparative institutional analysis, arguing that legal rules, by virtue of their distinct institutional structure, are used when they achieve a better transaction costs and transaction benefits profile compared to non-legal order. Although this model has not been operationalized in a social scientific sense, it is intuitively appealing, and can also be used to explain variations in legal rules across contexts. Indeed, this broader model can include the Hadfield–Weingast model and other game theoretic models.

## C) SELF-ENFORCING CONTRACTS

The common understanding of international law in the economics literature assumes that for international law to be effective, it must have the characteristics of a self-enforcing contract. The tools of analysis used by economics for particular legal rules or regimes is thus non-cooperative game theory, where it is assumed to be impossible to enter into exogenously binding contracts. Rather, the internal dynamics of the rule or regime must be structured so that it is endogenously binding – so that it has internal dynamics that will result in compliance.

Much of this analytical perspective is dependent on the definition of the scope of the game being played. For example, if the game is isolated as the reduction of tariffs on bananas game, or even as the broader trade liberalization game, then perhaps the requirement for self-enforcing contracts is appropriate. If instead, we understand the trade liberalization game as part of a broader general international law game, then it is not true that the trade liberalization component must itself be self-enforcing. Rather, the question is whether the general international law game is self-enforcing. Similarly, in domestic society, we do not need to ask whether the domestic environmental protection game is self-enforcing, because it is embedded in a broader legal and constitutional system. The domestic system starts out equally anarchic to the international system.

It is true that in anarchy, we must search for self-enforcing agreements, and even domestic law must be found to have roots in self-enforcing agreements.[49] As with the fundamental basis of domestic law, however, the self-enforcing character of international law must be assessed looking at the totality of the international law relationships between states, rather than by isolating individual relationships. There is a much greater possibility for reciprocity, and for stochastic symmetry, when we examine the entire set of relationships,

[49] Id.

and examine them across time, than when we examine a single obligation. The economists' perspective, expecting all legal rules or regimes to be self-enforcing when considered separately and in the short-term, is both ignorant of the networked power of law and impotent to address long-term, highly asset-specific, and asymmetric cooperation problems. As to both domestic law and international law, we might say that each individual thread of obligation may be weak or strong; if it is weak, it will be unable to sustain cooperation. However, once a variety of threads are woven together in a "fabric" of society, the fabric will be considerably stronger than any individual thread.

## D) LAW AND ORGANIZATION

Not all international law requires a discrete organization. Much, if not most, international law lacks a secretariat, surveillance, dispute settlement, decision making, and other organizational functions. One theoretical justification for international organizations is to reduce the transaction costs of international cooperation. This is the Coasean story of the market versus the firm, with the international organization playing the role of firm.[50]

In the Coasean theory of the firm, the reason for firms (in our case, organizations) is dependent on transaction cost reduction. The best way to think about this model is in terms of cost-benefit analysis. There are gains to be achieved from cooperation. Where the net gains from cooperation exceed the transaction costs of cooperation, we would expect to observe cooperation. States would be expected to seek to maximize their net benefits from cooperation by utilizing the institutional structure, from case-by-case cooperation to organizationally structured cooperation (analogous to the continuum between the market and the firm), that maximizes the transaction benefits, net of transaction costs.

In connection with international cooperation, transaction costs arise from two main sources. First, they are occasioned by the cost of establishing mechanisms to promote cooperation and avoid strategic behavior. If an organization can reduce these costs by, for example, supplying information, certifying information, or changing the structure of retaliation and the payoff from defection, then the organization may be justified. A second source of transaction costs is the complexity of identifying, evaluating, and negotiating a Pareto-improving transaction.

---

[50] See Joel P. Trachtman, "The Theory of the Firm and the Theory of the International Economic Organization: Toward Comparative Institutional Analysis," 17 Northw. J. Int'l L. & Bus. 470 (1997).

It is not possible to determine in the abstract whether an international organization would have greater net transaction benefits compared to those resulting from a simple treaty without a specific organization formed around the treaty. Rather, this question can only be answered in connection with specific cooperation problems. In important dimensions, the question of which would have greater net benefits is dependent on the question of the structure of the international organization.

However, given a complex area of cooperation, with many opportunities for uncertainty and defection, it is certainly possible that an organization may provide certain useful services. In particular, we might examine the possibility of strategic behavior. To the extent that the strategic context in which states find themselves maps into a prisoner's dilemma or another strategic model that could be resolved efficiently by a change in the payoffs effected through legal rules, an international organization might be useful. It would allow states to cooperate where cooperation is beneficial, and where it otherwise would not be possible.

Let us pursue the example of a prisoner's dilemma. Recall that the dominant strategy for any state in the prisoner's dilemma is defection. The only way to avoid the Nash equilibrium of defection by all parties is to change the payoffs. An international legal rule that entails some kind of informal or formal punishment, or other negative consequences of defection, can change the payoffs to change the game from a prisoner's dilemma to a coordination game, with a much greater likelihood of compliance. Organizations can serve to engage in surveillance, communication, and adjudication in order to implement rules that change payoffs.

Williamson, extending the Coasean theory of the firm, focuses on asset specificity as a basis for problems of opportunism and, in turn, as a basis for integration within a firm.[51] This type of problem arises after economic relations are entered, and arises from the fact that one party makes an investment in transaction-specific assets. The classic and apparently apocryphal example of the relationship between Fisher Body and General Motors is used to illustrate the utility of vertical integration to safeguard the party required to make the asset-specific investment from opportunistic behavior on the part of the other party.[52] In this example, an asset-specific investment is one that can only realize its full value in the context of continued relations with another party.

---

[51] *See generally*, Oliver E. Williamson, *The Economic Institutions of Capitalism* (1985).
[52] Benjamin Klein, Robert Crawford, & Armen Alchian, "Vertical Integration, Appropriable Rents, and the Competitive Contracting Process," 21 *J. L. & Econ.* 297 (1978). Klein, Crawford, and Alchian consider asset specificity only one explanation of vertical integration.

Williamson claims that "it is the condition of asset specificity that distinguishes the competitive and governance contracting models. These are the formal versus informal models. Contract as competition works well where asset specificity is negligible. This being a widespread condition, application of the competitive model is correspondingly broad. Not all investments, however, are highly re-deployable."[53] What makes a particular transaction in international law asset specific? Any transaction where one state advances consideration at a particular point in time – and must rely on one or more other states to carry out their end of the bargain at a later point in time – or experiences a significant loss in its expected value is asset specific.

Williamson sees transaction costs economizing as the main purpose of vertical integration – of formation of organizations. Vertical integration is seen as a governance response to a particular set of transaction dimensions, including high asset specificity as the principal factor. With *high asset specificity*, the value of contracting is increased, but the type of contract – and institution – depends on other factors.

Assuming asset specificity, it may be useful to establish devices to constrain opportunism in order to realize gains from cooperation, depending on the costs and benefits of these devices. Institutions may be used to constrain opportunism. Institutions entail transaction costs, as do market transactions. Institutions may specify discrete rules, but are, under positive transaction costs, always incomplete. Even the discrete rules are incomplete in their interpretation, application, and enforcement.

International law is often subject to the problem of incompleteness in a way that domestic contracts are not. Domestic contract disputes always have an answer: "the common law abhors a vacuum." In general international law, there are fewer institutional and legal structures to complete contracts. First, there is not a complete body of law that can be applied to supply missing terms to incomplete treaties. Second, there is no dispute resolution tribunal with mandatory jurisdiction. Informal mechanisms are more likely to apply. Thus, it is often difficult to rely on the ability to complete contracts through general international law.

Thus, complete contracts in international law are impossible. Rather, states must accept a degree of incompleteness. They may use a variety of methods to complete their contracts ex post. One method is simply to negotiate regarding new circumstances as they come up. This method may give rise to stalemates or strategic behavior. A second method is to provide for a legislative system that

---

[53] Williamson, *supra* note 51, at 42.

involves less than full unanimity, or that has other expediting characteristics. A third method, with a somewhat different domain, is to provide for dispute settlement, with all of the varieties of dispute settlement structure that may be available. In particular, it is possible to delegate greater or lesser discretion to dispute settlement, through lesser or greater specificity of treaty text.

In Chapter 9, I discuss the use of dispute settlement to complete contracts in the WTO context. I explain that it is sometimes efficient to have rules that are state contingent – that are desired to apply differently under different conditions that can best be assessed ex post. Under these incomplete contract circumstances, dispute settlement plays the role of assessing the state of affairs in order to determine whether the rationale for application of the rule is met. This type of state contingent adjudication may be understood as a mechanism for achieving greater precision in delegation of authority to international law. Although avoiding granting overall authority to international law, international law is applicable where its concerns are applicable. This may be understood as a dynamic mechanism for achieving a subsidiarity-based division of authority.

In addition, it is necessary to specify bureaucratic, legislative, or dispute resolution methods of completing contracts in order to avoid opportunism – to complete the contemplated transaction as intended. The higher the magnitude of asset specificity, the greater the incentives for opportunism and institutional integration – for the transfer of authority to bureaucratic, legislative, or dispute resolution mechanisms.

So, in determining whether an international organization would be useful, it would be important to evaluate the strategic setting, magnitude of payoffs, capacity for informal enforcement, and other aspects of the circumstances. It is a complex determination, as the types of commitments that would be appropriate are interdependent with the types of institutional structures that would be appropriate to enforce them, including the design of the international organization.

Dispute settlement is not just a method of completing an international contract; it is also a method of enforcing rules. These are separate functions and should be evaluated and structured separately. In the enforcement role, dispute settlement declares who is right and wrong, removing the subject treaty from the default international legal mechanism of auto-interpretation. This declarative role can have important informal effects, and these may be sufficient to induce the desired level of compliance. However, where the declaration alone is deemed insufficient to induce the desired level of compliance, dispute settlement can be the basis for imposition of penalties or authorization of retaliation against the violating state.

## E) CHAPTER CONCLUSION

International law is one method of international cooperation. International cooperation can be useful under a variety of circumstances, including externalities, public goods, economies of scale and scope, and network externalities. Although there is a domain for soft law, there are substantial limits on the ability of soft law to address cooperation problems with great depth – those that involve strong incentives to defect. In particular, where the cooperation circumstance is not a coordination problem, and where one party provides its performance in advance of the other, so that there is significant asset specificity, soft law will be unable to induce compliance.

So, the special role of international law will be to allow states to cooperate under these more difficult circumstances. As we will see especially in Chapters 7 and 8, in areas such as macroeconomic policy and global warming, international law may be able to address substantial asymmetries through inter-temporal cooperation arrangements whereby one party gives its consideration significantly in advance of the other. This is not very different from a loan agreement, where the lender gives its consideration early and then must rely on its legal rights to induce the borrower to repay. The critical question will be whether international law can be made reliable enough to induce compliance under this type of asymmetry.

## 3 International Law and Organization as a System for Transnational Political Linkage

> Applied to relations between nations, [the] bureaucratic politics model directs attention to intra-national games, the overlap of which constitutes international relations.
>
> Graham Allison (1971)[54]

Any understanding of international cooperation through law must be infused with respect for the practical, state-based political process by which formal cooperation occurs, and it must include a mechanism by which states would determine to create organizational structures to facilitate cooperation. It must develop a perspective on the interaction between multiple domestic political processes, and it must develop a theory of the creation of international organizations.

As noted in Chapter 1, international law will not grow to replace the state, but will grow to supplement the state as a form of government in a federal or divided powers sense. The future of international law is as a set of functional, nuanced, differentiated, and organic links between the political systems of different states. As these links grow in terms of their mandatory character, specificity, and institutional support, they will increasingly ascend the scale from a more contractual type of international law to mechanisms that appear to have more of the characteristics of government.

Mitrany observed as follows:

> Our social activities are cut off arbitrarily at the limit of the state and, if at all, are allowed to be linked to the same activities across the border only by means of uncertain and cramping political ligatures. What is here proposed is simply that these political amputations should cease. Whenever useful or

---

[54] Graham Allison, *Essence of Decision* 149 (1971).

necessary the several activities would be released to function as one unit throughout the length of their natural course.⁵⁵

However, Mitrany did not develop the full implications of the extension of politics across borders. International law is the formal mechanism by which such extension occurs in the modern world, and international legal rules and institutions make up the formal link between separate domestic political systems. International law may still provide uncertain and cramping political ligatures, but there is no particular reason why it cannot grow more certain and more capacious, as well as less political. Indeed, Mitrany's functionalism relies largely on informal administrative connections, rather than formal legal and political connections. However, these informal administrative connections seem unrealistically removed from national politics. They seem relatively apolitical and insensitive to distributive consequences of administrative action. Today, we may recognize that even expert and technocratic decision making has deep political and distributive consequences.

International relations and international law form a mechanism by which, as Allison suggests in the quote at the beginning of this chapter, the domestic politics of different states may be linked, modifying the otherwise applicable political equilibrium in different states. The interaction of states matters for domestic politics, and in fact is simply an extension of domestic politics. It is, however, an extension that constitutes functional cross-national political equilibria, and in effect, communities. These communities often require law, and increasingly require international organization.

## A) METHODOLOGICAL INDIVIDUALISM FROM UNILATERALISM TO MULTILATERALISM

The liberal theory of international relations, as articulated by Andrew Moravcsik, calls attention to the domestic sources of international relations preferences.⁵⁶ Thus, "the demands of individuals and societal groups are treated as analytically prior to politics."⁵⁷ Liberal theory focuses on preferences of states, resulting from the aggregation of individual preferences by the state's political mechanisms. Governments then act purposively in world politics on the basis of these preferences. Preferences are the cause of state behavior

---

⁵⁵ Mitrany, *supra* note 21, at 82 (1966).
⁵⁶ *See* Andrew Moravcsik, "Taking Preferences Seriously: A Liberal Theory of International Politics," 51 *Int'l. Org.* 513, 516–21 (1997) (giving an overview of the assumptions underlying the liberal theory and explaining how domestic politics exerts an influence in world politics).
⁵⁷ *Id.* at 517.

within a world system that provides constraints on the basis of other states' preferences.

States are dynamic systems, with individuals and groups of individuals vying with one another for influence. To the extent that these systems are assumed to be closed, it may be appropriate to expect a fairly stable equilibrium among these individuals and groups. Coalition politics may be relatively stable, with change occurring on the basis of demographic, technological, ideational, or other factors that disrupt the equilibrium. The market of international relations, in which states seek modifications of the behavior of other states, provides an additional dynamic source of stimuli that may disrupt otherwise extant national political equilibria. On the other hand, as the market of international relations becomes deeper and more efficient, it will increasingly be a part of a normal, and more stable, national equilibrium.

Thus, although as Robert Putnam explains, "it is fruitless to debate whether domestic politics really determine international relations, or the reverse,"[58] the relationship between domestic politics and international relations has a particular directional structure. Liberal theory envisions states entering the "market" of international relations to satisfy preferences.[59] The market is a constraint: all preferences cannot be satisfied. Similarly, a non-monopolist/monopsonist corporation entering the market cannot determine alone the price at which it sells and buys. As this chapter argues, the state is a dynamic aggregator of individual, group, and coalition preferences. We always begin with individual preferences and move up the vertical ladder of hierarchy according to the principle of subsidiarity in order to better satisfy those preferences. Of course, when a state is the counterparty from which modification of behavior is sought, it must determine through its domestic political process whether the benefits offered are sufficient to induce it to modify its behavior. It follows a similar but obverse process.

## B) THE DOMESTIC CAUSES OF ADHERENCE TO AND COMPLIANCE WITH INTERNATIONAL LAW

International law generally begins with the demands of a single state: plurilateralism and multilateralism begin with unilateralism. (There may be circumstances in which transnational civil society will have the depth and breadth

---

[58] *See* Robert D. Putnam, "Diplomacy and Domestic Politics: The Logic of Two-Level Games," 42 *Int'l. Org.* 427 (1988).

[59] *See*, Jeffrey L. Dunoff & Joel P. Trachtman, "Economic Analysis of International Law," 24 *Yale J. Intl. L.* 1, 13–14 (1999) (analogizing the "market of international relations" to the market of goods, except that states trade in units of power).

to initiate demands across states.) So we must examine domestic politics to identify the roots of international law.

A number of factors within the domestic politico-legal sphere may cause states to adhere to (accept obligations) and comply with international law. It is unlikely that any mono-causal explanation would be broadly successful, and this field would benefit from empirical evaluation of the relative causal power of different factors. The literature has focused on the following categories of causal factors: (i) domestic structure;[60] (ii) ideas and managerial factors;[61] (iii) domestic litigation and interest groups; and (iv) domestic interests and partisan politics. I focus on domestic interests and partisan politics, or preferences, simply because I speculate that a preference-based explanation of entry into and compliance with law will generally provide the greatest causal power. My speculation is supported by a broad consensus in social science that preferences have great (although definitely not exclusive) causal power. However, this is not on the basis of empirical validation, and I would expect other causal factors to be important in specific circumstances.

In his seminal 1978 article "The Second Image Reversed: The International Sources of Domestic Politics,"[62] Peter Gourevitch develops the implications of the fact that the international system can affect the structure of domestic politics. This is the second image (an image of the impact of domestic politics on international relations) reversed.[63] In his leading article, "Diplomacy and Domestic Politics: The Logic of Two-Level Games,"[64] Putnam focuses attention on the role of international pressure – foreign demands – in inducing domestic political change. Putnam saw that the "second image" approach – focusing on domestic causes of international relations – and the "second image reversed" approach – focusing on international causes of domestic political phenomena – were inadequate by themselves. He claimed that, "A more adequate account of the domestic determinants of foreign policy and international relations must stress *politics*: parties, social classes, interest groups (both

---

[60] Helen Milner & Peter Rosendorf, "Democratic Politics and International Trade Negotiations," 41(1) *J. Int'l Confl. Resol.* 117–46 (1997).

[61] *See*, Harold HongjuKoh, "Internalization Through Socialization," 54 *Duke L. J.* 975 (2005); Harold HongjuKoh, "Why Do Nations Obey International Law?" 106 *Yale L. J.* 2599 (1997); Abram Chayes & Antonia Handler Chayes, "On Compliance," 47 (2) *Int'l Org.* 175 (1993); Abram Chayes & Antonia Handler Chayes, *The New Sovereignty* (1995).

[62] Peter Gourevitch, "The Second Image Reversed: The International Sources of Domestic Politics," 32 *Intl. Org.* 881 (1978).

[63] The first image examines the role of individuals in international relations. Kenneth Waltz developed the idea of three images. The second focuses on the effects of domestic politics on international relations, whereas the third focuses on the effects of the international system on international relations. *See* Kenneth Waltz, *Man, The State, and War* (1959).

[64] Putnam, *supra* note 58.

economic and noneconomic), legislators, and even public opinion and elections, not simply executive officials and institutional arrangements."[65]

Putnam's two-level game theory suggests that the role of the national government in international relations is to mediate between two separate "games," the international game and the domestic game: "The unusual complexity of this two-level game is that moves that are rational for a player at one board (such as raising energy prices, conceding territory, or limiting auto imports) may be impolitic for that same player at the other board."[66]

Although this provides important insights, especially as to the position of government officials caught in between, another perspective might suggest that there is no real conflict between these games. Rather, opportunities in the international game shape the strategy for maximizing an aggregate basket of preferences in the domestic game. The state is always maximizing its preferences under constraint. It is as erroneous to say that there is an inconsistency between the international and the domestic as it is to say that a corporation entering the market is in conflict with the market. It seeks the benefits of the market, in terms of the ability to purchase and to sell.[67] The corporation must decide whether to make or to buy – whether to be satisfied with internal production – or whether to contract with others. It only contracts to buy where this is superior to making. Similarly, in Coasean terms, where outsiders impose an externality on the corporation, the corporation only contracts with the outsider where it achieves a better outcome than acting on its own. Putnam sees the opportunity for national gain in the market of international relations as the exception, rather than the rule: "On occasion, however, clever players will spot a move on one board that will trigger realignments on other boards, enabling them to achieve otherwise unattainable objectives."[68]

The unstated assumption in Putnam's theory is that the national negotiator has some measure of autonomy that allows the negotiator to compromise between domestic and foreign interests, and that the national negotiator is not concerned with maximizing the national interests outcome. However, there is no need to assume an agency problem. A more parsimonious approach might view the national negotiator as maximizing national interests under international constraint, with the additional possibility of agency problems.

Putnam is right in his core insight that if we examine the domestic game, we may find that there is an opportunity for a domestic equilibrium that would not exist except for the existence of the international game (what Putnam

---

[65] *Id.* at 432.   [66] *Id.* at 434.
[67] For a broader argument along these lines, *see* Trachtman, *supra* note 27.
[68] Putnam, *supra* note 58, at 434.

refers to as a "synergistic linkage").[69] This is not the exception, however, but the rule in international cooperation and international law. As Jongryn Mo points out, domestic bargaining is endogenous to international cooperation – it is affected by opportunities for international cooperation.[70] Domestic bargaining is constrained by the range of international opportunities, wherever the international opportunities allow a superior outcome compared to a purely domestic equilibrium. We must assume that international cooperation will only be efficient, and will only ensue, where it allows a superior aggregate outcome, either from a public choice or public interest standpoint.

It is important to focus on the role of realignments on the domestic board – on the fact that entry into, and compliance with, international law is always motivated by either the prospect of change in domestic coalitions that the new international law causes, or by the prospect of avoiding unattractive change from an existing coalition. It is also important to focus on the implications of these realignments for compliance. If international law did not modify domestic political coalitions, there would be no purpose for the international law; once it is accepted, as will be argued, that compliance is always a domestic political decision – the international law will only be effective if it modifies domestic politics.

Mo formalizes and extends Putnam's conjecture that greater domestic constraints can be a bargaining advantage in international negotiations.[71] As discussed previously, this conjecture seems dependent on a particular definition of the state's preferences, and on a particular definition of advantage. That is, constraint can only be seen as an advantage if constraint is separated, and understood to be independent, from the state's actual preferences. However, it is difficult to understand how this type of artificial constraint could arise.

Putnam seems to assume that the state's true preferences are distinct from those expressed in domestic politics, so it can be an advantage in achieving the true preferences if the constraint, which is visible and credible to counterparties in international negotiations, causes them to give up more of the surplus from agreement than they otherwise would. This concept of constraint as advantage would be more logical if the constraint were a false constraint, or a false negotiating signal.

Otherwise, domestic constraint can be understood more simply in terms of domestic preferences, and the power that domestic constraint confers is simply the power of the negotiation concept of best alternative to a negotiated

---

[69] Id. at 447–48.
[70] Jongryn Mo, "The Logic of Two-Level Games with Endogenous Domestic Coalitions," 38 J. Confl. Resol. 402, 402 (1994).
[71] Id. at 414.

agreement (BATNA). This power is actually the simple fact that where the surplus generated by a negotiated agreement is less than that generated by an alternative unilateral action, we can expect the actor to choose the alternative unilateral action.

Mo develops a formal bargaining model of the interplay between domestic and international bargaining. He examines the context in which the negotiator has preferences different from those of her domestic constituents: the case of conflicting domestic interests. The model presented is also an example of a nested game. We can think of international bargaining as consisting of domestic and international games that are played simultaneously. In the domestic game, the incentives of groups trying to form a domestic coalition are structured by the international game. Because groups need to make a proposal attractive to the foreign country, their incentives in choosing domestic coalition partners thus do not depend exclusively on domestic considerations.[72]

Mo's model also provides that each group prefers to receive the benefits of an agreement earlier, rather than later, making it costly to cause delay by proposing unacceptable terms. However, the more that the group values future benefits, the more willing it is to adopt a strategy of waiting for a better offer. Mo accounts for this with the concept of a "continuation value," which is the discounted value of the expected outcome in continuing play after rejection of the current proposal.[73] Players are expected to compare the continuation value to the value of the proposal, and choose the greater.

Mo's model depicts a bargaining game of alternating offers between two countries. Each country has three lobbies, including the government as one lobby, and each country can only make an international agreement if two of the three lobbies agree. The foreign country will seek to provide concessions that will be marginally sufficient to induce a marginally sufficient number of the domestic country's lobbies to accept its proposal. Domestic lobbies left out of the coalition are assumed to receive no benefits.

Note, however, that the assumed foreign-country strategy may be counterproductive at a compliance stage. If the foreign country offers concessions marginally sufficient to induce marginally sufficient political support, then small shifts in lobby preferences may result in insufficient political support for compliance. So, depending on the incremental force of lobbies whose support increases on adherence – which may include the government, international lawyers, and even other domestic players whose lobbying power is increased by the benefits they obtain from entry into the agreement – a foreign-country strategy to ensure compliance would focus on concessions

[72] *Id.* at 406.   [73] *Id.* at 410.

marginally sufficient to induce marginally sufficient support for future compliance, not just adherence.

## C) A MODEL OF ADHERENCE TO, AND COMPLIANCE WITH, INTERNATIONAL LAW

In this section, I begin to develop this chapter's model, based in part on the Grossman-Helpman political support model designed for use in connection with international trade negotiations.[74] In that model, incumbent governments are assumed to seek to maximize a political support function. This political support function is assumed to have two components. First, organized interest groups are assumed to make political contributions that can assist in reelection, providing an incentive for governments to implement policies that enhance organized interest-group welfare. Second, voters are assumed to respond in their voting behavior to their own welfare, so one can expect some incentive to implement policies that enhance voter welfare.[75] The government then sets its policy to aggregate a weighted sum of total contributions and aggregate social welfare. Politicians thus seek to please the "winning" lobbies and the electorate as a whole.

I adapt the Grossman-Helpman model of the lobbying process as follows: each lobby, representing a particular policy decision in connection with international law (whether for or against the adherence or compliance decision), confronts the government with a contribution schedule. The contribution schedule arrays contributions against policy decisions. The government then sets a policy and collects the appropriate contribution from each lobby. "An equilibrium is a set of contribution schedules such that each lobby's schedule maximizes the aggregate utility of the lobby's members, taking as given the schedules of the other lobby groups."[76] This model has the structure of a common agency problem: a situation where several principals seek to influence the behavior of a single agent. "The government here serves as an agent for the various (and conflicting) special interest groups, while bearing a cost for implementing an inefficient policy that stems from its accountability to the general electorate."[77]

---

[74] *See* Gene M. Grossman & Elhanan Helpman, "Trade Wars and Trade Talks," 103 *J. Pol. Econ.* 675, 678 (1995).
[75] It may also be that politicians are civic-minded, resulting in precisely the same motivation, assuming that the voter's utility is actually congruent with the politician's civic vision.
[76] Gene M. Grossman & Elhanan Helpman, "Protection for Sale," 84 *Am. Econ. Rev.* 833, 836 (1994).
[77] *Id.*

Here, for simplicity, I do not examine the distinction or the strategic relationship between legislatures and executives; I aggregate these components of government. I am interested here in focusing attention not on the governmental processes or the type of government, but on the constellation of political support. The lobbies make implicit offers relating prospective contributions to the policies of the government.

The Grossman-Helpman model is designed to explain the effectiveness of lobbying in regard to trade policy, and specifically, tariffs and subsidies.[78] Individual preferences over protectionism are assumed to arise from their sector-specific endowments. Following Mancur Olson, there are some owners of factors of production who are able to organize, and some who are unable to do so.[79] The unorganized owners of factors of production do not make contributions, and so lack this type of influence over policy. I assume that each lobby structures its contribution schedule to maximize the total welfare of its members. Similar to Grossman and Helpman, I am first "interested in the political equilibrium of a two-stage noncooperative game, in which the lobbies simultaneously choose their political contribution schedules in the first stage and the government sets policy in the second."[80]

An equilibrium will be a set of contribution schedules, one set for each lobby, such that each one maximizes the joint welfare of its lobby's members given the schedules set by the other lobbies and the anticipated political optimization by the government. The structure of this menu-auction problem is such that the policy vector chosen by the government is assumed to maximize the joint welfare of the lobby and the government, given the contribution schedules offered by the other lobbies.

The Grossman-Helpman model relates a lobby's equilibrium success in obtaining protection to: (i) the state of its political organization; (ii) the ratio of domestic output in the relevant industry to net trade; (iii) the elasticity of import demand; (iv) the relative importance to the government of campaign contributions versus voter welfare; and (v) the fraction of voters that belong to the lobby group. Items (ii) and (iii) are specific to the trade context, but one would expect to find other measures of lobby welfare in other international legal contexts.

---

[78] Grossman & Helpman, *supra* note 76, at 834 ("This paper seeks to explain the equilibrium structure of trade protection. We are interested in understanding which special interest groups will be especially successful in capturing private benefits from the political process.").

[79] *See* Mancur Olson Jr., *The Logic of Collective Action: Public Goods and the Theory of Groups* 53–65 (1965) (providing a model predicting under what conditions organized political groups are likely to emerge).

[80] Grossman & Helpman, *supra* note 76, at 838.

In their 1995 article, "The Politics of Free Trade Agreements,"[81] Grossman and Helpman extend their 1994 model to examine the conditions under which two states might agree to a free-trade agreement. This model uses assumptions about the welfare effects of trade liberalization and addresses the decision to adhere. Grossman and Helpman assume that the status quo prior to an international agreement is itself a domestic political equilibrium in each state.[82] This assumption seems appropriate.

Thus, the opportunity for an international agreement can be understood as an exogenous shock to the existing domestic equilibrium. The opportunity for an international agreement changes the relative prices. In the trade context, the possibility for foreign compliance with a commitment to liberalize makes the domestic political price of protectionism higher by engaging the concerns of domestic producers for export.

Grossman and Helpman, in the context of establishment of a free-trade agreement, find that in order for an agreement to be entered into, there must be a sufficient number of exporters in each country prepared to lobby for the agreement, on the basis of the welfare gains these lobbies would achieve by virtue of the performance by the other state of its obligations under the agreement.[83] They use the concept of a politically *Pareto efficient agreement*, meaning an agreement with the property that no party could gain politically except at the expense of the other.[84] After they establish the Pareto frontier, they develop a bargaining model that shows first that two states negotiating by making alternating proposals would reach an equilibrium somewhere along the Pareto frontier.[85] The specific equilibrium selected would depend, under perfect information, on the relative positions of the two states, including their discount factors or degree of patience, and each state's relative aggregate welfare under the status quo.

In the trade context where Grossman and Helpman develop their model, it is possible to assume that specific industry groups, or lobbies, have specific types of interests in trade policy. In the broader international law context, lobby interests will be more diverse, and preferences cannot be assumed to be

---

[81] Gene M. Grossman & Elhanan Helpman, "The Politics of Free-Trade Agreements," 85 *Am. Econ. Rev.* 667 (1995).

[82] *Id.* at 668–70.

[83] Grossman & Helpman, *supra* note 76, at 847–49 (describing under what conditions the interests of various lobbying groups may align to make trade agreements across coalitions and countries possible).

[84] *See* Gene M. Grossman & Elhanan Helpman, *Interest Groups and Trade Policy* 27 (2002) (describing the concept of a Pareto efficient agreement).

[85] *See* Grossman & Helpman, *supra* note 81.

confined to narrow wealth gains. However, there may be industry, ethnic, or other groups that have relatively narrow interests.

Whereas in the Grossman-Helpman model lobbies make their contributions contingent on trade policy, we may generalize to assume that lobbies make their contributions contingent on international legal policy. For example, within domestic societies there will be a lobby group that is interested in increased human rights in other states. Although this interest may be explained in terms of preferences, the types of preferences involved will depend on the particular legal rule involved, and this type of interest cannot be compared directly with other types of interests that may be measured in monetary terms. Nor are we able to make any assumptions about the utility function of any particular group. Rather, the only assumption that seems defensible is that each international law rule will harm some groups and help others. However, there is one type of lobby that generally appears to be in favor of international legal adherence and compliance.[86] That type of lobby is exemplified, in the United States, by the members of American Society of International Law (ASIL). I will discuss this type of lobby in greater detail.

It is important to recognize that, in this political Pareto efficiency-based model, "compliance can be rational even if the country as a whole pays for it more than benefits from it."[87] The converse is also true: compliance may be irrational, in the sense that it is not supported by sufficient political force, even if the country as a whole benefits from it in a welfare sense more than it pays. However, if public welfare is included in the government's utility function, as in the Grossman-Helpman model, through the mechanism of voting, then international legal rules that increase public welfare are more likely to meet with both adherence and compliance.

Turning to compliance, the question is, conditional on adherence to (entry into) an international legal rule at an initial time $(t_1)$, what are the circumstances under which a particular country will comply with that legal rule at a later time $(t_2)$? I also assume that domestic politics change, in an "obsolescing bargains"[88] sense.[89] Thus, the coalition that supports adherence at $t_1$ may not have the same structure or magnitude, and may not even support compliance, at $t_2$.

---

[86] Of course, there will be exceptions. For example, some rules of international law may be found to be objectionable by some portion of the membership of the ASIL.
[87] Xinyuan Dai, *International Institutions and National Policies* 6 (2007).
[88] *See* Raymond Vernon, *Sovereignty at Bay* 46–53 (1971).
[89] *See* Giovanni Maggi & Andrés Rodríguez-Clare, "The Value of Trade Agreements in the Presence of Political Pressures," 106 J. Pol. Econ. 574, 574–601 (1998) (examining the utility of trade agreements to assist governments in opposing changing political pressure).

I assume an international legal rule with some depth in the sense described by Downs, Rock and Barsoom:[90] the rule requires behavior that would not occur without the added inducement that arises from operation of the rule. In our context, the domestic political process by itself and without any effect of international law would not decide to conform national behavior to the rule. This is a slightly different issue from the question, addressed for example by Grossman and Helpman, of whether the domestic political process would result in a decision to adhere to an international agreement.

I further assume that in order for any state to decide to comply with an international legal rule, there must be a coalition of domestic lobbies that is strong enough to determine national behavior. This assumption can survive the diversity of national politics: it is not necessary to have a dominant interest-group-based politics such as that of the United States for this type of model to apply. Even autocracies involve sensitivity to political support, although the relative importance of political support compared to government policy may differ markedly. Furthermore, decision making may, in some circumstances, take place in arenas that are insulated from interest-group politics, and even from executive policy. This is the case with international legal rules that have direct effect, in which the decision is delegated exclusively to courts. I focus on lobbies more broadly, recognizing that other mechanisms, such as courts, may play the critical role in compliance.[91]

## I) *Information Problems*

Xinyuan Dai has developed a model of compliance with international law, incorporating both electoral leverage and informational advantage as sources of influence for a domestic lobby.[92] Dai models a government's compliance decision in the context of competing domestic lobbies. Dai emphasizes the information problem whereby lobbies cannot observe the government's action directly. The accuracy of the lobbies' inference about the government's action "depends on how much information they have about the policy process and how much resources they invest in monitoring the governmental action."[93] Dai thus develops a model in which a government's compliance decision

---

[90] See George Downs, David M. Rocke, & Peter N. Barsoom, "Is the Good News about Compliance Good News about Cooperation?" 50 *Int'l Org.* 379 (1996).

[91] Anne Van Aaken, "Effectuating Public International Law Through Market Mechanisms," 165 *J. Institutional & Theoretical Econ.* 33 (2009).

[92] Xinyuan Dai, "Why Comply? The Domestic Constituency Mechanism," 59 *Int'l. Org.* 363, 363 (2005).

[93] *Id.* at 365.

is determined by both the electoral leverage of the domestic lobby and the domestic lobby's informational position.

In Dai's model, interest groups differ in: (i) their preferences regarding compliance – for example, one group may prefer a low compliance level, whereas the other prefers a high compliance level; and (ii) their informational endowments. Dai models informational endowments as a separate variable, although it might be that information endowments vary with the magnitude of preferences. Her main concern is that interest groups do not perfectly observe compliance efforts.[94] However, we might speculate that in many international law areas, interest groups would perfectly observe compliance itself.

On the other hand, the government official's objective function includes both private interest in reelection and aggregate social welfare on the basis of altruism. The expected value to the government official of being reelected is discounted by the probability of reelection, and by a discount factor. The inclusion of aggregate social welfare is intended to separate this factor from concern for reelection, but is not necessary for the central result of Dai's model.[95] The government official's interest in reelection makes the government official's welfare dependent on how lobbies perceive the official's compliance policy.

As might be expected, because it is built into Dai's model, Dai finds that where the group that favors compliance has greater electoral leverage and monitoring ability, compliance increases.[96] Conversely, where the group that favors violation has greater leverage and monitoring ability, compliance decreases. Of course, if aggregate social welfare is included in the equation, these differences in leverage and monitoring ability are not necessarily by themselves determinative, and the model does not tell us how to commensurate among these different factors. Furthermore, as Dai points out, the value to the incumbent of reelection, and her discount factor, will affect the incumbent's susceptibility to influence by lobbies.[97]

Although recognizing the importance of Dai's reference to each lobby's informational advantage as a source of influence, I make the simplifying assumption that the informational advantage is either included in the measure of political strength, or is co-variable with the magnitude of political strength or preferences, and therefore I do not account separately for informational advantage. Furthermore, whereas Dai's approach assumes that lobbies have

---

[94] See id., at 368, 384 (explaining that domestic interest-group politics affects democratic governments' decisions to comply and how international organizations should use this observation to increase compliance).

[95] Id. at 369.    [96] Id. at 364.

[97] Id. at 374.

difficulty assessing the degree of effort expended by government to comply, I focus on actual measures of compliance rather than efforts toward compliance, and assume that actual compliance is easier to measure than efforts. This will not always be true, but it seems to be a reasonable simplification. In appropriate circumstances, separate accounting for information would be important.

## II) Reciprocity

A number of scholars have examined reciprocity, or retaliation, as a means of inducing compliance with international law.[98] This theoretical approach is elegant and compelling: states comply with international law in order to induce other states to comply, or in order to induce other states to continue to refrain from retaliation. In Keohane's "specific reciprocity" (as opposed to diffuse reciprocity) sense, there is little difference between reciprocity and retaliation.[99]

Most work in this area has arisen from a growing rationalist debate regarding compliance with customary international law.[100] Norman and Trachtman,[101] for example, developed a repeated multilateral prisoner's dilemma model of formation of and compliance with customary international law. This model is based on the potential for retaliatory defection. It focuses on the parameters of the multilateral prisoner's dilemma in the customary international law context, but its parameters would be equally relevant in the treaty context. These parameters include: (i) the relative value of cooperation versus defection; (ii) the number of states effectively involved; (iii) the extent to which increasing the number of states involved increases the value of cooperation or the detriments of defection, including whether the particular issue has characteristics of a commons problem, a public good, or a network good; (iv) the information available to the states involved regarding compliance and defection; (v) the relative patience of states in valuing the benefits of long-term

---

[98] *E.g.*, Robert O. Keohane, *After Hegemony* 104–05, 128–31 (2005); Andrew T. Guzman, *How International Law Works: A Rational Choice Theory* 211–12 (2008) (listing reputation, reciprocity, and retaliation as costs that deter states from noncompliance).

[99] Keohane, *supra* note 35.

[100] *See* Jack L. Goldsmith & Eric A. Posner, *The Limits of International Law* (2005); Andrew T. Guzman, "A Compliance-Based Theory of International Law," 90 *Cal. L. Rev.* 1823 (2002); Edward T. Swaine, "Rational Custom," 52 *Duke L. J.* 559 (2002); Pierre-Hugues Verdier, "Cooperative States: International Relations, State Responsibility and the Problem of Custom," 42 *Va. J. Intl. L.* 839 (2002). The Goldsmith and Posner book has spawned a rich responsive literature. *E.g.*, George Norman & Joel P. Trachtman, "The Customary International Law Game," 99 *Am. J. Int'l L.* 541, 541 (2005).

[101] Norman & Trachtman, *supra* note 100, at 548.

cooperation compared to short-term defection; (vi) the expected duration of interaction; (vii) the frequency of interaction; and (viii) the existence of other bilateral or multilateral relationships among the states involved.[102]

Norman and Trachtman highlighted some of the characteristics of different states' domestic politics that might affect their level of patience and resulting propensity to accept and comply with rules of customary international law. (In custom, the adherence phase and compliance phase may be less distinct than in treaty.) However, they did not analyze the decision-making process within states or the lobbying game within states. Other rationalist approaches focusing on retaliation are characterized by the same limitation.

I assume that a state's decision to adhere to and comply with international law is dependent on domestic politics. We must recognize that states have a variety of interests, represented by different interest groups. Certain domestic lobbies are motivated by the possibility of direct foreign reciprocity and other domestic lobbies are motivated by respect for international law. As will be discussed in more detail, it is possible that respect for international law may also be understood as a special kind of diffuse reciprocity.

A good example of the type of specific reciprocity and engagement of domestic interests that benefit from reciprocity comes from the trade context. As discussed by Grossman and Helpman,[103] exporters are a domestic constituency interested in foreign liberalization. Therefore, exporters are concerned with domestic compliance with liberalization commitments in order to ensure against reciprocal punishment in the form of protectionism abroad.

It is important to note that reciprocity may be complex: it is not necessarily tit-for-tat, where each state promises the same performance.[104] Indeed, the possibility for complex barter or package deals increases the set of possible transactions. For example, whereas State A may be concerned with human rights in State B, for any number of reasons, State B may be unconcerned with human rights in State A. However, State B may be concerned with trade liberalization in State A, perhaps because State A already has sufficient autonomous reasons for providing a satisfactory level of human rights. In fact, international law increases the opportunities for complex barter by allowing diverse performances to be linked and supported by broad fidelity to international law.

On the other hand, uncertainty as to which commitments the counterparty will suspend in response to a violation would limit the likelihood that the domestic lobby concerned with those commitments will lobby for compliance. There may be a collective-action problem among possible lobbies. One way

---

[102] *Id.* at 542.
[103] Grossman & Helpman, *supra* note 81, at 687.   [104] Putnam, *supra* note 58, at 446–47.

to reduce the effects of this collective-action problem would be to designate in advance, and specifically, the type of retaliatory action that the counterparty will take.[105]

### III) The Role of Government and the Public International Law Lobby

It is useful to examine two sources of influence that might have a broader effect on adherence to and compliance with international law. Each state will have a government interested in maximizing political support or welfare more generally. Each state may also have a private group interested in supporting the international legal system in general. This might be called the public international law lobby or PILL. The government and the PILL can be included in a model of the domestic politics of international law in the same way that other lobbies are included.

The availability of international law as a general tool is important to each government, because international law allows the government to deliver greater governmental services under policy "trade" than under policy autarky, enhancing overall government support. The international legal system is best understood as a tool for enhancing the effectiveness of government to deliver the services demanded by constituents. For this reason, each government will have at least some interest in supporting the international legal system in general. Indeed, there is a network externality effect with respect to international legal compliance. As international law becomes more extensive and intensive, and more important to the delivery of government services, the interest of government in maintaining the international legal system will increase. So, as international law grows, it grows stronger. Furthermore, as it grows stronger it will be more useful for a wider range of tasks, causing the scope of international law to become more extensive. These network externalities support some of the spillover ideas of the functionalists.

The PILL may be motivated by altruism, including a general idea that international law provides broad benefits along the lines suggested previously. It may be motivated in addition or instead by an expectation that more international law will bring more power and income to international lawyers. This could not only cause the PILL to argue for more international law, but also cause it to argue for more compliance, as more compliance would be expected to evidence the importance of international law. Evidence for the importance

---

[105] This would be one benefit of the type of "contingent liberalization commitments" suggested by Robert Lawrence as a structure for remedies in the trade context. Robert Z. Lawrence, *Crimes and Punishments? Retaliation under the WTO* 79–89 (2003).

of international law, in turn, would add to the prestige and income of international lawyers. Furthermore, more compliance with international law might result in more international law, further benefiting the PILL.

For example, the mission of the ASIL "is to foster the study of international law and to promote the establishment and maintenance of international relations on the basis of law and justice."[106] So, yet another group has incentives to lobby for adherence to and compliance with international law: professors who form a core leadership group within ASIL stand to gain from inducing greater study of international law. Furthermore, "establishment and maintenance of international relations on the basis of law" can and should be understood as promoting adherence to and compliance with international law.

The PILL would thus be expected to support compliance with international law under most circumstances. I say "most" rather than "all" because there is an occasional debate regarding whether legitimacy may trump legality, especially in connection with humanitarian intervention.[107] Putting those exceptional circumstances aside, we might consider the PILL effect as fairly constant across international law rules.

Furthermore, whereas the PILL might, for the reasons set out, generally advocate adherence to international legal rules, it would not advocate adherence in all cases. For example, it would not necessarily take a position with respect to a particular state's entry into further preferential trade agreements, into stronger intellectual property protection treaties, or into further bilateral investment treaties. On the other hand, the PILL might more broadly advocate adherence to more international law restraining the use of force or promoting human rights. However, one would expect the PILL to be more likely to advocate compliance with international law in all but the exceptional circumstances mentioned previously.

In addition to the public choice explanation of the PILL influence described, the PILL, and government officials, may have an altruistic or civic-minded position, related to the fact that compliance with international law in general may be broadly beneficial because of network effects among international legal rules. Although adherence to international law might have some network effects also, these would appear to be weaker. Importantly, this public welfare position may be held both by the PILL and by government officials. The PILL may seek to educate government officials on the public welfare effects of compliance with international law. The altruistic position might be

---

[106] American Society of International Law, Overview (2010). Retrieved from http://www.asil.org/mission.cfm.

[107] *See* Simon Chesterman, "Legality versus Legitimacy: Humanitarian Intervention, the Security Council, and the Rule of Law," 33 *Security Dialog* 293 (2002).

on the basis of facts or beliefs. It is in connection with the PILL, and with the government as a lobby itself as will be described, that the constructivist model may have the greatest power: ideas and engagement may support compliance through the PILL and government.

Indeed, it may be that a broad group of citizens holds the view that compliance with international law is important, affecting their voting behavior and therefore the behavior of government officials. A 2002 Chicago Council on Foreign Relations survey showed that 43 percent of Americans considered strengthening international law a "very important" foreign policy goal, whereas another 43 percent rated it as "somewhat" important.[108] In a more recent World Public Opinion survey, respondents in 17 of 21 countries placed compliance with international law above national interest.[109]

It is important to note that there may also be an anti-international law lobby.[110] To the extent that such a lobby exists, its effects can be netted against the PILL, and to the extent that the anti-international law lobby is stronger than the PILL, then the PILL variable would simply be negative.

## D) TOWARD A MODEL

The following discussion is intended to outline a model of how domestic coalitions in two countries would be affected by and would affect adherence to and compliance with international law.

Assume two states, $H$ and $F$. Assume $H$ and $F$ each has exactly four lobbies, and that the respective governments of $H$ and $F$ represent a fifth interest group, each with the policy goal profiles set forth. Assume perfect knowledge by each player of the policy preferences and magnitudes of each lobby. Magnitude is a measure of the political valence of each lobby, although as noted it could include knowledge endowment as to compliance. The model would involve four stages. In the first stage, the lobbies in each country set contribution schedules to influence their government. In the second stage, the governments negotiate an agreement. In the third stage, lobbies (perhaps including new or different ones, and perhaps with different magnitudes) lobby about compliance. In the last stage, governments choose whether or not to comply. In the following discussion, I focus on two stages: $t_1$, when the governments negotiate and enter into an agreement; and $t_2$, when the governments choose

---

[108] Chicago Council on Foreign Relations, *supra* note 43. *See also* Michael Tomz, *supra* note 43.
[109] World Public Opinion, World Public Opinion on International Law and the World Court 1 (2009). Retrieved from http://www.worldpublicopinion.org/pipa/pdf/nov09/WPO_IntlLaw_Nov09_quaire.pdf.
[110] *See* Peter Spiro, "The New Sovereigntists," 79 *Foreign Aff.* 6 (2000).

whether or not to comply. It is important to note that lobbies at the first and third stages would be expected to anticipate the situation at the second and fourth stages, and respond accordingly.

H lobbies:

- J: policy goal is $x$ (for example, either consumers seeking free trade in bananas imported to $H$,[111] or environmentalists seeking carbon reduction).
- K: policy goal is *not-x* (for example, either import competing producers seeking protection in bananas in $H$, or oil companies seeking to avoid carbon reduction).
- L: policy goal is $y$ (for example, either orange producer seeking free trade in oranges exported to $F$, or separate group of environmentalists seeking protection of the rain forest in $F$).
- $P_h$: policy goal is adherence to international law at $t_1$ ($P_{h1}$) and compliance with international law at $t_2$ ($P_{h2}$). Assume that $P_{h2} > P_{h1}$ (international law lobbies are harmed more by noncompliance than nonadherence).
- $G_h$: government of $H$ (excluding the effects already reflected by $J$, $K$, $L$, and $P_h$) as a separate interest group that seeks to maximize its voting support by maximizing general public welfare in connection, inter alia, with adherence and compliance and concern for reciprocity and retaliation in connection with nonadherence at $t_1$ ($G_{h1}$) and noncompliance at $t_2$ ($G_{h2}$). Assume that $G_{h2} > G_{h1}$ (there is greater concern for retaliation against noncompliance than nonadherence).

If domestic equilibrium at $t_1$ were $x$ (the preferred policy of $J$), that is $J > K$, then no international law would be needed to induce $x$. However, assume that at $t_1$, $K > J$. (We are assuming international law with depth.) Therefore, the domestic equilibrium at $t_1$ is *not-x*: $H$ would not enter into an international agreement binding it to $x$. However, assume that $J + L + P_{h1} + G_{h1} > K$. Therefore, international law that engages the lobbying power of $L$ could cause a shift from *not-x* to $x$ at the adherence stage ($t_1$), inducing adherence to a rule of international law. Once that rule of international law is established, there is a shift from $P_{h1}$ to $P_{h2}$, and from $G_{h1}$ to $G_{h2}$. According to our assumptions, these shifts would be expected to increase the tendency to comply. In order to

---

[111] These policies in parentheses are merely provided as examples. Any policy where reciprocity is valuable and the magnitudes are appropriate could be substituted. For example, y could be protection of the ozone layer, and x avoidance of terrorist attacks. The point is that within each domestic system, there is: (i) a lobby on each side of the contention regarding the domestic measure; (ii) a lobby that cares about foreign measures; (iii) a public international law lobby that cares about the growth of and compliance with international law; and (iv) the government which, aside from its interest in lobbies' support, is also interested in public welfare as a way to increase voting support.

determine actual compliance at any given time, we would need to examine whether at that time $J + L + P_{h2} + G_{h2} > K$.

It is important to note that in this model, international law only affects state behavior pursuant to the assumptions regarding relative magnitudes of lobbies. This model does not utilize "compliance pull" or other effects of international law, separate from the force of the national lobbies that care about compliance with international law. However, in assuming that $P_{h1} < P_{h2}$ and $G_{h1} < G_{h2}$, we are assuming a tendency to comply, conditional on adherence. The magnitudes of these differences tell us something about the level of vulnerability of continued compliance to changes in other factors.

Also, recall that the issue-specific lobbies are not the only determinants of public policy. Under the assumptions of the Grossman-Helpman model, broader public welfare enters the equation through G by virtue of voting.[112] Therefore, an international legal rule that increases public welfare is more likely to achieve both adherence and compliance.

As outlined, H's decision to adhere and comply is partially dependent on the decision of F to reciprocate, inducing L to lobby for adherence and compliance. The situation in F is a mirror image of H, with adherence and compliance by both increasing their joint welfare, according to the assumptions of this model. The F lobbies are now described.

F lobbies:

M: policy goal is y (for example, either consumers seeking free trade in oranges imported to F, or protection of rain forest).

N: policy goal is not-y (for example, either import competing producers seeking protection in oranges in F, or seeking to develop the rain forest).

Q: policy goal is x (for example, either banana producer seeking free trade in bananas exported to H, or oil companies seeking to avoid carbon reduction).

$P_f$: policy goal is adherence to international law at $t_1$ ($P_{f1}$) and compliance with international law at $t_2$ ($P_{f2}$). Assume that $P_{f2} > P_{f1}$ (international law lobbies are harmed more by noncompliance than nonadherence).

$G_f$: government of F (excluding the effects already reflected by M, N, Q, and $P_f$), as a separate lobby that seeks to maximize its voting support by maximizing general public welfare in connection, inter alia, with adherence, compliance, and concern for reciprocity and retaliation in connection with nonadherence at $t_1$ ($G_{f1}$) and noncompliance at $t_2$ ($G_{f2}$). Assume that $G_{f2} > G_{f1}$ (there is greater concern for retaliation against noncompliance than nonadherence).

[112] Grossman & Helpman, *supra* note 76, at 847–49.

Assume that at $t_1$, $N > M + P_{f_1} + G_{f_1}$, therefore domestic equilibrium is *not-y*. However, assume that $M + Q + P_{f_1} + G_1 > N$. The situation of $F$ then parallels that of $H$.

Therefore, and this points to the critical function of international cooperation, if $H$ and $F$ are considered separately, they have separate equilibria of *not-x* and *not-y*. However, at $t_1$, if $H$ and $F$ are considered together – their ability to interact is an exogenous shock to each of their separate equilibria – they are able to reach an international exchange of policy. This international exchange of policy is politically Pareto superior, as it results in greater support for each government.[113] We have assumed that $L$ and $Q$ (the parties in each of $H$ and $F$ concerned about the measures taken by the other state), when their respective influence is added to $J$ and $M$, respectively, is able to overcome $K$ and $N$, respectively. So, at $t_1$, under interaction, a new equilibrium arises, of $x$ and $y$, inducing adherence to an international agreement.

However, at $t_2$, the compliance phase, this structure may take on the characteristics of a prisoner's dilemma game. That is, if $H$ can defect and move to *not-x*, and $F$ plays $y$, it might be that $H$ can garner the most political support.[114] However, assuming all positions remain the same as at $t_1$, if $H$ defects, then $F$ can defect in response, resulting in a non-cooperative equilibrium. However, assuming that $P_2 > P_1$, and $G_2 > G_1$, the differences in these factors may be sufficient in magnitude, especially when aggregated over time or multiple cooperation contexts, to exceed the value of defection, avoiding the prisoner's dilemma.[115] In fact, as noted previously, concern regarding the integrity of the international law system to enable it to continue to produce political welfare-increasing agreements may be included in $P_2$ and $G_2$.

Note that at $t_1$, the forces in $H$ and $F$ supporting *not-x* and *not-y*, respectively, will be expected to oppose the creation of the international linkage that changes the equilibrium to their detriment. In addition, these forces will be expected to oppose the creation of international legal rules that will result in the shift from $P_1$ to $P_2$ and from $G_1$ to $G_2$, which these forces anticipate will entrench their disfavored policy. However, the fact that they anticipate these effects does not mean that they have the lobbying power to avoid them. Nevertheless, they may seek to engage sovereigntist or other generally opposing forces in order to supplement their policy position.

---

[113] It is not necessarily superior from a public welfare standpoint.

[114] Putnam suggests that policymakers generally have an incentive to cheat. Putnam, *supra* note 58, at 438 (*citing* Matthew E. Canzoneri & Jo Anna Gray, "Two Essays on Monetary Policy in an Interdependent World," (International Finance Discussion Paper 219, Feb. 1983).

[115] For a full discussion of the prisoner's dilemma dynamic in compliance with international law, and the circumstances under which it may be escaped, *see* Norman & Trachtman, *supra* note 100.

Further development and use of this model will depend on policymakers' ability to identify proxies for power and interest of lobbies. In international economic law areas, wealth and amount at stake may serve as a proxy. In other areas, such as human rights or international environmental law, size of membership in relevant groups – such as ethnic groups – and survey data regarding the magnitude of individual concern may be helpful. However, as a guide to negotiators and policymakers, this approach may be useful without further formalization. If it is helpful to know about compliance, there is no more complete or precise approach. The test of a model is not whether it answers every question perfectly, but whether it answers questions that need to be answered in a useful way and better than the other tools available.

What systematic features does this model exhibit? First, because we assume that $P_2 > P_1$, and $G_2 > G_1$, this model exhibits a systematic bias toward compliance, conditional on adherence. However, although this is a systematic bias, it cannot be expected to overcome changes in other parameters in all cases. Moreover, the magnitude of this systematic bias depends on the individual magnitude of $P_2$ and $G_2$ in each state. This focus on $P_2$ and $G_2$ may either supplement or supplant the liberal states theory, depending on the cause of $P_2$ and $G_2$. These differentials between $P_2$ and $G_2$ may also be understood within a reputation or reciprocity model, as determinants of the importance to the particular state of its reputation or diffuse reciprocity in determining whether to comply. In a prisoner's dilemma model, these differentials can be seen as a measure of the extent to which the shadow of the future, including compliance in connection with other rules, affects the behavior of the subject state.

Second, this model accepts that domestic lobbies may vary in intensity from $t_1$ to $t_2$. This variation may be for exogenous reasons, or it may systematically be that lobbies that achieve their preferences at $t_1$ become wealthier or otherwise stronger at $t_2$ as a result. If this is the case, we would again see a systematic bias toward compliance, conditional on adherence.

How can policy preferences change in ways that might give rise to noncompliance? In other words, in what ways are international cooperation arrangements not self-enforcing? First, the timing of performance by one state may differ from the timing of performance by another, and this may give rise to asset specificity after $t_1$ adherence. In this context, by asset specificity I mean that the investment in compliance by one party would be less valuable to that party if the other party does not carry out its side of the bargain. This is no different from any other asset specificity in contracting. However, under asset specificity, a greater role for a PILL, or governmental preferences for compliance, may be required to induce compliance with international law, as the $H$ lobbies that benefit from the asset specific investment by $F$ would have little reason to lobby in support of compliance after performance by F. Obviously, to the extent that performance is expected to take place symmetrically at multiple moments over an extended period of time, this type of asset specificity may be reduced. If the period of time is finite, it is still possible for cooperation to unravel in anticipation of the last period.

Second, either state may have acted strategically or opportunistically at the adherence stage, developing a coalition to adhere to in order to reap benefits that may arise from adherence, with no intent or political power to actually comply. This is a sub-case of the first type of change, as it assumes that the non-defecting state gives some performance after $t_1$ adherence, whereas the defecting state fails to comply at $t_2$.

Third, the political magnitude of various lobbies may change over time. A prediction made at $t_1$ regarding the lobbying valence of various lobbies may have a high probability of being accurate at $t_1$, but would be expected to become less likely to be accurate over time. Consider, for example, circumstances of sudden great political change, such as a revolution.

Fourth, this model suggests that uncertainty regarding domestic coalitions to support compliance would increase over time. It thus might suggest that governments may assess the value of reciprocal commitments over a delimited period of time, rather than over an indefinite period of time. This would reduce the magnitude of the shadow of the future in inducing compliance at any stage.

Fifth, we can show that international retaliation, reputation, and reciprocity cannot ensure compliance. Compliance will always depend on the constellation of domestic political forces in the relevant state.

Sixth, we may be able to suggest reasons for bilateralism versus multilateralism, mutatis mutandis. Bilateralism might allow for the construction of more nuanced political coalitions to induce compliance, individualized to the particular international legal transaction.

Seventh, we might be able to explain the use by domestic governments of international legal commitments at $t_1$ to lock in a policy that is supported by a domestic equilibrium at $t_1$, where there is a preference over future policy. Government at $t_1$ may do so by increasing the effect of $P$ and $G$ through adherence, and inducing support from a separate domestic lobby through reciprocity. I discuss the "lock-in" theory of international–human-rights law in Chapter 6.

Eighth, we may be able to assist in determining whether entry into a particular international legal commitment is done insincerely, without intent to comply. Counterparties would wish to evaluate whether there is sufficient domestic support for compliance with the commitments on which they rely.

## E) CHAPTER CONCLUSION

This chapter develops a policy-exchange contractual theory of international law, focusing on the advancement of domestic preferences through international law. It theorizes that international law is made by strategic states willing to reduce their autonomy along certain dimensions in order to increase the satisfaction of their preferences along other dimensions, where after the commensuration of these two dimensions each state's government counts itself better off. The mechanism of the state's decision making regarding this trade-off and commensuration is domestic politics. In this theory, when domestic coalition A stands to achieve a benefit greater than the loss expected by domestic coalition B, coalition A is able to enter the political arena and overcome coalition B, all other things being equal. Where an international transaction – one type of which is international law – could result in a political surplus, that surplus may induce a coalition to act to achieve it. Autonomous, sovereign states would be expected to enter into international law as an exercise of their efforts to maximize the achievement of their preferences.

This chapter has developed a rationalist theory of adherence to and compliance with international law that takes account of the internal decision-making process of states. It has always been true that the domestic public-policy process has formed coalitions in order to make public policy, and that there have always been dissenters. The international-relations context can be understood as an expansion of the possibilities for trade-offs and agreement – for formation of coalitions. The set of possible coalitions that may be formed is effectively increased by the ability to engage in international legal agreements.

Formation and compliance with international law is dependent on the identification and negotiation of efficient transnational political linkages. In an important sense, the scope of domestic politics is extended by the capability of entering into international agreements. Although we do not have a continuous transnational political system, international law forms a transmission belt that can link domestic lobbies transnationally. Indeed, by virtue of the expansion of the scope of the possibilities for Pareto-improving political transactions, the international extension of the scope of domestic politics, where it occurs, would generally be expected to increase domestic political welfare. Of course, the move from domestic political welfare to actual welfare depends on the extent to which domestic politics reflects actual welfare. In any event, a government that wishes to deliver the most to its people, or at least to get the most political support, will be required to enter the international law market for some transactions.

These transnational political linkages are the building blocks of the functionalism described in Chapter 1. International law is a tool for establishing functional transnational political linkages – or functional communities – to address particular issues.

The rationalist theory of adherence and compliance developed here provides a novel way of analyzing the possibilities for development of international law. It suggests a number of empirical research strategies that may be followed in order to evaluate and possibly revise or extend the theory developed. Perhaps more importantly, it provides a useful template by which states may evaluate the possibility that their counterparties will accept and comply with international legal obligations. As states approach important international public policy issues such as global warming, terrorism, and international financial crisis, this evaluative tool will allow them to be realistic regarding the possibility and utility of proposed international legal rules.

# 4 The Futurology of International Law

> Change is the law of life and those who look only to the past or present are certain to miss the future.
> John Fitzgerald Kennedy, Address in the Assembly Hall at Paulskirche in Frankfurt, June 25, 1963

This book addresses the future of international law. We must bear in mind that "it is impossible to predict the future, and all attempts to do so in any detail appear ludicrous within a very few years."[116]

Nevertheless, all law reform is necessarily predicated on expectations about the future, and we often act on the assumption that trends observed in the past will continue into the future. Therefore, all self-conscious law reform must be based on some degree of anticipation of future conditions. Although prediction may be deeply unreliable, it is inescapable. In order to speculate about the future of international law, we must examine first how existing international law fails to meet existing challenges, and also how it will fail to meet expected future challenges.

Changes in the fields of globalization, development, demography, technology, and democracy provide shocks to the existing equilibrium that change relative prices of different externalities, public goods, or other causes of international law. In this chapter, I suggest some of the broad trends that can generally be expected to increase the need for international cooperation, and to affect the tools available for international cooperation. I recognize also that some trends might reduce the need for international cooperation, and make international cooperation less likely. Other trends may reduce the need for formal law in international cooperation.

[116] Arthur C. Clarke, *Profiles of the Future* 13 (1973).

The overall effect of these changes will often make international law more valuable. Indeed, it appears reasonable to assume that they will make international law more valuable more often than they make international law less valuable. This is because the overall level of law in the world is unlikely to decline, whereas the ratio between international law and domestic law is likely to shift toward international law, for the reasons detailed in this and succeeding chapters. These changes can also change the cost of different types of international law, making it less costly to make and enforce international law. So, future changes will affect both the demand curve and the supply curve for international law.

In Chapters 5 through 9, I suggest how some of the changes described here affect the specific areas of law addressed in those chapters.

## A) PRESENT CONDITIONS AND FUTURE CONDITIONS

Existing law does not always seem to match existing conditions because laws are generally self-conscious responses, on the basis of analysis and ideas, to observed social conditions. That is, law can often be expected to lag social change. This type of conservatism might be understood in behavioral terms as a product of an *availability bias*: until we actually observe the problem, we are not motivated to act. The fundamental bias of government is conservative. This conservatism is often pragmatic, avoiding solutions to problems before they arise and thereby allowing responses to benefit from greater information about the concrete problem. Not all lags are good, however.

We might contrast this type of conservatism in law generally, and international law in particular, with a kind of utopian idealism that imagines that modifications to international law will themselves be the cause of a better future. Utopian idealism lacks credibility because it is not grounded in existing conditions or plausible future conditions. Utopian idealism has often made aggressive assumptions about future social conditions, or about the ability of law to effect social change. These assumptions are not necessarily false, but we have no way of knowing if they are true. However, it may be that the future is arriving more rapidly today than in the past. Indeed, the pace of technological change, at least, has accelerated greatly in recent years, and other changes, too, may be speeding up.

This book seeks to chart a middle course between utopian idealism and obstinate conservatism. It engages in an exercise in institutional imagination to suggest areas in which changes in international law will help us meet our current goals. In this chapter, it goes further by anticipating some likely changes in conditions in the near future, and suggesting how these changes may call for changes in international law.

It would be an exceedingly ignorant conservatism that would argue that the international law we have today or that was initiated in the 1648 Peace of Westphalia is the international law that we will have forever. Imagine if we still had the domestic laws, or the technologies, that existed then. Thus, the only worthy questions are of the pace and direction of change, and of the appropriate response.

In fields such as environmental protection, we have already learned to think of the future, and to plan for it. There would be no debate over global warming without anticipation of future problems. In other areas, international policymakers and lawyers seem like the ignorant generals of legend, always fighting the last war. However, one might well ask, given all the dire problems that we have to address today, why focus on the future? One answer, as in the environmental field, is that small adjustments today can make the future significantly better – indeed, the only way to achieve a good result may be to plan ahead, and with growing complexity more issues may require us to develop a longer horizon. Longer-run planning can only be motivated by intergenerational equity, and concern for our offspring. We would not want to avoid doing something today that could have a great return in terms of benefits to future generations.

Indeed, in domestic policy making, we already build the public goods such as power lines and airports, and internalize the externalities anticipated in the future. Although not all of these activities are thought of as legal, in the international setting, lacking a formal international government, legal rules often serve the same kinds of purposes as governmental-agency action does in the domestic sphere.

In this chapter, I briefly summarize predictions developed by others of potential change along five salient dimensions: (i) globalization; (ii) economic development; (iii) demography; (iv) technology; and (v) democratization. When discussing globalization, I include increasing economic integration in areas of trade in goods and services, investment, and migration. Economic development examines the potential for economic growth, and its distribution. Within demography, I focus on both aggregate changes and on the distribution of population change. Technology is an enormous category, but I focus on selected categories that may have the greatest effect on international law. By democratization, I mean to examine trends away from authoritarian rule, toward more accountable government.

To anticipate just one likely criticism, I understand that all of these trends or actual changes are plausibly reversible, and have indeed been reversed at

# The Futurology of International Law

times in the past. Any trend line suffers from our uncertainty as to whether the trend will continue. However, social change is not a random walk, and we can examine social forces that support the trends in determining whether they may plausibly continue. Indeed, international law may play either a progressive or conservative role, precipitating change or stabilizing either existing circumstances, or changed circumstances.

## B) HORIZON

As a practical matter, all law (except ex post facto law) addresses the future: law is intended to modify or at least respond to behavior in the future, and therefore always makes assumptions about future conditions. Most law, however, seems to be made with the near future in mind. Of course, from a practical standpoint, it is not useful to think far into the future, because it is too difficult to know how our decisions today will affect our position in a far-off future. More troubling, our tendency is to take inadequate account of the position of future generations: we are selfish vis-à-vis our heirs.

Global warming, financial crisis, war, and epidemic are all future events, and to varying degrees what we do today in international legal terms has an effect on whether and how these events affect us in the future. So in attempting to predict what international legal rules and institutions will serve us now and into the future, it is appropriate to choose both a short and medium horizon, of perhaps twenty and fifty years: 2032 and 2062. I am using assessments of the future developed by others, and they do not neatly match these specified horizons. These are the ranges I will investigate, however, and it would be foolish to pretend that estimates are precise.

What international legal rules will be needed in response to changing conditions and ideas? Table 4–1 summarizes the discussion, and provides some information for 1962 and 1912, as points of reference by which to see the broad scope of change going back 50 and 100 years. Coincidentally, 1912 closely preceded the First World War, and 1962 marked a high point in the Cold War.

## C) GLOBALIZATION

The world is experiencing a general and long-term (since the 1930s) trend toward globalization, in the sense of reduction of barriers to movement of goods, services, money, and people. As barriers drop, prices for all factors become more homogeneous, competition becomes more acute, economies of scale become easier to realize, and supply chains lengthen. Although there

TABLE 4-1. Changing conditions

| Horizon | Globalization | Development | Demography | Technology | Democratization |
|---|---|---|---|---|---|
| −100 = 1912 | Unprecedented integration from 1870–1914 | The world is relatively homogeneous, with most individuals near poverty | 2 billion. Early flexibility in free migration | Early days of electricity; airplane; radio | De-monarchization |
| −50 = 1962 | Beginning response to breakdown of globalization after World War II | Europe has recovered, and Latin America is not uniformly poor, but most of Asia and Africa are poor | 3 billion. Restricted migration | Nuclear; early computers; laser; man in space | Decolonization; resulting in greater number of countries, many of which lack economic viability |
| 2012 | Significant globalization allowing greater specialization and transfer of productivity-enhancing knowledge | Accelerating growth. Significant development in certain Asian and Latin countries; sustained high growth in China and India; 2 billion people remain in low-growth countries | 7 billion. Restricted migration, but greater demand for mobility | Networks and ubiquitous computing; biotechnology; broad cellular coverage; retrenchment on nuclear power | Increasing national democratization; social networking; transparency |

| | | | | | |
|---|---|---|---|---|---|
| +20 = 2032 | Continuing globalization caused by and causing development, technological change, consumer and citizen demand | China's economy catches up with U.S.; other developing countries improve significantly | 8 billion. Growth focused in developing countries. Urbanization; migration of 11 million from south to north annually | Continuing growth in computational and telecommunications power. Computers exceed man; international dispersion causes greater information regarding compliance; greater accuracy and power of weapons | More extensive national democratization |
| +50 = 2062 | Continued globalization | India's economy catches up with U.S.; continued homogenization of incomes, caused in part by globalization | Stabilization of population at 9 billion. Urbanization; slightly reduced migration | Much greater growth in computational and telecommunications power | Global democratization plus international democratic accountability |

have been reversals to globalization in the past, given the value of globalization, it is difficult to imagine significant and sustained reversals in the future. Furthermore, "both the scale of international trade and the globalization of technology and production distinguish the recent developments"[117] from those in the early twentieth century.

There is still significant enhanced welfare to be gained by extending globalization, especially in the field of migration.[118] Writing in 2012, with the Euro crisis and Doha Round of multilateral trade negotiations stark reminders that not all efforts toward globalization succeed when expected, with states increasingly attracted to capital controls, and viewing post-financial crisis anti-immigrant sentiment, we can still say that globalization seems likely overall to increase, although there will be important challenges and inevitable reversals.

Hirst and Thompson refer to these reversals, and to the fact that the current period of globalization is not unprecedented:

> Globalization has a history. The 50 years between 1950 and 2000 are not remarkable compared with the period 1850 to 1914 – when flows of merchandise trade, capital investment and labour migration were all comparable to or greater than those of today. Technological change in the form of international telegraph cables unified markets and led to price and interest rate convergence of a kind that has never been equaled since. Financial integration was far greater, and levels of capital export from the major lender countries unprecedented. Economic convergence in prices and wages across the Atlantic was largely achieved by vast flows of surplus labour from Europe to the New World. This process is not operating on the same scale today.[119]

We know that economic globalization can be reversed, because we have the experience of the first great globalization, during which there was unprecedented integration of markets. This globalization broke down in the aftermath of the First World War, and during the Great Depression and Second World War. However, it is possible that the development of the legal infrastructure of globalization can have a type of lock-in effect, making reversals less likely. It appears that the 2008 financial crisis caused less reversal of globalization than might have been anticipated, perhaps because of the restraining effects of international law, such as that of the WTO.

---

[117] Daron Acemoglu, *The World Our Grandchildren will Inherit: The Rights Revolution and Beyond*, MIT Department of Economics Working Paper 12–09, April 6, 2012, p. 9. Retrieved from http://ssrn.com/abstract=2037497.

[118] *See* Joel P. Trachtman, *The International Law of Economic Migration* (2009).

[119] Paul Hirst & Grahame Thompson, "The Future of Globalization," 37 *Cooperation and Conflict* 247, 248 (2002).

# The Futurology of International Law

Increased globalization will create demand for more, not less, international law to support and stabilize liberalization. International law and globalization are complements. Opportunities for trade make law-preventing barriers more valuable. "Economic growth always occurs in parallel with the development of political, legal, and regulatory institutions. One can think of this as applying to national, subnational, and international levels. It's a continuous process in which increments in economic capacity and the effectiveness of government complement each other."[120]

Globalization places important demands on international law:

- First, globalization makes the effects of one state's regulation, or lack thereof, more likely to have an impact on other states. For example, if food travels from Chile to the United States, then the United States will have a greater interest in Chilean food-safety regulation. The scope of policy externalities is amplified by globalization.
- Second, globalization makes the effects of one state's regulation, or lack thereof, more likely to have an effect, through the market (a pecuniary externality), on other states. For example, as discussed in Chapter 7, carbon "leakage" in the form of movement of carbon-intensive industries to states with less stringent regulation of carbon might hurt businesses in states with more stringent regulation.
- Third, globalization will increase industrialization and development, placing greater burdens on the environment, and increasing demand for goods and services.
- Fourth, globalization may increase communications and cosmopolitan feelings of community across states.
- Fifth, while globalization provokes interest in greater international law to facilitate globalization, it also provokes comparisons between the law of globalization and regulatory areas of international law that address externalities, pecuniary externalities, and public goods. For example, increased international trade law may provoke those concerned about international environmental problems to seek increased international environmental law. Thus, comparison may lead to further development of these other types of international law.

Neo-functionalists observe a feedback loop between increasing international transactions (in our context, globalization) and integration: "What has been found in empirical studies, again and again, is that European integration is

---

[120] Michael Spence, *The Next Convergence: The Future of Economic Growth in a Multispeed World* 39 (2011).

largely the product of a basic kind of Haasian feedback loop: (a) increasing cross-border transactions activates (b) supranational governance (dispute resolution and rule-making), which facilitate (c) a subsequent expansion of cross-border transactions, which translates into greater social demand for new forms of supranational governance (spillover)."[121] Thus, to the extent that globalization proceeds, it is to be expected that greater international law will be called for in response.

### D) DEVELOPMENT

"The average citizen of the world has a much higher income than was the case 100 years ago; we are about eight times richer than our grandparents who lived at the time."[122] Although income inequality has trended disappointingly upward in the twentieth century, over the next several decades, the world's middle class will grow substantially, both in absolute and relative terms. The middle class will also be globalized – extending deeply into many states that today are considered developing countries. There will be two main drivers of growth in developing countries: (i) knowledge transfer; and (ii) globalization. *Knowledge transfer* is the process whereby technology and know-how are acquired by developing countries from advanced countries. It is easier for them to acquire knowledge from advanced countries than to rely on purely indigenous knowledge creation. Knowledge transfer is promoted by globalization, often through the mechanism of foreign investment: "This process has also enabled much more rapid growth in economies such as China, which have been able to leverage their abundant low-wage labor, without having to go through the same investments and similar technological and institutional stages that advanced economies underwent in the 19th and early 20th centuries."[123]

Development has a synergetic relationship with globalization: greater globalization causes development, and greater development causes globalization. At some point, greater development will reduce a category of trade and globalization that is caused by price differentials between poor countries and wealthy countries, especially in labor markets.

Globalization allows developing countries to benefit from their competitive advantages. It allows them to specialize to a far greater extent than they would be able to if they addressed only the domestic market. Specialization allows greater productivity, as countries increasingly specialize in the goods

---

[121] Sandholtz & Stone Sweet, *supra* note 13.   [122] Acemoglu, *supra* note 117.
[123] *Id.* at 9–10.

and services where they have greatest efficiency. Moreover, technology and globalization have increased the scope of tradable goods and services, providing greater opportunities for development. One important example is the development of the business process and software-development outsourcing market in India, utilizing the Internet.

A recent report prepared by Price Waterhouse Coopers (PWC) predicts:

> In 2050, in U.S. dollar terms, China's economy will be almost as large as the U.S. economy. India's economy will have been the fastest-growing in the world for many years and the third largest in the world. China is expected to overtake the US as the largest economy in around 2025. India has the potential to nearly catch up with the US by 2050. The projected list of fastest growing economies to 2050 is headed by Vietnam, and the top 10 includes Nigeria, Philippines, Egypt and Bangladesh. The Brazilian economy will be as big as the Japanese. And the economies of Indonesia and Mexico will be larger than those of Germany and the U.K. The collective size of the "E7" economies (China, India, Brazil, Russia, Indonesia, Mexico, and Turkey) will be around 25 percent larger than that of the current G7 (U.S., Japan, Germany, UK, France, Italy, and Canada). Consumer spending in the E7 will be driving growth in the global economy as these countries catch up with living standards in the developed world. Living standards in India and Indonesia will be similar to those of South Korea and Spain in 2005, while those in China, Turkey, and Brazil will be at par with the G7.[124]

The decline in the G7 economies is relative, not absolute. In absolute terms, PWC suggests that the G7 will grow by about 150 percent between now and 2050, and a critical driver of this growth will be the demand for their goods and services from E7 economies.[125] These changes in economic leadership will translate into changes in international legal leadership, initially in connection with international economic affairs, but subsequently in other areas, as well.

Ian Morris offers a more long-term prediction when he says that by 2103, the Western economic lead will end, and the East will become powerful again.[126] In 2025, China's economic output will catch up with the United States, and by 2040, Chinese incomes will reach $85,000; Americans will be making $107,000.[127] Morris also predicts that between 2000 and 2050, social development will rise twice as much as it has in the prior fifteen millennia.

---

[124] PWC, "The World in 2050" (2006). Retrieved from http://www.pwc.com/gx/en/world-2050/growth-in-emerging-economies-oportunity-or-threat.jhtml.
[125] Retrieved from http://www.pwc.com/gx/en/world-2050/pdf/world_2050_brics.pdf. The "E-7" countries are China, India, Brazil, Mexico, Russia, Indonesia, and Turkey.
[126] Ian Morris, *Why the West Rules – For Now* 582 (2010).
[127] *Id.* at 588.

As countries develop, people tend to move from the countryside to urban areas, so development will cause an increase in urbanization. Urbanization contributes to pollution, democratization, and development. By 2025, 57 percent of the world population will live in urban areas,[128] and the world will add another eight megacities to the current group of nineteen – all except one of these eight will be in Asia and sub-Saharan Africa. More than half of Africa will live in cities, although the extent of urbanization will still be less than Europe or North America.[129] However, the United Nations Population Division (UNPD) estimates that the average annual rate of change of the urban population has been decreasing and will continue to decrease: 3.12 percent (1950) to 1.85 percent (2010), 1.54 percent (2030), and 1.05 percent (2050).[130] Meanwhile, the world rural population will peak in 2018, then fall to 2.8 billion by 2050.[131]

The number of people considered to be in the "global middle class" is projected to grow from 440 million to 1.2 billion or from 7.6 percent of the world's population to 16.1 percent over the next few decades, according to the World Bank.[132] Most of the new entrants will come from China and India. For example, in India the middle class share of the population was 5 percent in 2005, and is forecast to be 20 percent by 2015 and 40 percent by 2025.[133] Many changes are predicted because of this rising middle class. For example, car ownership in India is currently 14 per 1000 people, and is expected to grow significantly. By way of comparison, Australia and the United States have ownership rates of around 500 per 1000 people. India is projected to be the third largest automobile market in the world by 2030.[134]

What does this development, and convergence of incomes, mean for international law? First, convergence of wealth will lead to greater convergence of demand for global public goods. Reduced asymmetry of positions will make international agreement on provision of public goods easier. Movement to the middle class will increase domestic demand for environmental protection, human rights, political accountability, education, and other governmentally provided goods, as well as international law extensions of these goods. Today's

---

[128] Free World Academy Web site. Retrieved from http://www.freeworldacademy.com/globalleader/leader.htm.
[129] Laurence Smith, *The World in 2050* 32 (2010).
[130] UN Department of Economic and Social Affairs, Population Division, Population Estimates and Projections Section 2011 estimate. Retrieved from http://esa.un.org/unpd/wup/index.htm.
[131] Smith, *supra* note 129, at 35.
[132] Free World Academy Web site, *supra* note 128.
[133] "Our Future World: An Analysis of Global Trends, Shocks and Scenarios," Insights: Center for Future Studies. Retrieved from www.futurestudies.co.uk.
[134] *Id.*

developing countries will join with industrial countries in seeking greater environmental and health protection. They will find it less burdensome to accept international–human-rights commitments. They will seek greater legal rules facilitating free movement of goods, services, and money, and greater protection of intellectual property.

As we will see in Chapters 5–9, many international cooperation problems involve significant asymmetries, often between wealthy and poor countries. Along with greater symmetry will come greater opportunities for cooperation. However, in the nearer future, characterized by greater asymmetry, there will be greater need for international law that can overcome asset specificity to allow inter-temporal exchange of commitments: consideration provided early by wealthy states in exchange for consideration provided later by current poor states.

Second, greater sophistication, availability of information, and outward orientation will help citizens of today's developing countries seek greater human rights and accountability in their governments. Their governments will be increasingly required to enter the international relations market in order to maximize their ability to deliver the goods and services demanded of them.

Generally speaking, development will result in greater demand for international law. A mediating factor will be the fact that with growing symmetry, states will increasingly act autonomously, or be induced to act by soft law, making the role of international law less important.

## E) DEMOGRAPHY

In October 2011, the world's population reached 7 billion. The U.S. National Intelligence Council (NIC) predicts that by 2025, there will be 1.2 billion additional people on the planet. Asia, Africa, and Latin America will account for almost all population growth over the next twenty years; less than 3 percent of the growth will occur in the West.[135] Other analyses also suggest that the world population will reach 8.2 billion in 2030, will grow to 9 billion by 2050, and then stabilize and begin to decline after 2100.[136] According to the UNPD, two future projections for population growth exist:

> The high projection variant, whose fertility is just half a child above that in the medium variant, produces a world population of 10.6 billion in 2050

---

[135] Global Trends 2025: The National Intelligence Council's 2025 Project. Retrieved from http://www.dni.gov/files/documents/Newsroom/Reports%20and%20Pubs/2025_Global_Trends_Final_Report.pdf.

[136] Free World Academy Web site, *supra* note 128.

and 15.8 billion in 2100. The low variant, whose fertility remains half a child below that of the medium, produces a population that reaches 8.1 billion in 2050 and declines towards the second half of this century to reach 6.2 billion in 2100.[137]

The UNPD predicts that population aging will be unprecedented over the next few decades.[138] By 2025, one of every three people will be aging in the Western world. This is said to be caused by declining fertility and increasing life expectancy. The annual level of net immigration would have to double or triple to keep working-age populations from shrinking in Western Europe.[139] Marked differences exist between developed and developing regions in the number and proportion of older persons. In the more developed regions, more than a fifth of the population is currently aged sixty years or more and by 2050, nearly a third of the population in developed countries is projected to be in that age group. In the less developed regions, older persons account today for just 8 percent of the population, but by 2050 they are expected to account for a fifth of the population.[140]

Such aging of societies will have economic consequences. Even with productivity increases, slower employment growth from a shrinking workforce will reduce Europe's GDP growth by 1 percent. The cost of trying to maintain pensions and health coverage will squeeze out expenditures on other priorities, such as defense. Therefore, although Europe and Japan will have higher per capita wealth than India and China, they will struggle to maintain robust growth rates because the size of their working-age populations will decrease.[141] Other states, such as Afghanistan, Yemen, Nigeria, and Pakistan, will experience a youth bulge and will see an increase in their youth population. Unless employment rates increase, these states may experience political instability.[142] It is predicted that the United States will be a partial exception to the aging of populations in the developed world because it will experience higher birth rates and more immigration.

Russia's demographically aging and declining population is projected to drop below 130 million by 2025.[143] Similarly, in around 2015, the size of China's

---

[137] UN Department of Economic and Social Affairs, Population Division, Population Estimates and Projections Section 2011 estimate. Retrieved from http://esa.un.org/unpd/wpp/Other-Information/Press_Release_WPP2010.pdf.

[138] Retrieved from http://www.un.org/esa/population/publications/WPA2009/WPA2009-report.pdf.

[139] Free World Academy Web site, *supra* note 128.

[140] UNPD, World Population and Aging 2009, ST/ESA/SER.A/295. Retrieved from http://www.un.org/esa/population/publications/WPA2009/WPA2009-report.pdf.

[141] Free World Academy Web site, *supra* note 128.

[142] *Id.*  [143] *Id.*

working population is predicted to start declining, and by 2025, a large proportion of China's population will be retired or entering retirement.[144] By 2030, India may overtake China as the world's most populous country.

Given population trends and trends in labor-force participation rates, the U.S. workforce will continue to increase in size, but at a considerably slower rate than in the past. During the 1970s, the workforce grew 2.6 percent annually, declining to 1.1 percent growth in the 1990s. Between 2000 and 2010, the annual growth rate is projected to equal that of the 1990s, but it is projected to slow in the next decade to just 0.4 percent, and in the following decade to only 0.3 percent. However, the workforce will be more evenly distributed across ages.[145]

According to U.S. census bureau projections, the increase in the world's working-age population between 2010 and 2030 will be 900 million people, 400 million people fewer than over the past few decades.[146] Furthermore, although over the past few decades the increase in the world's working population centered on India and China, over the next twenty years this increase is predicted to center on sub-Saharan Africa, whereas other emerging economies will experience a decrease in their working-age populations.[147]

More specifically, young man power (between ages fifteen and twenty-nine) will increase by just 4 percent over the next twenty years, about a fifth of the increase over the past two decades. Eberstadt suggests that Russia could be an exception to these trends: Russia's working-age population and urban population will fall by 2030.[148] Meanwhile, in India, approximately 80 percent of the population growth will be in the working population. There will, however, be a demographic divide between the north and south of India: the north will be youthful, with a growing population, whereas the south will have an aging population, and growth will cease.

Europe will continue to attract migrants from Africa, and it is likely that the increased growth in India and China will make them attractive places for immigration, as well. According to the UNPD, approximately 11 million migrants will move from lesser-developed areas to more-developed areas in the middle term (2025–2030), and this number will fall to approximately 9 million migrants in the next few decades (around 2050).[149] All this migration

---

[144] Id.

[145] Rand Corporation, "The Future at Work – Trends and Implications," Research Brief 5070. Retrieved from http://www.rand.org/pubs/research_briefs/RB5070/index1.html.

[146] Nicholas N. Eberstadt, "Our Demographic Future," Foreign Affairs, November/December 2010.

[147] Id.   [148] Id.

[149] UN Department of Economic and Social Affairs, Population Division, Population Estimates and Projections Section, 2011 Estimate. Retrieved from http://esa.un.org/unpd/wpp/Excel-Data/migration.htm.

is estimated to be from less-developed parts of Africa and Asia to developed parts of Europe and North America. The rate of migration, however, is predicted to fall over the fifty-year period.[150]

By 2025, non-European minority populations could reach significant proportions – 15 percent or more – in nearly all Western European countries.[151] The NIC predicts that "[s]uccessful integration of Muslim minorities in Europe could expand the size of the productive work forces and avert social crisis. Lack of efforts by Europe and Japan to mitigate demographic challenges could lead to long-term declines."[152] Given growing discontent among native Europeans with current levels of immigrants, such steep increases are likely to heighten tensions. New migrants are likely to bring cultural and political change, and greater links to their homes, fostering globalization.

What do these demographic changes mean for international law? There will be greater pressure on states to promote migration to redress imbalances in population growth.[153] Greater migration will cause more cosmopolitan outlooks, and more cultural and political homogenization. With greater homogenization in political preferences, there will be greater possibilities for agreement on international legal rules to address many different issues. Greater urbanization will cause greater pollution, greater chances of epidemic, and greater concern for responsive international public goods.

### F) TECHNOLOGY

Technological change has accelerated in recent years, and a number of important innovations are on the horizon. Furthermore, technological development is often a dynamic response to problems, so a complete vision of future problems must take account of the ameliorating effect of technological responses. We can expect technological change along a number of dimensions,[154] and of course there are likely to be many surprises.

Computing power has grown geometrically according to Moore's law, and we can expect this growth in power to continue. By 2032, use of artificial intelligence will be widespread, and workplaces can be highly automated, delegating many administrative functions to computers.[155] Quantum computing should be available around 2037, vastly increasing computing power. If Moore's law continues to operate, by 2053, desktop computers will contain

---

[150] Id.
[151] National Intelligence Council, *supra* note 135.
[152] Id.
[153] For a discussion of the type of law that may result, *see* Trachtman, *supra* note 118 (2009).
[154] *See* National Intelligence Council, *supra* note 135.
[155] Futuretimeline.net. Retrieved from http://www.futuretimeline.net/21stcentury/2030-2039.htm.

artificial intelligence with the processing power of all existing human brains combined.[156]

This level of computing power, combined with advances in robotics, will eliminate the need for both manual and many types of white-collar human labor. Societies, and international society, would need to develop systems for allocation of wealth that are not necessarily linked to productivity, or even to ownership. Indeed, subject to environmental and social limits, society could afford to ensure that each individual has what we might consider today a very satisfactory level of material wealth. Obviously, this is a utopian fantasy, which might fail to be realized for all sorts of reasons, not least of which include warfare, environmental degradation, or disease.

Communications has kept pace, allowing computing power to be linked, and information to be shared through increasingly large and powerful networks. By 2032, Internet connection speeds, including wireless connections, may be as great as one terabit (a trillion bits) in many places. The connectivity brought by these networks has had significant effects on productivity, largely through transaction-cost reductions. "These technologies could radically accelerate a range of enhanced efficiencies, leading to integration of closed societies into the information age and security monitoring of almost all places. Supply chains would be streamlined with savings in costs and efficiencies that would reduce dependence upon human labor."[157]

Energy will also be affected by technological change. Safer nuclear energy, fusion power, algae biofuel, nanotech fuel cells, solar, and wind power will slowly replace fossil fuels,[158] reducing climate change and other pollution problems. This is too late to prevent significant climate change, resulting in a hotter world, and scarcities of fresh water and food. These scarcities may in turn induce conflict.

Of course, technological advance will increase globalization by reducing costs of transportation and communication. Technological advances in the area of communication can also promote democratization. They allow citizens of one state to see how others live and how other states govern, and to measure their own governments' performance by comparison. This enhances government accountability, and can also lead to greater use of international law to maximize delivery of government services.

The effects of these types of technologies on international law could be dramatic. They would give impetus to development, and to globalization because

---

[156] Id.
[157] National Intelligence Council, *supra* note 135.
[158] Futuretimeline.net, *supra* note 155.

of their facilitation of global supply-chain management. Greater globalization of this type – intensive networked production – may also reduce the possibility of conflict by raising the productivity costs of conflict. Ubiquitous universal translators would make negotiation of international legal rules less costly and more reliable.

These technologies, including a wide array of different types of sensing devices, as well as enhanced abilities to share information, would provide the power for much greater monitoring of compliance with varying types of international law.[159] A particular example is international law relating to pollution, which can be tracked much more accurately by remote sensing devices. The transaction costs of producing and enforcing international law would be greatly reduced. A range of legal rules that are today impractical because violation cannot be detected or ascertained would become more viable. On the other hand, the greatly increased power of the state would require mediation by constitutional rules, which may require international–human-rights rules for support.

Enhanced technology will present increased dangers, and these dangers will often be shared, or will allow one state to threaten another. Enhanced technology will have greater global effects – there will be greater externalities and greater public goods problems. Indeed, some might predict a dystopian future, on the basis of abuse of technology, and this is indeed possible. Great threats will come from ready access by individuals and terrorist groups to the most destructive technologies. This access will challenge individual freedoms and democracy, and may even challenge the dissemination of technology.

As discussed further in Chapter 5, further international legal rules will be useful to manage the coming technologies. Greater harmonization and more reliable compliance will be necessary to ensure states that others are taking appropriate care.

## G) DEMOCRATIZATION

By 2052, if current trends continue, the majority of countries around the world will be governed democratically.

In autocracies, the governing group generally focuses on maximizing its own position or wealth, rather than societal well-being. As discussed in Chapter 1, as states become less despotic, they will be more accountable to their

---

[159] Jennifer Shkabatur, *Global Panopticon? The Changing Role of International Organizations in the Information Age* (2011). Retrieved from http://works.bepress.com/jennifer_shkabatur/1.

citizens.¹⁶⁰ Communications technology will allow citizens to compare their circumstances to those of citizens of other states. Communications technology will also allow citizens to solve the collective-action problem associated with protest and rebellion, by coordinating action. Greater democratization is also consistent with reduced domestic conflict, which in turn is consistent with reduced international war.¹⁶¹

Citizens will demand efficiency in the provision of governmental services. Part of this efficiency involves determining the preferences of citizens. Democratic processes will allow governments to identify their citizens' preferences more readily, although this could also be accomplished through survey or other methods.

Future society will not be the property of the sovereign, served by the people. Rather, sovereigns will be understood as trustee governments, holding power only insofar as they are servants of the people. As such, the trustee government will be forced to admit that in order to serve the people best, there will be situations in which it must give up authority. Such a trustee government must give up authority sometimes to subnational units, to non-territorial but local social units such as professional associations, churches, or schools; global non-territorial and non–state-based social units; and multilateral, regional, or bilateral organizations of states. It will do so on behalf of the citizens, in the exercise of selfless subsidiarity, to allocate authority to the social organization best suited to exercise authority in the particular context. This can be expected to result in more international law.

Of course, some international organizations of states will suffer from their distance from democratic accountability – the democratic deficit. This will be one, but an important, parameter in determinations to allocate authority to such organizations. New international legal and organizational mechanisms for accountability and rights will be necessitated.

## H) CHAPTER CONCLUSION

Anticipated future developments will have important impacts on the demand and supply of international law. Development and demographic change will increase demands for the global public goods and other benefits that

---

¹⁶⁰ See Thomas Fujiawara, "Voting Technology, Political Responsiveness, and Infant Health: Evidence from Brazil" (December 2011). Retrieved from http://www.princeton.edu/~fujiwara/papers/elecvote_site.pdf (showing that greater democracy results in greater benefits to the enfranchised).
¹⁶¹ See Stephen Van Evera, *Causes of War* (Cornell University Press 1999).

international law can deliver. Democratization will increase the pressure on national governments to respond to these demands. Technological change will be a cause also of greater demand for international law, but it will also reduce the transaction costs of international law, by making it easier to negotiate and enforce.

Characteristics: holistic, fragmented, complex, asystematic } normativity beyond coercion, non-state actors

I am not sure above democratization

complex model necessarily original fragmented =

- International ⟷ local normativity

- Soft accountability sanction / expulsion from the "globalist club"

- Fragmentation of sovereignty =
  – military
  – commercial
  – technological / modern wars

Expansion of international laws / PIL / Fusion with common areas / widest/new methods and regional

How global is global? How the influence national states

## 5   Cyberspace and Cybersecurity

This chapter, and Chapters 6, 7, 8, and 9, examines particular areas of international engagement in order to analyze the cooperation problems raised in these areas, utilizing the framework of reasons for international law, and of domestic politics, developed in Chapters 2 and 3. I use the ideas about the future developed in Chapter 4 to suggest how these problems may change over the next twenty to fifty years. On the basis of this analysis, I suggest the role that international law may play in facilitating cooperation.

The rise of cyberspace presents challenges and opportunities to international law, and to global government. There are two main types of challenge that we can observe today. First, information is much more mobile than it was prior to the rise of cyberspace, crossing national boundaries without interruption and decreasing the costs of all sorts of interactions. Second, the rise of cyberspace enables a novel type of terrorism and warfare. Both of these phenomena challenge the continuing ability of the state to provide the kinds of services that it has traditionally provided. Often this will make it more valuable for states to cooperate with one another, and to use international law to do so.

This chapter explores the relationship between technological change and social change; between the technical production frontier and the structural production frontier.[162] These are the two components of the frontier of Pareto efficiency. In short, the technical production frontier is set by our technological capabilities, whereas the structural production frontier is set by our institutional capabilities. Lawyers, at their best, work to expand the structural production frontier. Cyberspace is best viewed as a bulge in the technical production

---

[162] Guido Calabresi, "The Pointlessness of Pareto: Carrying Case Further," 100 *Yale L. J.* 1211 (1991). *See also* Douglass C. North, "A Framework for Analyzing the State in Economic History," 16 *Explorations Econ. Hist.* 249 (1979).

frontier. In order to maximize its benefits, changes are required in the structural production frontier.

Our institutional structures, including sovereignty itself, determine the extent to which we reach the limits of the technical production frontier. In addition, and more saliently, changes in the technical production frontier, especially in communications, modify the structural production frontier. They do so by modifying the transaction costs of different institutional structures. This means that not only does cyberspace facilitate private activity, it also facilitates government activity. Not only does technology strengthen the tools of government, it can also strengthen the legitimacy of government through heightened transparency and democracy.

Furthermore, these technological changes affect the costs of achieving our preferences. Change in the cost of achieving preferences will differentially affect the extent to which we may satisfy some preferences and, more importantly, will affect the means used to achieve our preferences. This includes the question of whether we use the market or the state to achieve certain goals. We cannot predict the answer to this question simply by referring to cyberspace. Rather, the answer to the market versus state question is dependent on the confluence of a complex set of variables. Even if all variables other than the development of cyberspace were held constant, the development of cyberspace itself includes several variables, perhaps contradicting one another, which must be evaluated separately before being aggregated to form an answer.

How does cyberspace affect the relationship between individual sovereignty and state sovereignty? Certainly bidirectional communications are made more efficient, and therefore more frequent. Individuals may provide more information regarding their preferences to government through referenda, surveys, or market-mimicking mechanisms such as electronic highway toll collection. This information revelation function may serve to legitimate government action: it can be more strongly rooted in citizen preferences. The citizen can keep better track of government and thereby provide enhanced input as to the citizen's preferences. This revolution in availability of information risks overwhelming the citizen: representative democracy has roots in efficiency.

## A) CYBERSPACE, SOVEREIGNTY, AND JURISDICTION

In order to examine the relationship between the development of cyberspace and international law, it is important to examine how cyberspace relates to territoriality, the principal basis for allocation of authority in the international legal system. Territoriality as a principle for allocation of jurisdiction (the legal variant of authority) has many benefits, as well as costs, and may be an appropriate basis for allocation of jurisdiction in many circumstances. Territoriality is a type of formalism, and suffers from the same deficiencies as other formalist rules: underinclusiveness and overbreadth. However, under some circumstances, the costs of underinclusiveness and overbreadth may be less than the costs of unpredictability and adjudication in a greater number of cases.

A kind of conclusory, debate-halting claim of sovereignty is often paired with similarly conclusory claims of territoriality: the assumption that authority can and should be allocated on the basis of the territoriality of conduct. Under circumstances in which states are the only entities with claims to territory, territoriality excludes the possible authority of other legal rules and organizations. Furthermore, conclusory sovereignty, with its unsustainable assertion of unconstrained state power, requires territoriality as a basis to cabin the separate omnipotencies of multiple states.

In fact, territoriality is the constraint that unravels the assertion of unconstrained state power. The myth of unconstrained state power fails horizontally because territoriality constrains it. Furthermore, the territoriality constraint is radically indeterminate. Since Walter Wheeler Cook's legal realist attack on the vested rights theory in the 1930s and 1940s,[163] conflict of laws scholars have known that simple assertions of territoriality often fail to answer questions of allocation of power, given mobility of persons and cross-border effects. The assertion of unconstrained state power also fails vertically, because states at least agree on the existence of international law, including the international law rule that vertically limits each state's horizontal assertion of power on bases related to territory.[164]

Sovereignty has both horizontal and vertical determinants. A state's power vis-à-vis other states is the horizontal determinant. A state's power vis-à-vis sub-state and supra-state institutions (and individuals) is the vertical determinant. The vertical determinant is addressed by the concept of subsidiarity, which is often used, similar to sovereignty itself, as a conclusory epithet. The vertical allocation of plenary power to the state is also confounded by the inability to parcel out discrete powers horizontally. In order to manage a system where power cannot be allocated horizontally, states must share power through vertical structures. These vertical structures include the international legal order itself, as well as particular treaties, arrangements, and institutions by which states share power in the international legal system.

[163] *See* Walter Wheeler Cook, *The Logical and Legal Bases of the Conflict of Laws* (1942).
[164] Restatement (Third) of Foreign Relations Law § 403 (1987).

Nevertheless, it is not clear that "[c]yberspace radically undermines the relationship between legally significant phenomena and physical location."[165] Did the telephone, telegraph, television, or mail do so? Are they different from cyberspace, other than in terms of frequency, velocity, and cost? Conduct still occurs in territory. Individuals still reside in territory. Most importantly, effects are still felt in territory. Thus, although cyberspace may be a supraterritorial phenomenon that fractures both conduct and effects, supraterritoriality is not new, and conduct and effects have been fractured in the past. More importantly, the supraterritoriality of the medium only results in part in a supraterritorial society. Our problem is to determine to which society or societies regulation of a particular problem belongs. It is too easy to argue that regulation of cyberspace belongs to the cyberspace society. Why does not regulation of telephone, television, financial services, or pollution also belong to a separate supraterritorial society?

Cyberspace is a global network. It involves many linked computers located around the world. Its hardware and software structure are relevant to the question of how different states or international organizations may exercise power – in legal terms, jurisdiction – over cyberspace. The original *root file* of top-level domains – the list of domain names and their translation to numerical IP addresses that is consensually accepted as definitive – is physically located in the United States, on a server controlled by Internet Corporation for Assigned Names and Numbers (ICANN). It is ultimately under the control of the U.S. government. This is a source of power over other governments that depend on the root file for their national domain names. It is also a source of power over some of the most significant domains, such as .com, .net, and .org.

In other respects, the Internet is not subject to centralized power. Rather, it is a "network of networks," by which packets of data are transferred from one computer on one network to another computer on the same network or on another network. The critical power points are "backbone providers,"[166] and

---

[165] David R. Johnson & David G. Post, "Law and Borders: The Rise of Law in Cyberspace," 48 *Stan. L. Rev.* 1367, 1367 (1996). *See also* Lawrence Lessig, "The Constitution of Code: Limitations on Choice-Based Critiques of Cyberspace Regulation," 5 *Comm. L. Conspectus* 181, 184 n. 23 (1997). "In cyberspace, because code is so plastic and so powerful, and because law is so feeble and (on an international scale) so rigid, code has a comparative regulatory advantage over law. A gap in legal regulation will therefore emerge, and code will fill that gap." *Id.* at 184.

[166] Michael Kende, "The Digital Handshake: Connecting Internet Backbones" (FCC Office of Public Policy Working Paper No. 32, Sept. 2000). Retrieved from http://www.fcc.gov/Bureaus/OPP/working_papers/oppwp32.pdf.

Internet service providers and the routers they operate.[167] The *backbone*, which is the means of transmission from one network to another, is provided by backbone providers to Internet service providers. The backbones and *local loops* that form the physical conduits through which packets flow on the Internet are subject to the jurisdiction of the state in which they physically exist. Therefore, they are distributed among a number of jurisdictions – each country has control over the backbones and local loops physically located in its territory.[168] This does not necessarily mean that any particular country can block all Internet access in its territory: access through satellite or difficult-to-block international telephone connections do not flow through local backbones and local loops.

The United States has substantial power vis-à-vis other governments and legitimate businesses in Internet society because of its size and the value of its market, which would allow it to impose a change in standards for the United States that would be difficult for foreign persons to reject. In this sense, the United States is capable of unilateral action to regulate the Internet, but is also capable of providing incentives for other states to accept multilateral agreements along the lines of the U.S. standard: "uni-multilateralism."

The real jurisdictional novelty of cyberspace is that it will give rise to more frequent circumstances in which effects are felt in multiple territories at once. This development makes apparent a truth that existed before the development of cyberspace: effects are rarely neatly cabined within particular jurisdictions. Therefore, the allocation of jurisdiction to a particular state is not simply a technical issue; rather, it necessarily involves distributive or political choices. Thus, the development of cyberspace does not itself raise new problems, but frees us to think more clearly about problems of jurisdiction. However, as will be seen, the old problems are difficult enough. In fact, one may view the rise of cyberspace as a phenomenon that accentuates the old problems to a point where it is worthwhile to devise a more substantial institutional solution. Furthermore, whereas cyberspace accentuates the old problems, it also provides intriguing new potential solutions.

It is well recognized that the central and most difficult legal issue in cyberspace is jurisdictional. This jurisdictional issue is often recognized as a horizontal jurisdiction question: which state has prescriptive (or adjudicative or enforcement) jurisdiction over conduct in cyberspace? This issue is thought to arise from the fact that it is difficult to locate cyberspace conduct

---

[167] Markus Mueller, "Who Owns the Internet? Ownership as a Legal Basis for American Control of the Internet," 15 *Fordham Intell. Prop. Media & Ent. L. J.* 709 (2004).
[168] *Id.*

territorially. The latter fact arises from the dispersed nature of the computer network that comprises the Internet. Two conflicting prescriptions, with the choice dependent on the tastes of the author, are generally made.

> *Prescription 1.* The first prescription argues that because cyberspace cannot be neatly cabined in any single territory, and assuming that territoriality is the only basis for jurisdiction, no state should regulate cyberspace. This argument is obviously non sequacious; it proves too much. Nothing can be neatly cabined in any single territory. If we throw up our regulatory hands simply because we cannot establish territorial categories, the result would be anarchy. Although this may be congruent with the new medievalism, and with the Chicago school (and socialist) vision of the state, many of us still see a role for government.

> *Prescription 2.* The second prescription, on the basis of the same factual predicates, argues for global government. This global government may be described on three parameters. On the first parameter, it may have rules for allocation of jurisdiction among governments. On the second parameter, it may harmonize or coordinate rules. On the third parameter, it may create centralized organizations to engage in rulemaking and enforcement activities. Similar to the first prescription, the second is a non sequitur: the failure of territoriality indicates neither anarchy nor global government.

These two opposing choices are insufficient. It is obvious that not everything is for the market, as it is obvious that not everything is for international government, just as it is conversely obvious that not everything is for the state. However, some things are bound to remain for the state, whereas some things are for the market and other things are for international government. This is the true meaning of subsidiarity, and it leaves us in the existential position of having to analyze and choose, rather than being able to conclude debates by simple epithets.

There have always been many issues that one country cannot completely deal with on its own; cyberspace simply accelerates the realization of this fact. The development of cyberspace will only change our jurisdictional lives incrementally, and should not be viewed as a revolution that marks radical changes in our legal relationships. Nor should the development of cyberspace be viewed as a basis for either allocation of all social decisions to the market, or allocation of all social decisions to international governance. I will discuss the complex and contingent problem of discriminating among these choices in particular circumstances. However, the rise of cyberspace will induce more action among states to establish rules of prescriptive jurisdiction, harmonized or coordinated laws, and international organizations to apply these rules. Many recent initiatives in international regulation and the trade arena have done exactly this.

Coase explored the dichotomy between transactions in the market and allocational decisions within the firm. This dichotomy may be understood as a kind of institutional choice: which structure better allows people to produce more of what they want? The institutional choice may, however, be broadened to include not only the market and the firm, but also the state. I have proposed the further extension of this choice to the international organization.[169] Thus, institutional choice may begin with a determination of whether the particular issue is best addressed by the market, firm, state, international law, or an international organization. Of course, this is only the beginning of analysis, as there are many variations in the size, structure, and governance of each of these types of entity. Moreover, these structures always coexist and interrelate in subtle and complex ways.

It is important to evaluate the changes wrought by the rise of cyberspace. As we evaluate the choice between the state and the international organization as loci of power, we must give cyberspace its due: cyberspace works on the transaction costs side of the market, state, and international organization. It is here that the role of cyberspace may be viewed as revolutionary. Let us briefly enumerate the types of effects cyberspace may have on the information economics of governance. Before we examine some real effects, however, it is worth noting one alleged effect that is worth disputing. This is the argument that cyberspace is not technically susceptible to regulation. There is nothing to this argument: anything wrought by the mind of man is capable of regulation by the mind of man. Although there may be a lag between the private initiative and the regulatory response, again, this is not peculiar to cyberspace. Finally, cyberspace may raise the costs of regulation to the point where it is inefficient to regulate, but it has not been demonstrated that this is broadly the case and, at least in theory, one would expect the technological miracles that enable cyberspace to also enable its regulation.

First, cyberspace may tend to convert information from a private good to a public good. Whereas servers lack truly unlimited capacity, and the Internet can be creaky at times, information in cyberspace is largely characterized by nonrivalrous consumption. *Nonexcludability* refers to the relative ease or difficulty of preventing consumption by those who do not pay for the resource. Cyberspace continues to struggle with this problem, which is itself a transaction costs problem: what is the cost of excluding nonpayers? Thus, although the analysis is neither complete nor conclusive, cyberspace tends to convert

---

[169] Trachtman, *supra* note 50, at 470 (1997).

information from a private good to a public good. On the other hand, for those who have followed the battles over intellectual property rights in international trade, it is clear that even information that is ordinarily distributed in physical form already has public goods characteristics. Simply put, the rise of cyberspace seems to accentuate these characteristics.

Second, cyberspace makes the exchange of information faster and cheaper. This is the reason for the rise of commerce on the Internet, both commerce in physical goods and commerce in information goods. These technological advances are growing geometrically, and as enterprises realize their utility and establish network externalities by exploiting their utility in greater numbers, they will substantially decrease the cost of transacting. This decrease in the cost of transacting will have the effect of increasing the number of transactions effected.

Third, information will flow more cheaply to both the customer and the wholesale purchaser of goods and services, enabling information to also flow more cheaply from the purchaser to the seller. This has given rise to new forms of targeted advertising, as well as targeted product development.

Finally, and critically for our topic, if one thinks of government as a provider of goods and services, then there is no reason that government cannot have the same transaction cost reduction benefits enjoyed by the private sector. The theoretical core of this idea, and its possible extension, is that enhanced communication can allow citizens to more easily coordinate autonomously, without the intercession of formal governance. The citizenry may more readily organize spontaneously to supervise government, and thereby partially displace government as an independent decision maker. This is a fundamental change, and has been important in government from the Arab Spring to Wikileaks. However, note here that this story is incomplete, for although the transaction costs of spontaneous governance may be diminished, the strategic problems that may prevent spontaneous governance may actually be increased. That is, with reduced transaction costs, the cost of holdout-type conduct – and the collective action problem – may be increased. Thus, cyberspace is a technical production frontier development that has dramatically reduced the transaction costs of coordination in both the private and public sectors.

The structural production frontier is the place for institutional design. With the reduction of transaction costs by advances on the technical production frontier, what will be the reaction on the structural production frontier? On the structural production frontier, we create institutions to facilitate social relations – to maximize net gains, from the benefits and costs of social relations. In a market context, we refer to many types of social relations as transactions, and indeed the transaction is the basic unit of institutional economic analysis. The choice of institutions is determined by choosing the structure that maximizes social gain. If the rise of cyberspace differentially reduces the transaction costs implicated by various institutional structures, then it will affect the choice of institutional structure.

However, the suggestion that the rise of cyberspace will result in a victory of the market over the state, the international organization over the state, or the state over either of the others, makes an unwarranted assumption about the transaction cost profiles of the relevant institutions. Rather, particularism still rules. Although the world has changed, and transaction costs have been reduced, the world has never stopped changing, and transaction costs have generally been reduced continuously throughout history. We know that social relations – transactions – have become less costly, so we can expect them to become more dense, more frequent and more complex. This is why property rights are more complex and disputes more frequent than in the past. This is why international relations is more complex and varied. This is why we see greater moves toward the international law of cooperation.

Thus, the only learning we can really derive from the rise of cyberspace is that our methods of social relations will merit reexamination given the availability of these new methods of communication. One area that will certainly merit reexamination is the allocation of prescriptive jurisdiction. States have tried to resolve disputes over control of the commons, or of people, by reference to formal concepts such as sovereignty, territoriality, and extraterritoriality, but these concepts grow increasingly indeterminate. More importantly, even where determinate, they increasingly provide unsatisfactory responses to complex social problems. It is in this area that cyberspace has helped us, by educating us to the limited utility of concepts of sovereignty, territoriality, and extraterritoriality. Cyberspace has demonstrated the incompleteness of our social response to problems of jurisdiction, and has therefore made it incumbent on us to revise it.

Our fear of cyberspace is not wholly unwarranted. One dark side of cyberspace is its facilitation of private sector jurisdictional evasion and, at least in some contexts, its facilitation of regulatory arbitrage. Jurisdictional evasion might consist, for example, of securities fraud aimed into the United States from a Web site that is based at an offshore server. How is this different from a telephone call aimed into the United States from an offshore "boiler room" practicing securities fraud? It is not terribly different in jurisdictional terms, although there are important distinguishing features. The United States has legal rules, such as the effects doctrine, that address such offshore conduct. Whereas it may be argued that any act anywhere has some localized effect everywhere, the effects doctrine has always been selective and may grow more selective in the future. The rise of cyberspace may prompt greater selectivity, as a message posted on the Internet may have effects everywhere. From an economic standpoint, the role of jurisdictional rules is often to internalize externalities to the extent desired or alternatively to provide clear allocations of jurisdiction so that it may be reallocated through transactions among states.

There are times when it is useful to internalize externalities, and there are times when it is useful to constrain regulatory arbitrage. When the jurisdictional rules actually applied fail, we can refer to a jurisdictional mismatch, or gap. This type of *jurisdictional mismatch* – a mismatch between the actual governance structures and the governance structures that would allow states to achieve the internalization and regulatory arbitrage outcomes they desire – may be viewed as a lag in the structural production frontier. That is, the social institutions for allocation of jurisdiction have not changed to reflect the technological changes brought by the rise of cyberspace. Why have they not changed? Perhaps there are transition costs, on the basis of path dependence or network externalities, that form barriers to change. If so, the failure to change may be viewed as efficient from a global perspective, if not from a narrower perspective of the particular context. Perhaps the value of change has simply not been recognized. It is in this sense that lawyers, as structural production frontier workers, may help identify potential revised structures that may be adopted for greater benefits.

## B) CYBERSECURITY

This book avoids an in-depth discussion of the subject that first comes to mind for those who consider international law generally: the law restricting the use of force. Of course, the future of international law for some has always been the application of law to international relations to eliminate the scourge of war. This may indeed be the future of international law, but this future will be developed, as Mitrany predicted, only from organic functional development of relationships that both make war less attractive to aggressors and facilitate the avoidance of war.

We will not wake up any day soon to states agreeing to globally disarm, or even to create an international military force capable of deterring aggression. Rather, war between states will become less likely as states develop greater ties and interdependencies. This is the antiwar vision of the founders of the EU, Jean Monnet and Robert Schuman. So far, it has been borne out by the fact that war between France and Germany has not recurred since the founding of the EU. We might add that since the United States Civil War, the states of the United States have been deterred from making war on one another. By the late nineteenth century, local warfare was suppressed by central national governments throughout most of the world. So, although the late twentieth century and early twenty-first century have exhibited bloody civil wars, this functionalist vision may have some empirical support, depending on how the trend line develops.

However, cybersecurity is a novel issue, and has different characteristics from overall real-world security issues. Cyberspace is almost necessarily an international space, even where dictatorial regimes have sought to limit their people's access to information. As an international space, eliminating the natural distance and protection of geography, it presents novel security issues and fundamentally overrides and destabilizes the geopolitical security system. The central feature of cyberspace for our purposes is the fact that the technology of cyberspace permits virtually costless mobility. This mobility facilitates jurisdictional arbitrage, allowing those who wish to escape regulation greater freedom, and also makes surveillance and detection more difficult.

Indeed, the very creation of international economic, cultural, and social integration through cyberspace brings with it greater security threats. The leading example so far is the 2007 attack on Estonia's computer networks.[170] A cyber attack on Iran's nuclear facilities in 2010 provided evidence of both intent and capabilities to disrupt foreign real activities through cyberspace, although that attack may not have involved use of the Internet.[171] So, the development of cyberspace must be met with development of cybersecurity. Because of the international nature of cyberspace, and assuming that states are unwilling to deny their people the benefits of cyberspace and unwilling to or incapable of walling off their cyberspace frontiers, cybersecurity is an international issue.

Cybersecurity threats, such as the stuxnet virus – which was discovered in 2010 – or the flame virus discovered in 2012, may reduce the possibility for functional integration, perpetuating real-world security threats. Furthermore, cybersecurity threats can be posed by non-state actors more readily than real-world security threats. Of course, terrorism carried out by non-state actors is a real-world security threat, but non-state actors still lack the capability to pose the greatest threats in the real world, whereas they seem to compete with the power of states in the virtual world.

The rise of cyberspace has greatly facilitated all kinds of activity, including commercial, social, and governmental interaction. There is no doubt that

---

[170] Joshua Davis, "Hackers Take Down the Most Wired Country in Europe," *Wired*, Aug. 21, 2007. Retrieved from http://www.wired.com/politics/security/magazine/15-09/ff_estonia?currentPage=all.

[171] Ron Rosenbaum, "The Triumph of Hacker Culture," *Slate*, Jan. 21, 2011. Retrieved from http://www.slate.com/articles/life/the_spectator/2011/01/the_triumph_of_hacker_culture.html.

cyberspace today constitutes valuable real estate, indeed. We have also routed our control of many real-world processes through cyberspace. Because of this increased value, the security of cyberspace has grown in importance. In the near future, the value and importance of cyberspace will grow geometrically. All sorts of industrial, consumer, political, social, and military activities will be integrated with networks. Artificial intelligence and robotics will take over all kinds of work in these areas. The fantasies of science fiction writers regarding war and terrorism within networks, with real effects in the real world, will come true. Thus, cybersecurity will become real security, with tremendous complexity and great potential for danger.[172] This will challenge the state tremendously, just as prior changes in military technology have challenged earlier social orders.[173]

Cyberspace is both a tool and a target of terrorists. It could also be a tool against terrorists. Most critically, cyberspace is a tool of human interaction and commerce, whereas terrorism is the nemesis of human interaction and commerce. So, these forces, although similar in structure, are natural opponents.

The rise of terrorism, as one type of asymmetric and distributed warfare, has not only threatened the gains derived from cyberspace, but has also threatened the real-world activities and assets that now come to depend on communication through cyberspace infrastructure. Individuals and governments wish to ensure that they will continue to reap the benefits of cyberspace, and that cyberspace controls will not be turned against them.[174] Their enemies see cyberspace as a high-value target.

The remainder of this chapter analyzes the jurisdictional and organizational facets of international security against cyberattack, including both cyberterrorism and cyberwar. By "cyberwar" I simply mean a state-to-state conflict utilizing cyber techniques. Because state-to-state cyberwar in the context of an acknowledged war, where attribution is not a problem, does not present legal problems that are at a theoretical level very distinct from real war, I focus on cyberterrorism. I include in cyberterrorism any politically motivated attack designed to cause significant physical or network harm where the authorship of the act is either a non-state actor or is uncertain. Because of the great difficulty in attributing a cyberterrorist attack, uncertainty as to attribution will characterize much of the cyber threat, and will include many types of acts that are initiated or sponsored by states. Although the act may be difficult

---

[172] *See* Richard A. Clarke & Robert Knake, *Cyberwar* 70 (2010).
[173] *See, e.g.,* Phillip Bobbitt, *The Shield of Achilles* (2002).
[174] Stewart Baker, Shaun Waterman & George Ivanov, *In the Crossfire: Critical Infrastructure in the Age of Cyber War* (2010)

to attribute ex post, it may be possible to induce states to reduce their own capabilities to engage in cyberterrorism in a verifiable way ex ante.

In U.S. President Obama's May 2011 "International Strategy for Cyberspace," he envisions hopes for the following future:[175]

> This future promises not just greater prosperity and more reliable networks, but enhanced international security and a more sustainable peace. In it, states act as responsible parties in cyberspace – whether configuring networks in ways that will spare others disruption, or inhibiting criminals from using the Internet to operate from safe havens. States know that networked infrastructure must be protected, and they take measures to secure it from disruption and sabotage. They continue to collaborate bilaterally, multilaterally, and internationally to bring more of the world into the information age and into the consensus of states that seek to preserve the Internet and its core characteristics.

In order to examine the need for and potential structure of international cooperation to combat cyberterrorism, it is first necessary to examine several subsidiary questions. First, to what extent and in what contexts is governmental regulation appropriate to combat cyberterrorism?[176] This is the first level of the subsidiarity analysis: is government action necessary? Second, to what extent and in what contexts is domestic government action, although possibly necessary, insufficient to combat cyberterrorism? This is a second level of subsidiarity analysis: is local regulation sufficient/is international cooperation necessary? Third, what form shall international cooperation take: should it be in the form of ad hoc or nonlegal and non-organizational relationships among states, or should it be in the form of more formal law or organization? Fourth, what should be the content or responsibilities of this more formal law or organization?

As already suggested, where regulation is called for, the next question is a choice of levels of regulation: subnational, national, regional, international law, or international organization. This chapter provides a brief analysis of the problem of allocation of authority – of jurisdiction – over different components of cyberspace, both horizontally and vertically, and of the need for international cooperation in this field.

---

[175] Office of the President of the United States, International Strategy for Cyberspace (2011). Retrieved from http://www.whitehouse.gov/sites/default/files/rss_viewer/international_strategy_for_cyberspace.pdf.

[176] See Jack Goldsmith & Tim Wu, *Who Controls the Internet?* (2006) (arguing for government regulation). *But see* Jonathan L. Zittrain, "The Generative Internet," 119 *Harv. L. Rev.* 1974, 2029 (2006) (arguing for private measures).

As we attempt to describe some of the parameters of cyberterrorism, it is useful to establish an analytical framework for discussion. There are two main categories: (i) the value, vulnerability, and protection available with respect to the target (risk variables); and (ii) control over the target and potential attacker (control variables). In legal terms, we might consider these to be analogs of effects and jurisdiction, raising the question of the match between effects and jurisdiction that challenges all areas of regulatory practice.

Control variables will determine the response to risk variables, and can be used to reduce or increase the aggregate risk. The risk variable profile will affect the importance of control variables. So, the first analytical question is how big is the existing risk, to whom does it accrue, and how can it be modified? The second analytical question is who controls the target and the attacker, and do they have appropriate incentives and capability to respond to – to modify – the risk profile presented by the risk variables? The controlling person could be a private person, one or more governments, and/or an international organization. The choices of private persons may be constrained through legal rules, whereas the choices of governments may be constrained through international law.

Theory would suggest that states should seek an optimal level of congruence, which will be less than full congruence, between control and risk – between jurisdiction and effects. This is no different than saying that in domestic property-rights analysis policymakers seek to achieve an optimal level of internalization of externalities. Thus, our first analytical question regards the risk-adjusted value of a particular target, and the degree to which the risk may be reduced through a variety of protective actions.

As previously noted, advanced societies have come to depend more and more on electronic communications and information processing networks in order to communicate, coordinate production, and transmit all manner of information. Advanced societies are thus more vulnerable to cyberterrorism than less industrialized societies. This is one way in which cyberterrorism may be understood as a form of asymmetric warfare: the cost of disruption of cyberspace is greater to advanced societies. This asymmetry may make international cooperation more difficult, or suggest the requirement for linkages with other types of cooperation.

Threats, networks, contexts, and tools available to different private-sector actors and governments vary. Therefore, there is no universal best response at the private sector or governmental level to the risk of cyberterrorism. There is no such thing as a completely secure network, but there are several important tools. These include: (i) limitation of terrorist access to networks; (ii) ex ante surveillance of networks in order to interdict or repair damage; (iii) ex post identification and punishment of attackers; and (iv) establishment of more robust networks that can survive attack. For purposes of our analysis of jurisdictional and international cooperation issues, we assume that governments will wish to operate in each of these categories of response. Once the nature of the network and the threat against it is understood, it becomes important to evaluate issues of control: do the decision makers regarding protection – those with control – have appropriate incentives to take efficient protective action?

Cyberterrorism is not by any means limited to attacks on government. In fact, with critical infrastructure largely in the hands of private actors, cyberterrorist attacks on critical infrastructure will largely involve attacks on private networks. Therefore, protection against cyberterrorism will require protection of private networks, raising the question of whether private actors have sufficient capability and incentives to take appropriate precautions, or whether governmental intervention is required.

## I) Locating Cyberwar

Terrorists may be wholly independent, sponsored by a state, or directed by a state. Sponsorship or direction by a state, if identifiable, may provide a useful means of deterrent. On the other hand, the central purpose of state sponsorship of terrorism, instead of direct attack, is covert action and plausible deniability. The fact that cyberterrorism may be state sponsored, or part of a cyberwarfare campaign,[177] means that any framework for cooperation could break down just when it is most crucial to security. Therefore, in order to cooperate effectively, states that are potential enemies will either need to be able to provide one another with powerful assurances that they will not violate their commitments, or cooperate to promote early detection and suppression of cyberterrorism. These assurances may be similar to those needed in arms-control agreements, but the problem may be that cyberwarfare agreements may be even less verifiable than realspace arms-control agreements. Thus, the relationship between states that are potential enemies will differ from that between states that see themselves as long-term allies.

Of course, the location and nationality of the attacker determines much about amenability to jurisdiction and the possibility of physical, as well as virtual, interdiction. Here, of course, attackers may be mobile in terms of their location and nationality, raising important questions about the utility of sub-universal arrangements for control of cyberterrorism.

---

[177] Susan W. Brenner & Marc D. Goodman, "In Defense of Cyberterrorism: An Argument for Anticipating Cyber-Attacks," 2002 *U. Ill. J.L. Tech. & Pol'y* 1 (2002).

## II) Private Sector Responses to Cyberterrorism

Importantly, private action and order may transcend national boundaries. Therefore, international cooperation through private initiatives does not face the same array of jurisdictional barriers that government initiatives face. If private action or private order can respond efficiently to the threat of cyberterrorism, then there is no need for government intervention, or intergovernmental cooperation. In fact, a subsidiarity perspective would only call for governmental action to the extent that governmental action can achieve individual goals more efficiently. It is not possible to provide a complete analysis of comparative efficiency of private order compared with public regulation, even within the limited context addressed here. However, in this subsection, we will try to provide a suggestive analysis of the relative benefits of private versus public order in the cyberterrorism context.

Security against cyberterrorism may be understood as a public good. Many types of security against cyberterrorism would appear to be non-rival in the sense that consumption by one user of this type of security would not diminish the availability of security to others. Security against cyberterrorism appears generally non-excludible in the same sense as national security more broadly: it is impractical, and ethically suspect, to exclude some from its umbrella. There are ways in which security against cyberterrorism may be made excludible. For example, to the extent that the security is derived from software or hardware resident on the end user's computer, or can be provided by an Internet service provider through its servers and made available only to that ISP's customers, it is excludible. To the extent that security is excludible, then it is a "club good". Of course, to the extent that the Internet itself, and its breadth of inclusion, provides network externalities, damage to others' ability to access the Internet reduces its value even to those who retain access.

There may also be significant externalities in connection with the threat of cyberterrorism. A particular state or private sector entity may have relatively little at stake with respect to its network, but it may be that its failure to take care imposes risks on other states or other private sector actors. Indeed, some states may have incentives to be cyberterrorism "havens" that experience some benefits from hosting cyberterrorists, but do not experience the costs. Finally, and perversely, measures by one person to establish security may induce cyberterrorists to target other persons, imposing an adverse cost on the others.

Will individuals overcome the transaction-cost issues to develop mechanisms to provide this public good or internalize relevant externalities without government intervention, or is government intervention necessary? It is true that the Internet has substantial transaction-cost advantages that allow it to facilitate private coordination. Which group of individuals are we talking about: end-users or backbone providers and Internet service providers or both? The number of backbone providers and Internet service providers is relatively small, also facilitating coordination. Moreover, it may be that backbone providers and Internet service providers have appropriate incentives on the basis of their desire to maintain the value of their networks to service consumers. Business end users that depend on the Internet for business-to-business communication and business-to-consumer selling will also have high-powered incentives to ensure the security of the Internet. These incentives are likely to be highest in connection with wealthier countries.

It is possible that even end users would have appropriate incentives with respect to the protection of their ability to access the Internet. However, here the collective-action problem is significant, and we would expect underprovision of this public good, given the difficulties in coordinating.[178] On the other hand, as previously noted, software or hardware prophylaxis may be excludible and therefore may not be a public good. In that case, we would have greater reason to expect efficient provision of security.

Do private-sector actors have the tools to deliver security against cyberterrorism? Will private-sector responses result in an accentuated digital divide or other adverse social effects? It is possible that private ordering might focus on solutions to the cyberterrorism problem that will not be socially optimal. It appears that some kinds of cyberterrorism security issues may be amenable to private ordering solutions. These types of issues might include spam, viruses, worms, and other methods of attacking individual computers at the end-user level. Under circumstances of sufficient diversity, decentralization, resiliency, and redundancy, society could afford to accept the risk of this type of cyberattack. Computer scientists and others skilled in assessing risk would be required to evaluate the extent to which this type of response would suffice: the extent to which conditions of diversity, decentralization, resiliency, and redundancy are sufficiently satisfied to reduce risk to a socially acceptable level.

We must compare the risk-adjusted magnitude of damage with the cost of taking care. This is simple comparative cost-benefit analysis, where the magnitude of damage avoided constitutes the benefit. So, the subsidiarity question in this context is whether the risk-adjusted magnitude of damage

---

[178] *But see* Yochai Benkler, "Coase's Penguin, or, Linux and the Nature of the Firm," 112 *Yale L. J.* 369 (2002); David R. Johnson, Susan P. Crawford, & John G. Palfrey, "The Accountable Net: Peer Production of Internet Governance" (Berkman Center for Internet & Society at Harvard Law School Working Paper, March 25, 2004). Retrieved from http://cyber.law.harvard.edu/The%20Accountable%20Net%20032504.pdf.

under private ordering, plus the cost of private-ordering measures to take care, is greater or less than the risk-adjusted magnitude of damage under government regulation, plus the cost of government regulation to take care. Of course, the more nuanced, and likely, comparison will examine different public-private partnerships: multiple combinations of private ordering and regulation. The next level of subsidiarity analysis would be international cooperation, asking whether the risk-adjusted magnitude of damage under international cooperation, plus the cost of international cooperation, is less than both.

## III) Governmental Intervention to Secure Cyberspace

Thus, it is possible that private ordering could under some circumstances provide sufficient protection, but it is also possible that it would be efficient under some circumstances for its protection to be enhanced by public order, for example, in the form of law enforcement-type action. It appears that some kinds of cyberterrorism security issues, relating to essential infrastructures where risk is unacceptable – including military command and control networks – will benefit from isolation and redundancy designs. In these types of applications, the risk of loss is preemptive, and swamps the costs of taking care under any conceivable calculation. These networks must be made secure against terrorism – both cyberterrorism and realspace attack – and need not necessarily be integrated with other networks. Alternatively, firewall technology may be sufficient to isolate these networks from attack, at the same time permitting partial integration with other networks.

Therefore, it is a middle group of cyberterrorism security issues – where private ordering does not provide sufficient security, or could be assisted by supplementation, and where isolation is not acceptable or is not technologically feasible – that will require public order. These include protection of infrastructures that must remain attached to the network and where firewalls cannot provide sufficient protection. Examples include Internet backbone networks, Internet service provider networks, industrial control, banking and other financial services, telecommunications services, transportation services, health services, and fire, police, emergency, and other public services. How to protect the networks and end-user systems in these areas? Stronger firewalls, filters, and protected access to critical components seem worthy of consideration. It would be possible to establish a variety of levels of protection, dependent on the level of risk of attack, and the magnitude of loss expected to be incurred from a successful attack.

Would there be sufficient incentives for any one of these sectors, or for particular entities within these sectors, to develop appropriate protection, and to implement the protection? Whereas some types of protection may best be implemented on a decentralized basis, there may be types of protection – including surveillance and interdiction – that are best implemented collectively. Is this area characterized by a collective-action problem? Although not all public-goods problems or collective-action problems are suitable for governmental intervention, under some transaction costs and strategic circumstances, government intervention will be the preferred solution.

## IV) International Cooperation

As already noted, variations in contexts, threats, and potential responses indicate that we are likely to see variations in the determination by each state of its unilateral optimal response to the threat of global cyberterrorism. Some states may determine to do nothing. They may determine that the threat is to the private sector, that there are no potential externalities or information asymmetries that would justify regulation, and that it is up to the private sector to act.

Other states may determine that a regulatory response is merited. Under some circumstances, an effective regulatory response may require international coordination or cooperation. In this part, we examine the possible effectiveness of private ordering, the possible areas in which public regulation may be required, and the possible areas in which international coordination of public regulation may be required.

The degree to which public intervention is preferred will depend on the preferences of persons in different states, which will vary, as well as on the available governance structures and transaction-cost structures within the particular state. It is clear that law plays different roles in different societies, and the private-public balance is likely to be achieved in different ways in different societies. These differences produce a type of path dependency in which subsequent institutional choices are constrained.

As mentioned, some types of cyberspace security will have public-goods characteristics, and therefore may be under-provided without intervention of some kind. This will be an argument for governmental intervention. Interestingly, it will often (but not always) also be an argument for international cooperation, as the existence of public goods or collective-action characteristics that call for government intervention at the domestic level may call for governmental intervention at the global level. This is not to say that all arguments for regulation are arguments for global regulation.

Public-goods problems and collective-action problems are actually types of externalities, where the decision of one person has effects – beneficial or detrimental – on another, and that decision is not necessarily incorporated in decision making. There are many possibilities for externalities in connection with security against cyberterrorism. Most importantly, one person's insecure network may be used to mount an attack against another person's network. Second, because of the benefits of cyberspace network externalities, the failure of one person to protect his own network may have adverse effects on others.

One of the major arguments made by those who argue against all cyberspace regulation is that it is prohibitively costly, if technically possible, to regulate the "borderless" Internet. It is true that the Internet makes avoidance of national regulation by relocation easier. However, this argument militates both (a) against national regulation; and (b) in favor of international regulation. For example, Michael Vadis writes, "Given the global nature of the Internet, it is not surprising that computer crime is also global, with attacks crossing national lines with increasing frequency. Operational efforts to prevent and respond to computer attacks must therefore also be global."[179]

## V) Choice of Horizontal Public Order: a Transaction Costs Analysis of Prescriptive Jurisdiction in Cybersecurity

Once we accept that each state will have different preferences, and different ways of articulating those preferences, it becomes apparent that there will be some variety in the way states approach the problem of security against cyberterrorism. Clashes of values and methods will be significant. States may have sharply divergent goals, and there may be substantial externalities. If we think of cyberterrorism as a type of cyberwarfare, some states will take the view that they benefit from the insecurity of other states.

## VI) Territoriality and Aterritoriality

Just as possession is nine-tenths of the law of property, territoriality is nine-tenths of the law of jurisdiction. Of course, we must initially divide territoriality into categories of conduct and effects: territorial conduct and territorial effects. Few states question the basic rule that each state has prescriptive jurisdiction over territorial conduct. In realspace, but even more so in cyberspace, it may sometimes be difficult to distinguish conduct from effects. For example, where firms establish a cartel to fix prices outside a state's territory, and implement

---

[179] Michael Vadis, "International Cyber-Security Cooperation: Informal Bilateral Models," in *Cyber Security: Turning National Solutions Into International Cooperation* 1 (J. Lewis, ed., 2003).

the price-fixing agreement by virtue of the prices that they charge within the states' territory, is it conduct within the target state's territory? Even if it is not, few states would abjure the right to respond in legal terms to actions outside their territory that cause bad effects within their territory.

The novelty of cyberspace from a legal perspective stems from the fact that the cost of splitting conduct among multiple jurisdictions, or of locating conduct in a jurisdiction of choice, is much reduced.[180] This chapter adopts the fundamental analytical perspective that *prescriptive jurisdiction* – the right to make a state's law applicable to a particular matter – is analogous to property in a private context.[181]

States act to maximize state preferences. States will seek jurisdiction over matters as necessary to allow them to achieve their preferences. This is analogous to individuals seeking ownership of property that will allow them to achieve their preferences. In a primitive context, states encounter one another and may find it appropriate to engage in a particular immediate transaction. This transaction is similar to a "spot" market transaction in domestic markets. The international legal system is engaged at two moments. First, the international legal system is engaged to assign initial jurisdiction rights to the actors. Second, when these exchanges take place over time, when they are not spot transactions but longer-term transactions, requiring the security of treaty or other law, the international legal system is engaged to facilitate these transactions, through the law of treaty and other international law.

Although the international legal system contains some rules for allocation of prescriptive jurisdiction, these rules are unclear and incomplete. They are often unclear insofar as a rule, for example, territoriality, does not distinguish between territorial conduct and territorial effects – does not distinguish between what is conduct and what are effects. Furthermore, conduct may occur in multiple territories, as may effects. More importantly perhaps, rules for allocation of prescriptive jurisdiction are incomplete because they do not necessarily tell us the limits of a state's behavior in relation to its jurisdiction. For example, whereas states have jurisdiction over their citizens, international-human-rights law limits the scope of state exercise of this jurisdiction.

The international legal problem of jurisdiction over activities that may facilitate or prevent cyberterrorism may be understood as a problem of incompleteness of rules allocating jurisdiction: to what extent may the United States use its territorial sovereignty over top-level domain names or other parts of the

---

[180] Joel P. Trachtman, "Cyberspace, Sovereignty, Jurisdiction and Modernism," 5 *Ind. J. Global Legal Stud.* 561 (1998).
[181] Joel P. Trachtman, "Economic Analysis of Perspective Jurisdiction and Choice of Law," 42 *Va. J. Intl L.* 1 (2001).

Internet as a basis to demand changes in the way that Mongolia regulates Internet service providers who locate their servers in Mongolia? Of course, rules allocating jurisdiction may be efficiently incomplete. Under circumstances of low value, one would not expect property rights to arise: one would expect a res nullius regime. In a *res nullius* regime, as the property becomes more valuable, a common pool resource problem – or tragedy of the commons – may develop, and may provide incentives to develop property rights. Similarly, as the importance, or value, to states of regulatory jurisdiction rises with the rise of the regulatory state and enhanced transportation and communications, it is not difficult to imagine that there may be incentives to clarify rules of jurisdiction heretofore left unclear.[182]

This can be said to be the case in connection with security against cyberterrorism. With the rise in value of the Internet, and the rise in risk from terrorism, jurisdiction to address these risks has become more valuable, and it is likely that states will move from what is in effect a res nullius regime (at least as it addresses jurisdiction to regulate prior to an act of terrorism) to a system of property rights. Alternatively, we might say that the likely move will be from a system of jurisdiction on the basis of territorial conduct or nationality to one that more accurately reflects the risks to the jurisdiction of territorial effects.

Under circumstances where a relatively clear rule – such as one that accords exclusive jurisdiction to the state of territorial conduct – would minimize the transaction costs of reallocation, theory predicts that such clear rules would be chosen.[183] This might be the case, for example, where the conduct and effects are confined to a single territory.

This position assumes that it would be more costly to get the initial allocation right – to align allocation with states' preferences – than to establish a system that would allow states through their autonomous actions to get the reallocation right – to engage in subsequent transactions in order to align allocation with states' preferences. Territoriality is the leading jurisdictional

---

[182] See Harold Demsetz, "Toward a Theory of Property Rights," 57 *Am. Econ. Rev. Papers & Proceedings* 347 (1967); B. C. Field, "The Evolution of Property Rights," 42 *Kyklos* 319 (1989); Thomas Merrill, "Trespass, Nuisance, and the Costs of Determining Property Rights," 14 *J. Legal Stud.* 13 (1985); R. S. Hartman, "A Note on externalities and Placement of Property Rights: An Alternative Formulation to the Standard Pigouvian Results," 2 *Int'l Rev. L. & Econ.* 111 (1982); John Umbeck, "Might Makes Rights: A Theory of the Formation and Initial Distribution of Property Rights," 19 *Econ. Inquiry* 38 (1981); John Umbeck, "A Theory of Contract Choice and the California Gold Rush," 20 *J. L. & Econ.* 163 (1977); Terry Anderson & Peter Hill, "The Evolution of Property Rights: A Study of the American West," 18 *J. L. & Econ.* 163 (1975); David Ault & Gilbert Rutman, "The Development of Independent Rights to Property in Tribal Africa," 22 *J. L. & Econ.* 183 (1979).

[183] Trachtman, *supra* note 181.

principle today, but it might be argued that territoriality is under pressure from two sources. First, technology such as cyberspace makes territoriality less clear, as conduct relating to a particular matter may more easily occur in multiple territories. Second, territorial–conduct-based jurisdiction is increasingly inconsistent with territorial effects, giving rise to greater externalities. Under these circumstances, territoriality as a default rule seems less appealing. On the other hand, where it is not costly to determine which state should initially be allocated jurisdiction in order to maximize aggregate wealth, states should agree on these allocations in order to avoid the potential transaction costs of reallocation to reach these positions.

Thus, where one state is affected substantially more greatly than other involved states, and the costs of reallocation are positive, it might be best initially to allocate jurisdiction to the state that is more greatly affected. Under these transaction-cost circumstances, allocation of jurisdiction in accordance with effects might be selected. This would argue for allocation of authority necessary to prevent cyberspace terrorism to the United States, which (i) has the most to lose of any state; (ii) is a likely target; and (iii) has substantial expertise to address these problems. Alternatively, authority might be shared among the states with the most to lose. This would suggest an Organization for Economic Cooperation and Development (OECD)-based regime, or a facially multilateral regime driven by advanced country interests.

## C) THE ROLE OF ORGANIZATIONS

Under high transaction-cost circumstances one possibly appropriate strategy would be to establish an organization to hold and reallocate jurisdiction. Thus, it might be useful – it might be efficient in terms of maximizing overall welfare – to share jurisdiction over these types of problems in an organization. So horizontal jurisdiction problems may manifest themselves as subsidiarity problems, should the state retain jurisdiction or should jurisdiction be delegated to an international organization? Of course, when we ask this question, we must also ask about the governance structure of the proposed international organization.

More specifically, states would establish organizations where the transaction costs occasioned by allocation through the organization are less than those occasioned by allocation through ad hoc transactions, all other things being equal. High transaction costs of ad hoc transactions characterize circumstances in which it is difficult to make an initial allocation on the basis of effects, combined with high transaction costs in the formal reallocation of prescriptive jurisdiction.

Furthermore, where effects are dispersed, and holdout problems are likely in trying to negotiate a particular transaction in prescriptive jurisdiction, it may be useful to states to step behind a partial veil of ignorance by establishing an organization that has some measure of transnational power to address the relevant issue. By transnational, I mean that the organization's decisions are not subject to the control of each individual member, but are subject to some shared governance.

Note that any assignment that differs from the status quo would have adverse distributive effects on the states ceding jurisdiction. Of course, where there is no net gain from transacting, we would expect states to refrain from transactions. Where there is a potential net gain, some type of compensation may be required in order to induce states to cede jurisdiction. These distributive consequences would implicate strategic concerns along the lines we will now discuss.

## D) REGULATORY COMPETITION AND REGULATORY CARTELIZATION

We have seen, in international taxation and other contexts, the possibility that one state will attract market entrants, or the businesses in one state will find it efficient to export and will compete effectively against other states, because of lax regulation. Although there is still scholarly contention over empirical support for the pollution haven hypothesis, the theoretical basis for the hypothesis is unimpeachable. One of the factors that may make regulatory competition attractive – one of the assumptions in Tiebout's model – is costless mobility. The Internet provides something very close to costless mobility. Indeed, the Principality of Sealand, with hosting services administered by Havenco, is but one example of the possibility for states, or quasi-states, to position themselves at or near the bottom in terms of quantity of regulation.[184]

As discussed in Chapter 2, regulatory competition is thought to occur under certain conditions, suggested by the work of Tiebout. These conditions include, inter alia, mobility of citizens, knowledge of variations in regulatory regimes, and absence of spillovers. Where these conditions are met, Tiebout theorized, regulatory competition could lead to pressure on governments to improve regulation. However, if the regulatory competition is predicated on regulatory arbitrage by private actors that results in the regulating state failing

[184] Kim Gilmour, "Wish You Were Here? The Principality of Sealand Is a Self-Proclaimed Sovereign state in the North Sea. It's Also the Place to Host your Site if You want to Escape Draconian Internet Privacy Law," *Internet Magazine*, Dec. 1, 2002.

to bear the costs of its inefficiently lax (or inefficiently strict) regulation, leading to spillovers, regulatory competition can demean national regulation.

What has this to do with allocation of regulatory jurisdiction over the Internet? The rules for allocation of jurisdiction will determine the extent to which the regulating state will bear the costs (or experience the benefits) associated with its regulation. For example, a strict rule of territorial conduct will leave the regulating state unaccountable for extraterritorial adverse effects. Thus, the possibility of regulatory competition provides an additional source of enhanced welfare derivable from transactions in jurisdiction. Furthermore, under circumstances where externalities could cause unstable regulatory competition – races to the bottom – the availability of contingent intervention by a centralized authority, such as an international organization, can act to provide a stable equilibrium.[185] This latter insight provides an additional reason for states to form an organization to share jurisdiction under certain circumstances.

## E) STRATEGIC CONSIDERATIONS AND INTERNATIONAL LEGAL AND ORGANIZATIONAL RESPONSES

The previous discussion suggests some of the costs and benefits, including transaction costs, of international cooperation against cyberterrorism. The transaction-costs perspective that was outlined assumes nonstrategic action to maximize aggregate welfare. However, an additional analytical perspective examines the strategic context of cooperation to enhance security against cyberterrorism. The payoff structure that forms this strategic context will be affected by transaction costs and considerations of regulatory competition. Most importantly, as noted, different states will have different, and/or inconsistent, preferences over security against cyberterrorism. One reason is that cybersecurity will be less valuable to states that use cyberspace less. Furthermore, some states will view cyberterrorism or cyberwarfare as a strategic option in the event of war, and will view other states' security against cyberwarfare negatively.

Moreover, different phases or components of the cyberterrorism security issue will have different payoff structures, so will best be analyzed by analogy to different games. Some games will contain an efficient dominant strategy that will benefit each individual state, and therefore will have an efficient Nash equilibrium. Other games will be characterized best as coordination or assurance games, similar to the stag hunt parable. Still other games will be cooperation games, such as the prisoner's dilemma.

---

[185] Joel P. Trachtman, "Regulatory Competition and Regulatory Jurisdiction," 3 *J. Int'l Econ. L.* 331 (2000).

Of course, there is also the possibility that cooperation is inefficient, resulting in a deadlock game in which at least one player's dominant, and efficient, strategy is to defect.[186] Furthermore, it is likely that cyberspace security will involve asymmetric games, as cooperation will be more valuable to some players than to others.

It would be possible to generate a large number of individual games within the cyberterrorism security field. There are bilateral games and multilateral games, and a wide array of payoff structures, including some that are symmetric and some that are asymmetric. The problem of global cyberterrorism has a payoff structure that cannot be assessed without substantial empirical analysis. These game models are simply ways of depicting particular payoff structures. As will be seen, at least under some of these games, it may be possible for states to overcome coordination problems or cooperation problems in order to reach implicit or explicit agreements. We would only expect these agreements, if at all, under circumstances where the benefits to states as a group exceed the costs; where the agreements are Kaldor-Hicks efficient. Side payments may be necessary in order to reach Kaldor–Hicks-efficient transactions. Side payments are by definition outside the initial game, but may be understood as part of a broader strategic context, perhaps involving linkages to other areas.

It is necessary to limit the scope of our analysis. Therefore, I will focus on three potential contexts, and a possible game model for each. These analyses assume that in at least a significant number of cases, private initiatives are insufficient, and government intervention is necessary – but not sufficient – to provide an efficient level of security. They further assume that in some cases, national measures are insufficient to provide an efficient level of security. The three contexts are the following:

- The Cybersecurity Public Good Game
- The Cybersecurity Coordination Game
- The State Sponsorship of Cyberterrorism Game under Symmetric and Asymmetric Preferences

I will review each of these in turn.

## I) *The Cybersecurity Public Good Game*

To a certain extent, the same characteristics that make some aspects of security against cyberterrorism a public good within a domestic society may also make

---

[186] Kenneth W. Abbot, "Modern International Relations theory: A Prospectus for International Lawyers," 14 *Yale J. Int'l L.* 335 (1989).

it a global public good. That is, given the global nature of the Internet, and the global dimension of the non-rival and non-excludible nature of security against cyberterrorism discussed, there are certain aspects of global security against cyberterrorism that would seem to have the characteristics of a public good. Therefore, states may attempt to free ride on security measures taken by other states, resulting in under-provision of this public good. Of course, to the extent that it is possible not to share new technologies that prevent cyberterrorism, these may be understood as club goods, rather than public goods. However, there will be strong incentives to share these technologies once they are produced, including marginal cost pricing and the network externalities that derive from cyberspace.

The existence of a public good often gives rise to a collective-action problem: although the aggregate benefits of cooperating to produce the public good exceed the costs, each state expects the others to contribute, and fails to contribute itself. Some collective-action problems have payoff structures that make them prisoner's dilemmas: coordination to contribute is the optimal collective strategy, but the individual dominant solution is to decline to contribute. States may choose to contribute to the production of the public good, or to attempt to free ride.

How can this problem of cooperation be resolved? As a matter of fact, in many circumstances, including some relating to the global environment, states are able to reach implicit (customary) or explicit (treaty) agreements to cooperate, and to enforce these agreements.[187] They are able to do so among relatively patient states, under circumstances of frequently repeated, or linked, interaction over a long duration, where information about the compliance or failure of compliance of others is readily available. This problem is analogous to other global public-goods problems, which are most closely analyzed in connection with environmental protection. In Chapter 7, I develop a more complete analysis of problems of international cooperation in connection with international public goods. This analysis is also applicable to cybersecurity.

It may well be, also, that this component of the global security against cyberterrorism problem has characteristics of a network, in which the more states that take action to contribute, the greater the value to each state: payoffs increase with the number of states that participate. Under these circumstances, it may be easier to sustain cooperation among large numbers of states.[188]

---

[187] Norman & Trachtman, *supra* note 100. *See also*, Scott Barrett, *Environment and Statecraft: The Strategy of Environmental Treaty-Making* (2003).
[188] Norman & Trachtman, *supra* note 100.

TABLE 5–1. A stag hunt game[189]

|   |   | B | |
|---|---|---|---|
|   |   | Cooperate/Hunt stag | Defect/Hunt rabbit |
| A | Cooperate/Hunt Stag | 2,2 | 0,1 |
|   | Defect/Hunt Rabbit | 1,0 | 1,1 |

Finally, it is worth noting that a number of arms-control contexts may also have the characteristics of a prisoner's dilemma, with similar responsive dynamics.[190] Whereas there may come a time when cyberwarfare is sought to be subjected to arms control, any efforts along these lines will encounter substantial problems of verification.

## II) *Coordination Problem: the Global Cyberspace Stag Hunt*

In other areas, there is a different type of collective-action problem. It may be possible for each state to choose whether to protect its own networks in a less effective way, or to join together to protect global cyberspace. However, the effectiveness of the latter approach may be dependent on the extent to which other states make a similar decision. Under the stag hunt, which is a type of assurance game, each state may obtain smaller payoffs – a lower level of protection – by seeking to protect only its networks. If states are able to coordinate to forego settling for a lesser level of local protection or other local benefits in favor of global protection, they will each achieve a higher level of security. Cooperation may break down if players are uncertain about the preferences and strategy of others.

The stag hunt game, as described in Table 5–1, is derived from a Rousseauvian fable of cooperation among hunters.[191] Unless all hunters are committed to catching the stag, it will escape. Each individual hunter may be tempted by a passing rabbit. Each hunter prefers a share of stag to an individual portion of rabbit, but is uncertain about whether other hunters are sufficiently committed to capturing stag. The analogy to cybersecurity is as follows: each state prefers its share of global security against cyberterrorism (stag), but may

---

[189] See Abbot, *supra* note 186.
[190] George Downs, David Rocke & Randolph Siverson, *Arms Races and Cooperation*, 38 World Politics 118 (1985).
[191] Kenneth W. Abbot, "Collective Goods, Mobile Resources, and Extraterritorial Trade Controls," 50 *Law & Contemp. Probs.* 117 (1987).

be distracted by the opportunity to provide local security (rabbit), especially if it is unsure of the commitment of other states.

A stag hunt context requires a lesser level of international legal inducements to compliance compared to the prisoner's dilemma. There is no dominant solution to the game as depicted: neither action makes the actor better off no matter what the other actor does. However, mutual cooperation is the focal equilibrium because it results in higher payoffs.

It is possible that the parties would consider the probability of the other party cooperating, in order to determine whether or not they would cooperate. Sufficient clarity regarding the definition of the cooperative behavior, monitoring to ensure compliance, and modest penalties should be sufficient to induce cooperation. In addition, decreases in the gains from defecting, and increases in the gains from cooperating, would increase the chances of cooperation. Note that we are assuming symmetry of preferences: no player actually prefers rabbit, and no player prefers not to catch anything.

Imagine, however, a multilateral circumstance, in which the aggregation technology is weakest link, as may be the case in the cybersecurity field. If any of a large number of players is distracted by rabbit, no one catches stag. Under these circumstances, if the probability of cooperation for any player is independent of cooperation by others, greater assurance is needed to induce any player to cooperate. This is because the aggregate probability of defection by any one player is much greater than the probability of defection by a single player.

### III) State Sponsorship of Cyberterrorism: a Game of "Chicken" or "Bully"?

As noted, public goods and collective-action problems often involve externalities. In connection with security against cyberterrorism, we have a more direct international externality problem. It may be beneficial to state A to permit or encourage, or perpetrate, cyberterrorism against state B. Even where state A does not benefit from harm to state B, it may be that acts under the jurisdictional control of state A confer harm on state B without being taken into account by state A. The potential function of international law in this context is to internalize these externalities, where it is worthwhile to do so in substantive and transaction cost terms.

In the cyberwarfare context, we may understand this as a deterrence game. In this "chicken" game, as depicted in Table 5–2, neither player has a dominant strategy. In this particular case, there is no unique efficient equilibrium.

TABLE 5-2. A chicken game[192]

|   |            | B          |        |
|---|------------|------------|--------|
|   |            | Cyberpeace | Attack |
| A | Cyberpeace | 3,3        | 2,4    |
|   | Attack     | 4,2        | 1,1    |

Each player has two Nash equilibria: attack when the other plays peace, and play peace when the other attacks. However, both players wish to avoid the circumstance where they each play attack, and the even split in the northwest quadrant seems intuitively attractive, although it is unstable. In order to achieve it, they should each commit to playing "cyberpeace." International law or organization can be used to implement this commitment, by ensuring that the payoffs to defection are reduced to three or less through a penalty of one or more. It should be noted that, as with any deterrence threat, this strategy may suffer from lack of credibility: after the other party has attacked, the victim may not have incentives to retaliate.[193]

Each of the other models presented here assumes symmetrical preferences among states. This is obviously counterfactual. It is important to note the asymmetry among states in terms of the relative value to each state of security against cyberterrorism on the one hand and the relative value of cyberterrorism on the other hand. Poor states are unlikely to be as adversely affected by cyberterrorism as wealthy states. On the other hand, cyberterrorism is a weapon that may be more available to the poor than other weapons, so restrictions on cyberterrorism – such as restrictions on sleeping under bridges – may be less attractive to the poor.

In this bully game, as described in Table 5-3, B's dominant strategy is to attack. A does not have a dominant strategy, but if A understands B's dominant strategy to attack, it can increase its payoff from zero to one by playing cyberpeace when B attacks. If B understands A's dilemma, it will simply attack. If B does not understand A's dilemma, A may be able to convince B to compensate A for playing cyberpeace, as doing so increases B's payoff from two to three. This game may illustrate an asymmetric circumstance in which a global network breakdown would not harm the deadlock player much, relative to the chicken player.

---

[192] See, Steven J. Brams & D. Marc Kilgour, *Game Theory and National Security* (1988). This game was adapted from Brams and Kilgour.
[193] *Id.*

TABLE 5–3. A bully game involving asymmetric payoffs

|  |  | B (Deadlock Player) | |
|---|---|---|---|
|  |  | Cyberpeace | Attack |
| A (Chicken Player) | Cyberpeace | 2,1 | 1,3 |
|  | Attack | 3,0 | 0,2 |

However, if the deadlock player would not be harmed because it is poor and does not have valuable network assets, as opposed to because it is wealthy and advanced and has secured its network, it might be strange to attribute so much power to a poor country. In this isolated context, the poor country has the power of poverty, but if its situation is examined in a broader setting, we would not consider it to be powerful, and there would likely be sticks or carrots that a wealthy country could wield to secure its desired action.

## IV) Relative and Absolute Gains

Where enmity overcomes all other values, we might understand states as engaging in a game where winning in relative terms vis-à-vis other states is more important than absolute gains from interaction. This can be understood in standard rationalist absolute gains terms, by considering that the losses associated with falling behind – with losing – are unacceptably great.[194] This is a distinction between ordinary cybercrime and cataclysmic cyberterrorism. For example, the United States can afford to accept the risk of a few billion dollars loss owing to a particularly effective virus. It cannot afford to accept the risk of sabotage of its missile control system or of destruction of its financial system.

## V) Information Problems

In any real-world context, there will be serious information problems that will impede both the ability of particular states to determine an appropriate strategy, and the ability of states to join together in a cooperative arrangement. First, it will be difficult for one state to know another's preferences. Second, it will be difficult for one state to know another's strategy, where there are multiple available strategies. This presents a problem of coordination, even where cooperation is otherwise feasible. Law may be used to help to resolve this

---

[194] Robert Powell, "Absolute and Relative Gains in International Relations Theory," 85 *Am. Pol. Sci. Rev.* 1303 (1991).

coordination problem. Finally, as previously mentioned, it could be difficult to identify the true author of any attack, making real or cyberspace retaliation difficult.

## F) CHAPTER CONCLUSION

The previous discussion illustrates some of the reasons why states may determine to cooperate with one another to address cyberterrorism. This part discusses some possible international legal and international organizational tools available to effect cooperation, reasoning in part by analogy.

Much in the cybersecurity problem is analogous, both substantively and doctrinally, to pre-existing problems.[195] Those preexisting problems have preexisting solutions. It would be foolish to argue that we can learn nothing from analogs. However, it would be equally foolish to argue that there is nothing different about cyberspace and cybersecurity, or that existing solutions are presumptively sufficient. The differences may be characterized at least partially as differences of degree: of velocity and volume, and of human behavior induced by these initial differences. When do these differences merit a different response? It is important to note a degree of comparative-law path dependence. Not every society will require the same response, nor will every society require a response at the same time. This is a source of asymmetry even among states with the same fundamental goals.

Some have argued that through decentralized production of autonomous governance, individual actors will produce satisfactory governance. To the extent that this group has incentives to write code so that what would otherwise be legal concerns are addressed, then this autonomous "social norm" type of code may take the place of law. We know, however, that social norms do not preempt every type of law.[196] Rather, there are circumstances in which law is a more efficient solution to the problem of cooperation.

Law can also guide the development of social norms toward selected equilibria. In fact, the line between autonomous norms and law is not as clear as sometimes assumed. We might say that the state, and its powers, developed and are constantly changing through autonomous action, including governance mechanisms that we now bundle together as "the state." However, in appropriate historical and anthropological perspective, this is only different in degree from what we label "social norms."

---

[195] Trachtman, *supra* note 180.
[196] Kaushik Basu, "Social Norms and the Law" in *The New Palgrave Dictionary of Economics and the Law* 476 (P. Newman, ed., 1998).

It is clear that cyberterrorism poses a very great threat. There would seem to be important reasons for international cooperation in this area. Thus far, there seems to be little formal international activity comparable to that observed in other areas. Once the need for international cooperation is determined, it would be appropriate to consider mechanisms similar to those already implemented in order to counter maritime terrorism and terrorist financing, mutatis mutandis. For example, it would at least be worth considering a global certification scheme for ISPs and backbone providers, along the lines observed in the maritime and financing contexts. The utility of a certification scheme would depend on the degree to which actions taken at this level could prevent or ameliorate the consequences of cyberterrorism.

As the value of networks and the potential power of cyberterrorism inevitably increase, states will wish to develop ways of unilaterally securing their networks, but will also wish to pursue cooperation to reduce the possible threats from abroad. The greatest problem in establishing cooperation will be in verifying the cooperative actions of counterparties.

# 6 Human Rights

Over the past century, the legal instantiation of human rights has evolved. It has grown, and for reasons set forth in Chapter 4, can be expected to grow further. The role of "negative" human rights in this legal instantiation is, of course, the restriction of the power of the state. As "positive" human rights have developed, we see greater articulation of positive responsibilities of the state.

Thus, the essence of human rights is about the constraints and minimum responsibilities of states in their relationship to citizens. The legal, as apart from the ethical, idea of human rights arises from the idea of the limited authority of the state – from the rejection of the concept of unconstrained monarchic sovereignty – which constraint is at the heart of both constitutionalism and international law. When should these limits be a matter of domestic constitutionalism, and when should they be the subject of international law, and what is changing in society that might affect this balance?

International human-rights law is fundamentally concerned with *behind the border* issues – issues that only a short time ago would have been understood as outside the scope of international law because they were within an impermeable domestic sphere: the *domaine reservé*. In this sense, it is quite different from the international law of coexistence as described by Wolfgang Friedmann, except to the extent that coexistence has been concerned with the treatment of minorities in a particular state where another state has a special relationship to that minority group. However, international human-rights law is more difficult to see as part of the international law of cooperation – it raises the question of precisely what the international concern is, or what the international public good is, that is addressed by international human-rights law.

In order to evaluate the future of international human-rights law, this chapter addresses several questions. What are the externalities or public goods, or other bases for international concern, regarding domestic human rights? What

# Human Rights

causes states to request other states to enter into human-rights treaties? What causes states to enter into human-rights treaties, and to adhere to them? What are the effects of globalization, technological change, economic development, and other expected future changes in global society on human rights? How will changes in human rights affect the role of international law?

The assumption of this chapter is that human rights are not part of natural law, and are not universal, or at least are not completely universal. Rather, human rights are determined through political, constitutional, and essentially contractarian processes, which we can expect to differ to some extent in different states. However, with increasing globalization, democratization, and development, there are important forces militating toward greater convergence in human rights in the future. Still, it is important to recognize that different rights will have different levels of importance for different states. Furthermore, some of the extensions of human rights that have been proposed or even adopted in recent years may be less compelling than some of the earlier established human rights.

As we analyze international legal commitments that are symmetric in form, it is important to recognize that these commitments are often asymmetric in effect. By commitment, I refer to the smallest unit of international legal obligation – the promise to take a specific action or to refrain from taking a specific action. Treaties or groups of treaties may involve many different commitments, and these diverse commitments may balance the asymmetric effects of one another. It is also possible that entire treaties or groups of treaties may, on an aggregate basis, be somewhat asymmetric.

The main point is that each decision about how to combine different commitments within a treaty or among a group of treaties or even between international legal obligations and nonlegal forms of international transfers of consideration involves a complex weighing by each state party. Each state party must decide whether the package of commitments demanded of it is appropriately counterbalanced by the package of commitments granted to it: whether the combined effect of a particular set of commitments is politically Pareto efficient as to that state. It does so by aggregating its domestic preferences through its domestic political system, along the lines described in Chapter 4.

With respect to any particular commitment that is framed as a formally symmetrical obligation, it is likely that the commitment will be more politically costly for some states to accept and carry out than other states. With respect to any particular commitment, there will be high-depth states, low-depth states, and no-depth states (I will use low-depth to refer to both low-depth and no-depth states), with depth referring to the extent to which compliance with that commitment would cause the state to take action or refrain from taking action inconsistent with its purely domestic preferences.[197]

Some areas of human-rights law exhibit broad asymmetry, for example where human-rights obligations are framed in a way that is consistent with the purely domestic preferences of liberal democratic states, but are inconsistent with the purely domestic preferences of authoritarian states. In liberal democratic states, which are no- or low-depth states with respect to these types of human rights, the domestic political equilibrium largely supports these rights, whereas authoritarian states may be understood as high-depth states for these rights because their domestic political equilibrium would otherwise reject these rights.

For low-depth states, entry into a treaty, and compliance with the treaty, is not very costly, either in an economic or political sense. For high-depth states that by definition lack sufficient autonomous political support for human rights, compliance with a human-rights treaty is politically – and perhaps economically – costly, and therefore entry into a human-rights treaty is generally costly, assuming that they will comply or bear costs for failing to do so. However, there may be countervailing benefits. On the other hand, compliance is by no means certain, and violation not necessarily costly.

This scenario raises four critical questions.

1. *Demand for Accession and Compliance.* Why do low-depth states care about what happens in high-depth states? More generally, what are the externalities or public goods or other bases for international concern regarding domestic human rights in other countries? What causes demand for international human-rights law? I assume that, generally speaking, the same things that cause demand for compliance cause demand for accession, provided that accession causes compliance. Although under some circumstances accession may benefit low-depth governments in their relationships with certain domestic constituencies, regardless of compliance by high-depth states.

2. *Supply of Accession.* What causes high-depth states to enter into these treaties, when they get nothing of value in terms of changed human-rights performance from low-depth states? What causes supply of international human-rights law? This is a different question from the question of what causes high-depth states to become low-depth states. Acculturation, development, or other factors may cause high-depth states to change, developing an indigenous demand for human rights

---

[197] George Downs, David M. Rocke, & Peter N. Barsoom, "Is the Good News about Compliance Good News about Cooperation?" 50 *Int'l Org.* 379 (1996).

that overcomes indigenous resistance. I am concerned not with changes in preferences, but with why states enter into international legal commitments inconsistent with their human-rights preferences: why high-depth states enter into international human-rights treaties.

3. *Supply of Compliance*. What causes high-depth states to comply with international human-rights treaties? Again, this is different from the question of why states autonomously protect human rights. The question is, how do international human-rights treaties cause states to take actions that are inconsistent with their autarchic political equilibrium?

4. *Strategic Barriers*. How can supply meet demand? Focusing on commitment, assuming low-depth states generally care about human-rights performance in high-depth states, how can they induce high-depth states to enter into treaties? Can low-depth states overcome the collective-action problem of determining how to share the cost of inducing high-depth states to enter into these treaties? Even when demand and supply can otherwise intersect, there may be strategic barriers to transactions.

This chapter reviews existing literature on these four questions, suggesting a preference-based analytical approach to the demand and supply of international human-rights law.

## A) THE DEMAND FOR INTERNATIONAL-HUMAN-RIGHTS COMMITMENTS AND COMPLIANCE: WHY DO STATES CARE ABOUT THE HUMAN-RIGHTS PERFORMANCE OF OTHER STATES, OR THEIR ACCESSION TO HUMAN-RIGHTS TREATIES?

It is a continuing puzzle to explain international human-rights law, as opposed to domestic human-rights law.[198] If a human-rights treaty binds low-depth states, then it is largely superfluous, and we need an explanation of why other states requested the treaty. If the treaty binds high-depth states, we need an explanation other than agreement with the principles, because by definition, high-depth states do not agree.

In *Mobilizing for Human Rights*, Beth Simmons rejects the power of reputation, retaliation, or reciprocity to cause adherence to or compliance with human-rights treaties – effectively rejecting the influence of international relations. Focusing on the supply side, Simmons suggests that the main reason states enter into human-rights treaties as obligors is not reciprocity, but that they agree with the principles articulated. This proposition does not answer the

---

[198] Dennis Mueller, "Rights and Liberty in the European Union," 13 *Sup. Ct. Econ. Rev.* 1 (2005).

question of why some states desire that other states enter into human-rights treaties, or why states that agree with the principles feel the need to enter into a treaty articulating those principles.[199] In *Mobilizing for Human Rights*, Simmons does not explain why states would accept an international human-rights obligation at one time that will cause them to take unwanted action at a later time. If, alternatively, the requisite action is wanted, as opposed to unwanted, the treaty has no depth and is not very interesting from the standpoint of human-rights behavior. Simmons' argument supports the possibility of autonomous human-rights protection, but does not explain international commitments. *Mobilizing for Human Rights* fails to explain the use of international law to make commitments by low-depth or high-depth states.

Examining the possibility of reciprocity in this area, we might ask rhetorically, "Would Sweden really torture its citizens in response to torture by Syria of Syria's citizens?" However, this question is analogous to the question in the municipal realm, "Would one parent beat his child in response to the beating by another parent of his children?" Of course not, but this type of narrow reciprocity is not seen as a condition for the existence of domestic law, and it is not a condition for the existence of international law. In fact, in most areas of international law, international legal rules are characterized by either explicit or implicit asymmetry: the commitments of different states are diverse. This is because of the different situations of different states. Even in the field of trade, which is often thought of as exhibiting narrow reciprocity, different states agree to liberalize market entry for some products in exchange for liberalization by other states with respect to other products. In the field of investment, although bilateral investment treaties are formally bilateral, capital often flows largely in one direction, and only one of the states presents significant barriers or risks to investment.

It is possible that there is reciprocity within particular human-rights agreements, especially those largely among liberal democratic states. Even where human-rights agreements lack reciprocity within the agreement itself, however, there is a possibility of more diffuse reciprocity, involving denial of foreign aid, exclusion from free-trade agreements, refusal of military alliances, or other deleterious effects of non-accession or violation.

I now review some of the leading preference-based reasons why one state might request another state to improve its human-rights protections, and confirm its commitment to improve in a treaty. There is little empirical work

---

[199] Beth Simmons, *Mobilizing for Human Rights* (2009). Thus, if a state agrees with the principles, then it is not a high-depth state, and therefore can be expected to implement human rights of its own accord.

# Human Rights

linking these possible reasons to actual human-rights treaties, but some of the connections seem intuitively appealing.

## I) Physical Externalities

It is true that human-rights violations may cause significant international external effects, including refugee crises, ethnic or other conflict, certain types of regulatory competition – as in connection with labor rights – and more diluted external effects in terms of reduced economic growth. Human-rights violations may also certainly cause external effects through altruism: citizens of foreign states may suffer diminished utility from knowing of human-rights violations in other states.

First, human-rights violations may simply cause victims or those at risk to leave the perpetrating state. If this emigration is disorderly, excessively large, or politically unappealing in other ways, it may cause direct adverse effects outside the perpetrating state. The human-rights violations may create conditions that would result in civil war or a threat to international peace and security. Other states may wish to avoid a situation in which they would be compelled to intervene at great cost. Security Council actions with respect to Libya, Somalia, Haiti, Iraq, Rwanda, and the former Yugoslavia may be understood in this way.

The recently formulated *responsibility to protect*[200] may be understood as a proposal to address these types of external effects, as well as a proposal to give affected states some power to respond. It states that "each individual State has the responsibility to protect its populations from genocide, war crimes, ethnic cleansing and crimes against humanity." The international community may use diplomatic, humanitarian, and other peaceful means, and if those fail, may take "collective action, in a timely and decisive manner, through the Security Council, in accordance with the Charter, including Chapter VII, on a case-by-case basis" when "national authorities are manifestly failing to protect their populations" from these crimes.[201]

Another type of direct externality would involve appropriations of the property of foreigners. For example, there may be a human right to certain types of property, including intellectual property. Denial of certain property rights could have the character of a human-rights violation. A state may appropriate

---

[200] *See* Report of the International Commission on Intervention and State Sovereignty, "The Responsibility to Protect" (Dec. 2001). Retrieved from http://responsibilitytoprotect.org/ICISS%20Report.pdf.

[201] 2005 World Summit Outcome, G.A. Res. A/RES/60/1, 138, U.N. Doc. A/RES/60/1 (Oct. 24, 2005); Protection of Civilians in Armed Conflict, S.C. Res. 1674, 4, U.N. Doc. S/RES/1674 (Apr. 28, 2006).

property of foreigners, or otherwise abuse foreigners in a way that causes a direct external effect. Of course, this type of externality might be addressed simply by providing better-than-national-treatment to the foreign persons. Internalization of these externalities would thus not necessarily require that broad human rights be accorded to residents.

## II) Demonstration Effects

Another type of externality is ideational. That is, if one state abuses its citizens it may make it easier for another state to do so. International public opinion might not be so outraged, or its outrage might be diluted, by virtue of widespread violations. Concerns about responses by the United States to the September 11, 2001 attack might be understood in this way. Thus, fear of contagion would be one reason citizens of one state would be concerned about human-rights practices in another state. Conversely, it might be hoped that by spreading human-rights protection more broadly, it would be more difficult for one's government to engage in human-rights abuses. This perspective supports Simmons' argument that the reason states adhere to human-rights treaties is because they agree with the principles, but suggests why they agree with the principles for others, and support a treaty, as opposed to simply practicing human rights unilaterally. It is supported, to some extent, by Simmons' empirical finding that ratification by a particular country is often associated with ratification by other countries within that country's region.[202]

## III) Diaspora Externalities

Where there are important ethnic or religious relations between citizens of one state, and related ethnic or religious groups in a second state, it is not uncommon for these related citizens of the first state to be concerned about the treatment of their ethnic group in the second state. This type of concern arises frequently, with examples including the concerns of the U.S. Irish community regarding the British treatment of Northern Ireland, Indonesian concerns regarding the Israeli treatment of Palestinians, or Chinese concerns regarding the treatment of overseas Chinese.

## IV) Mobility

A plausible economic approach to human rights sees them as distributive claims, in which the rights holder is protected from certain types of majoritarian – or outside a democracy, authoritarian – impositions in the case

---

[202] Simmons, *supra* note 199, chapter 3.

of negative rights, or denials in the case of positive rights.[203] In this model, proposed by Dennis Mueller, rights are established where the likely majoritarian concern is small relative to the likely minority interest. For example, the right to a fair trial means a lot to the accused, and might be seen as a relatively minor imposition for the majority.

However, this approach does not suggest universality of human rights, but rather anticipates that different societies would develop distinct baskets of human rights on the basis of their own history and characteristics. Mueller raises the question, then, of why groups of states – such as the EU or even a wider multilateral group – would determine to harmonize rights, or to commit internationally to provide human rights. Another way of asking this question is to ask the optimal size of the regulatory unit for particular human rights. Interestingly, there is no reason to expect that the optimal regulatory unit would be the same for all rights, or for all states. Mueller's approach is focused on the direct concerns of a foreign citizen who may either move to the human-rights obligor state, or imagine himself in the position of a resident of the human-rights obligor state. It therefore does not address most cross-border externalities owing to human rights denial or provision. It is also dependent on some degree of expected mobility.

## V) Altruistic Externalities

Furthermore, the direct welfare of its own citizens does not necessarily exhaust the objective function of a particular state. Rather, it is entirely plausible, and common, for individuals – and by extension for their states – to have preferences regarding the welfare of others. For a domestic example validating the possibility of altruistic preferences, we need look no further than the preferences parents have regarding the welfare of their children. For international examples, we might look at private and public efforts to assist in the event of foreign natural disasters or famines.

Indeed, Mueller suggests a kind of Rawlsian veil of ignorance-based virtual mobility, in which a citizen of one state imagines himself as a citizen of another state, as a basis for concern regarding foreign human rights. This is an argument for ethical concern arising from a thought experiment; the point is that individuals might develop ethical concerns that would induce them to lobby their governments to request human-rights protections in foreign states.

Altruism may be accentuated by virtue of new information technologies that address the availability bias by which we feel concern for problems that are physically closer than those that are farther away. States and their citizens can

---

[203] Mueller, *supra* note 198.

cooperate for purely self-interested reasons, but we also observe more altruistic cooperation, where repetition is unlikely or where it is impossible to obtain reputational gains from cooperation.[204]

An availability bias may also highlight concerns for problems that are temporally or historically closer. Under the *availability bias* or availability heuristic, people respond irrationally to concerns that are present in their minds – either because of geographic proximity or perhaps temporal proximity – than to risks that are more distant, even if the risk is otherwise equal. It is not difficult to see the historical factors that led to the development of international human-rights law after World War II in this light. The experience of the Holocaust, the war itself and its aftermath, decolonization, and the commencement of the Cold War all contributed to the development of international human-rights treaties. Much began and was driven by the role of international human-rights law in the U.S. domestic political scene.[205]

## VI) *Positive Externalities and Global Public Goods*

Another reason for foreign concern regarding human-rights practices is the global public-goods aspect of some of the results of human-rights protection. High levels of human rights are conducive to economic growth and welfare.[206] Economic growth and welfare benefits other states, in particular through trade and finance channels. Therefore, the protection of human rights on a national level may confer positive externalities on foreign persons, or may be a partial global public good, insofar as its benefits are not all captured by the granting state. For this reason, it may be that human rights are under-provided, and an international cooperative regime would be useful in providing the optimal level of human rights. This may be especially true under national authoritarian governments, wherein the autocrat/kleptocrat can capture more welfare by denying human rights and enhancing his own power than by granting human rights that might increase total national welfare.

## VII) *Pecuniary Externalities*

Some types of human-rights violations – notably labor rights – may have an adverse effect through the price system, and thus would be understood as pecuniary or competitive externalities. For example, permission for child

---

[204] *See* Samuel Bowles & Herbert Gintis, A *Cooperative Species: Human Reciprocity and its Evolution* (2011).
[205] *See*, Elizabeth Borgwardt, A *New Deal for the World: America's Vision for Human Rights* (2005).
[206] Lorenz Blume & Stefan Voigt, "The Economic Effects of Human Rights," 60 (4) *Kyklos* 509 (2007).

labor, prohibitions on collective bargaining, or failure to set a minimum wage may provide bargaining power to employers that would enhance their ability to pay a lower labor cost, and therefore be more competitive in the international market. These types of pecuniary externalities may be accentuated by globalization – by the reduction of other barriers to competition. This is one reason we sometimes see labor-rights components to free-trade agreements. Thus, competitive or pecuniary externalities may be expected to produce increasing pressure on certain domestic human rights as globalization advances.

## VIII) Conclusion Regarding Demand

As suggested at the outset, there are not necessarily very strong reasons for demand by low-depth states for legal obligations or performance by high-depth states in the field of human rights. Nevertheless, we have seen significant growth in treaty commitments relating to human rights since World War II.

Of course, the level of demand will depend not just on the benefits described here, but on the costs. The costs to high-depth states will determine the supply of accession and compliance with human-rights obligations. The net benefits to low-depth states will determine the price that low-depth states would be willing to pay to high-depth states to adhere to and comply with human-rights treaties. Similarly, the net costs to high-depth states (we know that they are net costs by virtue of the definition of high-depth states) will determine the price they would be willing to accept in order to adhere and comply.

We know that most human-rights treaties have very limited mechanisms to ensure compliance, and perhaps this is because the low-depth states are only willing to expend enough to purchase a weak treaty, rather than a strong treaty. However, in some particular contexts, we have seen low-depth states willing to buy a strong treaty, conditioning important trade benefits on human-rights performance.[207] For example, the United States has conditioned entry into a preferential trade agreement with Colombia on certain core labor-rights protections.

## B) THE SUPPLY OF INTERNATIONAL HUMAN-RIGHTS ADHERENCE: WHY DO STATES ACCEPT HUMAN-RIGHTS OBLIGATIONS THAT REQUIRE THAT THEY CHANGE THEIR BEHAVIOR?

Analyses of why and when states commit to human-rights treaties seek to explain why high-depth states sign treaties they do not have to, when such

---

[207] Emilie M. Hafner-Burton, "Trading Human Rights: How Preferential Trade Agreements Influence Government Repression," 59 (3) *Int'L Org.* 593 (2005).

treaties are costly by virtue of the fact that they curtail state sovereignty and may require costly domestic changes. Recent empirical research has examined several main causes of commitment.

First, states may commit to treaties because the benefits of commitment exceed the costs. The benefits may be categorized as reciprocity, reputation, or the avoidance of retaliation. There may be diffuse reciprocal economic benefits, or there may be more direct benefits in terms of entry into a preferential trade agreement or other trade preferences, foreign aid, or military alliance. The costs include the lost autonomy owing to treaty constraints, whose costs are dependent on the extent to which the treaty will affect behavior, or will impose costs for violation. Importantly in the human-rights sphere, to the extent that human-rights violations are seen as useful for a government in keeping power, the possible costs of lost autonomy may be viewed by the government as very great.

Alternatively, the benefits may come from signaling, which might be considered a part of reputation, or considered separately. According to *signaling theory*, states find it useful to expend costs in order to signal their "type," so as to induce certain treatment or cooperation from other states. Some have recently argued that governments may use the entry into human-rights treaties to signal that they are willing to incur great costs – including the costs involved with response by other states to violation – in order to stay in power.[208] The idea is that they purposely make their human-rights violations more costly in order to demonstrate their resolve.

Second, governments of states may commit to international human-rights treaties in order to lock in a certain domestic political decision, protecting it from change under subsequent political equilibria. Third, particular historical circumstances – such as those surrounding the end of the Second World War or the decline of the empire of the former Soviet Union – may play an important causal role. Fourth, acculturation factors – such as how governments or states see themselves or their desire to mimic other governments or states or the adoption of new normative perspectives – may cause states to commit to human-rights treaties.

## I) Minimizing Costs

Oona Hathaway argues that states decide to ratify human-rights treaties on the basis of expected compliance costs – the higher the cost of commitment, the

---

[208] James R. Hollyer & B. Peter Rosendorff, "Why Do Authoritarian Regimes Sign the Convention Against Torture? Signaling, Domestic Politics and Non-Compliance," working paper dated June 2011. Retrieved from http://papers.ssrn.com/sol3/papers.cfm?abstract_id=1876843.

less likely it is that a country will sign a human-rights treaty. This commitment cost is a function of both "the extent to which a country's practices diverge from the requirements of the treaty and of the country's expectations regarding the likelihood that the costs will be realized."[209] This is a reference to the depth of the treaty. Hathaway argues that the decision to sign human-rights treaties depends on the cost of commitment, the enforcement structure of the treaty, and the nature of each country's governance regime.

Hathaway finds that democratic and nondemocratic countries have different commitment patterns because the former have stronger internal human-rights enforcement measures. The further a democratic nation's human-rights practices diverge from what a treaty requires, the less likely it will be to join. However, nondemocratic states whose human-rights practices diverge from a treaty's standards will be no less likely to commit than those whose human-rights practices do not diverge from treaty requirements. Furthermore, countries are less likely to sign treaties with stronger enforcement mechanisms, and therefore, Hathaway concludes by suggesting that measures to improve treaty monitoring and enforcement should be approached with care.

Jay Goodliffe and Darren Hawkins examine commitment to international human-rights treaties in the context of the Convention Against Torture (CAT), and – like Hathaway – also focus on the costs of commitment.[210] They argue that states incur three types of costs when they commit to treaties: policy change, unintended consequences and limited flexibility, and that consideration of these costs affects the decision to adhere.

## II) Maximizing Benefits

Of course, a more complete approach to explaining the decision to adhere would focus not just on costs, but also on benefits: what inducements in terms of reciprocity, reputation, or avoidance of retaliation affect the decision to adhere? Transactions and equilibrium prices depend both on supply and demand.

There are unlikely to be narrow reputational, reciprocal, or retaliatory incentives – within the particular human-rights commitment or even within the broader field of human rights – for high-depth states to make international

---

[209] Oona Hathaway, "The Cost of Commitment," 55 *Stan. L. Rev.* 1821 (2002–2003). In this study, Hathaway looked at empirical data from 166 countries over a period of 40 years. *See also* a later publication making the same argument, Oona Hathaway, "Why Do Countries Commit to Human Rights Treaties?" 51 (4) *J. Conflict Resol.* 588 (2007).

[210] Jay Goodliffe & Darren G. Hawkins, "Explaining Commitment: States and the Convention against Torture," 68 (2) *J. Pol.* 358 (2006).

human-rights commitments. With respect to treaties that may include diverse commitments, it is possible that a degree of intra-treaty reciprocity may apply, but for simplification purposes, let us assume a circumstance in which there is no intra-treaty reciprocity. By assumption, high-depth states lack sufficient domestic incentives to take the action demanded by the commitment with respect to which they are defined as high depth. Assuming that they are consistent over time, this suggests that they lack domestic incentives to enter into these human-rights commitments.

So, why do states enter into treaties that are costly to them? Even if costs are low, unless they are zero, the only preference-based reasons relate to reciprocity, retaliation, or reputation. Assuming insufficient domestic demand for international human-rights commitments – which assumption seems validated by the fact that in a high-depth state there is insufficient domestic demand for the relevant human rights – we would not expect high-depth states to enter into these treaties without some international payoff.

However, one international-based incentive within human rights that may be available to high-depth states is reciprocity with other high-depth states. If there is a negative competitive or pecuniary externality in connection with human-rights accession or protection, human-rights treaties may present an opportunity for collusion among high-depth states to avoid a race to the bottom in human rights. By inducing other high-depth states to protect human rights at the same time, the negative pecuniary externality that might be imposed on a single high-depth state moving alone to protection may be avoided. If the magnitude of these pecuniary externalities is great, this could be an important effect. Alternatively, if there is a competitive benefit that might be made available to high-depth states in exchange for human-rights accession or protection – such as preferential trade – then we might expect to see states that compete with a particular high-depth state mimicking its accession or compliance behavior in order to maintain a competitive position. This behavior would be consistent with Simmons' observation that regional accession is a good predictor of individual state accession.[211]

David Moore develops a signaling theory of human-rights treaty commitment.[212] He argues that countries enter into human-rights treaties because governments wish to signal particular messages to other governments. For Moore, such messages include a government's willingness to restrain the exercise of power in the medium-term for benefits in the long-term (its discount rate). States with low discount rates seek to cooperate with similar states. Other

---

[211] Simmons, *supra* note 199.
[212] David Moore, "Signaling Theory of Human Rights Compliance," 97 Nw. U. L. Rev. 879 (2002–2003).

influential factors include the cost of the signal, the payoffs of any signal, and the possibility of becoming a signal entrepreneur. Although signaling theory, to the extent that it does not include a full array of costs and benefits, may be limited in its scope, Moore seems to examine both the supply side and the demand side of the equation. Along similar lines, Geisinger[213] applies Guzman's rational-choice theory to human-rights treaty formation and compliance,[214] emphasizing the role of reputation in the decision to sign human-rights treaties.

Emilie Hafner-Burton and Kiyoteru Tsutsui[215] approach this question differently, but reach a similar conclusion. They use statistical analyses of a comprehensive sample of government repression from 1976 to 1999 to understand why states commit to treaties they do not have to commit to, and often do not comply with. Calling this the "paradox of empty promises," they argue that the institutionalization of international human rights creates a context in which "governments often ratify human rights treaties as a matter of window dressing,"[216] reaping benefits without expecting to incur costs. For this type of dissimulation to be attractive to high-depth states, there must be some international benefit that they expect to receive in response to commitment.

James Hollyer and Peter Rosendorff turn the conventional signaling approach on its head. They argue that authoritarian governments use signature of the CAT, followed by the willful violation of its provisions, as a costly signal to domestic opposition groups of their willingness to employ repressive tactics to remain in power.[217] They believe that this proposition is supported by their empirical findings that authoritarian governments that torture heavily are more likely to sign the treaty than those that torture less. However, they do not control for the possibility that states that torture heavily are also subject to greater demands that they sign the CAT than states that do not. The differential could plausibly come from the demand side of the equation, rather than from the supply side. Hafner, Tsutsui and Meyer find that "repressive states want the legitimacy that the human rights treaties confer on them more than non-repressive states because they are under tighter scrutiny for their practices."[218]

---

[213] Alex Geisinger, "Rational Choice, Reputation and Human Rights Treaties," 106 *Mich. L. Rev.* 1129 (2008).
[214] *See* Andrew Guzman, *How International Law Works: A Rational Choice Theory* (2010).
[215] Emilie M. Hafner-Burton & Kiyoteru Tsutsui, "Human Rights in a Globalizing World: The Paradox of Empty Promises," 110 (5) Am. J. Sociology 1373 ( 2005).
[216] *Id.* at 1378.　　　　　　　　　[217] Hollyer & Rosendorff, *supra* note 208.
[218] Emilie M. Hafner-Burton, Kiyoteru Tsutsui, & John W. Meyer, "International Human Rights Law and the Politics of Legitimation: Repressive States and Human Rights Treaties," 23 (1) *International Sociology* 115–41 (2008).

Furthermore, this type of costly signaling explanation can only be true if the costly signal brings benefits that are greater than the cost of the signal. In the CAT case, the costly signal of signing brings greater risk of cost to the government and its elites if it should be deposed, or if its elites travel to other states. On the other hand, Hollyer and Rosendorff suggest that, by signing the CAT, the government signals to domestic opposition its tenacity and willingness to incur great costs to retain power, with the result that domestic opposition reduces its activities, bringing increased benefits to the authoritarian regime.

Hollyer and Rosendorff do find reduced domestic opposition activity after signing the CAT, but some of this reduction could be caused by satisfaction with entry into the CAT or with other reforms – some of the opposition may reduce activity in response to reduced torture after signing. Hollyer and Rosendorff do not control for this, but discount it by arguing that the opposition would have no way to commit to diminished activity in response to signing, and therefore reduced opposition activity could not induce the government to sign the CAT. However, this argument is dependent on the existence of an opposition determined to overthrow the government, rather than one that simply seeks improved human-rights conditions. Different states will have different types of oppositions.

In fact, one proxy for domestic opposition that Hollyer and Rosendorff use, a calculation of battle deaths, could just as easily be appreciated as an indicator of reduced regime violence rather than reduced domestic opposition, plausibly caused by the same unobserved variable that caused entry into the CAT. The other measure that they use, a measure of riots, strikes, revolutions, demonstrations, and other antigovernment activities, shows statistically significant negative correlation only in the case of strikes, and in any event is subject to the same alternative appreciation. Nor do they develop any process–tracing-type evidence or survey evidence to suggest that the reason for reduced opposition is the effect that they claim.

The Hollyer-Rosendorff analysis also indicates reduced torture after signing the CAT. They suggest that the reason for this is reduced domestic opposition, but it is equally possible that the reduction results from the costs imposed on the regime by the CAT.

Without evidence that supports this creative but arcane interpretation, parsimony suggests that we revert to normal price theory, which suggests that authoritarian regimes sign the CAT because of inducements available to them, and comply with it because of the costs of violation. These propositions are supported by work of Beth Simmons and Richard Nielsen, showing that entry into the CAT may increase foreign assistance in the long run, and by work of Emilie Hafner-Burton showing that entry into preferential trade agreements with "hard" human-rights requirements is associated with improved human-rights performance.[219]

Along these lines, a more plausible form of benefit is in the form of payoffs, such as international respect or "soft power," availability of trade preferences or free trade agreements, or availability of foreign aid. This proposition is questioned by empirical work done by Simmons and Nielsen, suggesting that overall ratification of human-rights treaties does not produce significant payoffs for less-developed countries in terms of increased aid, trade, or foreign direct investment.[220] Their work controls for actual human-rights performance, so it is a narrow test of the effects of ratification – of the effects of entering into treaties as opposed to simply improving performance. Furthermore, it would tend to exclude examples of successful adherence – adherence that causes better human-rights performance. That is, by controlling for actual performance, they are in fact identifying circumstances where adherence was rewarded but did not result in improved performance. Importantly, their work also controls for free-trade agreements and trade preferences under generalized system of preferences (GSP) programs, eliminating from consideration some of the most important possible means of rewarding high-depth states for ratification. Hafner-Burton finds that trade agreements and GSP programs that condition trade preferences on human-rights performance can cause improved human-rights performance.[221]

## III) Lock In

International law may be useful to low-depth states in order to lock in reforms. In 2000, Andrew Moravcsik published a systematic study of binding international–human–rights-law agreements in postwar Europe,[222] and argued that governments (especially newly formed democracies) often committed to international–human-rights treaties because such commitments helped them "lock in" credible domestic policies. According to Moravcsik, this "self-binding" helps new democracies stabilize the domestic status quo and reduce the risk of nondemocratic threats. It must do so by adding the power of

---

[219] Emilie M. Hafner-Burton, "Trading Human Rights: How Preferential Trade Agreements Influence Government Repression," 59 (3) *Int'l Org.* 593 (2005).

[220] Beth Simmons & Richard Nielsen, "Rewards for Rights Ratification? Testing for Tangible and Intangible Benefits of Human Rights Treaty Ratification" (2012). Retrieved from http://papers.ssrn.com/sol3/papers.cfm?abstract_id=1451630.

[221] Emilie M. Hafner-Burton, "Trading Human Rights: How Preferential Trade Agreements Influence Government Repression," 59 (3) *Int'L Org.* 593 (2005).

[222] Andrew Moravcsik, "The Origins of Human Rights Regimes: Democratic Delegation in Postwar Europe," 54 (2) *Int'l Org.* 217 (2000).

international relations and international law to the domestic incentives to maintain the targeted domestic policies. This theory assumes that international law may have power to lock in reforms greater than that of domestic law or constitutional restrictions. It thus depends on some underlying reasons why national governments would comply with international law, including concern for compliance on the part of other states.

Goodliffe and Hawkins find little evidence supporting the lock-in theory.[223] On the other hand, Simmons finds, in the context of the CAT, that there is some evidence that may support lock-in theory.[224] Modern behavioral economics can supply a conjecture as to why states might accept human-rights treaties to lock in certain reforms. To the extent that the formulation of rights is on the basis of a considered or consensus-based philosophical formulation of the rights of individuals, behavioral economics would suggest a "nudge" comprised of simply allowing the so-called reflective system to overcome the passions of the moment that might be described as the "automatic system."[225] So, establishing human rights may be understood as a device that assists in restraining the automatic system and empowering the reflective system. In this sense, the formulation of human rights, in order to be legitimate (and not paternalistic), must conform to a reasonable consensus view of the content of human rights. Thus, human rights may be used as a device to assist in making decisions that conform to a consensus view of human rights, where behavior might otherwise follow the automatic system and thereby depart from this consensus. According to this explanation, international human-rights law is a means by which states may constrain their own behavior in a way that is attractive to them ex ante: a form of lock in.

## IV) The Effects of Globalization and Global Law: Locking in through Supplementary Human Rights

States may also determine to engage in a type of lock in in order to maintain a constant level of restraint on government despite the expansion of government powers under globalization. This is the converse of Mueller's proposal that mobility causes greater concern for human rights abroad, insofar as it involves concern not so much for the practices of other states, but for the practices of one's own state. Globalization has posed important challenges to human rights. One challenge is the question of which persons are owed human rights

---

[223] Goodliffe & Hawkins, *supra* note 210.
[224] Simmons, *supra* note 199, at 107.
[225] *See* Richard H. Thaler & Cass R. Sunstein, *Nudge: Improving Decisions about Health, Wealth, and Happiness* (2008).

by which governments under circumstances of mobility of individuals and global effects of government action. Under some circumstances, globalization can disrupt a stable domestic–human-rights equilibrium, resulting in a need to protect human rights internationally in order to maintain a preexisting quantum of human rights.

For example, regarding the United States' actions against terrorism after September 11, 2001, the question has arisen to what extent the human-rights constraints on U.S. governmental action that takes place domestically apply to action that takes place abroad, or to action that has connections with different territories. To the extent that government action is only constrained territorially, but government action can take place extraterritorially, there may be a gap in human-rights protections. This type of discontinuity between the broader-than-territorial scope of power and the territorial scope of rights-based constraint can leave a gap.[226] The gap may be filled by international human rights.

This potential marginalization of domestic human-rights regimes by virtue of globalization may give rise to demand for international human-rights law as a replacement. We might call this *supplementary human-rights*. Perhaps the best way to understand supplementary human rights is as a way to maintain a steady equilibrium of human rights in the domestic setting, under globalization. In order to maintain such a domestic equilibrium, it sometimes becomes necessary to protect or promote human rights at the international level.

Subsidiarity implies that under some changes in technological or social circumstances, the vertical level at which it is appropriate to guarantee certain human rights may change. Supplementary human rights respond to gaps in the domestic law human-rights framework that are created or accentuated by globalization. These gaps may take the form of failure to apply domestic human rights to circumstances that are factually difficult to distinguish from those to which domestic human rights ordinarily apply but that are outside the jurisdictional reach of domestic human rights, conflicts between the laws, including human-rights laws of different states, or the possibility of unstable or inefficient competition between rules of different states. One response to these phenomena is to agree on rules determining the scope of application of different states' human rights – we might call these "choice of human-rights law rules." An alternative response to these phenomena is to harmonize human rights, or to establish human rights at the international level.

Finally, consider various controversial U.S. actions in the war on terror that implicate transnational interests, including the extraordinary rendition of

---

[226] *See* Anne Peters, "Compensatory Constitutionalism: The Function and Potential of Fundamental International Norms and Structures," 19 *Leiden J. Int'l L.* 579 (2006).

suspected terrorists to states accused of committing torture and the commission of human-rights abuses against terrorist suspects by U.S. agents at sites outside the United States. As of this writing, the extent to which U.S. constitutional protections apply to these acts has not been definitively resolved.[227] If domestic courts ultimately determine that domestic constitutional protections do not apply to these sorts of fact patterns, we would expect renewed pressure for supplementary human rights in these areas.[228]

## V) Preference Modification Factors

Preference-modification factors underlie the constructivist approach developed by Thomas Risse and Katherine Sikkink,[229] as well as the sociological approach developed by Ryan Goodman and Derek Jinks. The preference modification class of explanations suggests that states commit to human-rights treaties because they agree, or come to agree, with the normative content of the instruments.

Of course, states that do so are no longer high-depth states, so preference modification factors that cause agreement with the principles of the

---

[227] See, Boumediene v. Bush, 553 U.S. 723 (2008) (Detainee Treatment Act unconstitutionally suspends rights of alien enemy combatants to petition for writ of habeas corpus); El-Masri v. United States, 479 F.3d 296 (4th Cir. 2007) (dismissing suit by individual allegedly detained as part of CIA's extraordinary rendition program and tortured on grounds that case could not proceed without disclosing state secrets), cert. denied, 128 S. Ct. 373 (2007); Arar v. Ashcroft, 532 F.3d 157 (2d Cir. 2008) (dismissing suit by alien against United States and government officials alleging that he was mistreated and then removed to Syria where he was tortured).

[228] Disputes over the extraterritorial reach of fundamental rights and constitutional norms are not new. See, e.g., The Insular Cases, 182 U.S. 1 (1901) (addressing whether U.S. Constitution applies in territory that is not a state). With globalization, increasing numbers of cases involving the extraterritorial application of fundamental rights are arising before international and domestic tribunals. See also Legal Consequences of the Construction of a Wall in the Occupied Palestinian Territory, 2004 I.C.J. Rep. 136 (July 9) (ICCPR "is applicable in respect of acts done by a State in the exercise of jurisdiction outside its own territory"); Case Concerning Armed Activities on the Territory of the Congo (Dem. Rep. Congo v. Uganda) 2005 I.C.J. Rep. 168 (Dec. 19) (international human rights and humanitarian treaties apply to acts in occupied territories); Öcalan v. Turkey, 2005-IV Eur. Ct. H.R. 131 (Grand Chamber) (overseas arrest of separatist leader); Bankovic v. Belgium et al., 2001-XII Eur. Ct. H.R. 333 (Grand Chamber) (legality of NATO bombing of Serbia); Ben El Mahi v. Denmark, 2006-XV Eur. Ct. H.R. (aliens abroad injured by hate speech in Denmark); Munaf v. Geren, 553 U.S. 674 (2008) (Constitution does not prohibit transfer of U.S. citizens detained by U.S. military in Iraq to Iraqi custody despite possibility of torture); Atamirzayeva v. United States, 77 Fed. Cl. 378 (2007), aff'd, 524 F.3d 1320 (Fed. Cir. 2008) (rejecting alien's claim for compensation when foreign government, with cooperation from U.S. government, took her land adjoining U.S. embassy).

[229] Thomas Risse & Kathryn Sikkink, "The Socialization of International Human Rights Norms into Domestic Practice: Introduction," in The Power of Human Rights: International Norms and Domestic Change (Thomas Risse, Steve C. Ropp, & Kathryn Sikkink, eds., 1999).

human-rights treaty leave open the question of why other states might be interested in commitments from these states that are now low- (or no-) depth states. Indeed, under these circumstances, we would also need to ask why the obliged state would incur the additional administrative or other costs of entering into a human-rights treaty. Preference modification that does not go far enough to convert high-depth states to low-depth states would, however, effectively reduce the cost of commitment to the high-depth state, by reducing the extent of policy change required, thereby reducing the level of other inducements necessary to cause them to commit.

Goodman and Jinks have proposed acculturation as a distinct causal mechanism in connection with compliance, but it may also help explain adherence. By *acculturation*, they mean the process by which actors assimilate beliefs and behavioral patterns of their culture. Acculturation is driven by identification with a reference group that generates cognitive and social pressures to conform to its behavioral expectations.[230] Goodman and Jinks argue that neither coercion-based nor persuasion-based accounts of the influence of international law are sufficient to explain the pattern of isomorphism and decoupling that is observed among states. *Isomorphism* refers to a tendency of states to have similar structures and commitments, whereas *decoupling* refers to departures from this similarity:

> Structural similarity exceeds that which might be explained by reference to the material incentives of target states, however, persistent decoupling strongly suggests an "incomplete internalization" inconsistent with persuasion-based explanations. The upshot is that coercion and persuasion-based accounts, however indispensable for a comprehensive theory of global social influence, require supplementation. The resultant, more comprehensive theory of global social influence further suggests several regime design principles that might guide the fashioning of more effective human rights law and institutions.[231]

As noted, Simmons, in *Mobilizing for Human Rights*, suggests that a primary reason why states enter into human-rights treaties is because they agree with the principles therein.[232] Again, the preference modification or acculturation approaches have difficulty explaining the role of international commitments.

---

[230] Ryan Goodman & Derek Jinks, "IncompleteInternalization and Compliance with Human Rights Law," 19 *Eur. J. Int'l L*, 725, 726 (2008).

[231] *Id.* at 727.

[232] Simmons, *supra* note 199. This argument is most clear in a working paper Simmons wrote in 2002, where she states that "there are clear cultural preferences, domestic legal traditions, and transitory political conditions that are associated with higher degrees of international human rights treaty commitment-making." See Beth Simmons, "Why Commit? Explaining

Goodliffe and Hawkins find support for norms as a motivation for commitment, on the basis that states within a regional grouping are more likely to sign and ratify the Convention Against Torture. They do not seem to control for the potential demand side of the equation, under which it might be that a particular region might be of more concern to low-depth states than other regions. They also do not control for the possibility that states within a particular region might compete more directly with one another than with others for trade preferences, investment, aid, or other benefits. Thus, the demand side presents a source of potential unobserved variable bias.

Wade Cole rejects the preference modification approach. Cole examines the relationship between the content of a treaty and the costs associated with committing to it, when it comes to a state's decision to sign and ratify a treaty.[233] Cole uses data from more than 160 countries between 1969 and 1999 to analyze the explanatory power of three dominant theories of treaty ratification: rationalism (according to which treaty ratification is a function of the costs of commitment), world polity institutionalism (according to which states ratify treaties to signal agreement with the dominant values of the international community), and what Cole calls the clash of civilizations perspective (where states sign treaties because they agree with the values embodied therein). Cole's analysis concludes that the rationalist and world polity theory are useful in explaining states' treaty behavior, whereas the clash of civilizations theory is not.

## C) COMPLIANCE: WHY DO OBLIGEES COMPLY WITH HUMAN-RIGHTS COMMITMENTS?

There is a similarly rich body of literature on the relationship between human-rights treaty commitment and compliance.[234] Some of these studies suggest that human-rights treaties can cause better human-rights conditions, although they proffer different mechanisms by which they work.

In *Mobilizing for Human Rights*, for example, Simmons suggests that international–human-rights treaties can produce behavioral effects because treaty ratification encourages changes in elite agendas, public law litigation, and civil society action that eventually improves human-rights protection and

State Acceptance of International Human Rights Obligations" (Berkeley Law Working Paper Series No. 02–05, 2002). Retrieved from http://www.law.berkeley.edu/835.htm.

[233] Wade Cole, "Sovereignty Relinquished? Explaining Commitment to the International Human Rights Covenants, 1966–1999," 70 (3) *Am. Sociological Rev.* (2005).

[234] In her book on compliance, Sonia Cardenas discusses what constitutes state compliance, and uses statistical analysis to determine what the domestic and international pressures for compliance and norm violation are. *See generally,* Sonia Cardenas, *Conflict and Compliance: State Responses to International Human Rights Pressure* (2007).

treaty compliance in countries.[235] She argues that international–human-rights law has its effect through these domestic mechanisms, as opposed to reciprocal mechanisms that may be operative in other areas of international law. Of course, although all international legal compliance is proximately caused by a domestic political decision, the important question for students of international law is the extent to which international legal consequences in the form of reciprocity, reputation, or retaliation contribute to the domestic political decision, or the extent to which international law is an instrument of acculturation.

Simmons' work provides an important analysis and empirical validation of the proposition that international–human-rights treaties can produce behavioral effects through these channels: changes in elite agendas; public law litigation; and civil society action. Her conclusion is buttressed by other studies. Eric Neumayer finds that human-rights improvement after treaty ratification is a function of how democratic the country is and the number of international nongovernmental organizations in which its citizens participate. Conversely, in very autocratic regimes with weak civil society, ratification can be expected to have no effect and is sometimes even associated with more rights violations.[236] Emilie Hafner-Burton, Laurence Helfer, and Christopher Fariss study derogations from human-rights treaties, and find that domestic politics – not international reciprocity, retaliation, or reputation – is the "crucial determinant of state compliance with international human rights law." Their conclusions are on the basis of comprehensive datasets of derogations and states of emergency around the world from 1976 to 2007.[237] Cardenas comes to a similar conclusion.[238] However, according to Hafner-Burton and Tsutsui, the impetus for compliance comes not from the treaty regime or state intent, but from the "global legitimacy of human rights experts and independent global civil society."[239]

One concern with these works that suggest that reciprocity is not important, and that treaties have domestic sources and domestic channels of causal effect, is the time-inconsistency problem: these authors seem to assume that high-depth state governments are ignorant of this effect of signing treaties, later causing them to do something they had wished to avoid.

---

[235] Simmons, *supra* note 199.
[236] Eric Neumayer, "Do International Human Rights Treaties Improve Respect for Human Rights?" 49 (6) *J. Conflict Resol.* 925 (2005).
[237] Emilie M. Hafner-Burton, Laurence R. Helfer, & Christopher J. Fariss, "Emergency and Escape: Explaining Derogations from Human Rights Treaties," 65 *Int'l Org.* 673 (2011).
[238] Cardenas, *supra* note 234.
[239] Emilie M. Hafner-Burton & Kiyoteru Tsutsui, "Human Rights in a Globalizing World: The Paradox of Empty Promises," 110 (5) *Am. J. Sociology* 1373 (2005).

On a somewhat different note, Hafner-Burton studies the impact of preferential trade agreements on human-rights protection, and develops an incentive-based theory of human-rights compliance. She argues that traditional human-rights treaties are often not complied with because they rely on persuasion alone, which is often not enough. Reciprocity – in the form of human-rights norms linked to preferential trade agreements (PTAs) – is far more effective.[240] She studies the experience of 177 states during the period 1972–2002, and validates 3 hypotheses: (1) state commitment to human-rights agreements and (2) PTAs supplying soft human-rights standards (not tied to market benefits) do not systematically produce improvement in human-rights behaviors, whereas (3) state commitment to PTAs supplying hard human-rights standards does often produce better practices.

Other studies are, however, skeptical of the relationship between treaty ratification and actual human-rights protection. Linda Keith argues that data about International Convention on Civil and Political Rights (ICCPR) ratifications and actual state behavior suggests that signing the ICCPR has very little to do with better human-rights practices. She examines data across 178 countries over an 18-year period (1976–1993) and across 4 different measures of state human-rights behavior. Her study suggests that "it may be overly optimistic to expect that being a party to this international covenant will produce an observable direct impact."[241] A similar study by Oona Hathaway suggests that ratification of human-rights treaties has little favorable impact on individual countries' practices, and may result in worse human-rights practices.[242]

## D) THE FUTURE OF INTERNATIONAL–HUMAN-RIGHTS LAW

How will future changes affect international–human-rights law? Let us examine projected changes in globalization, development, demography, technology, and democracy – as described in Chapter 4 – in order to evaluate the impact of these changes on human rights.

To the extent that interaction and a sense of community serve as a predicate for altruistic concern regarding the human rights of others, we might anticipate that increasing globalization and enhanced communications technologies will

---

[240] Emilie M. Hafner-Burton, "Trading Human Rights: How Preferential Trade Agreements Influence Government Repression," 59 (3) *Int'l Org.* 593 (2005).

[241] Linda Keith, "The United Nations International Covenant on Civil and Political Rights: Does It Make a Difference in Human Rights Behavior?" 36 (1) *J. Peace Research* 95 (1999).

[242] Oona Hathaway, "Do Human Rights Treaties Make a Difference?" 111 (8) *Yale L. J.* 1935 (2002) (offering suggestions for treaty design in the future, which include stronger monitoring and enforcement mechanisms). For criticisms of these conclusions, *see* Ryan Goodman & Derek Jinks, "Measuring the Effect of Human Rights Treaties," 14 (1) *Eur. J. Int'l L.* 171 (2003).

increase concern. As discussed, globalization and even the development of international legal structures may give rise to increasing need for international–human-rights law. In addition, for Mueller, the basis for concern about human rights in other states results from the anticipation of possible travel or relocation to other states – thus, increasing migration would be expected to increase concern for international–human-rights law. Increasing migration will accentuate the factor that Mueller focuses on: the possibility of migration gives rise to concern for human rights abroad.

There is some evidence that increasing globalization, at least in terms of trade in goods, is associated with increased respect for human rights. Although this might suggest a reduced need for international law, it may also suggest that entering into international legal commitments to protect human rights would come at a lower cost. Increasing trade in goods and services will accentuate the kinds of pecuniary externalities, especially in connection with labor rights, discussed. To the extent that one state may compete with other states by demeaning its human-rights protections, there may be concerns regarding a race to the bottom driven by increasing trade. There is a possible link between economic development and the development of national human rights. It is difficult to know whether one causes the other, or whether another factor causes both.

We have seen in the Arab Spring of 2011 and beyond the role of increased information technology in allowing human-rights campaigners to overcome collective-action problems and organize to demand human rights. Enhanced data processing and communications technology will also facilitate monitoring of human-rights abuses; for example, by allowing victims or others to report abuses anonymously, or simply to supply accessible data regarding abuses.

With the growth of democracy, we can expect an increase in human rights. In a theoretical sense, human rights are inconsistent with democracy, as human rights restrict democratic action at the expense of minorities. However, increasing democratization in the sense of government as servant of the people will also increase respect for human rights.

## E) STRATEGIC PROBLEMS IN MATCHING DEMAND AND SUPPLY OF INTERNATIONAL HUMAN-RIGHTS LAW

In order to induce high-depth states to adhere and comply, simple identical-performance reciprocity will often not be sufficient. Rather, it will be necessary for the low-depth states to expand the game through linkage or side payments in order to induce adherence and compliance. As previously noted, acculturation or other mechanisms for changing preferences in high-depth states may reduce the price to be paid. To be clear, what is really happening under acculturation is that a high-depth state is becoming a less–high-depth state, or perhaps even a low-depth state. The need to provide some consideration will not be eliminated unless the high-depth state is converted to a low-depth state. For a low-depth state, there seems to be little need for international law except to lock in reforms. There are countless examples of linkage between human-rights compliance and other arrangements, including preferential trade arrangements, foreign aid, and military cooperation. In order for this type of linkage to support human-rights adherence and compliance, the low-depth state must not have sufficient independent reasons for supplying the linked good: it must be individually rational, and therefore credible, that the low-depth state would deny the high-depth state the linked good. It may be that this is a matter of the structure of the domestic political-interest groups in the low-depth state: lobbies supporting providing preferential-trade arrangements, foreign aid, or military cooperation might remove their support for these activities under weak human-rights performance.

Let us examine a hypothetical arrangement in which a single low-depth state (ND) and a single high-depth state (HD) determine to enter into a PTA including hard human-rights standards. Assume five lobby positions in the low-depth state:

$H_{nd}$ = human-rights activists concerned about human rights in the high-depth state

$R_{nd}$ = realists who believe that the low-depth state is better off if it avoids addressing human-rights issues with the high-depth state

$C_{nd}$ = consumers interested in cheap imports from the high-depth state

$P_{nd}$ = producers who fear competition from cheap imports from the high-depth state

$E_{nd}$ = exporters interested in export opportunities in high-depth state

Assume mirror-image lobbies in the high-depth state (distinguished by the subscript $_{hd}$), except that instead of realists, $R_{hd}$ is a regime interested in maintaining power, and in which the political salience of each lobby differs as set out.

Assume that at an initial time, $R_{nd} < H_{nd}$ and $R_{hd} > H_{hd}$. Therefore, there is demand in the low-depth state for human-rights protection in the high-depth state, and the high-depth state is indeed a high-depth state, without autonomous reasons to supply human-rights protection. On the trade side, assume that $P_{nd} > C_{nd}$, with a protectionist equilibrium. However, if the interest of $E_{nd}$ can be precipitated through reciprocity with the high-depth state, assume that this will be almost, but not quite, sufficient when combined with $C_{nd}$ to overcome $P_{nd}$ such that we still have the outcome $E_{nd} + C_{nd} < P_{nd}$. However, the coalition for trade can be made stronger by adding the strength of $H_{nd}$, as follows: $H_{nd} + E_{nd} + C_{nd} > P_{nd} + R_{nd}$. This follows from the assumption that $H_{nd} > R_{nd}$. The implication is that, under this assumption, linking the PTA to human rights in the low-depth state, the low–depth-state coalition favoring the PTA is made stronger, and is able to overcome the combination of protectionist and realist interests. Conversely, assume that in the high-depth state, there is a strong coalition for free trade, but not for human rights. That is, whereas $R_{hd} > H_{hd}$, and even if $P_{hd} > C_{hd}$, $C_{hd} + E_{hd} > P_{hd}$ and $C_{hd} + E_{hd} + H_{hd} > P_{hd} + R_{hd}$.

Now there is a deal that can be done in both human rights and trade, whereas without linkage and cross-functional reciprocity, a deal between the high-depth state and the low-depth state could not have been made and policy in neither state would change. Note that without linkage, although ND was interested in a human-rights deal, and HD was interested in a trade deal, neither deal could be made. With linkage, a combined deal can be made, assuming there is enough surplus political power for human rights in ND and trade in HD.

What about compliance? The combined PTA/human-rights treaty can be structured to establish continuing cross-functional reciprocity, protected by arrangements for cross-retaliation. This is what has been done in the Colombia-U.S. PTA. Cross-retaliation will allow ND to retaliate in trade if HD violates human rights, and, perhaps less realistically, will allow HD to retaliate in human rights if ND violates in trade. We might also assume that there is a generalized but weak general incentive to comply with international law: once international law is made, government and other pro–international-law groups add their weight to the decision to comply.[243] I hasten also to add that human-rights treaties alone may have real constraining effect on high-depth states: ratification generally seems associated with improved human-rights performance in at least some fields.[244]

Assuming that there is sufficient supply and demand for human-rights law as developed, what may stand in the way of establishing increased international human rights? I illustrated how a single low-depth state might enter into a PTA/human-rights treaty with a single high-depth state. However, as pointed out by Beth Simmons[245] and Eric Posner, there is another problem.[246] The protection of human rights in high-depth states is, in a sense, a public good

---

[243] *See* Joel P. Trachtman, "International Law and Domestic Political Coalitions: The Grand Theory of Compliance with International Law," 11 *Chicago J. Int'l L.* (2010).
[244] Simmons, *supra* note 199.   [245] *Id.*
[246] Eric Posner, "Human Rights, the Laws of War, and Reciprocity" (University of Chicago Law & Economics Olin Working Paper No. 537, Sept. 27, 2010). Retrieved from http://papers.ssrn.com/sol3/papers.cfm?abstract_id=1693974 (last visited Aug. 18, 2011).

for the class of low-depth states. Low-depth states might operate together to achieve this public good. However, empirical work by Raechelle Mascarenhas and Todd Sandler finds in connection with donations of foreign aid, donors do not work together.[247] Of course, multilateral or regional aid mechanisms implicitly constitute instances of donors working together. Furthermore, it is possible that human-rights treaties present a different type of occasion for donors to cooperate. Finally, when the EU confers trade benefits on third countries, it does so as a bloc, pursuant to its common commercial policy.

Most of the reasons for concern in low-depth states are shared. If the high-depth states protect human rights, the benefits to low-depth states will be non-excludible, in the sense that all low-depth states may enjoy the benefits, and will also be non-exhaustible, meaning that the enjoyment by one low-depth state does not reduce the enjoyment by other low-depth states. If this is the case, this public good would tend to be undersupplied, and the low-depth states would need a mechanism by which to cooperate around the compensation of high-depth states for entry into and adherence to human-rights treaties. So, both games must be resolved simultaneously: (i) the high-depth states must be induced to adhere and comply; and (ii) the low-depth states must be induced to contribute. This type of public-good contribution problem exists in a number of other contexts, such as environmental protection, public health, and other areas of global public goods.

Perhaps the most likely way to address a public-goods problem of this nature is to have a coordinated signing, or a minimum number of ratifications before the treaty becomes effective. In this way, states that might otherwise attempt to free ride on the contributions of others may be induced to commit to contribute.

## F) CONCLUSION

Accession to and compliance with international law can usefully be understood in terms of supply and demand, which highlights the costs and benefits to both the demanding state and the responding state. International law is often reasonably symmetric in form – and perhaps in principle – but is often asymmetric in connection with particular commitments. That is, particular commitments often have greater effects on some states than others: they have greater depth for some states than others. Considering this asymmetry in its broadest terms, we might examine the generally asymmetric character of human-rights law in

---

[247] Raechelle Mascarenhas & Todd Sandler, "Do Donors Cooperatively Fund Foreign Aid?" 1 *Review of International Organization* 337 (2006).

# Human Rights

relations between liberal democratic states and authoritarian states. It is not immediately obvious why liberal democratic states care about human rights in authoritarian states, but this chapter provides a taxonomy of bases for concern. It is also not immediately obvious why authoritarian states would enter into human-rights treaties that constrain their actions. Although they may have domestic reasons to use international law to lock-in certain behaviors – assuming that international law serves this purpose – or to signal to either external audiences or internal audiences what type they are, these types of reasons seem less plausible and general than a simpler exchange-based model under which other states provide some valuable consideration or refrain from taking harmful action in exchange for human-rights protection.

As suggested in Chapter 3, international law can serve as a tool for exchange of consideration – for reciprocal and linked exchange – that disrupts existing political equilibria, allowing a superior political outcome for each state under asymmetry. International law may also address the collective-action problem that may arise among liberal democratic states as they determine how to share the costs of inducing authoritarian states to protect human rights.

For a number of reasons, we can expect greater protection of human rights in the future, with more states autonomously more likely to protect human rights. This will reduce the "cost" of international treaties requiring human-rights protection, although it may also reduce the demand. Increasing globalization and technology will increase demand for human-rights protection abroad, and therefore will increase demand for international–human-rights treaties.

## 7  Environmental Protection and Public Health

Environmental protection is a relatively new area for national governments, arising from greater industrialization, technological advance, and urbanization. International public health is also a relatively new field, and has grown in importance as congestion has increased the threat of national epidemics, and globalization has increased the threat of international epidemics. This chapter cannot survey the breadth of these important fields, but will focus on certain externalities and public-goods aspects of these areas of international law, suggesting how they give rise to demands for international law, and how those demands may, in general, be met.

This chapter will also highlight the distributive aspects of these topics. International environmental protection and public health raise, in a focused way, the problem of the distributive impacts of international cooperation. This area also raises important issues of cross-functional integration – of fragmentation – because there are important relationships between environmental protection and other areas of international law – such as trade – and between international public health and trade, intellectual property protection, and migration.

As industrialization grows and technological processes become more sophisticated, the danger of environmental harm can increase. With increased globalization comes an increase in competition among producers located in different states. These states can provide advantages to their own producers through less costly environmental regulation. To the extent that any individual state does not experience all of the detriments of its own decision regarding the extent of environmental regulation, it will have some incentives to regulate less strictly.

Global population growth, combined with increasing urbanization and the concentration of growth in poor countries, will intensify environmental problems. Population growth, combined with industrialization, will increase the global intensity of industrial processes, thereby increasing the intensity of pollution unless measures are taken to counter this tendency. Greater technology also presents two types of promise: first, the possibility of amelioration of pollution through new clean technologies; and second, the increasing possibility of enforceable international law by virtue of remote sensing and other surveillance technologies.

Increasing population and urbanization also increase the risk of epidemic. As a consequence of globalization – including particularly travel and migration, as well as trade in food – there is increasing global concern regarding infectious disease. An infectious disease that becomes dangerous in one country threatens people in other countries. Of course, technology provides important responses to disease, but there are difficult questions about the patenting and ownership of medicines.

## A) EXTERNALITIES AND ACCOUNTABILITY: THE INTERNALIZATION FUNCTION OF INTERNATIONAL LAW

As discussed in Chapter 2, international law can be used to cause states to internalize externalities, where this seems efficient. Absent international cooperation, national governments can be expected to act in their own narrow self-interest. Therefore, national policies may fail to internalize transboundary environmental harms or international epidemics. As discussed in more detail in Chapter 3, international law in this context can link the domestic political systems of multiple states, causing the domestic political system in the acting state to take account of effects on a foreign state. Of course, technically speaking, once what was an externality is caused to be taken into account by the actor, it is internalized and no longer an externality. So, as discussed in Chapter 2, international law can be used to eliminate inefficient externalities.

Interestingly, this type of internalization may extend the accountability of the acting state, but diminishes its responsiveness to purely domestic political concerns, insofar as the domestic political concerns on their own fail to take account of foreign effects. So, very importantly, what might be understood as a "democracy deficit" may be better understood in some cases as merely providing democratic accountability to foreign citizens who are affected by national actions. To some extent, the phenomenon referred to as the democracy deficit is a result of a narrow national frame of accountability.

It is readily apparent how inefficient externalities might arise in connection with cross-border emissions of pollutants. The classic example of an externality – environmental nuisance in the form of smoke from a factory affecting the productivity of a nearby laundry – has a similar structure. From an economic point of view, the efficiency question is identical; from a legal point of view, the international legal order provides a starkly different framework for analysis compared to the domestic law of nuisance. However, a similar type of black-letter legal regime has developed: the *Sic utere tuo ut alienum non laedas* principle[248] is argued by some to have developed into a binding principle of customary international law. It has now been codified, in the context of air pollution, in Principle 21 of the Stockholm Declaration: "No State has the right to use or permit the use of its territory in such a manner as to cause injury by fumes in or to the territory of another or the properties or persons therein, when the case is of serious consequence and the injury is established by clear and convincing evidence."[249]

However, this principle has several limitations. First, it does not generally benefit from mandatory adjudication or other effective enforcement mechanisms, leaving its enforcement highly uncertain. As discussed in Chapter 10, we might say that this principle is structurally subordinated to areas such as trade and investment, which may benefit from mandatory dispute settlement. Second, under existing institutional structures, it might best be understood as a liability rule, rather than a property rule or rule of regulation. The implication of this second limitation is that states may violate and incur an obligation to pay (which according to the first limitation they may never satisfy). If it were a property rule or regulatory rule, it would provide an ex ante prohibition. Third, this rule is not very specific, and leaves open the possibility of argument about whether or not it has been violated in any particular case. Given the lack of mandatory adjudication, the possibility for conclusive assignment of responsibility is limited.

Finally, and perhaps most importantly, this rule grows increasingly indeterminate under increasing cross-border effects. Given that most activities will have some cross-border effects – at a minimum in the way that the beating of the wings of a Beijing butterfly may affect climate in Canada – and given that these effects increase with intensity of industrial process, we can expect that most activities may in some way cause adverse cross-border effects. Of course, qualifiers such as "serious," or evidentiary standards, may reduce the scope of the principle, but it may be that it is efficient to internalize adverse effects that do not reach this level. The conclusion: greater specificity will be needed.

The optimal intervention in connection with environmental externalities, at least under certain transaction-cost profiles, is a *Pigouvian tax*, charging the

---

[248] Trail Smelter Case (*U.S. v Canada*) 1938, 1941 3 U.N.R.I.A.A. 1905 (Apr. 16, Mar. 11) (articulating, in dictum, *sic utere tuo* as a general principle of law. It has since been recognized by many as a rule of customary international law).

[249] Declaration of the United Nations Conference on the Human Environment (Stockholm Declaration) Principle 21, Jun 16, 1972, (11 I.L.M 1416) (1972 UNYB 319).

# Environmental Protection and Public Health

polluter the value of the external harm. Perhaps the standard of liability under sic utere tuo would amount to a Pigouvian tax. As already suggested, however, the imposition of such a tax on an international level would be difficult under the current state of international law. Although it is possible for a particular state to act unilaterally – for example, by applying a special border tax or tariff – the scope for unilateral action may be constrained by international trade law or other restrictions. This is a kind of fragmentation issue, discussed further in Chapter 10. The existence of extensive trade law may foreclose otherwise-available informal options for environmental order, inducing the creation of international environmental law, either engineered to be consistent with trade law or establishing an exception to trade law.

Furthermore, a Pigouvian tax would require a substantial international organizational infrastructure. The organizational infrastructure would need to have the ability to levy and enforce the tax, as well as to resolve disputes regarding the correct application of the tax. Even a quantitative restriction, a cap, whether or not combined with a trading regime, would require a mechanism to set national caps and to enforce these caps. One of the great limitations of the Kyoto Protocol has been in enforcement.

Of course, Coase criticized the Pigouvian approach with the insight that, under zero transaction costs, the parties would negotiate an efficient solution to an externality without governmental measures to internalize. However, it is also true that under positive transaction costs, which surely characterize the international market for allocation of authority, it is possible that a Pigouvian tax would be an efficient means to cause decision makers in polluting states to take account of the effects of their actions on others.

I will evaluate the cooperation problems in connection with three areas of international public goods: infectious disease, ozone-layer protection, and climate change. Recognizing that these types of cooperation problems have different structures, and often involve significant asymmetry, I develop an overall analytical framework for developing legal structures to respond to these problems.

## B) GLOBAL PUBLIC HEALTH: INFECTIOUS DISEASE EXTERNALITIES

The way a single state deals with emergent infectious disease can confer negative or positive externalities on other states. If a state takes appropriate action to avoid outbreaks, and deals quickly, transparently, and effectively with local outbreaks of infectious disease, it minimizes the risk to other states. However, the risk to other states may be very significant, and if it were taken into account, the state of outbreak might expend greater resources to prevent or address the outbreak. So, the state of outbreak might have insufficient incentives to efficiently address infectious disease, given the possibility for international epidemics.

The World Health Organization (WHO) has developed the International Health Regulations (IHR) in order to address the spread of disease. The WHO Constitution accords power to the World Health Assembly to adopt regulations "designed to prevent the international spread of disease." After adoption by the WHO Health Assembly, these regulations enter into force for all WHO Member States unless they opt out of them within a specified period. Interestingly, no state has ever opted out of an International Health Regulation.

Under the 2005 version of the IHR, states are obligated to develop certain minimum public health capacities to detect, assess, notify, and report events that may constitute a public health emergency of international concern as defined, and to notify the WHO of such events. Each state party is required to develop the capacity to respond promptly and effectively to public health risks and public health emergencies of international concern. Furthermore, the WHO director-general is authorized to declare a "public health emergency of international concern" and issue temporary recommendations. From both a constitutional and substantive perspective, this is a significant set of powers.

Although this structure seems reasonably well designed to address some portion of the external effects of infectious disease, especially by including requirements for minimum public health capacities, there will certainly be occasions when these capacities are insufficient. The decision of poor countries to invest less in public health than perhaps a wealthy country would, could mean that an outbreak of disease in the poor country threatens the wealthy country (not to mention the poor country). Greater harmonization of capacities, perhaps predicated on transfer of resources, could resolve this asymmetry.

Asymmetries in the health field can be exacerbated by issues relating to the availability of health technologies. This is an issue of fragmentation, in which it is impossible to address global public health completely without also addressing intellectual property rights. As discussed in Chapter 9, absent cooperation, states are likely to provide insufficient protection to foreign-produced intellectual property.

Patents on medicines are protected under the WTO's TRIPS Agreement and other international agreements, and it is unclear the extent to which these patents would prevent access to medicines during a public health crisis. In response, during the avian influenza outbreaks in late 2006, Indonesia refused to share virus specimens with the WHO, claiming it was unfair to give pharmaceutical companies access, in light of the fact that the pharmaceutical companies would not ensure fair access to resulting medicines.[250] In 2011, the WHO approved a nuanced nonbinding framework to encourage states to turn over specimens to the WHO, and to make medicines available to poor states. Under asymmetry, the solution was to provide a nuanced side payment to poor countries in order to induce them to cooperate. This solution is not unlike the response to asymmetry in human rights described in Chapter 6.

Infectious diseases represent a global public bad, and their suppression has characteristics of a global public good. The harm from infectious disease is non-rival and – putting aside quarantines, which are costly – non-excludible. The benefit from suppression is generally non-rival, although circumstances may differ from disease to disease and country to country, and depending on the mechanism of suppression, may be non-excludible. If the mechanism of suppression is a medicine or procedure for which access can be controlled, then suppression may be a club good, as described in Chapter 2. Alternatively, if the mechanism of suppression is an inoculation for which the formula is known, it may be non-excludible, depending on the application and strength of international patent law, including the WTO's TRIPS (Trade Related Intellectual Property Rights) agreement. Where suppression is a public good, we would expect it to be undersupplied, and states that experience emergent infectious disease to confer negative externalities on other states. One recent example is the level of reporting provided by the Chinese government with respect to the outbreak of severe acute respiratory syndrome in 2003.

As Sandler[251] describes, different diseases can be characterized by different degrees of universality of concern, with special focus on the level of concern of wealthy countries, and therefore different aggregation technologies. *Aggregation technology* refers to the structure of costs and benefits to individual states of providing the public good. For example, there are "best-effort" public goods that depend on the best efforts of an individual state, where the benefits to that individual state of providing the public good exceed the costs. Research to identify a vaccine or cure could be a best-effort public good. There are "weakest-link" public goods that depend on all states contributing sufficiently for any state to benefit; whereas the benefits to each state exceeds the costs to any individual state, no state benefits unless all states contribute. Efforts to eradicate a widespread disease might have the characteristic of a weakest-link public good. For weakest-link public goods, global efforts are only as successful

---

[250] *See* David P. Fidler & Lawrence O. Gostin, "The WHO Pandemic Influenza Preparedness Framework: A Milestone in Global Governance for Health," 306 J. Am. Med. Assn. 200 (2011).
[251] For more detail, *see* Todd Sandler, *Global Collective Action* 108–111 (2004); Barrett, *supra* note 33.

as the weakest efforts. A *summation aggregation technology* means that contributions of each state are cumulated, and that these efforts will be successful once a sufficient aggregate is reached. There are also *asymmetric public goods*, in which the aggregate benefit to all states would exceed the costs to all states, but for some states the individual costs would exceed the individual benefit. For these latter types of public goods, some compensation or compulsion mechanism would be required in order to induce provision.

Health measures taken today can have significant benefits in the future.[252] For example, the development of a cure for AIDS would benefit not only currently infected people, but all people in the future who might develop AIDS. Domestic governmental mechanisms often have trouble taking into account future harms or benefits, because of short-term election cycles. Because the development of international law depends on demands by national governments, we can expect international law to also fail to fully take future benefits into account.

With increasing globalization, intensification of agriculture, and urbanization, disease is likely to grow as an international-cooperation issue. International public health presents a number of different types of international-cooperation problems. Contagion of infectious disease presents the issue of externalities. Suppression or elimination of infectious disease – or development of a cure – may be subjected to a public-goods analysis – including issues of degree of excludability and rivalrousness – as well as issues of aggregation technology. I will now further develop the analysis of public-goods issues.

## C) GLOBAL ENVIRONMENTAL PUBLIC GOODS I: THE OZONE LAYER

Maintaining the ozone shield helps prevent skin cancer. The maintenance of the ozone shield is a pure public good, insofar as all states benefit regardless of the extent to which other states benefit (non-rivalrous consumption), and no state can be excluded from the benefits of the ozone shield (non-excludible consumption). Because it is a public good, it would tend to be undersupplied without cooperation: states can be expected to free ride on the efforts of others. However, there are different types of public goods, with different cost-benefit ratios, aggregation technologies, and degrees of homogeneity or asymmetry of national interests. So we would expect international legal responses to different public goods to vary.

---

[252] Sandler, *supra* note 251. *See also* Jack Hirshleifer, "From Weakest-Link to Best-Shot: The Voluntary Provision of Public Goods," 41 *Public Choice* 371 (1983).

No states stood to gain from depleting the ozone shield, and a few major countries – the United States, Japan, and the former Soviet Union – accounted for a large measure of cloro-fluoro-carbon (CFC) emissions, whereas twelve countries accounted for more than 78 percent of emissions.[253] Furthermore, technological substitutes for CFCs were readily available. For example, Sandler concludes that "for the United States... the benefits... minus the costs... to acting alone were positive."[254] Therefore, the dominant strategy for the United States was to reduce CFC emissions, and many of the national reductions required by the Montreal Protocol would have occurred without the treaty.[255]

The ozone regime followed a pattern of gradualism seen in other environmental treaty regimes. It began with the 1985 Vienna Convention for the Protection of the Ozone Layer, requiring scientific study of the effects of CFC emissions on the ozone layer. In this field, it was very important that the magnitude of the benefits of CFC reduction were relatively clear. Furthermore, the 1985 Vienna Convention might be understood as setting a focal-point goal around which states could begin to cohere. Few developing countries participated in the 1987 Montreal Protocol on Substances that Deplete the Ozone Layer, partly because their participation was not so important, and they had less to gain from participating.

Thus, although the ozone layer is a public good, because the payoffs were such that the dominant strategy for developed countries such as the United States was to unilaterally reduce emissions, this was not a difficult cooperation problem. It might be understood more as an information and coordination problem, where it became useful to share information and then set a focal point around which coordination could take place. For states that would benefit from their own CFC reduction more than this reduction would cost, international law was not a significant cause of their behavior.

## D) GLOBAL ENVIRONMENTAL PUBLIC GOODS II: CLIMATE CHANGE

The greatest unaddressed environmental threat of our time is climate change. Negotiations among states to replace the Kyoto Protocol have moved slowly. It seems clear that some degree of international cooperation is needed with respect to the control of greenhouse gases. Cooperation is needed because a stable climate is a global public good: it is inexhaustible and non-excludible.

---

[253] World Resources Institute, World Resources 1992–1993 (1992).
[254] Sandler, *supra* note 251, at 218.   [255] *Id.*

Moreover, the structure of this public-good problem is quite different from that of the ozone layer. Individual state action would not be expected to provide significant benefits even to that state, and there are powerful incentives to free ride, so cooperation is needed.

One critical aspect of the climate problem is that states have widely asymmetrical interests, and poor southern countries tend to be more vulnerable than rich northern countries. Some states will lose territory or be swamped owing to rising seas, others will experience increased disease or decreased agricultural productivity, whereas still others will benefit from reduced heating costs or increased agricultural productivity. In addition, different states will experience differing costs of carbon reduction or other mitigation.

In a national system, with a strong vertical sovereign, these types of differing preferences could be dealt with through national majority-voted legislation, perhaps including some redistributive logrolling. Logrolling should be understood in terms of linkage or compensation to those who would otherwise be harmed by action. In the international system, based as it is on individual state consent, it may be tougher to make rules that would bind free riders or those who may be hurt by carbon reduction. It would be critical to engage in appropriate linkage or compensation. Broadening bargaining through linkage should expand the range of potential agreements.[256]

States recognized the need for cooperation when they entered into the 1992 UN Framework Convention on Climate Change. As of May 1, 2012, the Framework Convention had 195 parties, and so has almost universal adherence. The Framework Convention is best understood as the beginning of a process – a process of gradual movement toward cooperation as the costs and benefits of climate stability, and their distribution, became more apparent. The Framework Convention provided for annual meetings called Conferences of the Parties. The original 1992 Framework Convention, which came into force in 1994, can be understood as a particular type of soft law: it is a binding treaty, but at least with respect to limits on greenhouse gas emissions it does not contain binding obligations. This was largely because of the refusal of the United States to accept a binding target.

At the third Conference of the Parties of the Framework Convention, in 1997, the Kyoto Protocol was adopted. It entered into force in 2005 in accordance with Article 23, after not less than fifty-five parties to the Framework Convention – incorporating parties included in Annex I that accounted in total for at least 55 percent of the total carbon dioxide emissions for 1990 of the

---

[256] *See* Lissandro Abrego et al., "Trade and Environment: Bargaining Outcomes from Linked Negotiations," 9 *Rev. Int'l Econ.* 414 (2001).

TABLE 7–1. Ozone and Carbon public goods

|  | Rivalry | Excludibility | Aggregation technology |
|---|---|---|---|
| **Ozone** | Non-rival | Non-excludible | Summation; cumulative benefits |
| **Carbon** | Non-rival | Non-excludible | Summation; cumulative benefits |

parties included in Annex I – deposited their instruments of ratification, acceptance, approval, or accession. This was a tough standard to meet, given that the United States did not participate. Under Article 3 of the Kyoto Protocol, Annex I parties were required to reduce carbon emissions by at least 5 percent below 1990 levels in the commitment period 2008–2012, as specified in limits assigned to each country. Countries not included in Annex 1 undertook no binding commitments. "Kyoto only limits the emissions of a relatively small number of countries by just a little bit for only a short period of time."[257] Even if extended to full participation, the Kyoto Protocol "can be considered as only a first and relatively small step towards stabilizing the climate."[258]

So why has action been difficult? It might be argued that international environmental cooperation is simply difficult, but we have the successful example of the ozone regime to disprove that generalization.[259] All global public-goods problems are not created alike. The three parameters of public goods are the degree of non-rivalry of consumption, excludability, and aggregation technology.

The basic parameters of the public-goods cooperation problems in connection with ozone depletion and carbon emissions are the same, as illustrated in Table 7–1.

Given that the basic public-goods parameters of ozone-layer maintenance and climate change are similar, what are the critical differences? Importantly, although many states will be harmed by global warming, some states will be helped in terms of agricultural productivity or other parameters. Second, although only a handful of states accounted for most CFCs, the generation of greenhouse gases (GHGs) is global. Indeed, the greatest increases in emissions of GHGs come from developing countries that generally wish to prioritize growth over emission reduction. Thus, there are many more states that must be induced to act to reduce emissions in the climate regime. Furthermore – and this is true of virtually all environmental benefits – different states will

[257] Barrett, *supra* note 33, at 91.   [258] *Id.*
[259] For a comparison of the carbon and ozone regimes, *see* Sandler, *supra* note 251, at 212–34.

have different preferences depending on their wealth, geographical position, and other factors.

As Sandler points out, whereas the dominant strategy for some key polluters in connection with ozone was to reduce ozone emissions, because the benefits of individual state reduction exceeded the individual state costs, this is not true in the climate-change field. Rather, in the area of climate change, the individual costs are expected to exceed the individual benefits, with the result that the dominant strategy for most states will be to pollute unabated.[260] Of course, the fact that the dominant strategy is to pollute does not mean that cooperation is impossible if the structure of payoffs can be changed. One principal way to change the structure of payoffs is through the establishment of enforceable legal rules. Another is to establish linkages to other areas of cooperation. These two methods can be combined.

In order to examine the possible role of enforceable legal rules in connection with global warming, the stages that are to be analyzed include: (i) adherence to an agreement to contribute; and (ii) compliance with the agreement to contribute. Under this two-stage game, adapted from Barrett's model,[261] the players choose in stage 1 whether to adhere to the agreement. In stage 2, adherents and non-adherents choose whether to comply.

For purposes of simplification, let us assume binding international law. Therefore, for any state that has adhered to the agreement there is no choice as to whether to comply, provided that there are other adherents who are in a position to enforce the initial adherent's obligations. This model assumes that any agreement to contribute is binding, that each player knows what happened at the prior stage, and that each player examines its choices at each subsequent stage when determining what to do at the first stage – whether to accept the agreement to contribute or not. By this process of backward induction, we can determine whether states would adhere to the agreement.

For simplicity, I begin with a two-person prisoner's dilemma game. I use the prisoner's dilemma here because it represents a context in which cooperation is tough to achieve. Here, the parties have incentives to defect. In other payoff structures, illustrated by games such as the battle of the sexes or stag hunt, the parties do not have similar incentives to defect.

The following analysis is adapted from Black, Levi, and de Meza.[262] Assume that the payoff to each state from creation of the public good of reduction of carbon emissions is $rb-c$, where $r$ is the number of states that contribute, $b$ is the benefit produced by each contributing state's contribution, and $c$ is the

---

[260] Sandler, *supra* note 251, at 224.   [261] *See* Barrett, *supra* note 187 (2003).
[262] Jane Black, Maurice D. Levi, & David de Meza, "Creating a Good Atmosphere: Minimum Participation for Tackling the 'Greenhouse Effect," 60 *Economica* 281 (1993).

cost to each contributing state of contribution. In this payoff structure, the aggregate benefits rise in proportion to the number of states that contribute. The aggregation technology is therefore summation.

The benefits of reduction are non-excludible: a non-contributing state gets the benefit of contribution by others without the cost of its own contribution. Thus, the payoff to a non-contributing state simply equals $rb$. Assume that $b$ is less than $c$. Otherwise, as was the case in connection with ozone for some of the most important states, there would be no need for a rule of international law: each state would by definition benefit from its own contribution in an amount greater than the cost of contribution. For example, with two players that both contribute, and assuming $c = 3$ and $b = 2$, the payoff to each state from contribution is 1, because $2(2) - 3 = 1$. If neither state contributes, then the payoff to each is 0. If one contributes and the other violates, the contributing state gets a payoff of $-1$, and the non-contributing state gets a payoff of 2. This is a prisoner's dilemma: under the assumptions of a non-cooperative game, neither state will contribute.

Now assume that states may agree to contribute in preparation for or in connection with the diplomatic convention for a carbon-reduction treaty. Recall that we are assuming that their agreement regarding contributions is strictly binding, so that it always results in compliance. Under the payoffs we have assumed, a non-adhering state will play the strategy of no contribution at stage 2; this is the dominant solution for a non-adherent. However, an adherent will be required to contribute pursuant to our assumption of binding international law.

In this two-player game, assume that one state adheres to the rule in stage 1. Because that state is the only adherent, (assume that) the rule either never comes into being or cannot be enforced against it, and so it declines to contribute in stage 2, as it anticipates that the other state will also play no contribution in stage 2. It understands the other state's dominant solution, and in fact is pursuing its own dominant solution. The outcome is that both play no contribution: the same type of inefficient equilibrium that we expect in a prisoner's dilemma. Here, however, there is a difference. There is an institutional mechanism for formally binding treaties.

Anticipating the inefficient solution to the prisoner's dilemma game, both parties examine their choices at stage 1. If one of the parties (A) adheres to the contribution agreement at stage 1, the other party (B) faces the following choice: if B declines to adhere, then A will play no contribution in stage 2, as discussed in the prior paragraph. B anticipates that it will receive a payoff of 0 if both parties play no contribution. On the other hand, if B adheres, irrevocably binding itself to contribute, A will also be bound to contribute, securing a payoff of 1 for B (as well as for A). So, in this setting, B will adhere.

TABLE 7–2. A public goods game

| Number of States that Contribute | 0 | 1 | 2 | 3 | 4 | 5 |
|---|---|---|---|---|---|---|
| Payoff for Non-Contribution | 0 | 2 | 4 | 6 | 8 | n/a |
| Net Payoff for Contribution | 0 | −1 | 1 | 3 | 5 | 7 |
| Aggregate Payoff | 0 | 7 | 14 | 21 | 28 | 35 |

We might understand A's adherence as an offer to contract, which B may accept by adherence. Adherence is a (weakly) dominant solution for both players in stage 1.

As suggested by Barrett, this model works well for a two-person game, and the two-person prisoner's dilemma when transformed into a cooperative game (in which binding agreement is possible) is easily resolved. This result is intuitive. In part, this two-player case is simple. Where only one player contributes, it receives no benefit, but only a detriment. So it is perfectly willing to revert to the Nash equilibrium solution: non-contribution. A *Nash equilibrium* is a set of strategies in which each player plays a strategy that maximizes its payoffs regardless of the actions of other players. The other player, realizing this, can adhere and thereby enhance both its own welfare and that of the other player. However, we are interested in plurilateral and multilateral international law. When this two-person model is extended to multiple persons, whether states will adhere to a multilateral agreement will depend on the structure of the payoffs.

The matrix in Table 7–2 depicts this circumstance of a prisoner's dilemma among five states.[263] For every state that contributes, a pure public good is produced, giving all states a benefit of 2 each, with a cost to the contributing state alone of 3. Each state can play either of two strategies: contribute or non-contribute. The dominant strategy is for each state to free ride and play non-contribute, because each of the payoffs for non-contribution in the second row is greater than the payoff for contribution in the third row. The Nash equilibrium is an outcome where no state contributes, although global welfare is maximized if all contribute. Under a prisoner's dilemma set of assumptions, we expect the Nash equilibrium: no contributions, and no aggregate payoff. The world loses significant potential welfare. However, if we assume instead that states may enter into binding agreements, the possibility for greater welfare emerges.

[263] Adapted from Todd Sandler, "Treaties: Strategic Considerations," 2008 (1) *Ill. L. Rev.* 155 (2008).

In a game with $n$ players, it may well be that a benefit is created through adherence by a coalition that is less than $n$. So reversion to Nash (non-contribution) may not be attractive to that smaller group. The two-person game previously discussed illustrates this circumstance. Depending on the nature of the required performance, and in particular on whether the benefit of contribution is non-excludible, as we have assumed, other states may have an incentive to free ride by declining to adhere to an agreement.

Using the same formula just provided, we recall that the payoff to a contributing state is $rb - c$, whereas the payoff to a non-contributing state simply equals $rb$. Recall that $r$ is the number of states that contribute, $b$ is the benefit produced by each contributing state's contribution, and $c$ is the cost to each contributing state of contributing. Under the assumption of binding international law, adherence results in contribution, provided that at least one other state adheres.

We assume that the payoff from nonadherence, assuming all others fail to adhere, is 0. Therefore, $k$ states will adhere (and therefore contribute) if $kb - c \geq 0$. Therefore, if the number of states $k \geq c/b$, then that number of states will adhere. Using the values of $c = 3$ and $b = 2$, if the number of states is greater than or equal to 1.5, they will adhere. So, in this example, two states result (as previously stated) in a payoff of 1, and because $1 > 0$, they will adhere. However, once the number of adherents reaches this level, assuming a serial process of adherence, other states will have no incentive to adhere – they will have an incentive to free ride. Adherence will result in costs incurred by the marginal adherents without affecting the behavior of other states.

Thus, in our two-stage game with the possibility of serial adherence to a binding contribution agreement, two states will be expected to adhere under these assumptions – that is, in equilibrium, the number of adherents is 2. This is because the payoff to non-adherents is greater than the payoff to adherents after two have adhered. For example, if three states adhere, the payoff is 3 to each adherent but 6 to each non-adherent (non-adherents do not bear the cost).

Barrett shows that under these assumptions (including the aggregation technology of summation), the gains from cooperation increase with $b$ (the benefit of compliance), and decrease with $c$ (the cost of compliance). This result is intuitive. However, less intuitive is the fact that the equilibrium number of state adherents increases with $c$, and decreases with $b$. This means that the equilibrium number of states will tend to be small when the gain from cooperation is large, and large when the gain from cooperation is small.[264]

---

[264] Barrett, *supra* note 261, at 204.

Furthermore, in equilibrium, non-adherents can free ride and get a higher payoff than adherents.

Of course, this assumes a serial process of adherence, under which incremental states may observe how many states have already adhered and subsequently decide whether to adhere. Much depends on the values of the costs and benefits to each state. Furthermore, it assumes an isolated adherence game, without the ability to subject states to scrutiny or punishment for unilateralism; that is, failure to join a plurilateral regime.

The core problem is one of free riding: some states may realize the benefit of contribution by others, without incurring any costs themselves. Indeed, each incremental state would prefer to free ride, if it could ensure that enough other states would adhere. This behavior assumes that there is a public-goods aspect to the cooperation problem. If, on the other hand, states that fail to comply can be excluded from sharing the benefits, the strategic challenge becomes smaller, although not trivial. If states can be excluded from benefiting from the cooperation of others, all states should then be willing to adhere. By adhering they would achieve a greater payoff than they would receive by failing to adhere.

However, even under non-excludability, a relatively easy solution may exist, under an assumption of simultaneous decision instead of serial decision. Under the circumstances previously described, the decision to adhere to the (binding) treaty would have the characteristics of a chicken game,[265] as described in Table 5–2.

As suggested in Chapter 5, under the chicken game payoffs, each state's best outcome is to abstain from agreement when others form a stable coalition that will generate the relevant public good. The second-best outcome is to adhere when others adhere. The worst outcome is if no state adheres. In this chicken game, neither player has a dominant strategy. In this particular case, there is no unique efficient equilibrium. Each player has two Nash equilibria: decline when the other adheres, and adhere when the other declines.

However, both players wish to avoid the circumstance where they each play decline, and the even split in the northwest quadrant of Table 5–2 seems intuitively attractive, although it is unstable. In order to achieve that even split, they should each commit to adhere. They may do so through a number of mechanisms. The simplest (in the treaty context) is a signing conference where each state signs a treaty simultaneously.[266] Only slightly more complex is a specification of a minimum number of adherents prior to entry into force.

---

[265] *See* Carlo Carraro & Domenico Siniscalco, "Strategies for the International Protection of the Environment," 52 *J. Public. Econ.* 309 (1993).

[266] It seems reasonable here to elide the distinction between signature and adherence, as signature brings certain obligations, including obligations to seek ratification.

These settings are comparable to the chicken game, but instead of two wild teenagers hurtling toward a cliff, we have sophisticated diplomats sitting eyeball to eyeball. Although there may still be incentives to try to avoid contributing, and these incentives may sometimes hold sway, the diplomatic context takes place in a simultaneous and broadly linked setting, where failure to contribute may be criticized and subject to punishment.

So, at least under symmetry in this context, it is possible to have a welfare-enhancing international legal regime in which states cooperate by ensuring that other states irrevocably agree to cooperate. Although international treaty law is never irrevocably binding, it is possible to design punishments that are sufficient to induce compliance. The use of linkage or financial sanctions to do so is discussed here and in Chapter 10.

E) LEAKAGE

A coordinated policy is essential to efficient response to climate change, and also for an efficient response to other health and environmental problems. I focus here on the dynamics of climate change. With respect to climate change, a coordinated policy is important because it is necessary to have uniform shadow prices, or values, of carbon emissions in order to ensure that the most efficient opportunities to reduce carbon will be exploited. With varying prices, mitigation might be applied where it is more costly, rather than where it is cheapest. Similarly, without uniform shadow prices, carbon leakage would occur, whereby high policy-imposed costs of carbon in one location drive activities to other locations.

Leakage occurs through three channels: price effects, slack-off effects, and capital reallocation effects.[267] *Price effects* result when reduced use of emissions-causing materials in one country causes reduced prices for these materials in the world market, inducing greater use of these materials in other countries. *Slack-off effects* result when the acts of one country cause sufficient benefits to other countries that they reduce their efforts to achieve their unilateral best level of emissions. *Capital reallocation effects* are caused by decisions to relocate production in states with lower prices for emissions-causing materials, or for emissions. Importantly, price effects and capital reallocation effects are exacerbated by economic integration. Globalization increases leakage;[268]

---

[267] *See* Jonathan Wiener, "Think Globally, Act Globally: The Limits of Local Climate Change Policies," 155 *U. Pa. L. Rev.* 1961, 1968 (2007).

[268] Onno Kuik & Reyer Gerlagh, "Trade Liberalization and Carbon Leakage," 24 (3) *Energy J.* 97, 98 (2003).

therefore, greater globalization will make it more important to cooperate in connection with climate change.

Although globalization would generally increase leakage, cross-border movement of technology – through globalization – can ameliorate leakage. This occurs when one country's investment in abatement technology becomes available to other countries with a strong enough effect to induce them to engage in greater abatement.[269]

Importantly, as with other areas of regulatory competition, the fear of leakage may cause the adverse effects of leakage: legislators fearful of leakage might reduce carbon abatement even if no leakage is likely to occur.[270] This seems to be the mechanism that caused the United States to decline to ratify the Kyoto Protocol in 1997. Conversely, international agreement that reduces concerns regarding leakage can promote national action.

## F) COOPERATION UNDER ASYMMETRY AND LEAKAGE

The ability to engage in cooperation will be made more difficult by two related complications. First, there is great asymmetry among states in terms of the degree of harm they will experience from global warming, their financial capability, and their attitudes. Second, under globalization, leakage will be accentuated by variation in mitigation.

The public-goods game analysis provided assumes symmetric states. However, especially in the context of climate change, states are not symmetric. As suggested, states may have different positions and preferences in relation to international environmental policy, such as climate change. These asymmetries make it more difficult to achieve a coordinated policy, and more difficult to reach agreement. In the environmental field, poor countries are likely to have less concern with environmental protection than wealthy countries, even where they may be subject to greater harm. The principle of "common but differentiated responsibilities" established in the UNFCCC and Kyoto Protocol recognizes that developing countries should not, and cannot, be required to sacrifice development opportunities in order to contribute to mitigation at the same level as wealthy countries. Whereas until 2004 the wealthy countries were the greatest source of GHG emissions, developing countries are now the larger sources, and are growing as sources.[271]

---

[269] Rolf Golombek & Michael Hoel, "Unilateral Emission Reductions and Cross-Country Technology Spillovers," 4 (2) *B.E. J. Econ. Analysis & Pol'y* 2 (2004). Retrieved from http://www.bepress.com/bejeap/advances/vol4/iss2/art3.

[270] Wiener, *supra* note 267, at 1972.

[271] U.S. Energy Information Agency, International Energy Outlook 2010, Figure 103. Retrieved from http://www.eia.gov/oiaf/ieo/emissions.html. *See also* Robert N. Stavins, "The Problem

# Environmental Protection and Public Health

It is necessary to recognize the different incentives of states in order to make entry into the agreement individually rational for each state. This will require research into the position of each state, and discussion to avoid strategic holdouts or overstatement of costs or of benefits. It will also require calculation of potential leakage.

Where states are not able to agree on a policy, we might assume that this failure to agree indicates that there is not a policy that would enhance all states' welfare. However, a market failure such as the type of public-goods problem discussed might prevent states from reaching a globally welfare-enhancing agreement. Furthermore, there may be potential Pareto-efficient agreements that would not benefit all states, but would benefit the benefitting states in an amount that would be more than sufficient to compensate the harmed state. If compensation takes place, and is done consensually, of course, this agreement would be Pareto efficient. "Where national net benefits are not positive, some form of side payment will be needed to attract participation."[272] A more limited side-payment arrangement has been agreed at the December 2011 Durban climate-change conference.[273] However, even if compensation does not take place directly, there may be circumstances in which compensation may take place indirectly.

Consider a circumstance in which there are two types of countries: (i) wealthy countries whose abatement would be less beneficial to the global commons (because the costs of further marginal abatement are high), and whose people have greater preferences for environmental protection; and (ii) poor countries whose abatement would be more beneficial to the global commons, but whose people have lesser preferences for environmental protection. Furthermore, for an equivalent level of abatement, fast-growing poor countries would have to give up more natural future growth than slow-growing wealthy countries. This structure is comparable to the asymmetry discussed in Chapter 6, with respect to human rights.

Under these conditions, side payments may induce the poor countries to enter into the agreement.[274] If the side payments are one-time payments made at the inception of the agreement, they would need to be combined with binding treaties that prevent parties from terminating early. On the other hand, if the side payments are continuing payments or performances, such as

---

of the Commons: Still Unsettled after 100 Years" (The Harvard Project on International Climate Agreements Discussion Paper 10–43, September 2010). Retrieved from web.hks.harvard.edu/publications/getFile.aspx?Id=607.

[272] Wiener, *supra* note 267, at 1977.
[273] *See* http://unfccc.int/meetings/durban_nov_2011/meeting/6245.php.
[274] Sandler, *supra* note 251, at 343.

annual financial assistance or trade liberalization, these agreements may be self-enforcing.

It is not a trivial problem to determine the appropriate magnitude of the required side payments. For example, how would states estimate the amount of future developing country growth that might be suppressed by required carbon abatement, and determine the appropriate monetary or other compensation for that future growth? It may be in the interest of the poor countries in this example to exaggerate their costs and understate their benefits during negotiations, and in the interest of wealthy countries to do the opposite. In order to solve these problems, some institutional mechanism may be needed, whereby states agree on the principles and then leave it to independent third parties to apply them.

In addition, under strong international law, it is not necessary that all transfers of consideration be contemporaneous: it is not necessary to have a self-enforcing agreement. As Spence suggests,[275] an intertemporal arrangement whereby wealthy countries contribute the greatest toward mitigation in the first twenty years, and developing countries begin to contribute after that period, might be the basis for an appropriate agreement, but would depend on the degree of confidence that wealthy countries have in the enforceability of long-term legal commitments by developing countries. Spence's analysis combines estimates of the growth patterns and emissions of developing countries with estimates of the advance of mitigation technologies, to develop the perspective that it indeed is not realistic to expect developing countries to contribute materially to mitigation in the early years. "The challenge is to define the differentiated responsibilities in such a way as to create a path to hit safe emissions targets without undermining developing country growth.[276]

Economy-wide carbon pricing will be necessary for efficient carbon reduction.[277] Leakage will only be completely prevented by homogeneous economy-wide carbon pricing. So the more complete solution would be to implement economy-wide pricing, with separate compensation payments to developing countries. However, this approach may be impractical in the short-term. If developing countries are excluded from mitigation obligations at first, leakage would remain a substantial problem: industries in wealthy countries would reduce their regulated emissions by relocating their production to unregulated poor countries, with no necessary global reduction in emissions.

---

[275] Spence, *supra* note 120, at 209–21.   [276] *Id.* at 214.
[277] Gilbert E. Metcalf, "Market-Based Policy Options to Control U.S. Greenhouse Gas Emissions," 23 J. Econ. Persp. 5 (2009).

It is possible to make some efforts to contain leakage without uniform mitigation. Let us consider slack-off effects, price effects, and capital reallocation effects. Slack-off effects would be addressed ex ante by determining appropriate differentiated responsibilities. Price effects, in which GHG-intensive inputs become cheaper because of restrictions on their use in developed countries, inducing intensification of their use in developing countries, could be addressed through special border-tax adjustments or simply tariffs on developing country imports of these goods. Capital allocation effects, in which GHG-intensive production migrates to developing countries, could be addressed by rules that restrict investment in GHG-intensive production in developing countries.

Indeed, if a proposed treaty had sufficient mechanisms to contain leakage, it would deprive non-cooperating states of some of the benefits of non-cooperation, and thereby tend to reduce the number of non-cooperating states. This fact motivated the inclusion of a trade restriction on CFCs in the Montreal Protocol.[278]

A coordinated abatement agreement must be interactive, so that abatement obligations may be bought and sold between states in order to result in the most efficient, or cost-effective, abatement. A mechanism such as the Clean Development Mechanism included in the Kyoto Protocol, which allows wealthy countries to get credit for mitigation that they carry out in developing countries, would engender more efficient mitigation. So, whereas developing countries might not have early obligations to mitigate, the developed-country obligations could be met through mitigation in developing countries.

### G) COMPLIANCE AND LINKAGE

In light of the structure of the global-warming abatement public-goods game, including these important concerns regarding leakage, it is difficult to imagine an uncoordinated response to global warming. Indeed, it is difficult to imagine a response that does not use significant requirements of coordinated reduction, with significant punishments for failure to comply. There are two stages to address: adherence and compliance.

Given the character of punishments that seem to be required, and the fact that these punishments might otherwise violate other international-law commitments – such as free-trade commitments – the consent of each state, or at least a majority of states, to be regulated would appear to be preferable. If there are holdouts, it might be possible to utilize the consent of the majority

---

[278] Barrett, *supra* note 187, at 313.

of states – including all the most powerful states – to coerce the holdouts, but it would be difficult to do so without the consent of the majority.

However, the critical problem in an intertemporal arrangement is that it would not constitute the kind of contemporaneous self-enforcing agreement that some theoreticians believe is the sine qua non of effective international law.[279] Rather, the wealthy countries would be providing consideration in the early period in exchange for commitments by the poor countries to provide consideration later. However, as argued in Chapters 2 and 12, this perspective – expecting all law to be self-enforcing in the short-term – although common among social scientists, is ignorant of the networked power of law and the possibility of institutional design and linkage that can overcome the failure of any particular agreement to be self-enforcing on its own. This perspective is dangerous because it leaves us impotent to address long-term, highly–asset-specific, and asymmetric cooperation problems. In addition, the poor countries are expected to become wealthier, so both their capacity and their desire to address climate change and other environmental problems should be greater later.

In fact, Barrett shows that with the inclusion of substantial trade restrictions as punishment for nonadherence (and noncompliance), it is fairly easy to reach a cooperative agreement. Under this structure, when the number of signing countries is low, every country prefers to be a non-signatory because they would otherwise have to engage in punishment by trade restriction that is costly to them. On the other hand, when the number of signing countries is high, every country prefers to be a signatory because they obtain the benefits of abatement, and avoid substantial losses in trade terms. "The benefit that non-signatories derive from free-riding is overwhelmed by the loss they suffer in being unable to trade with the majority of other countries."[280] With trade restrictions, the cooperation problem is not a chicken game, but a simple coordination game that can be solved by having a minimum participation condition for effectiveness of the treaty.

Of course, there are unanswered questions regarding the legality under WTO law of environmentally motivated trade restrictions. Under existing WTO jurisprudence, it is likely that trade restrictions rationally designed to support a needed multilateral environmental-protection regime would be found to be permitted. However, this area of overlap, or fragmentation, might benefit from greater clarification.

---

[279] See Barrett, *supra* note 187; Giovanni Maggi, "The Role of Multilateral Institutions in International Trade Cooperation," 89 (1) *Am. Econ. Rev.* 190 (1989). See the discussion of this point in Chapters 2, 10, and 12.

[280] Barrett, *supra* note 187, at 318.

## H) CHAPTER CONCLUSION

International health and environmental protection present interesting problems of international externalities and public goods. These represent important areas of cooperation. Under globalization, and technological and demographic change, governments will find it increasingly difficult to deliver the protections and services their citizens demand without cooperation. Importantly, the reciprocal need to take account of the concerns of foreign states may precipitate erroneous criticisms of the democratic accountability of governments that enter the international market in order to obtain the arrangements their citizens need.

This chapter has further developed the analysis of the role of international law to respond to international externalities and public goods, under circumstances of asymmetry and leakage. Under highly asset-specific types of arrangements, in which international agreements cannot be self-enforcing and provide the greatest efficiency, it will be necessary to ensure that international legal institutions are strong enough to induce compliance. Only under this circumstance will efficient international contracting be possible.

# 8 Global Regulation of Finance

As suggested in Chapter 2, international law should generally play a subsidiary role to domestic law. The principle of subsidiarity in its most rational form is best understood as a principle of efficiency. It holds that the state should intervene in civil society – should regulate – only where its involvement improves welfare, and that in turn, international law and organizations should be established only where they improve welfare.[281] It is appropriate to adopt a subsidiarity-based – or efficiency-based – method, examining first the circumstances in which it appears that states should regulate, and second the separate and different reasons why international law of regulation may be appropriate.

Thus, domestic regulation may be needed when firms do not bear all the risks of their actions or when the managers who are delegated control of firms do not bear all the risks of their actions. The recent crisis illustrates both types of problem. Building on the subsidiarity concept at a higher level of organization, international regulation is needed when states do not bear all the risks of their regulatory actions, where states acting individually would otherwise underinvest in a global public good, or where states may regulate more efficiently by working together. "The global financial crisis demonstrated that our globalized world has reached a level of international connectivity that far exceeds the reach of national policies and the effectiveness of the global architecture."[282]

## A) EXTERNALITIES OF FINANCIAL REGULATION

The financial regulation (or deficiencies therein) in one state may be associated with adverse or beneficial effects (negative or positive externalities) in

---

[281] For my more general analysis of this topic, *see* Trachtman, *supra* note 27. *See also* Thomas Cottier, "Multilayered Governance, Pluralism, and Moral Conflict," 16 *Ind. J. Global Legal Stud.* 647 (2009).

[282] Spence, *supra* note 120.

other states. Externalities may be addressed through rules of jurisdiction that accord the affected state control over the injurious behavior.

Domestic financial regulation may also cause adverse effects in other states by being too strict with respect to the entry of foreign financial services into the national market, or too lax with respect to domestic financial institutions, resulting in competitiveness effects (pecuniary externalities). Externalization through regulation that fails to protect foreign interests (or that implicitly subsidizes by failing to protect local or foreign interests), pecuniary externalization through strict regulation that has protectionist effects or through lax regulation that may be viewed as a subsidy, and subsidization itself may all be viewed as questions of prescriptive jurisdiction: which state – or international body – will have power to regulate which actions?

An example of a principle of international financial-regulatory jurisdiction that seems problematic from this standpoint is contained in a January 2009 proposal from the Group of Thirty, entitled "Financial Reform: A Framework for Financial Stability."[283] This report recommends, with respect to private pools of capital such as hedge funds, that "the jurisdiction of the appropriate prudential regulator should be based on the primary business location of the manager of such funds." However, the jurisdiction assigned responsibility under this principle might not include the primary location of investors, or of others who might be harmed by actions of the funds. Under these circumstances, the affected state might be denied control over the injurious behavior.

The externalization problem is accentuated by the diversity of states' positions. Some states may be regulatory havens that impose lax regulation because the adverse effects of the lax regulation will largely be felt externally, whereas the positive effects in terms of tax revenues and employment can be enjoyed by the regulatory haven. Certain jurisdictional rules, such as rules of regulatory recognition, might allow such externalization. On the other hand, jurisdictional rules of national treatment, or of managed recognition,[284] can reduce the possibility for such negative externalization. Similarly, in connection with capital controls, exchange-rate management, and convertibility, "these policies are adapted to local conditions but have external effects."[285]

Furthermore, one state's strict regulation might provide positive externalities to other states, both in terms of avoidance of contagion and avoidance of consequent economic disruption. Because this is a positive externality, the first state would require some incentive – in terms of some type of narrow or

---

[283] Group of Thirty, "Financial Reform: A Framework for Financial Stability," (2009). Retrieved from http://www.group30.org/images/PDF/Financial_Reform-A_Framework_for_Financial_Stability.pdf.

[284] *See* Nicolaïdis & Trachtman, *supra* note 28.  [285] Spence, *supra* note 120.

diffuse reciprocity – as compensation. International cooperation can set the terms of such reciprocity.

## B) PUBLIC GOODS

One type of cooperation problem in international-financial regulation relates to international public goods.[286] Examples of public goods in this area include the international financial and payments system, international financial stability, and global economic growth. Financial stability and the resultant economic growth may be viewed not just as a domestic public good, but also as a global public good, owing to contagion and systemic effects. That is, the benefits of stability are available to all states, and the enjoyment of stability by one state does not reduce its availability to others. At the financial level, under interconnectedness, regulatory cooperation may reduce the scope of systemic risk that each state's financial institutions experience. The 1974 Herstatt Bank crisis was an early example of this type of international contagion risk. At the economic level, a U.S. economic slump has repercussions around the world through the mechanism of trade and investment. Most recently, the Greek economic crisis raises questions about the financial situations of Portugal, Italy, and Spain.

States affected by externalities, or states that observe the possibility of underproduced international public goods, may thus determine to seek to alter other states' activities, through their own regulation or by seeking changes in the first state's regulation.

## C) ECONOMIES OF SCALE AND SCOPE, AND NETWORK EXTERNALITIES

As discussed in Chapter 2, additional potential sources of gains from cooperation may arise from economies of scale and economies of scope, as well as network externalities. Given the increasingly global nature of international finance, and of problems such as the international financial crisis, it seems likely that there would be economies of scale, under some circumstances, in the regulation of these matters.[287] There may be institutional economies of scale and scope: development of institutions may make it more likely that more issues will be addressed by those institutions. Network externalities may

---

[286] See *Providing Global Public Goods* (Inge Kaul et al., eds., 2003), *supra* note 33.
[287] Of course, the fact that it is efficient to regulate activity from a global perspective does not mean that only one regulator should exist; rather, it is a problem of contracting and establishing the most efficient institutional structure in response to technical or contextual factors. A similar caveat applies with respect to economies of scope.

increase savings with increases in the number of states that are party to an institution or a rule.

Economies of scale in international finance have a number of components. First, states may enjoy economies of scale in contexts where they regulate transnational actors. For example, there may be efficiencies gained through coordinated rule making, surveillance, and enforcement activities. In the absence of these transactions, states face heightened risks of evasion, detrimental regulatory competition (which can be driven by externalization), and unnecessary regulatory disharmony, all resulting in inefficiencies.[288] Second, there may be technological economies of scale, relating to equipment, acquisition of specialized skills, or organization. Certainly, as finance has become more complex, there may be greater economies of scale in developing the necessary regulatory capacities. Economies of scale may provide motivation for integration, in the sense that the economies of scale tilt the cost-benefit analysis in favor of integration.

D) REGULATORY COMPETITION

Technological advances, globalization, innovation, and growth have combined to make finance both actually and virtually rather footloose. Mobility exists both on the producer and consumer side of the equation. On the other hand, Joseph Stiglitz has argued that the part of the financial system that is critical to the real economy – the part that lends to Main Street business – is not as footloose as the more speculative part of the financial system.[289] Prior to the 2008 financial crisis, there had been some evidence of movement away from U.S. capital markets, arguably because of increasingly stringent regulation. However, no one has identified a move from the United States as being motivated by a desire for more onerous regulation. Indeed, the crisis may turn out to prove that we cannot rely on the capacity of private actors to leave a jurisdiction with inadequate financial regulation. The class of persons protected by regulation seemed in this case to lack the ability to evaluate and identify inadequate regulation.

The broader a financial institution's powers, the lower its capital requirements, and the greater the government safety net, the more profitable it is likely to be. Increased powers permit greater profits, lower capital requirements impose lower costs, and the government safety net operates as a subsidy. Therefore, a financial institution exclusively regulated by a jurisdiction that

---

[288] *See* Trachtman, *supra* note 30 (1993).
[289] Joseph Stiglitz, "Watchdogs Need Not Bark Together," *Financial Times* (Feb. 9, 2010). Retrieved from http://www.ft.com/intl/cms/s/0/3ebddd1e-15b7-11df-ad7e-00144feab49a.html#axzz2o90pqevy.

is more liberal in connection with capital or powers regulation, or that provides a stronger safety net, can be expected to be more competitive – all else being equal – than a more-constrained or less-supported financial institution. So there is a competitive, or pecuniary, externality arising from certain types of financial regulation. Moreover, this externality will often involve nonpecuniary elements, where the relevant financial institution may operate internationally and the risk of its failure may be detrimental to people outside its home jurisdiction. This is inefficient regulatory competition driven by externalization.

Thus, unilateral action alone, perhaps by use of national market-access restrictions that might prevent an inadequately regulated bank from doing business in a more vigilant jurisdiction, does not appear to be sufficient to establish appropriate rules. Furthermore, it may be difficult to distinguish such unilateral action from protectionism, raising fragmentation issues between regulation and trade. Therefore, discourse on the basis of regulatory expertise, toward multilateral essential harmonization, seems appropriate in this area; again, assuming that we are able to overcome uncertainty as to appropriate regulatory action. Of course, there is another type of uncertainty that is more difficult to overcome: uncertainty regarding the appropriateness of a particular regulatory rule across different legal, financial, and social systems. This is similar to the issue discussed in Chapter 9 with respect to national treatment and proportionality standards in international trade. However, under circumstances of increasing globalization, greater homogenization and mobility of abuse will militate toward essential harmonization of financial regulation rules in this area. Both types of uncertainty suggest state-contingent treaties, of the type developed in the trade-law context, as discussed in Chapter 9.

To the extent that we continue to operate under uncertainty regarding the appropriate structure of regulation, diversity may allow us to learn from further experience. On the other hand, where we believe that diversity is driven more by externalization or protectionism than by good-faith regulatory views, then there can be no assurance that diversity will be beneficial. As discussed in Chapter 2, the beneficial or detrimental nature of regulatory competition is recognized to be dependent on the question of regulatory jurisdiction, in the form of questions of positive and negative externalities that may limit the utility and domain of the Tiebout model.

## E) FRAGMENTATION AND COOPERATION

At the international level, we have an additional set of overlaps with other functional areas, or fragmentation issues. These fragmentation issues are in addition to those relating to functional separation, for example, among commercial bank regulation, securities regulation, insurance regulation, corporate governance, bankruptcy, consumer regulation, and commodities regulation. Of course, the resolution of fragmentation issues at the international level is made more difficult by the fact that there is no single institution that serves as forum or legislator for all of the relevant issues.

## I) Macroeconomic Management

If the root cause of pressure on domestic regulatory mechanisms, and eventual failure, is macroeconomic imbalances, then it may be more efficient to address these imbalances rather than to make changes to regulation. Regulation alone has not shown itself capable of preventing the adverse effects of instability. Some types of macroeconomic management may assist in preventing crises. It is likely to be necessary to do both. The correct balance would depend on an overall cost-benefit analysis of each mechanism. Macroeconomic imbalances might be caused, in turn, by savings-rate differentials, distorted exchange rates, or other factors.

> The financial system seems periodically to become unstable.
>
> During periods of instability, systemic risk rises, assets become highly correlated, debt rises as a contributing factor, normal risk-mitigation strategies such as diversification and insurance (various hedging models) either don't work or work much less well than usual. Drastic intervention is required to prevent indiscriminate destruction of businesses as credit channels close and credit dries up completely.[290]

The international problem is that national macroeconomic-management measures cause policy externalities. These externalities are not limited to financial-system contagion. For example, in response to the 2008 financial crisis, some states implemented a stimulus program. However, these programs conferred positive externalities on other states through the trade channel, so the establishment of an optimal stimulus was impeded by the fact that beneficial effects were expected to be absorbed by other states, at the cost of the stimulating state. A coordinated set of stimulus packages, in which each state was allocated a share of the cost, would have been a better cooperative outcome.[291] However, it would have been quite difficult to arrange.

This work cannot fully address the issue of currency management, involving the relationships between surplus countries and deficit countries. Multilateral

---

[290] Spence, *supra* note 120, at 141.  [291] *Id.*

surveillance by the IMF has not been sufficient to create monetary order. Such surveillance:

> [ ... ] has failed to avoid periods of widely perceived currency misalignment during the 1980s, 1990s and 2000s, or periods when fiscal imbalances generated significant global macroeconomic disequilibria. It has failed to avoid or neutralize spillover effects, with the principal international financial crisis of the 1980s – the Third World debt crisis – in part reflecting the externalities from recession in industrial countries. It also failed to avoid the series of interrelated currency and financial crises in the 1990s in emerging economies.[292]

It seems clear that states cannot be persuaded to take account of policy externalities that arise from their national monetary policies through mere surveillance.[293] The IMF Articles of Agreement attempted to provide stronger tools through Article VII, the so-called scarce currency clause, which could be used to authorize states to apply trade restrictions to limit exchange transactions with countries running chronic surpluses. However, the scarce currency clause has never been applied. Thus, the IMF has little power to induce chronic surplus countries, or deficit countries that can finance their deficits without resort to IMF facilities, to modify their policies.[294]

Spence suggests that the existing system worked until recently because it met the needs of diverse economies. Emerging countries were permitted to build surpluses, but the external economic effects were small enough to ignore, whereas developed countries have floating exchange rates, independent monetary policies, and generally no reserves accumulation.[295] However, the rise of China, India and Brazil has challenged this system, because their monetary policies have large external effects. Spence concludes:

> This is a cooperative game on a giant scale that we are trying to learn how to play, a complex one because of asymmetries among the players. The chances that asynchronous moves and separate agreements on distinct issues will lead to a fully cooperative outcome are very low. More likely is a noncooperative outcome with attendant suboptimal results and instability.... The challenge of developing a new rules-based system that accommodates divergent conditions and stages of development, but which safeguards global stability and ensures equitable outcomes, is entirely before us. It is one of the main design

---

[292] Graham Bird & Thomas D. Willett, "Multilateral Surveillance: Is the IMF Shooting for the Stars?" 8 (4) *World Econ.* 167, 171 (2007).
[293] *Id.* at 174.
[294] Joseph Gold, *Legal and Institutional Aspects of the International Monetary Fund*, I, 294–95 (1980).
[295] Spence, *supra* note 120 at 97–99.

challenges facing us if a reasonably cooperative process of globalization is to be maintained.[296]

A rules-based system would probably allow developing countries to use monetary policy to accumulate surpluses until such time as they reach a specified level of development, and then to gradually reduce their surpluses. Such an intertemporal agreement would be highly asset specific, and would require strong international law to ensure that it is reliable.

Rodrik describes an important link between monetary policy and trade policy. He suggests that after China's accession to the WTO, China responded to increasing competition from imports and increasing limits on its ability to promote exports by suppressing the appreciation of its currency.[297] So, assuming that WTO law does not otherwise restrict this type of currency practice, effective international trade law may require effective international monetary law.

## II) Trade

As is well known, one of the important pressures on the United States to relax its Glass-Steagall and other powers regulation – allowing its banking organizations to engage in insurance, investment banking, and other activities – came from demands by European and other states for reduced impediments to access to the U.S. market. Of course this pressure operated under uncertainty, or at least disagreement, regarding the utility of these components of powers regulation. Putting that political pressure aside, a state was nevertheless free to engage in unilateralism regarding powers criteria for market access. In the general international system, as contrasted to the EU, there is no rule of exclusive regulation by the home country. So, a potential host country could block market entry by the laxly regulated foreign financial institution. On the other hand, however, states such as the United States found their financial institutions disadvantaged in terms of operations in more lax foreign markets, where the U.S. financial institutions were subject to extraterritorial home-country restrictions, whereas native or other foreign financial institutions enjoyed a broader range of powers. So, cross-national regulatory differentials will have some distortive effect on trade, and may cause some states to close their borders to market access from other states that have less onerous regimes.

On the other hand, liberalization and globalization generally may change our definition of "too big to fail," which is the rationale often given for financial-institution rescues. If there are low barriers to market access, then a foreign firm may stand ready to acquire or supplant a failing domestic firm.

[296] Id. at 268.   [297] Rodrik, supra note 3.

## III) Development

Different states have different needs at different times. A developing state might need the right to regulate in order to promote growth under circumstances in which the risk of a resulting banking crisis is small in relation to the benefits of resulting development. So, there may be cross-national diversity as to the ideal level of regulation. Therefore, in any international regulatory response that includes some degree of harmonization, recognition, or enforcement cooperation, there may be some need to create a mechanism that recognizes appropriate diversity for development purposes. The IMF, in its role as development agency, and the World Bank have established a significant body of semisoft financial law. States that seek access to IMF and World Bank facilities are required to demonstrate a satisfactory level of compliance with these standards and codes.[298]

## F) FUTURE CHANGE AND ITS IMPACT ON REGULATORY REFORM

Of course, it is not possible to anticipate all aspects of the future stresses on financial institutions, but it will be important to do so as far as possible. On the basis of the discussion of future conditions in Chapter 4, we can identify some broad trends, and suggest how these may affect the themes of financial regulation discussed above. I focus on globalization, technological advance, financial innovation, and economic growth.

## I) Globalization

Globalization in finance and financial services has grown dramatically, in large measure because of technological advances. Because we have historical instances of globalization being reversed in the early part of the twentieth century, it is not possible to predict that globalization will continue to increase. However, enhanced technology over time and the expected economic benefits of globalization are likely to continue to drive increasing globalization.

Practically by definition, globalization results in greater competition, potentially reducing margins and thereby making local financial institutions more vulnerable to the risk of commercial failure. Reduced margins might indicate a need for closer supervision, greater capital requirements, or perhaps even the imposition of restrictions on competition in order to maintain the stability

---

[298] *See* International Monetary Fund & the World Bank, "The Standards and Codes Initiative – Is it Effective? And How Can it Be Improved?" (2005). Retrieved from http://www.worldbank.org/ifa/ROSC%20review%202005.pdf.

of financial institutions. This is the concept of overbanking that in some states has been used as a basis to limit market access to newcomers.

Further, globalization, by increasing the mobility of firms, would be expected to accentuate regulatory competition, depending on how globalization is structured. Regulatory competition could be benevolent or malevolent, depending on whether it is a race to externalize – in which the regulating state is imposing costs on outsiders – or to efficiency – in which the regulating state is seeking more efficient regulation.

This same mobility that allows honest firms to move to reduce costs can allow dishonest operators to seek out under-regulated markets, engaging in a perverse transfer of defalcation technology. This means that, under globalization, states cannot wait for indigenous fraudsters to appear, but must protect against imported fraud. Developing countries may consider this phenomenon as they determine to open their markets to competition in financial services. The risk of imported defalcation suggests a greater role for imported regulatory structures.

Greater competition owing to globalization, combined with a safety-net doctrine for companies "too big to fail" (TBTF), is a dangerous combination. Thus, under globalization, at the same time that regulatory competition may have induced reductions in regulatory stringency, increased cross-border inter-firm competition has reduced margins, driving financial institutions to seek more profitable, and more risky, activities.

In other dimensions, globalization provides opportunities both for greater stability and risks of contagion, depending on the structure of financial institutions and risk. Globalization may provide opportunities for greater stability by increasing the size of the market and reducing barriers to entry. If a firm is TBTF in a smaller market, it may not be TBTF given the readiness of foreign competitors to enter the market and acquire the firm or otherwise take over its market niche. This readiness may be enhanced by liberalization of trade in financial services, especially in connection with commercial establishment by foreign financial-service providers through acquisition.

On the other hand, globalization increases the risk of contagion,[299] with the result that a firm that might not be too interdependent to fail from a purely national perspective might be so from a global perspective. This could occur where the firm has few local obligations, but greater foreign ones. This effect raises increasing problems of externalities and collective action. In the

---

[299] *See* Jorge A. Chan-Lau, Donald J. Mathieson, & James Y. Yao, "Extreme contagion in equity markets," 51 (3) IMF Staff Papers, 386 (2004); Olivier De Bandt & Philipp Hartmann, "Systemic Risk: A Survey" (European Central Bank Working Paper Series No. 35, November 2000). Retrieved from http://www.ecb.int/pub/pdf/scpwps/ecbwp035.pdf.

crisis, the collapse of Lehman Brothers destabilized many other financial institutions, and American International Group (AIG) raised the spectre that its failure could damage European banks and insurance companies, as well as money market funds.

Globalization can also increase risk by making the process of regulation, including supervision and enforcement, more difficult. Increasing globalization places pressure on regulators to coordinate, and to assist one another in surveillance and enforcement. In order to encourage such assistance, it may be useful to harmonize rules.

Finally, the very mobility of capital that is a hallmark of globalization could be damaging in a procyclical way, or even in an inaccurate way, where a run on particular financial institutions, or on financial institutions in a particular country, might be precipitated or accentuated by mobility, with the result that those financial institutions or that country is destabilized.

## II) Technological Advance

Finance is dependent on information and communications, as well as on information processing. As technological advance proceeds, it not only contributes powerfully to globalization, but to greater efficiency and competition by reducing transaction costs, reducing information asymmetry, and increasing effective market access. This effect would be expected to reduce margins and, along with globalization, make finance not only systematically cheaper but also more homogeneous in price. Technology and globalization promote the effectiveness of the law of one price.

One approach to financial regulation would take advantage of decentralized technologically structured networks to procure, organize, and disseminate information.[300] This might help address information asymmetries in connection with bank regulation, as well as in connection with securities offerings. Indeed, as information asymmetries are reduced, we can expect even greater disintermediation in financial markets.

## III) Financial Innovation

It is true that the 2008 financial crisis has given financial innovation a bad name, and it may be that certain types of innovation have increased risk, but it is important to remember that financial innovation has increased welfare

---

[300] See "Rethinking Financial Regulation: Simple Transparency, Open Source, and XML," Next Big Future (Mar. 14, 2009). Retrieved from http://nextbigfuture.com/2009/03/rethinking-financial-regulation-simple.html.

broadly and deeply by allowing worthwhile projects that could not have been developed prior to financial innovation to be financed after innovation, and by broadly allowing more efficient financial markets. It is tempting to say that we have already innovated enough and that all future innovation would only add to excessive complexity and uncompensated risk. However, just as with innovation in physical technology, it is to be expected that innovation in financial services will improve our lives in the future. Consider for example the rise of microfinance, which is still to some extent a frontier, but which is promising for alleviation of poverty.

What are the dangers of innovation? Innovation often involves increased complexity, making each step of the regulatory process more difficult, and making it more and more difficult for different types of market intermediaries or consumers to evaluate financial services products. Innovation in investments will require intellectual suitability standards that forbid sale to investors who lack the ability to evaluate the relevant complexity, or alternatively, requirements for prospectuses to explain the complexity in a usable fashion. Greater innovation will therefore put greater pressure on regulation.

Innovation through swaps, derivatives, and other devices has already had significant impacts on globalization, by allowing financing to cross borders more easily. Globalization, in turn, has resulted in greater need for innovation in order to allow companies to reduce the risks involved in international payments flows – the development of the swaps market was initially driven by the desire for arbitrage across markets. Furthermore, advances in information technology allow for greater innovation.

The existence of government safety nets is deeply problematic from an incentive standpoint, and gives rise to problematic regulatory efforts, such as capital requirements and powers regulation. However, the rise of information technology and financial innovation has moved us far beyond the days of banks as principally depositary institutions and payments facilitators. It may be that technology and innovation have made deposit insurance less important, making it easier to apply market disciplines that were not operative under the shadow of government safety nets for financial institutions. Under these circumstances, it may be time to wean most of the financial architecture off government support, providing for narrow banks or even something akin to a postal savings system to allow consumers who require or choose governmental support to obtain it, at reduced returns. Obviously, the implementation of such a solution would need to be evaluated separately, and customized, for each adopting state. However, if some states were to withdraw their safety nets and others did not, this might raise issues of externalization of risk and regulatory competition.

## IV) Economic Growth

Economic growth can be expected broadly to increase demand for financial services. It can also be expected to increase globalization and education, and enhance information infrastructure. Thus, economic growth can be expected to increase the need for enhanced regulation in emerging market states, and also increase the need for international cooperation. Greater homogenization in the economic position of states, and in their needs for financial markets, may make harmonization of financial regulation more attractive.

## G) APPLYING THE SUBSIDIARITY METHODOLOGY TO INTERNATIONAL FINANCIAL REGULATION COOPERATION

In this section, I examine how the reasons for international cooperation, issues of fragmentation, and expected future developments – all previously discussed – affect possible regulation of: (a) executive compensation; (b) capital regulation; (c) powers regulation; (d) safety nets, bailouts, and resolution; (e) disclosure; and (f) rating agencies. Here, given an understanding of national policy in light of what we now know about the 2008 financial crisis and expected changes, we are able to evaluate the possible utility of international cooperation.

## I) Corporate Governance and Compensation

In connection with existing and proposed caps on bankers' pay, banks have argued that caps in one jurisdiction will cause highly skilled personnel to move to jurisdictions that lack caps. Given the competition among financial centers for the tax revenues, economic growth benefits, and prestige that comes with dominance as a financial center, it is not difficult to imagine that states would find it difficult to impose pay caps unilaterally, at least over the long-term. Failure of states to coordinate with respect to pay caps would be a test of whether the market, supplemented by corporate governance systems, is capable of providing adequate discipline with respect to compensation.

If it were possible to devise compensation systems that provide adequate incentives for performance without incentives to take on excessive risk, then assuming effective corporate governance or market mechanisms, we would expect investors to discipline firms using these mechanisms and avoid excessive compensation.[301] Market disciplines by virtue of investor voice or exit seem

---

[301] *But see* George Akerlof & Rachel Kranton, "It is Time to Treat Wall Street Like Main Street," *Financial Times* (Feb. 24, 2010). Retrieved from http://www.ft.com/intl/cms/s/0/

to have failed to prevent corporate governance problems. Nor has regulatory competition provided an effective response.

It might be argued that if it is impossible for the market to devise such systems, then it is likely to be equally impossible for governments to square that particular circle. Therefore, this argument would run, governmentally imposed caps are likely to provide inefficiently low incentives for performance. Whether compensation restrictions are nevertheless valuable because they also avoid offering excessive incentives to take on risk would depend on the magnitude of each effect. An opposing argument would point to information asymmetries that make it difficult for shareholders to evaluate the effects of compensation arrangements, or to broader social externalities that would not be taken into account by shareholders in policing compensation arrangements.

Corporate governance problems might have prevented the development of systems under which leading executives would have been required to bear greater downside risk, such as systems providing for deferred payment of bonuses in the form of equity or subordinated debt, with retention obligations.[302] Finally, the correct blend of incentives would depend to some extent on the social, legal, and financial context in which each firm operates. There is therefore likely to be some cross-national diversity in the optimal response.

So, in order to craft an appropriate international response, it would be necessary to balance the utility of cross-national diversity, plus the utility of beneficial regulatory competition and experimentation that might yield a superior solution, against the possibility of adverse regulatory competition that might yield insufficient discipline on compensation. The process of negotiating an international regime would help establish the right balance, most likely in terms of essential harmonization allowing a degree of national diversity.

To the extent that the financial crisis can be understood as a failure of corporate governance, or of other national financial regulation, it suggests that mere market forces harnessed to regulatory competition are insufficient to ensure a good result. In a very real sense, we have now experienced the results of a laissez-faire approach to regulatory competition, and have found them starkly unattractive. After all, in the run-up to the crisis, investors did not broadly migrate from United States to Canadian mortgage-backed securities,

---

3a8c9e76-217c-11df-830e-00144feab49a.html (arguing that incentive compensation is less likely to improve performance than is commonly thought).

[302] *See* Financial Stability Forum, "Financial Stability Forum Principles for Sound Compensation Practices" (2009). Retrieved from http://www.financialstabilityboard.org/publications/r_0904b.pdf.

nor did they migrate to investments in firms that had sufficient capital, or that avoided risky investments.

## II) *Capital*

In the field of capital regulation, we already have an international soft law regime. There are important international regulatory aspects of capital regulation. First, because financial institution stability and broader market stability are global public goods, we would expect them to be undersupplied without a cooperative arrangement. Second, we have some experience of states engaging in competitive reductions of capital requirements in order to promote their own financial services firms. There is broad agreement also that unrestrained regulatory competition would result in inadequate capital requirements. Indeed, all of our observations with respect to powers regulation also apply to capital regulation.

So, it seems important to coordinate capital requirements for financial institutions. The Basle Committee on Bank Supervision (BCBS), acting under the auspices of the Bank for International Settlements (BIS), has done so since 1988, although the degree to which it has created a level playing field is still uncertain.[303] Indeed, we might understand the Basle process as a technique of essential harmonization, which will develop a degree of harmonization, but which has left and will leave significant latitude for national regulatory diversity. We have also found an increasing need to take account of broader types of risks. Most recently, the BCBS has found the need to focus on risk arising from choice of counterparties and magnitude of relationships with counterparties.

Furthermore, in the 2008 financial crisis, we found that financial institutions that were not subject to the Basle capital requirements were able to engage in activities in competition with financial institutions that were subject to these requirements: the so-called perimeter issue. It can also be understood as an inter-functional leakage problem. In addition, not all states have accepted the Basle capital requirements. So, there is a dual problem of regulatory competition, or leakage, by virtue of competition from entities subject to less stringent regulation, either because of functional distinction or because of jurisdictional differences.

---

[303] *See* Patricia Jackson et al., "Capital Requirements and Bank Behavior: The Impact of the Basle Accord," (Basle Committee on Banking Supervision Working Paper, No. 1, April 1999); Hal S. Scott & Shinsaku Iwahara, "In Search of a Level Playing Field: The Implementation of the Basel Accord in Japan and the United States" (Group of Thirty Occasional Paper 46, 1994).

Leakage may be addressed by further harmonization or restrictions on competition. That is, where unregulated entities seek to compete, they can be subjected to regulation – this is harmonization. The United States and other states have used national restrictions on foreign bank entry to limit the ability of weakly regulated entities to compete in the U.S. market.[304] Unilateral restrictions on competition would evidently be inconsistent with globalization, and with the liberalization of trade in financial services sought at the WTO. On the other hand, internationally sanctioned restrictions on competition might thereby be understood to be "laundered" of protectionist intent, and may serve as an appropriate "line of equilibrium" between prudential regulation and liberalization.[305] In the EU context, essential harmonization is often combined with mutual recognition; that is, under EU single-market arrangements, essential harmonization is structured as a predicate for agreements to open the markets of Member States to competition from firms in other Member States.

Any level of harmonization will raise the question of implementation, and whether national supervision and enforcement of capital requirements will yield a sufficient level of effective harmonization. Different states might supervise and enforce, and fill in the details of regulation, in different ways. These differences could undermine efforts to harmonize. One institutional response to this question would be to provide an international supervisory and enforcement mechanism that would be structured to act independently of domestic political concerns.

Finally, but by no means least important, capital requirements, leverage ratios, loan-to-value ratios, and liquidity requirements may be utilized by regulators to reduce the possibility and magnitude of asset bubbles. It is important to note that this macroeconomic rationale is a distinct function for these types of regulation, but these types of regulation seem well-designed for this function.[306] Furthermore, this rationale and function suggests that within particular governments, it may be appropriate for monetary policy makers to be in charge of at least these components of regulation. However, the dual function of these types of regulation might suggest a dual responsibility, with the minimum requirements being set as the higher of the requirements laid down by the prudential regulator or monetary policy maker.

---

[304] *See* the Foreign Bank Supervision Enhancement Act, 12 U.S.C. § 3101.

[305] Appellate Body Report, "United States – Import Prohibition of Certain Shrimp and Shrimp Products (US – Shrimp)," WT/DS58/AB/R (Nov. 6, 1998).

[306] Stijn Claessens et al., "Lessons and Policy Implications from the Global Financial Crisis," 17 (IMF Working Paper No. 10/44, February 2010). Retrieved from http://ssrn.com/abstract=1562412.

## III) Powers

Putting aside for a moment corporate governance problems and perverse incentives that may derive from a safety net and compensation schemes, the greater a financial institution's powers, the more profitable it is likely to be. This is because one would not expect a fully market-disciplined financial institution to exercise powers that are not profitable, taking full account of risk. So the powers that would be exercised absent regulatory restrictions are likely to increase profits. Conversely, under these assumptions, regulatory restrictions decrease profits, and financial resilience.

Therefore, under these assumptions, a financial institution exclusively regulated by a jurisdiction that is more liberal in connection with powers regulation can be expected to be more efficient, and more competitive, than a more constrained financial institution. What is more, even where we relax the assumption of full market discipline by allowing a governmental safety net, we can expect the beneficiary unconstrained financial institutions to be more competitive. This is because they benefit from an implicit subsidy by virtue of the government absorption of risk. So there is definitely a competitive, or pecuniary, externality arising from lax powers regulation. Moreover, this externality will often involve nonpecuniary elements, where the relevant financial institution may operate internationally and the risk of its failure may be detrimental to people outside its home jurisdiction. So, a race to the bottom may be fueled by the possibility of externalizing adverse consequences.

Barry Eichengreen recommends the establishment of a "Global Glass-Steagall" rule that would separate traditional functions of banks in terms of providing a repository for household savings and operating the payment system from riskier functions such as derivatives trading. He argues that any move along these lines would have to be global, rather than national, because of these types of externalities.[307]

Of course, at least in the general international system, as opposed to, say, the EU, there is no rule of exclusive regulation by the home country. So, as a possible alternative to a Global Glass-Steagall, a potential host country could block market entry by the laxly regulated foreign financial institution. On the other hand, however, there are incentives for states to reduce inefficient or even merely uncompetitive regulation. As noted, states such as the United States that formerly imposed greater limits on the powers of their institutions found them disadvantaged in terms of operations in more lax markets, where the

---

[307] Barry Eichengreen, "Out of the Box Thoughts About the International Financial Architecture" (IMF Working Paper WP/09/116, 2009). Retrieved from http://www.imf.org/external/pubs/ft/wp/2009/wp09116.pdf.

U.S. financial institutions might have enjoyed a broader range of powers. Thus, unilateral action alone, by virtue of market access rules, does not appear to be sufficient to establish appropriate rules. Furthermore, it may be difficult to distinguish such unilateral action from protectionism.

Therefore, discourse on the basis of regulatory expertise, toward multilateral essential harmonization, seems appropriate in this area, again, assuming that we are able to overcome uncertainty as to appropriate regulatory action. Of course, there is another type of uncertainty that is more difficult to overcome: uncertainty regarding the appropriateness of a particular regulatory rule across different legal, financial, and social systems. However, under circumstances of increasing globalization, greater homogenization and greater mobility of abuse will militate toward essential harmonization of financial regulation rules in this area.

To the extent that we continue to operate under uncertainty regarding the appropriate extent of powers regulation, diversity may allow us to learn from further experience. On the other hand, where we believe that diversity is driven more by externalization than by good-faith regulatory views, there can be no assurance that diversity will be beneficial. By contrast, if there were no uncertainty that principal trading by financial institutions that benefit from a safety net is in theory and practice highly likely to cause such financial institutions to take on excessive risk, there would be a strong argument for international harmonization of a restrictive rule.

## IV) Safety Nets, Bailouts, and Resolution

Deposit insurance is a critical part of a government safety net, and would obviously reduce financing costs for beneficiary banks. During the crisis, modifications of deposit insurance by Ireland provoked concerns regarding regulatory competition, and speedy coordination within Europe.

As we have seen, much of the need for bank regulation stems from the fact that banks in many contexts benefit from a government safety net. If government, either legally or practically, cannot allow a bank to fail, then there is a critical incentive problem that must be addressed. In addition, governments find themselves in a time inconsistency bind, in which they may wish to say ex ante that they will not bail out a bank, but ex post are unable to avoid doing so. Of course, to the extent that banks or their owners understand this bind, they will take advantage of it.

Strangely, in the 2008 financial crisis, only a handful of major U.S. financial institutions had their equity holders wiped out. The equity holders of Citigroup and Goldman Sachs, for example, were bailed out when the government might instead have decided to take over full equity ownership. However, even if equity holders were wiped out when their banks fail, this would not fully address the incentive problem. As long as they have the opportunity to profit from risk, where there are external losses – such as to the financial system in general or the economy – they will not have sufficient incentives to take care. So, it is not just a corporate governance problem, but a regulatory problem to determine how to ensure that bank owners take full account of the social cost of bank operations.

During the crisis, questions arose in Europe regarding the extent to which government bailouts of their financial institutions might be considered illegal subsidies. In an open letter to the *Financial Times*, dated April 22, 2009, the EU Directorate General for Competition made the following statements:

> We are applying the tried and tested code of good economic governance that the EC Treaty's state aid rules represent to ensure four things: 1) that banks receive sufficient support to avoid financial meltdown; 2) that Member States' cures for their own banks do not put those banks in an artificially advantageous competitive position that would kill off banks in other Member States; 3) that banks are restructured to ensure their future long-term viability so that the mistakes of the past are not repeated, that taxpayers' money does not disappear down a black hole and that lending to the real economy is secured; 4) that the Single Market is preserved, with no discriminatory conditions attached to aid and no barriers to entry for cross-border banking. This is because the Single Market is crucial to ensuring Europe's economic recovery.

Resolution or bankruptcy proceedings for multinational financial institutions present special cooperation problems.[308] During the 2008 crisis, we saw the example of UK authorities "ring-fencing" assets of Icelandic banks available in the UK, for the benefit of UK depositors; German authorities ring-fencing Lehman Brothers' assets in Germany; and Lehman Brothers' insolvency being addressed in both U.S. and UK courts. Few bailouts, resolutions, or bankruptcy proceedings were internationally coordinated, and there were often powerful political incentives to secure local assets in order to maximize returns to domestic claimants. On the other hand, we saw the U.S. bailout of AIG

---

[308] International Monetary Fund and World Bank, "An Overview of the Legal, Institutional, and Regulatory Framework for Bank Insolvency," (April 17, 2009) (prepared by the staffs of the IMF and WB). Retrieved from http://www.imf.org/external/np/pp/eng/2009/041709.pdf (mentioning a forthcoming report on the issue); Working Group on Reinforcing International Cooperation and Promoting Integrity in Financial Markets (WG2), Final Report (Mar. 27, 2009). Retrieved from http://www.astrid-online.it/Dossier-d1/Documenti/The-London/G20_wg2_27_03_09.pdf; Basle Commission on Banking Supervision, "Report and Recommendations of the Cross-Border Bank Resolution Group" (Mar. 2010). Retrieved from http://www.bis.org/publ/bcbs169.pdf.

conferring a remarkable positive externality on Europe, by virtue of the fact that it prevented many European banks from failing.

In resolution and bankruptcy proceedings, the classic tension between territoriality and universality will continue to play itself out, representing the tension between local public policy preferences and local claimants on the one hand, and cross-border fairness and comity on the other hand. This tension has been difficult to address in ordinary bankruptcy, and will raise similar issues in financial institution resolution. At the London Summit in April 2009, the G-20 leaders welcomed action by the IMF, Financial Stability Board (FSB), World Bank, and BCBS to develop an international framework for cross-border bank resolutions. Although no formal action has been taken at the date of this writing, the BCBS issued a set of recommendations in 2010.[309]

## V) Securities Disclosure Regulation

Because issuers and underwriters located in one jurisdiction might be able to sell securities to investors located in another, there are significant issues of externalities and public goods in connection with securities law reform. For example, if the United States were to establish a disclosure rule requiring detailed information regarding loan-level data,[310] including analysis of the probability of default and the magnitude of default that would exceed the applicable credit support, financing costs for U.S. issuers might be higher or lower. They might be higher if this information is not valued in the market, and the requirement provides only costs without benefits to the issuers. They might be lower to the extent that this information is valued in the market, and the resolution of relevant uncertainty allows for cheaper financing.

If the financing costs are higher, but the social value of this disclosure is greater than the incremental costs, the United States would be conferring a positive externality on foreign beneficiaries. On the other hand, another state that did not establish this type of regulation would be conferring a negative externality on foreign-securities purchasers. If the financing costs are lower, then it might be possible for U.S. issuers to capture a sufficient amount of the benefits to compensate them for the increased costs of preparing the disclosure.

Economies of scale or network externalities might arise from a uniform standard worldwide, allowing investors to compare and evaluate securities

---

[309] Basle Committee on Bank Supervision, *supra* note 308.
[310] Committee on Capital Markets Regulation, "The Global Financial Crisis: A Plan for Regulatory Reform," E 22–24 (May 26, 2009). Retrieved from http://www.capmktsreg.org/pdfs/TGFC-CCMR_Report_%285-26-09%29.pdf (recommending that issuers of mortgage-backed securities be required to provide loan-level data).

without experiencing costs of dealing with different disclosure regimes. The stability that might arise from better information might be a global collective good, and therefore might be undersupplied without a cooperative agreement to supply it in concert. Future globalization, economic growth, and financial innovation will all militate toward greater cooperation in securities disclosure regulation.

## VI) Rating Agencies

Prior to the crisis, the conventional wisdom was that rating agencies would be adequately disciplined by market forces; after all, the only thing they had to sell was their reputation for integrity and diligence. For the rating agencies, it is difficult today to choose between being perceived as knaves or fools. During the boom in mortgage-backed securities, the rating agencies appear to have suffered from conflicts of interest, and perhaps competitive pressure, as well as a lack of financial foresight that allowed them to rate these securities as investment grade with insufficient regard for their dependence on prices in the housing market. Is there an international dimension to this problem? Regimes of registration, liability rules, and limitations on conflicts of interest may be somewhat useful. Here, one would also expect that there would be a race to the top. Any rating agency that can establish a good reputation should be able to sell its services, and it may be that appropriate government regulation would assist in the development of a good reputation. So it does not seem that international coordination is necessary.[311]

## H) SELECTING STRUCTURAL FEATURES IN INTERNATIONAL LAW AND ORGANIZATION

The previous analysis suggests a number of areas in which international law might be useful to establish cooperative solutions to regulatory problems. There are a number of parameters of choice in connection with the structuring of international law and organization. This section is intended to review some of the basic issues and describe some of the existing organizations that address regulation of finance.[312]

---

[311] *But see* Committee of European Securities Regulators, Press Release: "CESR Advises the European Commission to Take Steps and Offers Its Proposals to Enhance the Integrity and Quality of the Rating Process," (May 19, 2008). Retrieved from http://www.esma.europa.eu/system/files/08_404.pdf.

[312] For a useful extended analysis, *see* Eric J. Pan, "Challenge of International Cooperation and Institutional Design in Financial Supervisions: Beyond Transnational Networks," 11 Chic. J. Int'l L. 243 (2010).

## I) Hard Law, Soft Law, and Networks

There are many who believe that soft law is the best tool for international-financial-regulatory cooperation.[313] As discussed in Chapter 2, by soft law, many refer to rules that are specifically made nonbinding in formal terms. However, soft law can only be appropriate where its net benefits after costs exceed those of hard law. We would expect this to be the case where soft law can be legislated with sufficient coverage, and where there are sufficient reputational or retaliatory tools available to generate a sufficient degree of compliance.

As to the question of the ability to generate a sufficient degree of compliance, we would have to assess the magnitude of possible incentives to defect in comparison to the magnitude of incentives to comply. There certainly may be circumstances where soft law would do the trick. Networks of regulators with diffuse reciprocity and temporally linked reciprocity may provide powerful incentives. However, we would also expect to be able to identify circumstances where the incentives to defect are great enough to overcome the incentives to comply; for example, in circumstances where by doing so a state can ring-fence a sufficient portion of a failed financial institution's assets to be able to avoid a political disaster at home. It is likely that hard or formal law would carry greater incentives to comply, placing the integrity of the legal system at stake. Furthermore, with formal law, it is more natural to be able to establish formal penalties, and of course the remedies under the customary international law rules of state responsibility would operate by default.

## II) Specificity

The advantage of the EU technique of essential harmonization is that it seeks an optimum level of specificity that will allow appropriate national diversity when sufficiently addressing the relevant cooperation problem. The Basle Accord also left significant room for national diversity, and in some ways this may have diminished the utility of the Basle Accord as a tool of cooperation.

## III) Surveillance

If states are serious about compliance, regardless of whether soft or hard law is to be used, then it is necessary to have mechanisms by which to observe whether other states comply. Reporting requirements may be sufficient, or more involved mechanisms may be necessary. Much would depend on the relative incentives to defect. Furthermore, with greater penalties, less surveillance

---

[313] Chris Brummer, "Why Soft Law Dominates International Finance – And Not Trade," 13 J. Int'l Econ. L. 623–43 (2010).

is necessary. Surveillance may be carried out directly by an international organization, be done by individual member states acting on their own, or be effected through a process of peer review, as suggested by the Financial Stability Board.[314]

### IV) International Dispute Settlement

Experience in certain other areas where states can externalize costs to other states, such as the regulation of trade and foreign investment, shows that dispute settlement can be necessary to clarify what are necessarily incomplete international law obligations, and to establish the predicate for and limit the scope of retaliation. So, if German banks examine the way that Japan applies international capital requirements or powers regulation – or the way it distributes assets in a resolution – and finds a violation of international legal obligations, it would seem appropriate to give the German government – or the European Commission – a formal forum for complaint and dispute settlement.

### V) Adaptation to Change

In order to avoid holding a Maginot Line, and allowing the causes of future crises to evade regulation, it will be necessary to continue to be vigilant regarding growing risks, as well as having the adaptability to address them. Thus, international law or organization in this area must have the capacity to observe, analyze, and adapt as necessary. Normal methods of making international law by custom or treaty are likely to be too slow, and too politically charged, to be feasible. Rather, some degree of delegation to a regulatory agency appears necessary, combined with the resources and tools to promote effective action.

### VI) Economies of Scale and Scope

There may be important benefits that can be obtained by sharing regulatory capacity among states in particular areas. For example, smaller countries may benefit from economies of scale by sharing regulatory capacity among themselves, or with larger countries. Insofar as financial services operations are

---

[314] Financial Stability Board, "FSB Framework for Strengthening Adherence to International Standards" (Jan. 9, 2010). Retrieved from http://www.financialstabilityboard.org/publications/r_100109a.pdf.

increasingly global, although the default structure of regulation is national, modifications to regulation to make it more international may yield important benefits. One significant benefit is in the ability to engage in coordinated international surveillance and audit, in order to identify accounting irregularities, other violations of rules, or defalcation.

There may be important economies of scope that can be obtained from combining different financial-services regulation functions. Not only would this allow more coordinated regulation of financial conglomerates, but it would also make it easier to identify perimeter problems and leakage. Furthermore, to the extent that identification of fragmentation shows relationships and synergies between prudential regulation of financial services and macroeconomic regulation, development policy, investment regulation, or trade, it may be possible to capture further economies of scope.

## VII) Organizations

Once states determine what types of commitments for cooperation would be appropriate, they will be able to determine what organizational features are appropriate to support those commitments. They will be able to determine whether to house the commitments within an existing international organization, establish a new organization, or alternatively, split responsibilities among different international organizations.

There are a number of international organizations with responsibilities relating to prudential regulation of finance. It is worthwhile to consider the existing responsibilities of these organizations, as well as their capacities and competences, in connection with an assessment of the possibilities for international cooperation with respect to prudential regulation.

Eichengreen has suggested the establishment of a World Financial Organization to serve in the area of finance much as the WTO serves in trade: as a nexus in which states could negotiate, implement, and enforce specific commitments.[315] Concentrating functions would be helpful, but a clearer argument must be made regarding cooperation needs and institutional responses. To the extent that more law is needed, perhaps legislative capacity utilizing majority voting would be appropriate. To the extent that state-contingent international legal rules are desirable, as discussed in Chapter 8, applying rules differently to distinct situations, then adjudication may be appropriate. If enforcement will be assisted by independent declaration of disputed rights and responsibilities, then again, adjudication may be appropriate. I discuss these issues in Chapter 11.

---

[315] Eichengreen, *supra* note 307.

## I) CHAPTER CONCLUSION

It will take some time for economic historians to sort out the causes of the recent crisis. However, some major themes of possible national reform are emerging. States must carefully review the scope of their commitment to bail out financial institutions. They must make firm commitments not to bail out certain financial institutions. Those financial institutions that benefit from the safety net must be firmly regulated as to corporate governance, capital, and powers. Corporate governance must be structured to ensure that managers manage in the best interests of the firm, including its strict compliance with regulatory requirements. Capital requirements must be restructured to minimize their procyclical effects in downturns. Securities offerings of complex financial products must be accompanied by reasonably accessible disclosure that addresses risks with specific analysis, and not simply boilerplate warnings. Similarly, rating agencies must incorporate specific risk analysis into their ratings.

Because of existing globalization and future increases in globalization, financial innovation, and information technology and growth, these reforms will require greater international coordination. The international coordination is necessitated by increasing capacity to externalize risk, as well as increasing scope of financial global public goods.

We have an increasingly global society. This society must recognize the role of government regulation in providing and protecting efficient capital markets that will allow us, individually and together, to save and invest efficiently for important projects. There is no evidence yet of a beneficial regulatory competition in the case of the crisis. Shareholders and creditors do not seem systematically to have identified regulatory inadequacies, migrating to stronger regulatory environments. So, competition-based discipline on lax regulation seems not to have worked. Further research will be needed in order to determine whether just the opposite occurred: a race to inappropriate laxity. In order for each state to make its citizens better off, and to reduce risk, we must work together to avoid cross-border harm that is not fully taken into account in national decision making, and to avoid detrimental regulatory competition. We must work together to make rules, but we must recognize that our vision of the future is limited, so we must establish institutions that will allow us to revise our rules, and our institutions, as necessitated by unfolding change.

# 9 Economic Liberalization: Trade, Intellectual Property, Migration, and Investment

*Economic globalization* is the integration of markets for trade in goods and services, labor, capital, and intellectual property. Free movement of the factors of production generally increase overall public welfare, and constitute public goods. Although the optimal extent of protection of intellectual property depends on the context, protection of intellectual property can also increase welfare, and constitute a public good. However, it is possible for states to confer negative externalities on other states through the imposition of barriers to movement of these factors, or through the failure to protect intellectual property. Furthermore, each reduction of barriers to trade produces both winners and losers, so each reduction is asymmetric in its benefits. This chapter evaluates how international law can respond to these externalities and distributive concerns, and promote the efficient creation of global public goods. Free movement of factors and protection of intellectual property cannot be separated from one another, nor can they be separated from other global concerns, including protection of the environment, human rights, health, and security.

As in other areas, when we examine the reasons for international law in this area, we must recognize the distinction between economic welfare (public interest) and political welfare (public choice). As in Chapter 3, we assume that economic welfare is one vector in determining political welfare, and that in different states there will be different degrees of congruence between economic welfare and political welfare.

In the fields of economic liberalization addressed in this chapter, we see important reasons for establishing international law, and for establishing some components of international organization. These reasons will grow as potential globalization increases because of economic and technological change, making legal regulation more valuable. In important ways, as integration becomes more extensive, international law becomes more necessary to regulate the state's exercise of traditional sovereign prerogatives, such as health regulation of products and services, or immigration.

In this field, however, we see the development of nuanced, state-contingent international law, whereby the application of restrictions is conditioned on the existence of particular states of affairs. Power is not delegated by states wholesale, but only where necessary to avoid harm to other states that exceeds the value of the power delegated. In order to maximize the net benefits of these transactions, it is sometimes necessary to distinguish in a nuanced, state-contingent way between circumstances in which power should be delegated and those in which it should not. That is, in order to determine what activities are legal ex post, states may enter into treaties that can be assimilated to incomplete contracts. Under these incomplete contracts, adjudication may be used to assess the relevant costs and benefits, in order to determine whether a particular activity shall be permitted. The result is nuanced, state contingent, and dynamic subsidiarity.

## A) ROLE OF COOPERATION IN TRADE IN GOODS AND SERVICES

There has been much commentary on the economics and political economy of trade in goods and services. I now adapt the leading economic and political economy theories to develop a rationale for cooperation, and international law, in the area of trade in goods and services.

### I) *Tariffs*

Global welfare would be increased substantially if all countries removed all explicit barriers to trade in goods and services. (With respect to regulatory barriers that have other purposes, it may be that welfare could be impaired by removing them.) Of course, there are political barriers to such a move, partly because whereas global welfare would increase substantially, particular industries and workers would experience a reduction in welfare. Although we know that there would be enough of an increase in global welfare to compensate those who were harmed, we also know that states generally lack a mechanism to provide effective compensation.

### II) *A Welfare-Based Cooperation Problem*

Moreover, we also know that some states – those with market power – have the ability to use tariff barriers to improve their own welfare at the expense of foreign persons. States with market (terms of trade) power in a particular good are able to affect the prices charged by exporters to their markets. By setting a tariff that causes these exporters to absorb some of the costs of the tariff, they are able to transfer wealth from these exporters to the importing state's treasury. So, to the extent that a state has this ability, it can improve its own welfare at the expense of the welfare of the exporters.[316]

Thus, among states with this ability, the tariff-setting decision may have the attributes of a prisoner's dilemma. Of course, the payoffs in the prisoner's dilemma game are simply assumptions consistent with the idea that each state may harm the other, but if both avoid harming the other by liberalizing, they would both be better off than if both harm each other. For each state acting individually, the dominant solution is to impose a tariff, because it is better off imposing a tariff no matter what the other state does. However, because each state acts in accordance with its dominant solution, both are worse off than if both liberalize. Thus, the function of international law in this context is clear: provide for penalties or incentives that will change the payoffs sufficiently to cause both states to liberalize.

## III) A Public Choice-Based Cooperation Problem

Of course, with respect to any particular good, only some states have the type of market power required by the terms of trade-based theory of welfare-based trade barriers set out previously. So, we might posit that a public choice or political welfare-based model is needed to explain protectionism in states that lack market power, and that this model is also capable, a fortiori, of adding to the explanation of protectionism in states that have market power. This public-choice model, on the basis of the initial ideas of Mancur Olson,[317] generally assumes that manufacturing interests, including firms and labor, are better organized for political influence than are consumer interests. Thus, states tend to prefer protectionism – by tariffs or other means – over liberalization. However, states also have firms and labor interests that seek export opportunities – that desire liberalization abroad. If they are able to include in the domestic political matrix this desire for liberalization abroad, and link it to domestic consumer desires for liberalization at home, liberalization would

---

[316] Ossa develops a model that shows that: (i) for the United States, the optimal tariff using its terms of trade power averages 66 percent; (ii) with retaliation in a trade war, the world average tariffs would be 63 percent; and (iii) the restraint of this behavior under the WTO produces a welfare increase that averages 4.4 percent. Ralph Ossa, "Trade Wars and Trade Talks with Data," (Working Paper, July 11, 2011). Retrieved from http://faculty.chicagobooth.edu/ralph.ossa/research/trade%20wars.pdf.

[317] Mancur Olson, *The Logic of Collective Action: Public Goods and the Theory of Groups* (1965).

have a greater chance of overcoming protection in the domestic political process. Chapter 3 used the domestic politics of trade to illustrate the domestic political sources of international law.

Of course, from the national government's standpoint, the greatest political support would arise if it is able to obtain liberalization abroad, declining to provide liberalization at home. Therefore, the public-choice model also suggests a game with the characteristics of a prisoner's dilemma. Again, the function of international law is relatively clear: modify the payoffs so as to cause states to achieve the (in this case, politically) efficient equilibrium of liberalization. So, it makes sense for states to enter into binding agreements to reduce tariffs, and we see this action in the General Agreement on Tariffs and Trade (GATT) beginning in 1947, and in the WTO. However, with the rise of the regulatory state, there are other types of measures that can have similar protective effects, and that are more difficult to address.

B) NON-TARIFF BARRIERS

The most intractable type of nontariff barrier is a regulatory measure or tax that either discriminates against imported goods or that otherwise disproportionately burdens commerce. Domestic regulatory autonomy can be used to restrict trade, and therefore there will be circumstances in which international legal restrictions on domestic regulatory autonomy will make sense. However, much more nuance is required than in addressing tariff barriers.

From a social-welfare perspective, national product regulations are measures that can be justified as instruments to deal with specific market failures.[318] Possible rationales for product regulation include imperfect information, uncertainty, market power, and other sources of externalities in production or consumption. Although product regulation can improve welfare if it succeeds in internalizing spillovers at acceptable transaction costs (i.e., improves allocative efficiency), this need not be the purpose or outcome. The intervention may also allow incumbent firms in an industry to exploit market power. Regulation may reduce the contestability of a market, because potential entrants find it less attractive to compete or enter. The greater the barriers to entry created by the regulation for foreign firms, the greater the beneficial profit-shifting effect of the product regulation measure for the domestic firms or industry, all other things equal. Thus, regulation can be employed strategically to shift rents.

---

[318] For a more complete discussion, see Bernard Hoekman & Joel P. Trachtman, "Continued Suspense: WTO Discipline of Domestic Regulation and the Relationship Between Non-Discrimination and Risk Assessment," 9 (1) *World Trade Rev.* 151 (2010).

The negative trade effect of an *efficient* nondiscriminatory product regulation – that is, one that addresses the information problems or consumption externalities that give rise to market failure at a global cost that is less than the global benefit – on foreign producers is not something that should be dealt with through a change in the regulation that is applied, as (by construction – given that the regulation is efficient) that would result in the local externality no longer being efficiently offset.[319] If the problem is a local consumption externality or market failure and the product regulation deals with that problem in an efficient manner, the importing country has achieved the first best solution.

In general, given differences in circumstances, social preferences, and risk attitudes across countries, product regulation will need to differ. This is important today, but will grow less important as wealth converges over the next fifty years. It is in practice very difficult to identify what constitutes an efficient regulation, and international cooperation can induce regulating states to take into account the costs imposed on foreign persons. This suggests that international cooperation can be beneficial by increasing information and scrutiny of the effects, efficacy, and equivalence of specific product regulations.[320]

However, absent agreement that countries will accept products that meet certain minimum standards, the fact that governments are free to adopt idiosyncratic norms will always bring with it differential trade effects, as firms will confront differences in market-specific costs of contesting different foreign markets. Absent a willingness to agree to abide by international norms or accept mutual recognition (both of which may result in inefficiency at the local level), the challenge confronting trading states is to ensure that national norms indeed are directed toward dealing efficiently with national consumption externalities, taking into account effects on foreign persons.

It is easy to see how international trade law might come to address domestic regulation. After agreeing on tariff–reduction-based liberalization, trade negotiators would be correct to be concerned about defection from the agreed commitments through protectionist regulation. After all, legal restrictions do not reduce the demand for protection from competition. The first line of defense against regulatory protectionism is to agree not to discriminate in the application of domestic tax and regulatory measures (i.e., abide by national treatment), but there is both de jure and de facto discrimination. De jure discrimination, which is generally explicit in its nature, is relatively easy to

---

[319] *See* Joel P. Trachtman, "Trade and... Problems, Cost-Benefit Analysis and Subsidiarity," 9 *Eur. J. Int'l L.* 32 (1998).

[320] *See* Robert Howse, "Democracy, Science and Free Trade: Risk Regulation on Trial at the World Trade Organization," 98 *Mich. L. Rev.* 2329 (2000).

identify and prohibit. De facto discrimination is more difficult to identify reliably, because it is possible to write facially general rules that have differential, and protectionist, effects.

Horn notes that a complete contract that specifies permissible policies in all possible states of the world is simply infeasible: the costs of writing and enforcing any such agreement are prohibitive even assuming heroically that governments are able to specify ex ante all the regulatory needs that may arise in the future.[321] The provisions of international trade agreements that require national treatment, or require proportionality[322] or a scientific basis, can be regarded as components of a state-contingent contract, delegating to the dispute-settlement process the task of determining the state. However, these provisions refer to a state that is described by virtue of conditions such as like products, less-favorable treatment, least trade-restrictive alternative, lack of scientific basis, and so forth. The implication is that adjudication or other decision making will be required on a case-by-case basis to determine the degree to which state contingencies result in beneficial internalization of externalities – the degree to which the regulation is justified from a welfare standpoint.

Horn develops a model in which for given tariff commitments, a marginally binding national treatment provision will increase government welfare, but moving beyond this and further tightening restrictions on national autonomy may reduce welfare. The problem caused by tariff bindings combined with a hypothesized strict national treatment rule (one that is unable to use legitimate regulatory categories to distinguish between products) is that insofar as imported products cause externalities, governments can no longer use the tariff to offset these. Instead they must use domestic instruments, which – because of national treatment – must apply equally to local and imported goods. As a result, an importing country that is being forced to abide by an equal domestic taxation or regulation requirement will set a uniform tax or regulation that is, from an international-efficiency point of view, too high with regard to the domestic product, and too low with regard to the imported product. As a consequence, provided the externality problem is sufficiently severe, the imposition of national treatment may be internationally inefficient.[323] Horn explains that

---

[321] Henrik Horn, "National Treatment in the GATT," 96 (1) *Am. Econ. Rev.* 394 (2006).

[322] A proportionality requirement in this context would ask whether the national measure is the least restrictive means to achieve the purported goal.

[323] Costinot develops a model showing that national treatment results in standards that are excessively restrictive, because of failure to take account of the interests of foreign producers exporting to the regulating market. On the other hand, under a regime of mutual recognition – in which each state undertakes to accept as satisfactory the regulation of the home state of the exported

information about government preferences is at the core of the problem that national treatment is intended to solve:

> If we were to assume that such information [regarding government preferences in order to determine the first-best solution] is verifiable, in the context of the present model there would exist an even simpler solution than the market access rule: a provision simply requesting the parties to "set internal taxes to their first-best levels.... Presumably, the reason why we do not see such a provision lies in the difficulty to prove whether a set of taxes that benefits domestic interests, and harms foreign interests, is chosen to exploit neighbors, or because the importing government's preferences are such as to make the chosen taxes efficient from a global point of view.[324]

The question raised by Horn is precisely the one discussed regarding the ability to determine whether domestic regulators are engaging in first-best regulation or protectionism. How do we determine the intent behind de facto discrimination? How do we get closer to a requirement to set internal regulation at its first-best level? Although there is no international–trade-law requirement that domestic regulators set internal regulations to their first-best levels, proportionality or scientific-basis requirements achieve a closer approximation of this test than mere national treatment. Indeed, national-treatment analyses as applied in international trade law have shaded over into assessments of proportionality or scientific basis.[325]

The negotiators of a trade agreement might decide that the history of application of national-treatment rules provides too much flexibility to judges to determine whether a national measure is impermissibly de facto discriminatory, and inevitably requires the judges to evaluate the good faith, or the prudential regulatory basis, of the domestic regulation. It is possible, however, to give the judges more guidance, and to discipline a broader range of national measures where it may otherwise be difficult to identify discrimination and determine the first-best measure. In addition to prohibiting discrimination, the negotiators might agree that they will also make sure that a certain category of regulatory measures where they expect a high level of protectionism – domestic political pressure for protection – is supported by a prudential regulatory basis – that it has an objective and sufficient non-protectionist aim or purpose. They might agree that all regulation in this category will be required to meet a test of proportionality or have a scientific basis.

good – standards will be too low, owing to a race-to-the-bottom effect, in which the regulating government fails to account for foreign externalities. See Arnaud Costinot, "A Comparative Institutional Analysis of Agreements on Product Standards," 75 J. Int'l Econ. 197 (2008).

[324] Horn, *supra* note 321, at 402.     [325] See Hoekman & Trachtman, *supra* note 318.

As states develop increasingly complex economies, with increasingly sophisticated technology, we can expect a greater total amount of national regulation. As tariffs are progressively reduced or eliminated, we can also expect states to turn to product regulation as an alternative method of protectionism. With increasing globalization, we can also expect increasing backlash, seeking protection from foreign competition. Thus, it is to be expected that these additional types of international legal restrictions – antidiscrimination obligations, proportionality requirements, or requirements for a scientific basis – will be increasingly important. In order to promote trade and increase welfare, states will increasingly need to turn to more refined international legal devices to restrain regulatory protectionism.

## C) INCOMPLETE CONTRACTS

To varying degrees, both negative integration in the form of national treatment, proportionality requirements, or scientific-basis requirements, and positive integration such as the harmonization requirements of the TRIPS Agreement (to be discussed), can be seen as attempts to internalize what would otherwise be policy externalities imposed by the pursuit of policies based purely on national interest. However, in the case of each national treatment, proportionality, scientific basis, and harmonization, there is always a degree of contractual incompleteness: it is impossible to specify explicitly the treatment of every anticipated circumstance, and it is also impossible ex ante to anticipate every possible circumstance. How can we explain the existing level of incompleteness of the WTO "contract" with respect to national treatment, proportionality, scientific-basis requirements, or harmonization? What are the implications of this incompleteness?

Horn, Maggi, and Staiger have argued that the WTO can be viewed as an incomplete contract whose form is endogenously determined.[326] They note that the WTO agreement displays both rigidity as well as discretion: whereas trade instruments such as tariffs are largely bound (and therefore rigid), domestic instruments are largely left to the discretion of governments, except that they have to abide by specified standards, such as national treatment.

Horn, Maggi, and Staiger examine the GATT, finding that it includes an interesting combination of "*rigidity*, in the sense that contractual obligations are largely insensitive to changes in economic (and political) conditions, and *discretion*, in the sense that governments have substantial leeway in the setting of many policies." They observe that "there is a *wide array of*

[326] *Id.*

*policy instruments* – border measures and especially 'domestic' measures – that should be constrained to keep in check each government's incentives to act opportunistically."[327]

Horn, Maggi, and Staiger argue that national discretion is less likely to require constraint where domestic instruments are less available to manipulate the terms of trade, or where the importing country has less market power in connection with the imported good. Under these circumstances, we would expect less use of domestic measures to manipulate the terms of trade, and therefore require less legal constraint.

Under significant uncertainty as to the future state of affairs, states would wish to establish complex state-contingent contracts. In the area of domestic regulation, the magnitude of domestic benefits from the regulation, and the magnitude of harm to foreign persons, is uncertain. However, contracting is costly, limiting the ability to specify state contingencies in detail. On the other hand, by specifying general standards, and delegating to dispute settlement bodies the responsibility to apply these standards, states are able to include complex state contingency in their contracts, with significantly less variable contracting costs.

The need for state-contingent contracting in order to promote efficiency in the trade-off between domestic regulation and international trade suggests that dispute settlement in international trade will continue to be an important institutional feature. That is, it is not so much that there are unexpected disputes because of a failure to agree clearly on specific rules. Rather, it is efficient not to agree on more specific rules, and to leave determination under specific circumstances to dispute settlement. In these cases, it is better to have general standards rather than more specific rules.

## D) INTELLECTUAL PROPERTY

The establishment of certain minimum levels of intellectual–property-right (IPR) protection might be seen as an even deeper level of discipline on domestic or "behind the border" regulation. As previously discussed, the first level of discipline is a requirement of national treatment,[328] whereas a second level of discipline is a proportionality requirement or scientific-basis requirement.[329] A third level is a requirement for harmonization, as was included for IPRs in the TRIPS Agreement established during the Uruguay Round of trade negotiations, which concluded in 1994. The TRIPS Agreement resulted in a

---

[327] *Id.* at 394.
[328] Horn, *supra* note 321.
[329] Hoekman &Trachtman, *supra* note 318.

significant increase in the degree of IPR protection available in most of the developing world. These three levels do not neatly map into either magnitudes of discipline or degrees of specificity of obligation. However, all three may be understood, similar to much international law in this area, as addressing policy externalities that may arise from actions of an importing regulating state. Harmonization of IPRs addresses a somewhat different type of policy externality from the regulatory protectionism discussed.

As previously discussed, national treatment requirements may be understood as protecting imports from differential treatment motivated by protectionist goals, and proportionality or scientific-basis requirements might be understood either as supplementing national treatment or as imposing an additional requirement of rationality in regulation as applied to imports. These disciplines can be understood as *negative integration* in the sense that they prohibit certain types of national measures.

On the other hand, the establishment of minimum levels of IPRs under TRIPS recognizes that each state may have an incentive to enact a level of protection that falls below the globally efficient level. The fact that nations have incentives to under-protect intellectual property does not necessarily imply that it is efficient to equalize the degree of IPR protection in all nations. Indeed, although such harmonization of IPRs is called for under TRIPS, Grossman and Lai have argued convincingly that such harmonization is neither necessary nor sufficient for achieving global efficiency.[330] In other words, in an open global economy, although each nation will generally undersupply IPR protection and attempt to free ride on the protection provided by other countries, efficient IPR reform does not require all nations to adopt the same set of IPR policies, as nations are heterogeneous with respect to innovative capacity, market size, and a variety of other relevant variables.

Of course, all international law restricts the autonomy of states, and all international-trade law may be understood in terms of management of policy externalities. The TRIPS is no exception. As pointed out by Grossman and Mavroidis:

> In a non-cooperative world regime of intellectual property protection, externalities might come in two main forms. *First*, governments may have a national incentive to discriminate against the intellectual property rights of foreign citizens. This explains the requirements for national treatment that are included in *TRIPs*, and in the *Berne Convention* and *Paris Treaty* before it. *Second*, even with national treatment, national governments may choose to

---

[330] Gene M. Grossman & Edwin L.-C. Lai, "International Protection of Intellectual Property," 94(5) Am. Econ. Rev. 1635 (2004).

provide insufficient protection for intellectual property relative to the strength of protection that would be globally efficient.[331]

The consensus calculus of optimal patent protection in a closed economy follows Nordhaus's argument that the optimal policy must balance the marginal benefit of inducing more innovation against the marginal static loss imposed by extending monopoly power.[332] More recently, Grossman and Lai have provided a thorough analysis of optimal patent policies in a two-region (North-South) open-economy context. It turns out that the presence of international trade matters a great deal. More specifically, they highlight two reasons why patent protection will be too weak in an open-economy setting when countries choose policies to maximize their own welfare. These two reasons are as follows:

> *First*, national governments do not take into account in their cost-benefit calculus the benefits that accrue to foreign citizens when protection induces additional investments in intellectual property. *Second*, national governments do not consider as an offset to the static cost of granting patent and copyright protection the monopoly profits that accrue to foreign rights holders. For both these reasons, a global regime of independently chosen patent and copyright policies will provide too little incentive for investment in intellectual property relative to the aggregate reward that would maximize world welfare. In effect, countries have an incentive to free ride on the intellectual property rights protection provided by their trading partners.[333]

This is a public-goods problem. It may be that states differ in the extent to which their citizens are benefitted by either investment in intellectual property or monopoly profits of rights holders. Importantly, also, the magnitudes of: (i) the benefits to foreign citizens from investment induced by protection; and (ii) the monopoly profits that accrue to foreign rights holders are uncertain.

To some extent, intellectual-property protection below the globally efficient level would impose its policy externality in a way similar to a tariff, although the market mechanism can be rather different. By their very nature, IPRs bestow market power on rights holders. Therefore, any meaningful discussion of the effects of IPR enforcement (or the lack of it) has to recognize the market power of rights holders. This is important because all countries have the ability

---

[331] *See* Gene M. Grossman & Petros C. Mavroidis, "United States – Section 110(5) of the US Copyright Act, Recourse to Arbitration under Article 25 of the DSU: Would've or Should've? Impaired Benefits Due to Copyright Infringement," 2 (2) *World Trade Rev.* 233 (2003).

[332] *See* William D. Nordhaus, *Invention, Growth, and Welfare: A Theoretical Treatment of Technological Change* (1969).

[333] Grossman & Lai, *supra* note 330.

to affect the degree to which rights holders can exercise their market power locally, by controlling the degree of IPR protection available in their respective markets. In other words, even small countries that we would ordinarily assume to lack market power for purposes of benefiting from imposing tariffs have sufficient market power to benefit from reduced protection of IPRs.

For example, when faced with an import tariff in a foreign market characterized by market power, a monopolist will typically find it optimal to absorb some of the tariff and not pass it on entirely to foreign consumers. Although a tariff directly affects the effective price collected by a monopolist or a rights holder, the lack of IPR protection can lower the market price for the rights holder's good by creating competition in the local market. The competition created by the infringing product necessarily implies a reduction in the price of imports, allowing domestic infringers to profit at the expense of foreign intellectual-property owners. Indeed, the competition created by the failure to protect IPRs benefits local consumers in the short run and is one reason many analyses of IPR protection in a global economy find that allowing for some level of imitative activities can be in the interest of countries that do not possess significant innovative capacity themselves.

International trade agreements are generally intended to cause states to internalize policy externalities. The policy externalities that arise from domestic decisions regarding intellectual-property protection may deprive foreign intellectual-property owners of the monopoly profits they would otherwise derive from intellectual property protection. In connection with intellectual property protection, even a state that lacks traditional market power on world markets may be able to impose terms of trade externalities on other states by reducing its protection of intellectual property below the global optimum. For this reason, and because of the international public-goods aspects of intellectual property, states have incentives to undersupply intellectual property protection. At least in part, TRIPS seems to be an attempt to reduce these policy externalities, because it basically requires all WTO members to adopt the same level of IPR protection as that which prevails in the industrialized world.

Intellectual property protection is one type of domestic measure. Interestingly, IPR protection is different from normal trade measures, insofar as any state, even a state without conventional market power, can impose terms of trade externalities on exporters from other states by declining to protect their intellectual property rights. As previously noted, this is because IPRs create market power that gives individual sellers the ability to influence prices, and this ability can be manipulated by importing countries by altering the product market conditions faced by such sellers in their markets. This fact seems to accentuate the observation of Horn, Maggi, and Staiger to the effect that, with rising volumes of trade, and consequent increasing costs of allowing discretion, there is an increasing need to constrain domestic policies.[334]

E) MIGRATION

Given existing wide disparities in wage rates across borders, global welfare would be greatly increased by permitting greater mobility of labor. As wages converge, because of development,[335] the opportunity to increase global welfare through migration will diminish. However, in the next twenty to fifty years, there will still be great opportunities to increase welfare. So why is it that we do not see greater liberalization of migration, and international legal commitments for liberalization?[336]

Is the Grossman-Helpman approach to international trade relations, described in Chapter 3, adaptable to migration?[337] Migration does not display the same pattern of domestic interests as trade. In the migration context, destination-state manufacturers, both for domestic consumption and export, would generally be expected to be in favor of liberalized immigration. Facchini, Mayda, and Mishra[338] suggest that migration politics is strongly affected by political contributions by manufacturers, as well as by labor union activity. However, destination-state manufacturers may experience difficulties in organizing, as the breadth of interest in immigration could result in collective-action problems unless immigration policy is selective by sector.

Some destinations, such as the United States, EU, Canada, Australia, and other wealthy states, undoubtedly are attractive to immigrants. Part of this attraction arises from the wages that can be earned in these destinations, presumably owing to high levels of productivity. This strong attraction may give rise to market power, in the sense that supply of immigration opportunities is limited, demand for immigration opportunities is high, and the governments of the destination countries have control of entry. Do these leading destination states use market power to extract welfare gains from immigrants or from home states? Consider the following possibilities.

- *First*, states with market power in this context may exert that power by accepting immigrants and effectively denying the home state of the immigrants

[334] Henrik Horn, Giovanni Maggi, & Robert Staiger, "Trade Agreements as Endogenously Incomplete Contracts," 100 (1) *Am. Econ. Rev.* 394, 406 (2010).
[335] Spence, *supra* note 120.   [336] *See* Trachtman, *supra* note 118.
[337] Harry R. Clarke, "Entry Charges on Immigrants," 28 (2) *Int'l Migration Rev.* 338 (1994).
[338] Giovanni Facchini, Anna Maria Maida, & Prachi Mishra, "Do Interest Groups Affect Immigration?" (IMF Working Paper WP/08/244, Oct. 2008). Retrieved from http://www.imf.org/external/pubs/ft/wp/2008/wp08244.pdf (last visited Aug. 19, 2011).

the ability to tax those migrants by declining to assist in enforcement. By doing so, the destination state may impose a negative externality on the home state.

- A *second*, related, way by which states with market power may exert their power is to accept only highly skilled immigrants – those who will make a positive contribution in terms of an immigration dividend and a fiscal contribution. Thus, we can interpret brain drain as a negative externality imposed by the destination state on the home state.
- *Third*, it is also possible that destination states could use their market power to impose discriminatory taxes or other burdens on immigrants, or to deny immigrants public benefits that are available to natives, causing immigrants to give up some of the surplus from migration that they might otherwise capture.[339]

The second and third types of measures are likely to provide disincentives for migration, in a way that may reduce global welfare insofar as migration would otherwise be efficient. Indeed, it may be that a sufficient rationale for states to cooperate in this area is simply to agree to suppress these types of measures in order to increase volumes of migration, and thereby enhance global welfare. According to this rationale, states could agree to increase international migration, and thereby increase global welfare, provided that they are able to agree on the distribution of the gains.

Note, however, that the home state is not necessarily directly harmed by the destination state exercise of market power, or does not feel the full welfare loss caused by the destination-state policy, and may not be sufficiently motivated to negotiate to protect its emigrants. On the other hand, if home states sought more actively to tax their emigrants, they might understand refusal by destination states to enforce these taxes as harmful, and discrimination may reduce amounts available for remittances or to be used for investment on return. Temporary migration arrangements may provide greater incentives for home states to protect their emigrants; under these arrangements, the goal of the home state is to have migrants send remittances home and then return with capital, skills, and contacts.

As suggested, in the trade model addressing terms of trade externalities, the role of international law is to allow states credibly to commit to exercise reciprocal restraint. Even in a model that does not include terms of trade externalities – in which states are failing to achieve optimal volumes of

---

[339] Sam Bucovetsky, "Efficient Migration and Income Tax Competition," 5 (2) *J. Pub. Fin. Theory* 249 (2003).

# Economic Liberalization

trade – and therefore are failing to achieve maximum global welfare, international law could play a similar role in allowing states to credibly commit to exercise restraint, or to make compensation, as appropriate.

This type of cooperation problem has often been modeled, assuming a certain structure of payoffs, using the prisoner's dilemma game. The assumption is that the states could be better off if neither of them defected, but that each is individually better off if it defects when the other cooperates, and is worst off if it cooperates when the other defects. The dominant solution – the expected behavior – is defection by all states. However, by using international legal rules to change (make negative) the payoffs from defection, states are able to achieve the collectively optimal outcome of mutual cooperation.

If, in the migration context, home states saw themselves as harmed by the kinds of negative externalities described imposed by destination states in connection with migration, and if the positions were symmetrical, a similar set of payoffs might arise. Alternatively, if states saw themselves as harmed by global failure to achieve optimal volumes of migration, a similar strategic setting, on the basis of a public-goods problem, might arise. On the basis of the example of trade, we might too quickly assume that international migration agreements could play a similar role. However, the explanations developed in connection with the political economy of trade do not neatly map into the migration context: although the welfare economics analysis bears some limited similarities, and the international setting may be comparable, the domestic political-economy parameters are different. There are important reasons why we do not yet observe more extensive international agreements for liberalization of migration.

In order to develop a simple schematic of the possible coalition dynamics in the political economy of the destination state regarding migration, comparable to the model of the political economy of the importing state regarding trade already described, it is necessary to make a number of simplifying assumptions and exclude much detail. For simplicity's sake, I largely exclude from this schematic factors other than economic welfare and political representation in connection with economic welfare.

As described in Chapter 3, there is a domestic coalition-building game, and a linked international-cooperation game. The question is whether governments may find it useful to enter into international agreements in order to induce the formation of domestic political coalitions in support of liberalization. I describe the domestic coalition-building problem textually, and show how it may drive an international coordination or cooperation game. I show that – at least under certain hypothesized circumstances – where without international agreements, pro-liberalization forces would not be successful in inducing formal liberalization, international agreements may increase the possibility of formation of pro-liberalization coalitions.

The schematic uses the assumption, on the basis of the Heckscher-Ohlin theory, that unskilled labor would migrate to where it is scarce, and skilled labor would migrate to where it is scarce. Opposition also follows Heckscher-Ohlin theory: the scarce factor in the destination state has the most to lose in terms of pricing power in connection with immigration. The schematic further assumes that wealthy country labor has no interest in migrating to poor countries. Under this schematic, potential reciprocity within migration policy would play no role, as wealthy-country labor would not seek access to poor-country markets. This schematic is structured in bilateral terms. Obviously, multilateral arrangements will be more complex.

Assume that domestic and foreign labor are asymmetric in skill level: labor in State A is largely high skilled; labor in State B is largely low skilled. Wages are significantly lower in State B. Under this assumed asymmetry, there are significant gains from trade: aggregate welfare in both State A and State B can be increased by reciprocal liberalization. This is an important part of each government's utility function, and may help induce the government to enter into international legal commitments to unlock this welfare increase.

Given that these states have asymmetric labor markets, under Heckscher-Ohlin, mobility (if made available without selectivity between classes of labor) is likely to benefit skilled labor in State A and unskilled labor in State B. Conversely, it is likely to harm unskilled labor in State A and skilled labor in State B. Actual positions – here and in connection with other factors – would depend on cross-elasticities of substitution among the various factors of production. Therefore, we would expect unskilled labor in State A to oppose liberalization, whereas skilled labor in State B would oppose liberalization.

Besides the migrants themselves, capital is the main beneficiary of liberalization of immigration. Here, under asymmetry, there are greater cross-country price differences, strengthening capital's support for liberalization. Except to the extent that they compete with immigrants for consumption opportunities, consumers would be likely to benefit in welfare terms from immigration. Here, under asymmetry, there are greater cross-country price differences, strengthening consumer support for liberalization. However, as in trade, consumers are not well-organized to articulate this preference in destination-country politics.

Pursuing the Heckscher-Ohlin approach, abundant labor may benefit from liberalization by virtue of increased immigration of complementary types of workers. These complementary workers may increase the returns to the abundant types of workers. These are not powerful incentives to advocate liberalization. Under circumstances of equal productivity in State A and State B, the abundant factor would believe that it would benefit from its own international mobility, allowing its workers to emigrate to where they are scarce, in search of higher prices. This benefit could give plentiful labor an added incentive to seek foreign liberalization. Thus, the added possibility of reciprocal foreign liberalization could induce the formation of a coalition among capital, the abundant labor factor, and consumers to overcome the scarce labor factor's opposition to liberalization of immigration.

However, note that whereas capital supports liberalization of immigration at home, it is less likely to support increased emigration by virtue of liberalization of immigration abroad, at least with respect to scarce labor factors. So, we would expect to see some diversity of position within capital: some employers would benefit from increased immigration; others would be harmed by increased emigration. Thus, *unselective reciprocal* liberalization may actually reduce capital's support. *Selective* reciprocal liberalization – by which the partner state liberalizes its immigration policy only with respect to factors abundant in the first state – would help overcome this problem.

Under these circumstances of equal productivity, each state would generally have strong interests in liberalization by the other state, but would prefer – in terms of political contributions and votes from scarce labor – to avoid its own liberalization. This strategic setting may give rise to a prisoner's–dilemma-type situation, in which each state is best off protecting when the other state liberalizes, but both states are better off if both liberalize than if both protect. In this asymmetric schematic, international legal rules could play a role in migration similar to that already described with respect to international legal rules in trade: international legal rules could be entered into by states in order to resolve the prisoner's dilemma, allowing states to achieve greater welfare.

A reciprocal agreement to liberalize would create increased surplus, possibly allowing government to utilize this surplus to redistribute to those harmed (the scarce factor). Arrangements within each state in order to compensate previously scarce labor for the loss of its market power may be necessary to induce agreement. If the gains accrue largely to capital, it may be appropriate to tax capital in order to acquire funds to provide adjustment assistance. If the gains accrue largely to migrants – which is likely – it may be useful to impose some type of charge or tax on migrants in order to capture a sufficient portion of the surplus to be able to provide adjustment assistance.[340] If these domestic institutional arrangements could be made, a wider range of reciprocal commitments to liberalize would become feasible.

---

[340] Timothy Hatton & Jeffrey Williamson, *Global Migration and the World Economy* 382 (2006).

TABLE 9–1. Asymmetric one-way flow: Unequal productivity (position of country of immigration)

|  | Scarce labor | Abundant labor | Capital | Consumers |
|---|---|---|---|---|
| **No Reciprocity** | Strongly opposed to liberalization | Weakly in favor of liberalization | Strongly in favor of liberalization | Weakly in favor (dispersed) |
| **Reciprocity** | Strongly opposed to liberalization | No change – no interest in emigration | Still in favor with enhanced benefits for investment | Weakly in favor (dispersed) |
| **Reciprocity with Side Payment** | Less opposed if side payment is used for adjustment or increase in export opportunities | More favorable if side payment is used for increase in export opportunities | Increased support if side payment provides increased investment or trade opportunities | May increase support if side payment is used to reduce taxes |

However, despite Heckscher-Ohlin theory, there is some reason to believe that for citizens of popular destination states, there may not be great interest in migration to the typical sending states. Under some circumstances,[341] both skilled and unskilled workers may flow toward the high-skilled country – the wealthy country.[342] "This is, of course, what happens in the real world, suggesting that richer countries do indeed enjoy superior technology to poor countries, and that endowments alone cannot explain differences in income, or for that matter trade patterns and factor flows"[343] Under these circumstances, some type of non-migration side payment – made to the wealthy country – would be required in order to realize an efficient solution. This situation is depicted in Table 9–1.

Although a side payment might result in an efficient solution, it might also be unappealing for poor states to make financial compensation to wealthy states. However, it is possible that if, for example, the poor states were willing

---

[341] Daniel Trefler, "International Factor Price Differences: Leontief was Right!" 101 *J. Pol. Econ.* 961 (1993); Daniel Trefler, "Immigrants and natives in general equilibrium trade models," in *The Immigration Debate: Studies on the Economic, Demographic, and Fiscal Effects of Immigration Policy Options* 206 (J. P. Smith & B. Edmonston, eds., 1998).

[342] Gordon Hanson, "The Economic Logic of Illegal Immigration," Council on Foreign Relations: Council Special Report No. 26 14 (2007).

[343] James R. Markusen, "Factor Movements and Commodity Trade as Complements," 14 (3–4) *J. Int'l Econ.* 341 (1983).

to liberalize in relevant high–value-added services sectors, under the General Agreement on Trade in Services (GATS): (i) wealthy-country capital might find this opportunity valuable; and (ii) wealthy-country skilled labor might benefit from opportunities to be employed or otherwise provide services to the poor state. A similar type of side payment or linkage could arise from investment liberalization in the poor state, providing opportunities for wealthy-state capital and skilled labor.

In fact, now that wealthy states have few tariff barriers – whereas developing states still have substantial tariff barriers, as well as barriers to services trade and investment – the outlines of a grand bargain toward a virtuous cycle of efficiency may be described: wealthy states allow greater immigration of skilled and unskilled workers, and poor states reduce tariffs and barriers to investment and high–value-added services.

Another alternative or additional type of side payment is to allow wealthy states to achieve compensation by imposing a special fee or tax on immigrants:[344]

> [B]ecause most of the gains from immigration accrue to the immigrants rather than to the residents of destination countries ... there is little incentive for destination countries to ease immigration restrictions. The only way I can think of to increase the receptivity of destination countries to accept more immigrants would be to redistribute the benefits of immigration so that a greater share of the benefits flow to natives and a lower share of the benefits to immigrants.[345]

Of course, the problem with a migration fee alone is that it would not necessarily provide incentives for any particular political group to lobby for liberalization of immigration. So, the migration fee might be used to fund adjustment assistance in the destination state, and perhaps development assistance in the home state. Thus, the institutional capacity of home and destination states to jointly charge a migration fee might allow them to enjoy a greater portion of the surplus from migration. This capacity might transform the payoff structure of the migration schematic into more of a collective-action problem between states, with greater incentives for cooperation.

This analysis suggests that different states will have different strategic positions, that different economic sectors within these states will have different strategic positions, and even that different occupational groups will have

---

[344] Richard B. Freeman, "People Flows in Globalization" (NBER Working Paper No. 12315, June 2006). Retrieved from http://www.nber.org/papers/w12315.pdf (last visited Aug. 16, 2011); H. R. Clarke, "Entry Charges on Immigrants," 28 (2) *Int'l Migration Rev.* 338 (1994).

[345] Freeman, *supra* note 344, at 33.

different strategic positions. Thus, it is clearly impossible to specify a single arrangement for international cooperation, or even to predict whether international cooperation will occur. However, we know that in the aggregate, liberalization is expected to provide increased surplus and, assuming: (i) that there are mechanisms that can be devised to overcome the strategic problems that may exist between different domestic constituencies, and between different states; and (ii) that the increased surplus exceeds the cost of its capture, we would expect states to move to do so. That they have not made these moves generally thus far does not mean that such moves are not available; it would be difficult to argue that the international legal system as we see it is already efficient. Some may argue that capital markets, with their clear pricing, narrow profit motives, and numerous transactions, are already efficient, and that therefore new transactions cannot result in profits. However, the international legal system is far less efficient, so we may expect that new transactions – of the nature already described – could make the parties better off.

In order to move forward, it will be necessary to analyze different states, different sectors within states, and different occupations within those sectors, in order to understand the strategic position of each. Then, once we know what game is being played, we can evaluate which international legal rules, if any, are useful in order to allow for the maximum net payoffs. A framework agreement that allows for states to agree on the structure of reciprocity, to allow sending states to share in the benefits of liberalization through a tax or other mechanism, to make side payments through linkage to other areas of liberalization, and to make side payments through immigration fees, would establish an appropriate institutional framework – would minimize the transaction costs – for states to negotiate optimal arrangements.[346] Assuming that liberalization of migration is potentially Pareto efficient, it may be that states are unable to achieve the efficient liberalization unless a move is made toward actual Pareto efficiency – toward compensation of states and individuals that are otherwise made worse off.

The national political economy of international migration is complex, and mediates imperfectly the welfare considerations, which are themselves complex. However, even an imprecise assessment of the interplay of interest and power yields insights into the possibility that international legal rules may play a role in committing other states to act, in order to support domestic coalitions that will support liberalization. The game theoretic abstractions developed here are merely conjectures as to the possible interplay of interest and power.

[346] *See* Trachtman, *supra* note 118.

## F) INVESTMENT

International legal constraints on domestic prerogatives with respect to foreign investment are generally only appropriate to the extent that there is a risk of states acting to harm the interests of other states. Therefore, in order to evaluate the utility of constraints on domestic regulation, we must examine the potential incentives of states to use regulation to restrict or otherwise harm foreign investment. There are three main types of goals or incentives to restrict foreign direct investment: (i) protecting domestically owned or other preexisting enterprises from competition; (ii) maintaining domestic ownership of certain types of enterprises for purposes of economic nationalism; and (iii) rent seeking in the form of drawing value from foreign-owned investment, such as expropriation or creeping expropriation.

The political economy of investment seems somewhat different from that of trade, intellectual property, and migration. That is, there seems to be less political pressure in host countries to construct protectionist barriers to investment than there is to construct barriers to imports of goods and services. Perhaps this is because although foreign investment may threaten domestic capital,[347] it may promote domestic employment: there are fewer interests to protect from foreign investment than from foreign imports. Furthermore, foreign investment may bring positive externalities in addition to employment, in terms of growth, education, technology, demand for inputs, and other factors.

In fact, many countries seem to have policies oriented toward the promotion of foreign investment, constituting a change since the 1960s and 1970s, in part resulting from the debt crisis of the 1980s. Thus, there may be fewer incentives to defect from liberalization commitments in the investment field than in the trade field, and hence, less reason for international legal protection. On the other hand, experience with negotiations in GATS suggests that states have substantial reasons for protection in connection with trade in services in the form of *commercial presence*, which generally entails investment in service areas such as financial services, telecommunications, or tourism.

Other kinds of economic nationalism may apply in the foreign-investment area, including concern regarding local control of the economy. This concern is especially acute in developing countries. There may be related concerns that foreign investors would do several things differently from local investors:

> *First*, they may import more raw materials or intermediate goods – certainly, intra-enterprise trade is a very significant component of global trade, and

[347] *See* Raghuram Rajan & Luigi Zingales, *Saving Capitalism from the Capitalists* (2003).

therefore one would expect some relationship between trade protectionism and concerns regarding foreign investment.

*Second*, there may be concerns that foreign investors would act with less regard for the local environment, labor force, and other social values than would local investors. This concern may give rise to suggestions of special extra-regulatory corporate social responsibility. This assertion of responsibility would presumably discriminate between local investors and foreign investors. It is predicated, in part, on either an assumption that the host-state regulatory capacity is otherwise incapable of managing the negative externalities caused by the investment, or a more paternalistic position that the local regulatory motivations are otherwise inappropriate.

*Third*, foreign investors are likely to repatriate profits and, at some point, capital.

*Fourth*, foreign investors may seek diplomatic protection, and may seek better arrangements than those available to local investors.

*Finally*, there may be special concerns, such as national security concerns, regarding foreign ownership of certain types of properties or industries.

Some of the incentives a state may have to restrict or mistreat foreign investments through regulatory measures may be valuable to be addressed through international treaty commitments, for two reasons. First, commitments may be valuable to capital-exporting states in order to reduce the risk and cost to their investors. Second, commitments may be valuable to capital-importing states for the same reason – and to provide incentives to foreign investment, to the extent that foreign investment is viewed as valuable. In this sense, international investment agreements may be viewed as commitment devices for capital-importing states.[348]

Along the lines described by Rajan and Zingales in connection with foreign investment in the financial sector, host states may restrict foreign investment in order to protect entrenched enterprises from competition.[349] Their story is one of crony capitalism, in which entrenched capitalists fear the competition of local and foreign investors in new enterprises. Another source of opposition to foreign investment is workers, who may fear increases in productivity that might result from foreign investment, reducing employment.

These international investment agreements are amenable to some of the same incomplete contracts analysis applied to trade agreements earlier in

---

[348] *See* Zachary Elkins, Andrew T. Guzman, & Beth A. Simmons, "Competing for Capital: The Diffusion of Bilateral Investment Treaties, 1960–2000," 60 *Int'l Org.* 811 (2006).
[349] Rajan & Zingales, *supra* note 347.

this chapter. In particular, some of the general standards in international-investment agreements have been the subject of important litigation to determine how much autonomy for regulation states retain, and to what degree they are constrained by these agreements. This litigation has addressed issues such as the scope of national treatment obligations, the meaning of the required international-law minimum standard of treatment, and what constitutes an expropriation.

The core foreign investment issue of expropriation is a distinctive concern of foreign-investment agreements. Expropriation is an important concern in the foreign investment context. It may be amenable to an analysis similar to the market-power analysis of intellectual property discussed earlier in this chapter: host states may be able to exercise expropriatory market power in a way that results in a direct transfer of wealth from foreign investors to the local government. There would be great incentives for host states to do so, absent either an informal constraint in terms of reduced future foreign direct investment, or a formal legal constraint. However, states require regulatory autonomy in order to engage in welfare-increasing regulation. Thus, state-contingent contracting seems like a reasonable response.

## G) CHAPTER CONCLUSION

Increasing globalization will increase demands for international law to facilite globalization by reducing national autonomy to impose barriers to trade. On the other hand, states will wish to retain as much national autonomy as possible, at the same time foreswearing protectionism. This is an incomplete-contracts problem that seems to be addressed in several instances by general standards applied by judges, allowing a directed state-contingent evaluation of the global costs and benefits of the national regulation. Much international law in this area seems intended to cause regulating importing states to take account of the interests of exporting states in their policy making. The problem is that, left to their own discretion, states may have incentives to set regulatory standards that are inefficiently high, imposing unjustified costs on exporters.

The discussions of trade, intellectual property, migration, and investment in this chapter indicate that there is an important role for international law in this area. International law has developed gradually in these areas, as globalization has proceeded, increasing the demand for international law. International law has also generally developed on the basis of reciprocity, where states make commitments to one another that are seen by states to be reasonable in response to those of their counterparties. Reciprocity often requires diverse commitments, as opposed to what we might describe as "mirror image" commitments. Even within the trade field, states make liberalization commitments with respect to different products or services. This provides an argument for *cross-sectoral linkage*, by which two efficient policy changes that do not have the political support to be effected alone may be viable together under linkage. This is similar to what is believed to have happened within the trade field, where mercantilism balances mercantilism.

However, liberalization commitments must be qualified by exceptions that permit efficient national regulation. Although no trade or investment treaty today specifies that states may only regulate imported products or foreign investment in a first-best way, standards such as national treatment, proportionality, or scientific-basis requirements seem to approximate this goal in ways that may be justified given limitations on judicial ability to determine first-best requirements.[350]

---

[350] See Trachtman, *supra* note 319.

[handwritten: 1º (see p. 84)]

## 10 Fragmentation, Synergy, Coherence, and Institutional Choice

Prior chapters have shown a need for an increase in international law in a variety of areas, as well as an increasing overlap among different areas of international law: the international legal terrain is definitely becoming more congested. With congestion comes collision. This chapter examines the occasions for collision, the meaning of collision, and the possible responses to collision. Collision of this type can occasion concern, as connoted in the term often used for this phenomenon: fragmentation. Collision, however, is less often considered as an occasion for *synergy* – in which the interaction of different areas of law produce better outcomes than if there were no interaction.

It is unlikely that increasing density of international law will cause significant compliance problems because of the potential of forum shopping. However, there will be increasing need for legislative capacity to deal with multiple substantive areas at once, as well as adjudicative capacity to deal with multiple substantive areas, both in a way that is capable of optimizing across multiple areas. The legislative capacity will often be applied to create more specific rules about, for example, the way that trade liberalization relates to environmental protection. The adjudicative capacity will apply broader standards in a context-contingent way so that, for example, in the trade and environment context, the aggregate benefits of trade liberalization *and* environmental protection are maximized. These problems will not often be capable of solution through setting up one set of values – such as those associated with trade, environment, human rights, or labor regulation – as the dominant value.

Fragmentation arises when there are overlaps between policy measures in the international legal setting. Some general examples of policy conflict will help frame the issue. In the area of trade and environment, there are important concerns that international trade law might prevent states from acting unilaterally, or even multilaterally, to avoid leakage of high carbon activities from states that restrict use of carbon to states that do not. Some worry that international trade law or international investment law will be used to prevent states from taking appropriate actions for economic development, environmental protection, or human rights.[351] Some international legal responses to terrorism have conflicted with human rights.

The discussion of state-contingent contracting developed in Chapter 9 is relevant here. Different treaties, or different areas of international law, express different values. These values must often be compromised with one another. The best compromise may be established through negotiated treaty provisions or informal comity or deference. However, it is also possible to establish compromise through state-contingent dispute settlement, determining which policy shall take priority in particular circumstances. In theory, an optimal method of compromise would be simple cost-benefit analysis: how can these values be compromised to maximize the resulting aggregate benefits? However, cost-benefit analysis is challenging for courts, and so treaty negotiators, and courts, have often developed simpler standards for commensurating between values.[352]

Formal conflict can arise when a dispute is submitted to multiple dispute fora and potentially inconsistent norms from different international legal regimes are applicable. For example, the Chile-EU swordfish dispute was submitted to WTO dispute settlement and a Special Chamber of the International Tribunal for the Law of the Sea. Chile charged EU fishermen with failure to comply with obligations under the Law of the Sea Convention; the EU charged Chile with prohibiting importation of the swordfish caught by EU fishermen, in violation of WTO law.[353]

Notably, this form of conflict is not limited to interstate disputes; the proliferation of human rights and investment tribunals has enabled private parties to pursue identical or related claims in multiple fora, either simultaneously or sequentially. One of the problems with the availability of multiple fora to address a single circumstance is that the individual fora may have limited mandates with respect to the law that they are permitted to apply. Multiple litigations arising out of the same facts raise serious efficiency and finality concerns as well as, of course, the very real possibility of conflicting judgments.[354]

---

[351] See, e.g., Rodrik, supra note 3.        [352] See Trachtman, supra note 319.

[353] See Marcos Orellana, ASIL Insight: The EU and Chile Suspend the Swordfish Case Proceedings at the WTO and the International Tribunal of the Law of the Sea (February 2001). Retrieved from http://www.asil.org/insigh6o.cfm.

[354] For one particularly notorious example of inconsistent judgments, compare *Lauder v. The Czech Republic* (U.S./Czech Republic BIT) UNCITRAL Final Award (Sept. 3, 2001) (London arbitral tribunal finds that state action did not constitute expropriation, not violate obligation to provide fair and equitable treatment and not breach duty to provide investor with full protection and security) with *CME Czech Republic B.V. v. The Czech Republic* (The Netherlands/Czech

# Fragmentation, Synergy, Coherence, and Institutional Choice 219

Similarly, conflicts can arise when bodies located in one specialized area of international law, with limited mandates relating to that area, are asked to apply norms generated in other specialized areas of law. For example, in the *Beef-Hormones* dispute, the EU asked the WTO's Appellate Body (AB) to apply the "precautionary principle" in the context of the EU's ban on beef from cattle treated with certain hormones.[355] The AB exaggerated the existing degree of fragmentation by suggesting that the precautionary principle might be part of "international environmental law" but not general international law, and in any event was not applicable to the dispute. Similarly, in the genetically modified organisms (*GMOs*) dispute, a WTO panel declined the invitation to refer in interpretation to an international environmental treaty,[356] and in the *Soft Drinks* dispute between the United States and Mexico, the AB declined to determine rights and duties under the North American Free Trade Agreement NAFTA.[357] These disputes suggest that the same case might be resolved differently in different tribunals, depending, inter alia, on the law that they are charged to apply.

There are good reasons for concerns regarding collision, or fragmentation. For some, fragmentation raises questions about "[international law's] stability as well as the consistency of international law and its comprehensive nature."[358] As the international legal system has developed so far, it has had little experience with fragmentation, and its rules have not evolved to deal with fragmentation in a satisfying way. Indeed, fragmentation seems to be a developmental problem of the international legal system. In this chapter, I first characterize the problem of fragmentation and describe the mechanisms currently available in the international legal system to address fragmentation. I then suggest the characteristics of mechanisms that would address fragmentation in a more complete way, lending coherence to the international legal system as the phenomenon of congestion and collision grows. Congestion is, as argued in earlier parts of this book, inevitable, but collision is not. Rather, it

---

Republic BIT) UNCITRAL Final Award (Mar. 14, 2003) (Stockholm tribunal, considering same fact pattern, finds state action to constitute expropriation, violate fair and equitable treatment, and deny investor full protection and security).

[355] Appellate Body Report, EC Measures Concerning Meat and Meat Products (Hormones), WT/DS26/AB/R, WT/DS48/AB/R, adopted Feb. 13, 1998.

[356] Panel Report, European Communities – Measures Affecting the Approval and Marketing of Biotech Products, WT/DS291/R, WT/DS292/R, WT/DS293/R, Add.1 to Add.9, and Corr.1, adopted Nov. 21, 2006.

[357] Appellate Body Report, Mexico – Tax Measures on Soft Drinks and Other Beverages, WT/DS308/AB/R, adopted 24 Mar. 2006.

[358] International Law Commission, Report of the International Law Commission on the work of its fifty-second session, Annex para. 144, U.N. Doc. A/55/10 (2000).

is possible to design international legal rules addressing the scope or domain of particular rules, or determining hierarchy under conflict, in order to provide for more orderly interaction.

Finally, I suggest how linkages can be constructed to provide synergies, circumstances in which a better outcome is produced by linking diverse international legal rules. These synergies are derived from the possibility to make possible bargains that would not be politically feasible without linkage. They also come from the fact that linkage of diverse legal rules can make the enforcement of each legal rule stronger.

## A) FRAGMENTATION AND THE ALLOCATION OF AUTHORITY

Authority may be allocated in two directions: horizontally and vertically. *Horizontal allocation* of authority within a system of states determines which state will exercise authority over a particular person, activity, or thing. This is the main concern of international law, as discussed in prior chapters.

*Vertical allocation* of authority determines at which vertical level of society authority will be exercised: (i) individual freedom; (ii) municipality; (iii) substate entity; (iv) state; (v) plurilateral organization; or (vi) multilateral organization. An attractive normative approach to vertical allocation of authority is expressed in the principle of subsidiarity. As discussed earlier, the principle of subsidiarity holds that the state should intervene in civil society – should regulate – only where its involvement improves welfare, and that in turn international law and organizations should be established only where they improve welfare.[359]

Thus, domestic regulation may be needed when firms do not bear all the risks of their actions or the managers who are delegated control of firms do not bear all the risks of their actions. Building on the subsidiarity concept at a higher level of organization, international regulation is needed when states do not bear all the risks of their regulatory actions, where states acting individually would otherwise underinvest in a global public good, or may regulate more efficiently by working together.

The role of law in society generally is to determine allocation of formal authority; its social role is to answer the question, "Does the regulated person have the authority to take certain action, or is the regulated person authoritatively required to take certain action?" International law is an important mechanism for determining allocation of authority under circumstances where multiple states are involved. Vertical allocation of authority between states

---

[359] For my more general analysis of this topic, *see* Trachtman, *supra* note 27.

and international law or organization can be guided by the principle of subsidiarity. There is no single term for the normative principle of allocation of authority horizontally among states, although we might simply say that we seek efficiency in horizontal allocation of authority among states.[360]

Nor is there a single term for the principle of allocation of authority horizontally among international legal rules or international organizations. The developing term for the problem of uncoordinated authority among international organizations, and among treaties or other sources of international legal rules, is fragmentation, but we also need a term that would be the horizontal counterpart to the vertical concept of subsidiarity. What shall we call the concept of efficiency in horizontal allocation of authority among international legal rules or organizations? We could simply use the term "efficiency in horizontal allocation," and so forth, or we could refer to "horizontal subsidiarity." Interestingly, vertical subsidiarity will be affected by horizontal subsidiarity: the vertical level at which it is efficient to regulate a matter will depend, in part, on which international organization or international legal rule would be assigned responsibility for the matter.

One issue in horizontal subsidiarity is the question of whether uncoordinated international legal rules or organizations is efficient, or whether it would be more efficient to establish coordinating rules – defragmentation rules – among international legal rules or organizations. This is really an issue of vertical subsidiarity between: (i) supranational international law or organization on the one hand; and (ii) supra-supra national rules or organizations to allocate authority among these international legal rules or organizations.

Fragmentation as a descriptive concept is best understood as an artifact of the existing decentralized structure for making international law – the decentralized nature of global government. The international system – unlike most domestic legal systems – lacks a single centralized legislator, but relies instead on specialized and separate treaty-making conferences and venues. This may be a survival of the "international law of coexistence," which did not address a broad scope of subjects. Under the "international law of cooperation," it makes sense to evaluate the extent to which greater centralization – through which legislators or treaty negotiators might establish greater mechanisms for coherence – would be appropriate.

As a pejorative term, fragmentation is a critique of the failure of mechanisms for reconciliation to keep up with increasing congestion and enforceability of international law. From a normative perspective, fragmentation may be understood as a kind of inter-regime externality, dependent in some cases

---

[360] See Trachtman, supra note 27.

on supra-regime governance to appropriately prioritize across governmental functions.

Fragmentation may thus be understood as a developmental problem of the international governmental system, in which there is a lag between congestion and measures to produce coherence. It is only to be expected that early cooperation would be ad hoc, and cabined in specific subject-matter contexts. However, as the frequency, intensity, and cumulation of these instances of cooperation increase, it is also to be expected that economies of scale and scope, arising from a number of sources, would suggest some degree of movement toward coherence. With increasing substantive interactions brought about by globalization, states would naturally find it useful to coordinate on issues of governing rules, regulatory cooperation, and regulatory competition. With increasing instances of coordination, states would naturally find it useful to ensure that the interactions among diverse rules is sorted out in a productive fashion.

Therefore, greater coherence, in the form of rules or judicially applied standards for mediation between different subject matter rules or institutions would in some cases be in order. In light of the increasing density of international law predicted elsewhere in this book, we can anticipate that the future of international law will include greater efforts toward coherence. What forms will they take? There are two major categories of mechanisms: legislative and judicial, and the judicial category is dependent on explicit or implicit legislative delegation.

Prior chapters have described possibilities for international cooperation in a number of areas, referring also to the possibility of collisions or fragmentation in connection with these areas. Fragmentation in this sense may be benign where action in one functional area may support policy in other areas, and may be potentially malignant where rules in one functional area conflict with, or impede the achievement of policy, in another functional area. The question of whether fragmentation is in fact malignant in a particular circumstance depends on whether the "losing" policy is more valuable than the "winning" policy, or whether the right compromise of policies is established: whether, indeed, the conditions for horizontal subsidiarity are met. Assuming intentionality, it depends on whether fragmentation is used by interest groups or powerful states to frustrate welfare-maximizing action that governments or international organizations would otherwise take.

This chapter develops an institutional analysis of fragmentation, focusing on the problem of allocation of authority, and draws inferences regarding institutional responses to fragmentation. This chapter also develops an institutional analysis of synergies between diverse functional legal rules, and potential linkages between rules.

# Fragmentation, Synergy, Coherence, and Institutional Choice

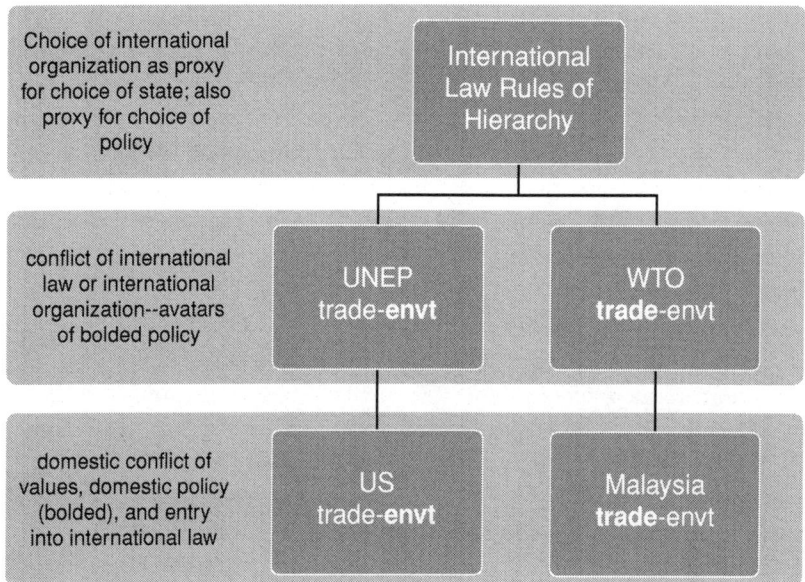

Figure 10–1. Horizontal and Vertical Dynamics of Fragmentation

Fragmentation problems always begin with conflicts of values. Interestingly, these conflicts of values will begin to be observed in domestic politics, and will have a particular outcome in domestic politics. As discussed in Chapter 4, domestic politics determines the desirability of international cooperation. All issues of international cooperation – as discussed in prior chapters – are, first, questions of allocation of jurisdiction horizontally among states; and, second, questions of allocation of jurisdiction vertically between states and international organizations, of subsidiarity. Third, and of growing importance, is the question of fragmentation, addressing the allocation of jurisdiction horizontally among international legal rules or international organizations. However, the question of fragmentation must continually be traced back to disputes regarding horizontal allocation of authority between states, because the outcome of a fragmentation dispute will have efficiency and distributive consequences horizontally between states. The second-level horizontal dispute – the fragmentation dispute – may indeed replicate the horizontal dispute between states. The diagram in Figure 10–1 illustrates these relationships.

International-law rules are often more durable or inflexible than domestic-policy positions, so whereas a prior policy might subsequently be reversed within the domestic sphere, it may continue to operate in international law or organization. In fact, this is the essential role of international law: to enable states to agree today to constrain later behavior. This constraining role is a signal feature of international law – the constraint does not necessarily change with any particular state's domestic policy, otherwise it would be no law at all. This persistence of international law commitments is one reason for fragmentation: a particular state may enter into conflicting commitments at different times. It may enter into these commitments with varying groups of other states, but we will see that the doctrinal essence of the fragmentation problem in international law arises from variation in the groups of states that establish international legal rules or organizations.

So, we move from: (i) domestic conflict of values; to (ii) domestic policy; to (iii) conflict of values between states; to (iv) international law; to (v) conflict of international law (fragmentation); and, perhaps, to (vi) rules for coordination or defragmentation between diverse sources of international law. The question is, how do we move from conflict of international law to a coherent global policy? To illustrate this question, let us examine in Figure 10–1 a hypothetical conflict between the United States and Malaysia. Assume that within U.S. domestic politics on a particular issue, environmental protection has trumped free trade. This may be partly because the costs of reducing free trade are partially externalized to exporting states, but the reason is not essential. In Malaysia, the domestic politics on the same issue has had the opposite results: free trade has dominated environmental protection. This also may be because the costs of reduced environmental regulation are partially externalized to other states.

So, Malaysia supports free trade in this case, whereas the United States supports environmental protection. Both states have previously become party to the WTO treaties, and to, for example, the United Nations Environment Program (UNEP) Basle Convention on Transboundary Movement of Hazardous Wastes. Assume a dispute between the United States and Malaysia, in which the international environmental law supports the U.S. position, but trade law supports the Malaysian position. Note that the minority domestic group in each state may seek a second chance to dominate in the international context – this is the domestic politics component of fragmentation; it involves a type of vertical forum shopping.

It should be noted at this stage that this dispute arises because of the incompleteness of reconciliation between the WTO treaties and the Basle Convention when they were written. We might say that this incompleteness could be resolved by use of formal application of the doctrinal rules of the Vienna Convention on the Law of Treaties, or alternatively by informal diplomacy, just as we might say that domestic contracts are not fully incomplete because they may be interpreted by domestic courts. So, fragmentation arises from incomplete contracts at the borders between functional areas. Recall the discussion of incomplete contracting, and state contingency, in Chapter 9. As will be discussed, the Vienna Convention fails to provide a complete, or satisfactory, response. Courts and others charged with completing these contracts thus have incomplete instructions.

The U.S. environmental interests – having won in U.S. domestic politics – seek, and therefore the United States seeks, determination of the dispute under international environmental law – perhaps in a UNEP discussion forum. Conversely, the Malaysian trade interests – having won in Malaysian domestic politics – seek, and therefore Malaysia seeks, determination of the dispute under WTO law. (Obviously, it is a simplification to say that the UNEP will always uphold environment over trade, or that the WTO will do the opposite.) The formal question that arises from fragmentation is how this type of dispute will be resolved, where the determination of which law to apply is outcome determinative.

This question, the reader will note, is analogous to the question of choice of law in private law: the parties dispute which law to apply where the determination of applicable law will be outcome determinative. Indeed, where the choice is one of organization – as opposed to rule – this choice is analogous to choice of forum in private trans-jurisdictional litigation: the choice of forum determines the applicable rule (or at least the forum rules by which the applicable law will be chosen), and the applicable rule determines who wins. As in the private law field, this type of dispute arises because of the incompleteness of the rules for determining choice of law and forum in transjurisdictional cases. As in the private law field, this type of dispute may be resolved according to choice of law or forum clauses – if these are negotiated – and if the law involved is considered private law. *Private law* is law that the parties are free to modify – it is facultative, as opposed to mandatory. With respect to public law, parties are not free to modify it, presumably because violation of public law imposes externalities on others in society. This analogy is relevant in connection with fragmentation: one question is the extent to which states may decide, inter se, to modify existing law between them. It is somewhat analogous to the private law–public law distinction. The category of *jus cogens* includes international law that states are not free to modify by treaty.

Importantly, the initial allocation of authority is comparable to three-dimensional chess. A joint determination must be made regarding the vertical allocation of authority and the horizontal allocation of authority. Thus, it is not enough to determine that the state is the appropriate vertical level – we must also determine which state. Similarly, it is not enough to determine that the multilateral organization is the appropriate vertical level of authority – we must also determine which multilateral organization. This is a joint determination, not a sequential determination. That is, the choice of vertical level is also dependent on the choice of horizontal allocation among different functional rules or organizations. It is also important to note that there is a choice of legislative determination versus judicial determination within a particular organization.

## B) THE PAST AND THE FUTURE OF FRAGMENTATION

Where there is little international law, there would be little need for cross-functional coherence. Furthermore, the international law of coexistence (in Wolfgang Friedmann's framework) was internally coherent: it was only when we began to develop the international law of cooperation that coherence became an issue. Fragmentation is a phenomenon of congestion.

Furthermore, when customary international law was the primary means for making international law, and its products were generally universal, fragmentation was a significantly less pressing issue. This is because, first of all, a customary international-law rule had the ability to be nuanced, and to take into account varying concerns – after all, it was socially rooted in behavior, not produced at diplomatic conferences narrowly focused on a particular issue. Second, to the extent that customary international law was universal, we did not experience the problem of multiple legislators: the world community was a single unified legislator. Fragmentation is largely an artifact of treaty law made in different fora, with different groups of parties.

Fragmentation may be understood as an "infant disease" of the international governmental system. It is to be expected that early international cooperation would be ad hoc, and cabined in specific subject-matter contexts. It is not surprising, as Friedmann described, that international law developed first in connection with security diplomacy and war: these were the primary areas in which cooperation was desirable. Until other areas developed sufficiently to motivate international cooperation, there was no fragmentation.

Thus, it is to be expected that the mechanisms for cross-functional coherence would be rudimentary where there is seldom a need for cross-functional coherence. It is necessary to recognize, however, that incoherence is not necessarily bad, and that all international law, like all contract and statute, is incomplete. However, this does not tell us the optimal level of completeness in this area. We must be careful, then, that the drive for coherence does not override more substantive goals – that it not become a drive for foolish consistency (the hobgoblin of small minds).

Also, aspirations of international law toward a nirvana image of coherence needs to be tempered by recognition that even in the municipal legal system – with its gold standard of more centralized legislators, courts, and executives – there is much fragmentation in terms of federalism, specialized courts, specialized agencies, and so forth.[361] Although this cannot quite constitute proof that it would be inefficient or otherwise undesirable to eliminate or reduce fragmentation, it is at least proof that the efficient level of fragmentation is probably greater than zero. By leaving fragmentation without an institutional or legal solution, we are simply leaving it to states in the market for international relations to negotiate over the relevant issue. Furthermore, as we examine international fragmentation, we must recognize that international coordination or coherence will be dependent on national coordination or coherence. It is difficult to imagine that the scope of international fragmentation would be less than the average scope of domestic fragmentation.

The issue of fragmentation exists without international organizations, but it can be accentuated by the existence of international organizations. Greater formalization makes fragmentation more acute. Assuming a progressive view of international relations – with increasing demands for cooperation – and increasing congestion of international law, we would expect functional integration to take on increasing subtlety and complexity. Although there would, of course, be practical difficulties of integrating the work of varying organizations with varying expertise, epistemic communities, and formal rules, the value of functional integration will grow with the value of increasing cooperation within different functional areas.

That is, as regulation becomes more dense because of greater complexity of production, greater production externalities and consumption externalities, and increasing technology, and as globalization and economic development causes greater dissemination of regulatory density among countries, we would expect to see more collisions and synergies between functional rules, and more instances of potential cross-functional coordination, or moves to increase coherence. This occurs domestically, but it is also replicated where international cooperation is effected in these regulatory areas.

With increasing substantive interactions brought about by globalization, technology, development, and other factors – as discussed earlier in this book – states would naturally find it useful to coordinate on issues of governing rules, regulatory cooperation, and regulatory competition. With increasing instances

[361] For the U.S. situation, *see* Jody Freeman & Jim Rossi, "Agency Coordination in Shared Regulatory Space" (Harvard Public Law Working Paper No. 11–09, March 4, 2011), 125 *Harv. L. Rev.* (Forthcoming 2012). Retrieved from http://papers.ssrn.com/sol3/papers.cfm?abstract_id=1778363.

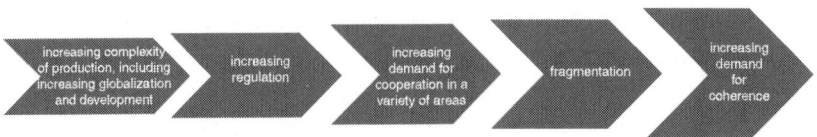

Figure 10–2. The Fragmentation Cascade

of cooperation among states, states would also find it useful to ensure that the interactions among diverse rules is sorted out in a productive fashion. Indeed, as the frequency, intensity, and cumulation of instances of cooperation increase, it is to be expected also that not only collisions, but also synergies and economies of scale and scope, arising from a number of sources, would suggest some degree of movement toward coherence. This set of relationships is depicted in Figure 10–2.

Thus, as international law and organization increase – largely through treaty and increase in functional variety – the "space" for international law becomes more congested, resulting in increased circumstances of collision between rules. As the number of international organizations and courts[362] increases, we also have increased opportunities for collisions. It is well understood that collisions are inevitable, because measures that are labeled "human rights," for example, or "finance" will inevitably overlap with measures that are labeled "security" or "trade." It is not possible to cabin legal rules within a particular functional label; it is a false assumption that measures within one functional area do not have effects on the achievement of the goals of another functional area. It is the increasing collisions, and the increasing inefficiency of collision, that makes it appropriate to redress fragmentation. Therefore, some coherence in the form of rules for mediation between different subject matter rules or institutions for mediating between different subject matter rules – some defragmentation – would be in order.

Whereas these mechanisms may be formal or informal – as the formal enforceability of international law increases – there may be greater need for formal mechanisms of coherence, or defragmentation. Indeed, to the extent that cooperation in particular areas is formal, it would be doctrinally strange to have integration across areas take place informally. For example, if you have a tribunal charged with application of the law of the sea, and a tribunal charged with application of international trade law, to the extent that these areas overlap

---

[362] *See* Benedict Kingsbury, "Foreword: Is the Proliferation of International Courts and Tribunals a Systemic Problem?" 31 N.Y.U. *J. Intl L. & Pol.* 679 (1999); Robert Howse & Ruti Teitel, "Cross-Judging: Tribunalization in a Fragmented but Interconnected Global Order" (New York University Public Law and Legal Theory Working Papers: Paper 112, 2009). Retrieved from http://lsr.nellco.org/nyu_plltwp/112/.

and there is no formal method for resolution of conflicts, the possibility of conflicting formal positions undermines formal legality. Formal mechanisms for resolving conflict could take the form of legislative or adjudicative rules or institutions. On the other hand, to the extent that international law depends on informal methods of interpretation and enforcement, there might be reduced need for formal mechanisms for cross-functional coherence. Thus, there will also be instances in which fragmentation is left unaddressed in the formal system, and states and international organizations are called on to address it through informal means.

Within domestic statutory systems, some states utilize a "last in time" rule to mediate among statutes, assuming that the legislature, by legislating later, intended to override earlier inconsistent legislation. Within the international legal system, a last in time rule – although appearing in a limited fashion in Article 30 of the Vienna Convention on the Law of Treaties – and perhaps more appealing than no rule at all, is not as attractive as in a domestic system with a more centralized legislative process. Furthermore, within at least the U.S. domestic administrative system, there is no last in time rule, and other more deliberate processes have been suggested for mediation, including "structural integration of agency functions, procedural consultation requirements, memoranda of understanding and mandated joint policymaking" between separate regulatory agencies.[363]

If we understand a particular international legal regime – such as, for example, the WTO – as the agent of the states party to that regime, and assuming for a moment perfect agency, we may ascribe the interests of the collective principals to the agent. Further assuming for a moment that other regimes have identical parties and different mandates, we may understand the issue of fragmentation first as a bureaucratic problem of coordination among multiple mandates by the same principal, each represented by separate agents. The collective principal – the states party to the different legal regimes – can resolve this problem simply by determining how to prioritize its goals, albeit at some transaction costs.

So, under the assumption of identical parties and perfect agency, fragmentation is best understood as a problem of bureaucratic coordination, or transaction costs. This does not mean that it is a simple problem, or that it lacks distributive consequences. The domestic example shows that it is both

---

[363] Freeman & Rossi, *supra* note 361, at 3, *citing* Jeffrey S. Lubbers, *A Guide to Federal Agency Rulemaking* 359–61 (2006). For an argument that similar types of devices may address issues of coherence among different international courts, *see* Chester Brown, *A Common Law of International Integration* (2007).

complex and contested.³⁶⁴ It is not surprising that there would be areas of overlap that either: (i) are not anticipated; or (ii) are not deemed worthwhile to resolve at the time that one or more of the regimes was created. In fact, if we understand the establishment of each regime as a kind of incomplete contract, and understand the interaction between the regimes as a part of this incompleteness, we can see that there would be contention over how to "complete" the contract when an issue of overlap arises.

However, once we relax the assumption of perfect agency, we see that the bureaucratic politics of separate agents who may be in a competitive position will impose additional agency costs. Fragmentation can give rise to inter-organizational competition, which might be beneficial or detrimental, depending on the structure of the competition – essentially depending on whether one organization is able to advance its mission at a cost to another organization's mission that exceeds its benefits.

Fragmentation and its responses have welfare costs and benefits. First, the concerns in one area of law may be of greater value than the concerns of other relevant areas of law. Second, different organizations bring different types of expertise, and it may be that one organization's expertise is more important in making a decision on a fragmented issue than another's. Third, different states may have different degrees of influence in different areas of international law, or different organizations. Fourth, fragmentation can give rise to flexibility that may be beneficial in responding to problems, but may do so at the cost of uncertainty both in advance of a dispute arising, and after a dispute arises.

Fragmentation in the sense of increasing numbers of rules can have important beneficial effects – there may be economies of scale and network externalities from the proliferation of international law. Although Daniel Drezner suggests that increasing congestion of international law – giving rise to increasing opportunities for the powerful to avoid compliance by virtue of forum shopping – demeans the force of international law,³⁶⁵ an opposite effect might arise and could be greater. The opposite effect arises from the expanded opportunities for barter and the creation of opportunities to create efficiency-enhancing international law that would not otherwise be created, as well as the expanded possibilities for cross-issue retaliation that could create greater incentives to comply with, and therefore to create, international law.³⁶⁶

---

³⁶⁴ Freeman & Rossi, *supra* note 361.
³⁶⁵ Daniel Drezner, "The Tragedy of the Global Institutional Commons" (Working Paper, March 2010). Retrieved from http://danieldrezner.com/research/InstitutionalProliferation.pdf.
³⁶⁶ Norman & Trachtman, *supra* note 100.

## C) RESPONSES TO FRAGMENTATION: INCOMPLETE CONTRACTS AT FUNCTIONAL BORDERS

There are four types of hierarchy among different legal rules: (i) informal; (ii) adjudicated; (iii) structural; and (iv) normative. *Adjudicated hierarchy* refers to determinations made by courts – where courts have jurisdiction – regarding the hierarchy of particular rules. *Structural hierarchy* refers to organizational structures – including dispute settlement and enforcement mechanisms – that may de facto prioritize one norm and subordinate another. *Normative hierarchy* refers to an order of priority – established legislatively or through treaty provisions – for different types of norms.

### I) Informal Mechanisms

Of course, there are multiple institutional options for allocating jurisdiction among international legal rules or international organizations. The default option is simply to leave these organizations in a state of nature, and thereby allow informal diplomatic mechanisms to deal with fragmentation. Under these circumstances, where organizations exist, they would negotiate with one another regarding particular instances of conflict, and in addition, negotiations would take place among constituent states, reaching varying degrees of resolution. This approach may be less than satisfactory, because the international organizations most likely would not have a mandate for compromise: they could discuss and coordinate, but they could not, on their own, provide exceptions from or modifications of their rules. Where organizations do not exist, states would take the leading role.

Furthermore, informality, or incoherence, benefits those with greater ability to navigate incoherence. Thus, fragmentation may have distributive consequences, insofar as states more adept at forum shopping may benefit from incoherence.[367] To the extent that they do, they would naturally resist attempts to increase coherence. For example, using Figure 10-1 as an illustration, if the U.S. is able to determine, or disproportionately to influence, the choice of applicable international rule or organization (with the choice of organization serving as a proxy for the choice of rule, including the choice of procedure), then its ability to have its conduct regulated under environmental law instead of trade law can be seen as a simple exercise of power.

---

[367] Drezner, *supra* note 365; Eyal Benvenisti & George Downs, "The Empire's New Clothes: Political Economy and the Fragmentation of International Law," 60 *Stan. L. Rev.* 595 (2007).

## II) Judicial Response under Existing Vienna Convention Rules: Conflict

A second institutional option is simply to refer fragmentation disputes to dispute settlement under the general rules of public international law. These general rules of international law are specific enough to constitute "rules" along the rules-versus-standards continuum to be described.[368] However, these rules lack substantive content, and whereaas they may be predictable enough in their application, they may result in outcomes that seem inefficient or otherwise normatively unattractive.

Although Article 30 of the Vienna Convention on the Law of Treaties (VCLT) provides a *lex posterior* or "last in time" rule, it generally only applies where all the parties to the earlier treaty are also party to the later treaty. In other cases, Article 41 (modification) of the VCLT applies. Consider the existing doctrinal response to fragmentation as expressed in Article 41. In order to sharpen the discussion, I will address the application of Art. 41 in the context of the WTO and its relationship with other international treaties.

Art. 41 allows inter se modifications where they: (i) are not prohibited by the multilateral treaty; (ii) do not "affect the enjoyment by the other parties of their rights under the treaty or the performance of their obligations"; and (iii) do "not relate to a provision, derogation from which is incompatible with the effective execution of the object and purpose of the treaty as a whole."

We must preliminarily recognize that any treaty is capable of contracting out of these rules of customary international law, so the policy question is whether it is useful to do so in any particular case, and furthermore, whether other generally applicable rules would be superior. In any specific existing context, such as that of the WTO, we must investigate whether the relevant treaty did contract out of the generally applicable international-law rules.

It appears that Articles IX and X of the WTO Charter, possibly combined with Article XVI:4, are best understood as contracting out of any possible permission for inter se modification under Article 41 of the VCLT. These provisions do not explicitly prohibit inter se modification, but they seem intended to provide an exclusive and preemptive means of modification of WTO law. Article XVI:4 seems to provide a continuing obligation for a state to conform its laws, including, arguably, its international legal obligations to its WTO obligations.

However, even assuming that Article 41 of the VCLT applies, inter se modifications would only be permitted if they were not prohibited by the treaty.

---

[368] *See* Joel P. Trachtman, "The Domain of WTO Dispute Resolution," 40 *Harv. Int'l L. J.* 433 (1999).

By virtue of the provisions discussed, there is a strong argument that inter se modification or waiver is implicitly prohibited by the WTO treaty.

In addition, with respect to the last two conditions of Article 41 – effects on third-party rights and consistency with the object and purpose of the treaty – there are strong arguments that many of the kinds of inter se modifications we are likely to see would violate these conditions. We may even understand Articles IX and X of the WTO Charter – providing third-party rights to approve waivers and amendments – as themselves violated by any inter se modifications or waivers. Importantly, as previously noted, Article X:2 specifies that these provisions may only be amended by unanimous decision, making it clear that the member states of the WTO did not think it appropriate to avoid these provisions even by a majority. If the provisions for amendment and waiver cannot be amended by a subgroup, how can it be argued that there is room left for amendment or waiver to be effected by the means specified in Article 41 of the Vienna Convention?

Furthermore, there are other third-party rights and treaty purposes that would be prejudiced by inter se modification or waiver. First, the WTO Charter recites that its purposes include not just bilateral trade relations, but the increase in global standards of living, employment, and demand: we might interpret this as a public good relating to volume of trade. If states were to agree inter se to violate WTO law in a manner inconsistent with this goal, it would adversely affect the enjoyment by third parties of their rights. Second, economic analysis shows that import restraints in one country may have important trade effects in third countries. An example of a dispute of this nature is the *Semiconductors* case, where the European Communities complained about a U.S.-Japan voluntary-restraint agreement.[369] Article 3.5 of the WTO Dispute Settlement Understanding (DSU) requires that any solutions to matters raised thereunder, even if consensual, must be consistent with the covered agreements. Third, the *Bananas* decision[370] of the Appellate Body recognizes a broad scope of state interest in violations by other states of their obligations. Article 3.8 of the DSU similarly expresses broad scope of prima facie nullification or impairment arising from violation.

Some commentators suggest that WTO law is best understood as "reciprocal" as opposed to "integral," and from this distinction draw important conclusions to the effect that WTO law can be modified by inter se agreements.[371]

---

[369] GATT Panel Report, "Japan – Trade in Semi-Conductors," 35 BISD 116 (1989), adopted May 4, 1988.

[370] Appellate Body Report, "European Communities – Regime for the Importation, Sale and Distribution of Bananas," WT/DS27/AB/R, adopted Sep. 25, 1997.

[371] Joost Pauwelyn, *Conflict of Norms in Public International Law: How WTO Law Relates to Other Norms of International Law* (2003).

The implication of this argument is that inter se environmental or human rights or other international law would always supervene WTO law. This position is not necessarily efficient or normatively attractive. Doctrinally, the reciprocal–integral distinction should be understood as merely a shorthand description of other features, and must defer to the more specific analysis of the Vienna Convention provided, as well as to the exclusive provisions for amendment and waiver contained in Articles IX and X. So, neither normative nor doctrinal consequences flow from the mere characterization of an agreement as reciprocal versus integral. Second, I have suggested why it is a mistake to characterize WTO law generally as reciprocal.

So, to conclude this argument about what happens in cases of conflict between WTO law and other international law, it seems quite incorrect to say that WTO law is generally trumped by international environmental, human rights or labor agreements. Rather, in the general international legal system, we are stuck with the messy and often normatively incoherent rules of lex posterior, as reflected in Art. 30 of the Vienna Convention and questions about how multilateral treaties may be modified by custom or other multilateral treaties with different membership under Arts. 41 and 58 of the Vienna Convention. It is not easy to think of a general rule that would be superior to the Vienna Convention rules, but that does not mean that the Vienna Convention rules are satisfactory. The general rules may be modified by more specific rules, fashioned in response to particular contexts, as discussed further.

### III) *Judicial Response under Existing Vienna Convention Rules: Interpretation*

Article 31.3(c) of the VCLT specifically instructs that interpreters shall "take into account... any relevant rules of international law applicable in the relations between the parties." This provision itself has been interpreted in recent jurisprudence at the WTO.

In the *EC-Biotech* case, a WTO panel determined that, "Article 31(3)(c) should be interpreted to mandate consideration of rules of international law which are applicable in the relations between all parties to the treaty which is being interpreted."[372] The panel found as follows: "The rules of international law applicable in the relations between 'the parties' are the rules of international law applicable in the relations between the States which have consented

---

[372] Panel Report, "European Communities – Measures Affecting the Approval and Marketing of Biotech Products," WT/DS291/R, WT/DS292/R, WT/DS293/R, Add.1 to Add.9, and Corr.1, adopted Nov. 21, 2006, para. 7.70.

to be bound by the treaty which is being interpreted, and for which that treaty is in force." Thus, the panel said, "The rules of international law to be taken into account in interpreting the WTO agreements at issue in this dispute are those which are applicable in the relations between the WTO Members."[373]

Because the complainants (as well as many other WTO Members) had not ratified the Biosafety Protocol, the panel found that the language of Article 31.3(c) did not require it to take the Biosafety Protocol into account in the interpretation of the WTO treaty.[374] Therefore, only those international legal rules to which all WTO Members are party, such as general customary international law or treaties that include all WTO Members, would be required to be taken into account. The panel thus limited the extent to which a WTO panel can take into account other international law, a position that was subsequently criticized in a report of the International Law Commission.[375]

The panel in the *EC-Biotech* case nonetheless left open the possibility that a panel could take into account another international treaty where the parties to the dispute had each ratified that other treaty.[376] In addition, it recognized that other rules of international law might inform the interpretation of WTO

---

[373] *Id.*, para. 7.68.
[374] Argentina and Canada had signed the Biosafety Protocol but not ratified it, whereas the United States had not signed it. Argentina and Canada had signed and ratified the underlying Convention on Biodiversity, whereas the United States had signed it but not ratified it.
[375] *See* Study Group of the Int'l Law Comm'n, "Fragmentation of International Law: Difficulties Arising from the Diversification and Expansion of International Law," 226–28, 237–39, U.N. Doc. A/CN.4/L.682 (Apr. 13, 2006) (finalized by Martti Koskenniemi):

> The panel buys what it calls the "consistency" of its interpretation of the WTO Treaty at the cost of the consistency of the multilateral treaty system as a whole. It aims to mitigate this consequence by accepting that other treaties may nevertheless be taken into account as facts elucidating the ordinary meaning of certain terms in the relevant WTO treaty. This is of course always possible and, as pointed out above, has been done in the past as well. However, taking "other treaties" into account as evidence of "ordinary meaning" appears a rather contrived way of preventing the "clinical isolation" as emphasized by the Appellate Body.... A better solution is to permit reference to another treaty provided that the parties in dispute are also parties to that other treaty. In addition, it might also be useful to take into account the extent to which that other treaty relied upon can be said to have been "implicitly" accepted or at least tolerated by the other parties "in the sense that it can reasonably be considered to express the common intentions or understanding of all members as to the meaning of the... term concerned.

[376] *Id.*, para. 7.72:

> It is important to note that the present case is not one in which relevant rules of international law are applicable in the relations between all parties to the dispute, but not between all WTO Members, and in which all parties to the dispute argue that a multilateral WTO agreement should be interpreted in the light of these other rules of international law. Therefore, we need not, and do not, take a position on whether in such a situation we would be entitled to take the relevant other rules of international law into account.

law as applied to a particular factual context, rather than as rules of law. The Appellate Body in the early *U.S.-Gasoline* report memorably wrote that the GATT "is not to be read in clinical isolation from public international law."[377] The interpretation of Article 31.3(c) of the Vienna Convention was discussed in the Appellate Body decision in *EC-Aircraft*, but the Appellate Body did not reach any determination regarding the question of whether other treaties that did not include all WTO parties, but included the parties to the dispute, could be referenced for purposes of interpretation. It stated as follows:

> In a multilateral context such as the WTO, when recourse is had to a non-WTO rule for the purposes of interpreting provisions of the WTO agreements, a delicate balance must be struck between, on the one hand, taking due account of an individual WTO Member's international obligations and, on the other hand, ensuring a consistent and harmonious approach to the interpretation of WTO law among all WTO Members.[378]

Similarly, in the *U.S.-Shrimp-Turtle* case, the Appellate Body referred to "modern conventions and declarations" in order to interpret the terms "exhaustible" and "natural resources" in Article XX(g) of GATT.[379] The Appellate Body did not mention that it was doing so pursuant to Article 31.3(c) of the VCLT, but its decision clearly took into account other international law. The *EC-Biotech* panel also maintained, although in a more circumscribed manner:

> Other relevant rules of international law may in some cases aid a treaty interpreter in establishing, or confirming, the ordinary meaning of treaty terms in the specific context in which they are used. Such rules would not be considered because they are legal rules, but rather because they may provide evidence of the ordinary meaning of terms in the same way that dictionaries do.[380]

In this way, the WTO Appellate Body can reduce the tension between the WTO and other regimes in a fragmented international law system and seek to limit political backlash against its decisions that touch on environmental, social, or other political issues, the potential of which is reinforced and signaled by such other regimes. From this perspective, WTO jurists may be persuaded by and internalize principles and norms from neighboring international law

---

[377] Appellate Body Report, "United States–Standards for Reformulated and Conventional Gasoline," WT/DS2/AB/R, adopted May 20, 1996, para. 11.

[378] Appellate Body Report, "European Communities and Certain Member States – Measures Affecting Trade in Large Civil Aircraft," WT/DS316/AB/R, adopted June 1, 2011, para. 845.

[379] Appellate Body Report, "United States – Import Prohibition of Certain Shrimp and Shrimp Products," WT/DS58/AB/R, adopted Nov. 6, 1998, para. 130.

[380] *EC-Biotech*, *supra* note 372, at para. 7.91.

regimes, and incorporate those principles and norms into their reading and application of WTO texts.[381] However, there are significant limits on the extent to which an international judicial body can achieve accommodation without seeming to exceed its mandate.

Although it is clear that a limited mandate for the Appellate Body's and panels' jurisdiction accentuates fragmentation, it is also possible that states would prefer different types of dispute settlement mechanisms for different types of international law. Thus, the acceptance of this type of fragmentation could be viewed as an acceptance of an institutional choice made by states: a choice to differentiate among different types of international law in terms of the available institutional infrastructure – to create a structural hierarchy among different types of international law.

### IV) Implicit Legislative Response: Structural Subordination

Today, because of the relative softness of their law and the weakness of their dispute resolution, as well as the imbalance between adjudicative capacity and legislative capacity in the international system as a whole, the WTO's competitors do not seem to be contesting the WTO's authority strongly, at least in formal terms. Informally, and in the world of nongovernmental organizations and public opinion, of course, the WTO's authority is strenuously debated. However, we might say that in the formal system, non-WTO law is structurally subordinated to WTO law: WTO law generally has greater mechanisms for dispute settlement and enforcement. A similar point might apply to investment tribunals under bilateral investment treaties.

Structural subordination is an implicit response to fragmentation. However, as greater commitments are made in other areas, and international cooperation requires greater institutional infrastructure by way of adjudication and enforcement, this structural subordination will diminish. When it diminishes, it will leave greater problems of conflict to address. So in the future, we can expect more demand for conflict clauses and other more direct means by which to address conflict.

Another possible technique of structural subordination, and one with some foundation in existing international legal doctrine, is on the basis of the conflict rule of *lex specialis*, which gives priority to the more specific rule. Assuming the operation of this rule, states could determine hierarchy through differential specificity. The problem is that specificity is a rather incoherent concept, because each competing legal rule would give an equally specific disposition

---

[381] *See* Teitel & Howse, *supra* note 362.

of any particular case. So, a lex specialis rule depends on the ability of judges to distinguish between different levels of ex ante specificity, presumably by counting the number of words, or measuring the narrowness of the applicable rules. A second problem, and a circular one, is that states do not seem to use relative specificity as a technique by which to denote hierarchy, so this rule has little normative attraction.

## V) Normative Responses: Conflict Clauses Allocating Authority between International Legal Rules or Organizations

Perhaps the most direct type of response to fragmentation is to specifically agree to rules addressing the hierarchy among international legal rules. These "secondary rules" (in the H.L.A. Hart sense) might be of different types. One type would establish a general hierarchy, as does the existing international law rule of jus cogens. A second type might simply specify in particular narrow circumstances which rule would take precedence. A third type might establish a heuristic by which to determine the hierarchy in a state-contingent setting, perhaps in order to promote maximization of the overall achievement of state goals, and may assign the task of applying this heuristic to a court.

There are no nirvana responses to fragmentation, just as there are no nirvana responses to the fact of our individual multiple concerns. Some have proposed normative hierarchical structures as a way to mediate among different sources of law, for example extending the concept of jus cogens or simply arguing that certain types of law – such as human rights – should take general precedence over other types of law – such as economic law. These hierarchical responses will be unsatisfying in most cases. Of course, jus cogens, such as constitutionally protected rights in the domestic system, is and perhaps should be understood as a type of supervening law. However, the scope of desirable supervening law would ordinarily be rather narrow, and there would be a broad class of subordinated law, with no way to decide how to address conflicts between subordinated legal rules, or for that matter between jus cogens rules.

Second, states may determine to establish narrower conflict rules. For example, if states wish to make an arrangement permitting, definitively, compliance with the Basle Convention on Transboundary Movement of Hazardous Waste, even where such compliance may violate WTO law, the most effective way to do so is to include in WTO law a specific reference to, and exception for, compliance with the Basle Convention. The effect of such a clause would be to establish a particular kind of response to fragmentation claims: one of integration of the relevant environmental norms with the relevant trade norms. NAFTA's provision stating that certain multilateral environmental agreements trump NAFTA's norms provides a precedent for a specific "carve-out" or "conflict clause."[382]

We might also postulate that recognition could be applied in inter-organizational allocation: one organization may recognize a norm or status developed by another, within the other's field of greater expertise or dominance. The GATT-WTO system has informally deferred on occasion to the International Labor Organization and the World Health Organization,[383] and has relationships of limited formal deference to the IMF.[384] The WTO Agreement on the Application of Sanitary and Phytosanitary Measures specifically allocates a measure of jurisdiction to Codex Alimentarius, the International Office of Epizootics, and the International Plant Protection Convention. These are more subtle and variegated mechanisms than across-the-board deference or across-the-board assertion of dominance.

Third, states may establish a heuristic for dealing with conflict in a state-contingent manner. Recall the relationship between interstate conflict, as in the hypothetical Malaysia-U.S. dispute discussed at the beginning of this chapter, on the one hand, and inter-functional conflict as between trade law and environmental law. Although as shown in Figure 10–1, horizontal conflict between international legal rules always replicates horizontal conflict between states. It is not the same for the United States and Malaysia to dispute jurisdiction over Malaysian shrimp trawlers as it is for the WTO and the UNEP to contend over the same thing, but these two types of contention have some dynamics in common. Both sets of organizations, after all, represent people seeking to achieve certain trade and environmental goals, albeit at different vertical levels.

These heuristics for determining the allocation of jurisdiction horizontally between international organizations or international legal rules would play a function similar to choice of law rules in the private setting, or prescriptive jurisdiction rules in the international public setting. Of course, the allocative options are somewhat different from those in the case of interstate conflict. For example, in the context of functional, as opposed to regional, international organizations, there is no territoriality. Furthermore, an analysis of effects would be somewhat different from that anticipated in the interstate setting.[385]

---

[382] North American Free Trade Agreement, art. 104, Dec. 8, 1992 (107 Stat. 2057) (32 I.L.M. 289 (1993)).
[383] See "Thailand – Restrictions on Importation of and Internal Taxes on Cigarettes," DS10/R, 37 B.I.S.D. 200 (Nov. 7, 1990).
[384] For a discussion of the relationship between the WTO and the IMF, see Frieder Roessler, "Domestic Policy Objectives and the Multilateral Trade Order: Lessons from the Past," in *The WTO as an International Organization* 213 (Anne O. Krueger, ed., 1998).
[385] See Trachtman, *supra* note 27.

However, as with states, we might evaluate effects in terms of the impairment or facilitation of the entity's ability to achieve the preferences sought to be achieved (by people) through that entity – of its mission. In private international law, Baxter developed the "comparative impairment" test for determining choice of law: apply the law of the state whose policy would be impaired the most by failure to apply its law.[386] We may imagine a similar test in the context of allocation of authority between international legal rules or organizations: in the case of conflict, apply the rule the nonapplication of which would cause the greatest harm. This would be a rule of horizontal subsidiarity, seeking the trade-off that provides greatest welfare.

## VI) Specific Rules versus General Standards

Of course, a concept of comparative impairment such as that discussed is not self-executing. Baxter developed it for application by courts. Alternatively, it could be a guide to legislative or treaty-making action, which would solve the problem of determining the value of the interests at stake by simply having legislators or treaty writers use it as guidance to decide which policy is to have priority.

As previously suggested, when negotiators agree to conflict clauses, or even to exceptional clauses, they have a choice of how specific to make the clause. By making the clause perfectly specific, they determine in advance all cases of conflict between different rules. By making the clause imperfectly specific, they implicitly defer to later informal processes or possibly to later adjudication. In the case of adjudication, the degree of generality of the clause may be understood as setting the terms of an implicit delegation of decision-making authority to courts. How would we expect negotiators to determine how specific to make the conflict clause or exception?

In the rules-versus-standards literature, a *law* is a rule to the extent that it is specified in advance of the conduct to which it is applied.[387] Thus, a law against littering is a rule to the extent that "littering" is well-defined. Must there be an intent not to pick up the discarded item; are organic or readily biodegradable substances covered; is littering on private property covered; is

---

[386] William F. Baxter, "Choice of Law and the Federal System," 16 *Stan. L. Rev.* 1, 3 (1963).

[387] For an introduction to the rules-versus-standards discussion in law and economics, *see* Louis Kaplow, "General Characteristics of Rules," *in Encyclopedia of Law and Economics* (B. Bouckaert & G. De Geest, eds., 1998); Louis Kaplow, "Rules Versus Standards: An Economic Analysis," 42 *Duke L. J.* 557 (1992). *See also*, Cass R. Sunstein, "Problems with Rules," 83 *Cal. L. Rev.* 955 (1995).

the distribution of leaflets by air covered? Any lawyer knows that there are always questions to ask, so that every law is incompletely specified in advance, and therefore incompletely a rule.

A *standard*, on the other hand, is a law that is farther toward the more general end of the spectrum, in relative terms. It establishes general guidance to both the person governed and the person charged with applying the law, but does not specify in detail in advance the conduct required or proscribed. Incompleteness of specification may not simply be a result of conservation of resources. It may be a more explicitly political decision to either agree to disagree for the moment – to avoid the political price that may arise from immediate hard decisions – or cloak the hard decisions in the false inevitability of judicial interpretation. It is important also to recognize that the incompleteness of specification may represent a failure to decide how the policy expressed relates to other policies. This is critical in the trade area, where often the incompleteness of a trade rule relates to its failure to address, or incorporate, non-trade policies.

Rules are more expensive to develop than standards ex ante, because rules entail specification costs, including drafting costs and negotiation costs, as well as the strategic costs involved in ex ante specification. In order to reach agreement on specification–in order to legislate specifically–there may be greater costs in public-choice terms.[388]

Rules are generally thought to provide greater predictability. There are two moments at which to consider predictability. First, is the ability of persons subject to the law to be able to plan and conform their conduct ex ante, sometimes known as *primary predictability*.[389] The second moment in which predictability is important is ex post, after the relevant conduct has taken place. Where the parties can predict the outcome of dispute resolution – where they can predict the tribunal's determination of their respective rights and duties – they will spend less money on litigation. This type of predictability is *secondary predictability*. Both types of predictability can reduce costs.

Although rules appear to provide primary and secondary predictability, tribunals may construct exceptions in order to do what is – by their lights – substantial justice, and thereby reduce predictability. It may be difficult to

---

[388] *See* Gillian K. Hadfield, "Weighing the Value of Vagueness: An Economic Perspective on Precision in the Law," 82 *Cal. L. Rev.* 541, 550 (1994), *citing* Linda R. Cohen & Roger G. Noll, "How to Vote, Whether to Vote: Strategies for Voting and Abstaining on Congressional Role Calls," 13 *Pol. Behav.* 97 (1991).

[389] For this use of the terms "primary predictability" and "secondary predictability," *see* Baxter, *supra* note 386, at 3.

constrain the ability of tribunals to do this. Furthermore, as will be noted, game theory predicts that some degree of uncertainty – of unpredictability – may enhance the ability of the parties to bargain to a lower-cost solution. Thus, simple predictability is not the only measure of a legal norm; rather, we must also be concerned with the ability of the legal norm to provide satisfactory outcomes. In economic terms, we must be concerned with the allocative efficiency of the outcome. We now consider allocative efficiency as we consider the institutional dimension of rules and standards.

As we consider the relative allocative efficiency of potential outcomes, we must recognize that there is a temporal distinction between rules and standards. Standards may be used earlier in the development of a field of law, before sufficient experience to form a basis for more complete specification is acquired. In many areas of law, courts develop a jurisprudence that forms the basis for codification – or even rejection – by legislatures. With this in mind, legislatures may set standards at an early point in time, and determine to establish rules at a later point in time.[390]

Kaplow points out that where instances of the relevant behavior are more frequent, economies of scale will indicate that rules become relatively more efficient. For circumstances that arise only infrequently, it is more difficult to justify promulgation of specific rules. In addition, rules provide compliance benefits: they are cheaper to obey, because the cost of determining the required behavior is lower. Rules are also cheaper to apply by a court: the court must only determine the facts and compare them to the rule.

Another distinction between rules and standards, often de-emphasized in this literature, is the institutional distinction: with rules, the legislature often "makes" the decision, whereas with standards, the adjudicator determines the application of the standard, thereby "making" the decision. Again, it is obvious that these terms are used in a relative sense. Economists and even lawyer-economists seem to assume that the tribunal simply "finds" the law, and does not make it. Of course, courts can make rules pursuant to statutory or constitutional authority: the hallmark of a rule is that it is specified ex ante, not that it is specified by a legislature. However, in general, rules are largely made by treaty, and standards are largely applied by tribunals.

However, the difference between legislators and courts is an important one, and may affect the outcome.[391] The choice of legislators or courts to make particular decisions should be made using cost-benefit analysis. Such a cost-benefit analysis would include – as a critical factor – the degree of

---

[390] See Kaplow, General Characteristics of Rules, supra note 387, at 10.
[391] *See* Neil Komesar, *Imperfect Alternatives* (1994).

representativeness of constituents: which institution will most accurately reflect citizens' desires? There are good reasons why such cost-benefit analysis does not always select legislatures. First, there is a public-choice critique of legislatures. Second, even under a public-interest analysis, legislatures may not be efficient at specifying ex ante all of the details of treatment of particular cases. Third, the rate of change of circumstances over time may favor the ability of courts to adjust. Finally, we must analyze the strategic relationship between legislators and courts. Thus, in order fully to understand the relationship between rules and standards, the tools of public choice or positive political theory[392] should be brought to bear to analyze the relationship between legislative and judicial decision making.

It is not possible to consider the costs and benefits of rules and standards separately from the strategic considerations that would cause states to select a rule as opposed to a standard. Johnston analyzes rules and standards from a strategic perspective, finding that, under a standard, bargaining may yield immediate efficient agreement, whereas under a rule, this condition may not obtain.[393] Johnston considers a rule a "definite, ex ante entitlement" and a standard a "contingent, ex post entitlement." Similar to Kaplow, he does not here consider the source of the rule, whether legislature or tribunal.

Johnston notes the "standard supposition in the law and economics literature ... that private bargaining between [two parties] over the allocation of [a] legal entitlement is most likely to be efficient if the entitlement is clearly defined and assigned ex ante according to a rule, rather than made contingent upon a judge's ex post balancing of relative value and harm."[394] Johnston suggests this supposition may be incorrect:[395] "[W]hen the parties bargain over the entitlement when there is private information about value and harm, bargaining may be more efficient under a blurry balancing test than under a certain rule."[396] This is because under a certain rule, the holder of the entitlement will have incentives to hold out and decline to provide information about the value to him of the entitlement. Under a standard, where presumably it cannot be known with certainty ex ante who owns the entitlement, the person not possessing the entitlement may credibly threaten

---

[392] See, John Ferejohn & Barry Weingast, "A Positive Theory of Statutory Interpretation," 12 *Int'l Rev. L. & Econ.* 263 (1992).
[393] Jason Scott Johnston, "Bargaining under Rules versus Standards," 11 *J. L. Econ. & Org.* 256 (1995).
[394] *Id.* (citations omitted).
[395] *See also* Carol Rose, "Crystals and Mud in Property Law," 40 *Stan. L. Rev.* 577 (1988); Joel P. Trachtman, "Externalities and Extraterritoriality," *in* Jagdeep Bhandari & Alan O. Sykes, *Economic Dimensions of International Law* 642 (1998).
[396] Johnston, *supra* note 393, at 257.

to take it, providing incentives for the other person to bargain. Johnston points out that this result obtains only when the ex post balancing test is imperfect, because if the balancing were perfect, the threat would not be credible. This provides a counterintuitive argument for inaccuracy of application of standards.[397] Interestingly, further research as to the magnitude of strategic costs under rules and standards might suggest that over time, rules provide some of the strategic benefits of standards. This might be so if tribunals develop exceptions to rules in a way that introduces uncertainty to their application. This increased benefit would of course be countervailed to some extent by the reduction of predictability that the development of exceptions would entail.

It is easy to see a standard as a way to complete incomplete contracts, ex ante, in a way that can under particular circumstances minimize costs of contracting. As discussed in Chapter 9, Horn, Maggi, and Staiger examine the GATT, finding that it includes an interesting combination of *"rigidity*, in the sense that contractual obligations are largely insensitive to changes in economic (and political) conditions, and *discretion*, in the sense that governments have substantial leeway in the setting of many policies.[398]

Under significant uncertainty as to the future state of affairs, states would wish to establish complex state-contingent contracts. For example, the magnitudes of: (i) the benefits of environmental protection; and (ii) the benefits of unimpeded free trade in particular products that may violate environmental rules are uncertain. However, contracting is costly, limiting the ability to specify state contingencies. On the other hand, by specifying general standards, and delegating to dispute settlement bodies the responsibility to apply these standards, states are able to include complex state contingency in their contracts with significantly less variable contracting costs.

## D) DEFRAGMENTATION: LINKAGE AND SYNERGY

Section C has discussed the methods available to states by which to respond to fragmentation. Its focus has been on natural linkages, whereby rules from different areas of law naturally collide with one another. However, there is also an important artificial, or constructive, role for linkage. These artificial linkages may actually improve the ability of states to realize joint gains through two mechanisms. First, at the negotiation stage, linkages may overcome asymmetries and allow states to establish reciprocally beneficial arrangements.

---

[397] *Id.* at 272.
[398] Horn, Maggi, & Staiger, *supra* note 334, at 406.

Second, to the extent that linkages can persist in overcoming asymmetry after adherence, they can enhance the enforceability of international legal rules. Enhanced enforceability can increase the value of international legal rules, making their use more attractive. These two effects were shown in the example provided in Chapter 3.

## I) Synergetic Bargains

Considering again the domestic political framework for entering into and complying with international law, there is the intriguing possibility that two efficient policy changes that do not have the political support to be effected alone may be viable together under linkage. This is similar to what is believed to have happened within the trade field, where mercantilism balances mercantilism. That is, the willingness of one state to liberalize in one product or service is balanced by the willingness of its counterparty to liberalize in another. Indeed, as suggested in Chapter 9 with respect to the relationship between liberalization of migration and liberalization in other areas of trade, now that wealthy states have few tariff barriers or explicit barriers to trade in services, and developing states still have substantial tariff barriers and barriers to trade in services, the outlines of a grand bargain between migration and trade toward a virtuous cycle of efficiency may be identified. Wealthy states allow greater immigration of skilled and unskilled workers, perhaps also agreeing to enforce a Bhagwati tax; poor states reduce tariffs and barriers to investment and high–value-added services.

We might make a similar suggestion in the case of intellectual property and the linkage of the TRIPS Agreement to liberalization in agriculture and textiles in what has come to be called the grand bargain that concluded the 1994 Uruguay Round. Assuming for a moment – as discussed in Chapter 9 – that some states might have incentives to apply a globally inefficiently low level of intellectual property protection, it was not possible to induce them to increase their intellectual property protection by offering incentives within the intellectual property field. However, by offering them incentives in liberalization of trade, it was possible to cause them to move to more efficient intellectual property laws, causing their counterparties to move to more efficient liberalization in agriculture and textiles. Whereas it is technically possible for these types of bargains to be perverse instead of benevolent, and the TRIPS (and perhaps this bargain seen as a whole) has perversely reduced welfare in poor countries, the choice between welfare gains and losses would be expected to tend to be made in the welfare-increasing direction. Chapter 6 showed the utility of linking human rights to other areas, such as trade. The scope of possible linkages is only limited by our imagination.

## II) *Redistributive Linkage: Embedded Liberalism*

In the "embedded liberalism" sense explained by Karl Polanyi and John Ruggie,[399] liberalization has distributive effects that make it necessary, in order for liberalization to be sustained, to effect redistributive regulation. This may be seen as a special type of linkage – in effect, a particular case of the idea that in international society, agreement on a matter may have differential distributive effects, and require some side payment in order to be accepted. Under this concept, mechanisms for redistribution through regulation are a price to be paid to those who would otherwise lose from liberalization, in order to ensure the continuity of the benefits of liberalization. The WTO is both a result and cause of greater global interdependence, and of the development of global society. To avoid disruption of this global society by démarches in trade, economic catastrophes or violent upheavals in member states, or terrorism, it is morally and politically necessary to develop mechanisms to enhance the position of the poor.[400]

## III) *Compliance Enhancements*

Formal or informal linkage among different rules may promote compliance with any particular rule. International cooperation in different sectors may be mutually supportive, and there may be a kind of network effect that makes each additional instance of cooperation more attractive than it would be absent existing instances. This game-theoretic perspective provides support for the early neo-functionalist hypotheses regarding international economic integration, and suggests the potential value of cooperation for its own sake or in order to facilitate further cooperation.[401]

---

[399] John G. Ruggie, "International Regimes, Transactions, and Change: Embedded Liberalism in the Postwar Economic Order," 36 *Int'l Org.* 379 (1982). Ruggie modernizes and adapts a perspective earlier elucidated by Karl Polanyi. *See* Karl Polanyi, *The Great Transformation: The Political and Economic Origins of Our Time* (1944). Dani Rodrik has considered the application of this perspective to modern global markets. *See* Dani Rodrik, *Has Globalization Gone Too Far?* 7 (1997). *See also* Robert L. Howse, "From Politics To Technocracy – and Back Again: The Fate of the Multilateral Trading Regime," 96 *Am. J. Int'l. L.* 94 (2002).

[400] Joel P. Trachtman, "Legal Aspects of a Poverty Agenda at the WTO: Trade Law and Global Apartheid," 6 *J. Int'l Econ. L.* 3 (2003).

[401] *See* Norman & Trachtman, *supra* note 100.

# Fragmentation, Synergy, Coherence, and Institutional Choice 247

In game-theory studies of cooperation over time, one of the critical factors that can cause cooperation is the shadow of the future. The shadow of the future refers to the possibility that non-cooperation today will produce retaliation in the future. The power of the shadow of the future is affected by the degree of linkage among issues, and the frequency and magnitude of future opportunities for retaliation. The frequency may be increased – and its power thereby magnified – by expanding the scope of issues that are linked to one another. Thus, for example, if the game is not the narrower game of prescriptive jurisdiction in antitrust, but the broader game of prescriptive jurisdiction more generally – or the even broader game of international-law compliance – the play is repeated more frequently, allowing greater opportunities for retaliation and greater incentives for compliance.

One of the assumptions underlying the prisoner's dilemma is that the game is self-contained. Casual observation of international society suggests that there are many linkages,[402] however, with the result that few issues can be isolated.[403] Players can bind one another in a variety of ways, including by linking the present game to other games in a "supergame."

Firms – and states – operate in multiple markets and encounter other firms, or states, in multiple contexts: as competitor here; as supplier there; as coconspirator elsewhere. Industrial-organization economists studying the effect of multimarket contact have found that this cross-sectoral activity may support cooperation.[404] For example, Giancarlo Spagnolo has noted that in the case of multimarket contact, cooperation "can be viable in a set of markets even when in the absence of multimarket contact it could not be supported in *any* of these markets."[405] This is a powerful corrective for scholars who

---

[402] See Robert O. Keohane, *After Hegemony: Cooperation and Discord in the World Political Economy* 91 (1984); Ernst Haas, "Why Collaborate? Issue Linkage and International Regimes," 32 *World Pol.* 357 (1980); Michael D. McGinnis, "Issue Linkage and the Evolution of International Cooperation," 30 *J. Conflict Resolution* 141 (1986) (showing formally that in a prisoner's dilemma "multisupergame," players may adopt strategies that create linkages across time and games, providing opportunities for cooperation, whereas cooperation would not be possible for isolated games); Robert D. Tollison & Andrew D. Willett, "An Economic Theory of Mutually Advantageous Issue Linkage in International Negotiations," 33 *Int'l Org.* 425 (1979).

[403] See Giancarlo Spagnolo, "Issue Linkage, Credible Delegation, and Policy Cooperation" (Center for Economic Policy Research Discussion Paper No. 2778, May 2001). Retrieved from http://ideas.repec.org/p/cpr/ceprdp/2778.html.

[404] *See*, B. Douglas Bernheim & Michal D. Whinston, "Multimarket Contact and Collusive Behavior," 21 *Rand J. Econ.* 1 (1990); Corwin D. Edwards, "Conglomerate Bigness as a Source of Power," in *Business Concentration and Price Policy* 331 (1955); Hitoshi Matsushima, "Multimarket Contact, Imperfect Monitoring, and Implicit Collusion," 98 *J. Econ. Theory* 158 (2001); Giancarlo Spagnolo, "On Interdependent Supergames: Multimarket Contact, Concavity and Collusion," 89 *J. Econ. Theory* 127 (1999).

[405] Spagnolo, *supra* note 403, at 128.

examine individual international law rules or treaties to inquire whether they are self-enforcing.[406]

One important difference between the commercial context and the international relations context is that state relations in the international context almost always cross a number of sectors.[407] States relate to one another in a variety of contexts, with varying roles in each context. In one context, a particular state may be concerned about the scope of its prescriptive jurisdiction, whereas in another context it may be concerned about the scope of its responsibilities to protect foreign diplomats. As a result, although there may be a carbon reduction game that is separate from the trade liberalization game, these games can be linked. In fact, states regularly link issues in international relations, with the result that it is not possible to establish precise boundaries for any particular game.

Defection in one area may therefore have consequences in another, with the possibility of cross-sectoral punishment. Thus, it is not enough to examine whether states have sufficient incentives for compliance within a particular sector or arrangement; one must also analyze the effect of activity in other sectors. Matsushima argues that multimarket contact can take the place of perfect information as a basis for a stable equilibrium of implicit cooperation. He shows that with multimarket contact, cooperation can take place even under circumstances of relatively high discount factors.[408]

In their study of the behavior of medieval merchants, Milgrom, North, and Weingast explain that "if the relationship itself is a valuable asset that a party could lose by dishonest behavior, then the relationship serves as a bond."[409] Thus, the shadow of the future effect is intensified by multimarket contact and perfect information. The broader this effect, the greater the likelihood that individual states will respect particular rules. The greater the likelihood of compliance, in turn, the greater the likelihood that states will use international law to achieve goals that are important to them. The result is a benevolent cycle of more international law producing greater compliance with individual rules, which in turn induces the creation of more international law.

This discussion suggests that international cooperation in different sectors may be mutually supportive, and that there may be a kind of network effect that

---

[406] See the discussion of this issue in Chapter 2.
[407] See Guzman, *supra* note 100, at 1869–70; Duncan Snidal, "Coordination Versus Prisoners' Dilemma: Implications for International Cooperation and Regimes," 79 Am. Pol. Sci. Rev. 923, 939 (1985).
[408] Matsushima, *supra* note 404, at 164–65.
[409] Paul R. Milgrom, Douglass C. North, & Barry R. Weingast, "The Role of Institutions in the Revival of Trade: The Law Merchant, Private Judges and the Champagne Fairs," 2 Econ. & Pol. 1 (1990).

makes each additional instance of cooperation more attractive than it would be absent existing instances.[410] This game-theoretic perspective provides support for the early neo-functionalist hypotheses regarding international economic integration.[411]

## IV) Broader Economies of Scale and Scope in International Organizations

Broader organizations may offer economies of scale and scope. On the other hand, broader organizations could reduce the domain of inter-organizational competition. A Ronald Coase or Herbert Simon perspective recognizes the essential fungibility between internal-organizational arrangements and contractual arrangements in a market. In the present context, this means that it does not necessarily matter whether functions are separated in function-specific international organizations or are integrated within a single organization, such as the United Nations (UN) or perhaps the WTO. Within a single organization, the critical question will be how these different concerns or functions are integrated. Furthermore, under path dependence, given that the WTO exists, and no World Environmental Organization yet exists, there may be actions – such as adding functional environmental responsibility to the WTO – that make sense today but would not make sense were the starting point different. Aaditya Mattoo and Arvind Surbramanian have recently suggested that certain obligations under the IMF Articles of Agreement be subjected to dispute settlement under the WTO.[412]

Negotiations in the WTO context may provide an advantage over negotiations in a multilateral environmental agreement, UNEP, the International Labor Organization (ILO), or another functional context: the greater possibility of linked package deals. Whereas institutional linkages may be made between discrete functional organizations, under some circumstances doing so within a single organization may enhance administration and legitimacy.[413] The WTO already contains much scope for package deals. "With all side

---

[410] *See* Barbara Koremenos, Charles Lipson, & Duncan Snidal, "The Rational Design of International Institutions," 55 *Int'l Org.* 761, 764–65 (2001).

[411] *See*, Ernst B. Haas, *Beyond the Nation-State: Functionalism and International Organization* (1968); Jeppe Tranholm-Mikkelsen, "Neofunctionalism: Obstinate or Obsolete?" 20 *Millenium: J. Int'l Stud.* 1 (1991). Neofunctionalism hypothesized that increasing cooperation would accelerate, as cooperation would create the conditions for its own extension.

[412] Aaditya Mattoo & Arvind Subramanian, "From Doha to the Next Bretton Woods: A New Multilateral Trade Agenda," 88 (1) *Foreign Aff.* 15 (2009).

[413] *See* Andrew T. Guzman, "International Antitrust and the WTO: The Lesson from Intellectual Property," 42 *Va. J. Int'l L.* 933 (2003); Michael P. Ryan, "The Function-Specific and

payments prohibited, there is no assurance that collective action will be taken in the most productive way."[414] However, it is worth noting that the WTO system, with its effective requirements of unanimity for amendment, results in greater requirements for package deals than a system that relies on majority voting for new legislative rules.

Surely, it is appropriate at least in some circumstances for international organizations to be subjected to competitive pressure,[415] but international organizations must also cooperate with one another in appropriate circumstances. Moreover, international organizations exist in a context of both horizontal and vertical competition. That is, international organizations such as the EU compete for political or regulatory authority not only with organizations such as the North Atlantic Treaty Organization, the BCBS, or the WTO, but also with their member states. The EU also cooperates with these other organizations in various ways. In aspirational theoretical terms, this competition and cooperation constitute a search for the optimal jurisdictional area: what vertical and horizontal governance satisfies the constituents' preferences most?[416]

## V) Competition among Legal Rules and Organizations

As suggested, in order to allow regulatory competition to develop a stable and efficient equilibrium, it is – inter alia – necessary to develop a structure that can reduce interjurisdictional externalities. In the interstate setting, we think of a *hegemon* or a central government that can intervene as necessary to require the internalization of externalities. What structure would play this role in interorganizational competition? Perhaps the UN or International Court of Justice (ICJ), if granted appropriate jurisdiction, could fulfill this role. In order to induce states to provide the UN or ICJ with this power, it would be necessary to convince states that they would individually benefit. Some facets of the UN, including the role of the Security Council and Article 103 of the UN Charter, suggest that it plays a partial role as "superior" international organization.

---

Linkage-Bargain Diplomacy of International Intellectual Property Lawmaking," 19 *U. Pa. J. Int'l Econ. L.* 535 (1998).

[414] James M. Buchanan & Gordon Tullock, *The Calculus of Consent* 153 (1962).

[415] *See* Kenneth E. Scott, "The Dual Banking System: A Model of Competition in Regulation," 30 *Stan. L. Rev.* 1 (1977); Henry N. Butler & Jonathan R. Macey, "The Myth of Competition in the Dual Banking System," 73 *Cornell L. Rev.* 677 (1988).

[416] *See* Henry N. Butler & Jonathan R. Macey, "Externalities and the Matching Principle: The Case for Reallocating Environmental Regulatory Authority," 14 *Yale L. & Pol'y Rev.* 23, 33 (1996); Daniel C. Esty, "Toward Optimal Environmental Governance," 74 *N.Y.U. L. Rev.* 1495 (1999).

## E) CONCLUSION: THE FUTURE OF FRAGMENTATION

As we consider fragmentation, it becomes clear that it involves a special type of institutional choice. As new forms of cooperation arise, and as cooperation intensifies, we can expect greater pressure to engage in this type of institutional choice. This chapter has suggested several mechanisms for managing fragmentation. As an initial matter, states might determine, either legislatively by rules or through standards that serve as instructions to judges, how best to allocate authority among functional rules or organizations. The choice between use of rules or standards would depend on the factors discussed.

In addition, states might be guided by some of the welfare aspects of their choice. First, they may determine – or might instruct courts – to allocate authority to the international legal rule or organization that would suffer the greatest impairment of its mission if it were to lack authority. Obviously, this requires some assessment of the magnitude of impairment, which could better be done by legislators than by courts, but there may be reasons to assign this task to courts for determination on a casuistic basis. Assignment to courts might be facilitated by simplification of the analysis, as compared with an extensive cost-benefit analysis.[417] Second, it is important to defer to relevant expertise. Third, it may be useful to devise systems for inter-organizational coordination, in order to limit conflicts and resolve as many as possible through more informal means.[418]

We may ask the same initial question about the international organization that Ronald Coase asked in 1937 about the business firm: why does it exist, and if its existence is justified, why is there not just one big one? Recognizing the utility of making trade-offs among different issue areas,[419] we ask what institutional structure best facilitates these trade-offs.

This chapter has viewed fragmentation problems as institutional problems associated with the allocation of jurisdiction along horizontal, vertical, and functional dimensions. This chapter has tried to suggest a method of analysis of these problems that understands them first as issues of horizontal allocation of jurisdiction, second as issues of vertical allocation of jurisdiction, and third as issues of horizontal allocation of jurisdiction among international rules or organizations.

In the fragmentation context, constitutionalization[420] – as discussed in Chapter 11 – can be seen as a way of introducing hierarchy and order – or at

---

[417] Trachtman, *supra* note 319.
[418] *See* Freeman & Rossi, *supra* note 361.
[419] *See* Spagnolo, *supra* note 403.
[420] *See Ruling the World: Constitutionalism, International Law, and Global Governance* (Jeffrey L. Dunoff & Joel P. Trachtman, eds., 2009).

least a set of coordinating mechanisms – into a chaotic system otherwise marked by proliferating institutions and norms. Hierarchically superior norms and coordinating mechanisms can manage or resolve legal conflicts and thereby produce greater predictability and certainty for actors subject to the rules.

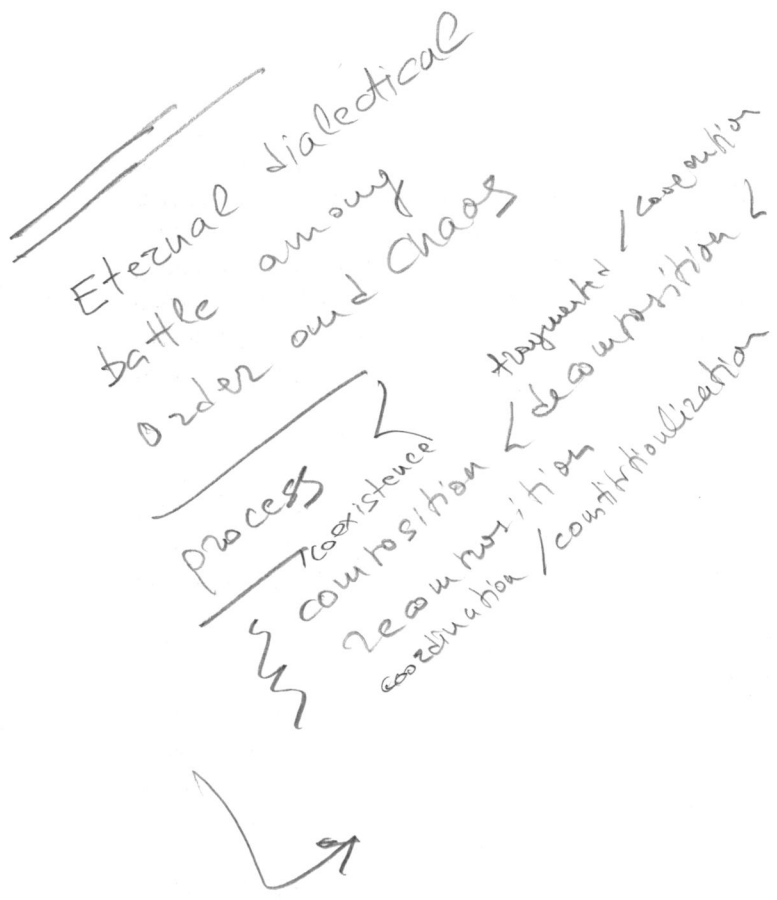

## 11  International Legal Constitutionalization

Earlier portions of this book have shown that existing and reasonably expected conditions suggest increasing demand for international law: both substantive international law in a variety of areas, and international law to address issues of coherence, as discussed in Chapter 10. Technological and social change yields greater possibilities for beneficial international interactions, including prominently international commerce, but also including international environmental stewardship, international health cooperation, human rights, and so forth. International legal rules become more valuable to achieve the increased benefits of these international interactions.

There will be increased demand both for more international law and for more international organizational capacity to provide mechanisms for legislative or decision-making action, secretariat functions including surveillance, agenda setting, and negotiation support, and dispute-settlement functions. Increasing demand for production of international legal rules gives rise to increasing demand for international constitutional norms and processes in order to increase supply. This chapter is concerned with these international constitutional norms and processes.

The future of international society implies an increase in the quantity, complexity, and variety of international cooperation issues, and therefore increased demand for international legal responses. What would a supply response to this increased demand look like? It is possible that states would increase their resources devoted to international relations. Certainly, if the proportion of government services that involve international relations compared to autarkic activities increases, it would make sense for governmental resources to shift, as well. It is also possible that states would decide to provide greater legislative, adjudicative, and executive authority to international organizations, or to the international legal system as a whole. These actions to provide greater governmental authority, and to selectively constrain this increased governmental authority, can be understood in constitutional terms.

## A) THE FUNCTIONAL DIMENSIONS OF INTERNATIONAL CONSTITUTIONALIZATION: ENABLING CONSTITUTIONALIZATION, CONSTRAINING CONSTITUTIONALIZATION, AND SUPPLEMENTAL CONSTITUTIONALIZATION

In this section, I begin to develop a functionalist approach to defining and analyzing constitutions at the international legal level.[421] The functionalist approach that I develop, as suggested in Chapter 1, is on the basis of a new institutional and constitutional economics perspective, which focuses attention on the way that constitutional structures address real-world cooperation problems. The fundamental question is how do constitutional structures enhance welfare?

This functionalist perspective avoids deifying constitutions, and avoids associating constitutions with nationhood or peoplehood. A functionalist approach is consistent with a constitutional patriotism perspective. The concept of constitutional patriotism recognizes that the traditional social bases of common identity – including ethnicity, language, culture, and a common tradition – are unavailable to support what Habermas describes as a global "lifeworld" that can regulate the complex and interrelated international economic and political systems.[422] *Constitutional patriotism* is allegiance to a particular constitution itself, supplanting nationalism. Constitutional patriotism of this type also facilitates *constitutional pluralism*. That is, once we determine that we value a constitution's features and characteristics, rather than the polity it constitutes, nothing is lost in dividing constitutional functions; in fact, presumably, something may be gained. I acknowledge that a functionalist perspective might be criticized for paying insufficient attention to the relationship between constitutions on the one hand, and identity and citizenship on the other hand, and the ways in which constitutions have a constitutive effect on society itself. However, one of the functions of constitutions, especially in the international setting, is to form a basis for allegiance and social coherence that can enable society to rise above more limited systemic goals.

---

[421] This discussion is based in part on my work with Jeffrey Dunoff in *Ruling the World: Constitutionalism, International Law, and Global Governance* (Jeffrey L. Dunoff & Joel P. Trachtman, eds., 2009).
[422] Jurgen Habermas, The Postnational Constellation (2001).

For current purposes, I wish to highlight three important functions that international constitutional norms play: (i) enabling the formation of international law ("enabling constitutionalization"); (ii) constraining the formation of international law ("constraining constitutionalization"); and (iii) filling gaps in domestic constitutional law that arise because of globalization ("supplemental constitutionalization"). This section explains these three functions. I draw a bright line between measures designed to achieve these three functions on the one hand, and ordinary international law on the other hand. To the extent that a measure performs these functions, it is a rule of international constitutional law. Earlier parts of this book have focused on ordinary international law, the vocation of which is to constrain states in particular ways. *International constitutional law* is distinct from ordinary international law, insofar as it facilitates and constrains the production and application of ordinary international law. After setting out the functions of international constitutional law, I explain how each of these functions is articulated through seven mechanisms that are commonly associated with constitutionalization: (i) horizontal allocation of authority; (ii) vertical allocation of authority; (iii) supremacy; (iv) stability; (v) fundamental rights; (vi) review; and (vii) accountability or democracy.

Any discussion of international constitutional law must confront threshold definitional challenges. Indeed, the literature reveals virtually as many definitions of the terms "constitution," "constitutionalism," and "constitutionalization" as there are commentators. The divergent definitions found in the literature reflect, in part, different approaches to difficult conceptual issues, and in part, the considerable variation in substantive content and institutional machinery found in constitutions across time and space.

However, for reasons that will become clearer, I do not believe that an adequate conceptual analysis of international constitutionalization must necessarily be premised on a definition setting forth a group of necessary and sufficient conditions that definitively determine whether a given legal order is constitutional or not. This "check list" approach to constitutionalization has a tendency to push discourse in the direction of terminological disputes, and thereby divert attention from analysis. The checklist approach can also mistakenly suggest that international constitutionalism is a binary, all-or-nothing affair. The following discussion of enabling constitutionalization, constraining constitutionalization, and supplemental constitutionalization shows that constitutional rules are a type, not a quantum, of rules.

First, some constitutional norms enable the production of ordinary international law ("enabling constitutionalization"). Legal norms that endow international bodies with the ability to create ordinary international law fall into this category. For example, the treaties establishing the EU set forth complex procedures for the creation of secondary Union legislation, and the UN Charter empowers the Security Council to create, under certain circumstances, norms that are binding on UN member states. These are prominent examples of what we understand as enabling constitutionalization. Also, international tribunals sometimes engage in enabling constitutionalization. Landmark European Court of Justice decisions, such as *Costa vs. ENEL*[423] or *Van Gend en Loos*,[424] are examples of international bodies effectively reallocating lawmaking authority both among various international actors and between national and supranational actors.

From the perspective of new institutional economics, including constitutional economics, enabling constitutionalization may be understood as an aggregate allocation of authority, in the sense that it allocates authority over multiple decisions at once, in a general or nonspecific way. Enabling constitutionalization determines allocations of authority, rather than the content of the specific exercise of authority. Because of this aggregate nature, and because constitutional mechanisms operate over time, these are also allocations under a veil of uncertainty as to the distributive outcome of the aggregate allocation: the distributive consequences of the specific rules that will be established are unknown in advance. The institutionalization associated with this allocation of authority becomes valuable where it enables relevant actors to cooperate more effectively: where it reduces either transaction costs or strategic costs of cooperation or enables these actors to enter into cooperative arrangements that would otherwise have been unavailable.

Second, some international constitutional norms constrain the production of ordinary international law (constraining constitutionalization). Thus, for example, the European Court of Human Rights has consistently held that European Convention on Human Rights norms take precedence over other treaty commitments made by member states. The Convention has a constitutional dimension insofar as it constrains the making of inconsistent international law. Similarly, any number of foundational international legal norms – we might think of the constitutional commitment to state sovereignty and international norms of a jus cogens character – act as constraints on the production of ordinary international law.

Constraining constitutionalization limits the scope of international law, and thereby constrains the ability of states to use international law to achieve

---

[423] Case 6/64, *Costa v. ENEL* [1964] ECR 585.
[424] Case 26/62, NV *Algemene Transporten Expeditie Onderneming van Gend en Loos v Nederlandse Administratis der Belastingen* [1963] ECR 1.

# International Legal Constitutionalization 257

certain purposes. On the other hand, constraining constitutionalization when matched with enabling constitutionalization simply cuts back on, and makes more precise and limited, the scope of the enabling constitutionalization. Furthermore, there could be circumstances under which constraining constitutionalization would preserve state autonomy and, to the extent international law has direct effect on individuals, individual autonomy.

The notion of constraining constitutionalization outlined here suggests a rather different approach to the relationship between human-rights law and international constitutionalization than that found in most of the literature. Most arguments regarding the constitutional nature of international human-rights norms focus on the vertical dimension of human-rights law and, specifically, the ways in which human-rights norms empower individuals and protect them from certain forms of state action. For our purposes, however, this corpus of law should be considered ordinary international law, as it constrains domestic action. However, to the extent that international norms constrain international legal or international organizational action, they should be considered international constitutional law: constraining constitutionalization.[425] Under this understanding, it is a category mistake to characterize as international constitutional law those forms of international law designed to constrain domestic action. Imposing constraints on state action is the function of ordinary international law, although it is certainly true that these norms may be understood as performing a constitutional function at the state level.

We would expect to see greater demands for constraining constitutionalization as international law becomes more demanding and intrusive, and especially with any moves toward arrangements for international-law legislation without unanimous state consent, or strong international adjudication. To the extent that there is a hard core of sovereignty – a domaine reserve – that international law should not affect, this rule of sovereignty can be understood as a subsidiarity-based rule of constraining constitutionalization: one that limits the production of international law.

There are growing fears that the increasing scope and density of international norms reduces, or threatens to reduce, the effect of domestic

---

[425] *See* International Law Association, "Report of the International Law Association Committee on Accountability of International Organizations" (2004). Retrieved from http://www.ila-hq.org/en/committees/index.cfm/cid/9 (last visited Aug. 20, 2011); Andrew Clapham, *Human Rights Obligations of Non-State Actors* (2006) (discussing, inter alia, human rights obligations of UN, World Bank, WTO and other international organizations). For recent work on the responsibility of international organizations, *see* Giorgio Gaja, "First Report of the Special Rapporteur," UN Doc. A/CN.4/532 (2003); Giorgio Gaja, "Second Report of the Special Rapporteur," UN Doc. A/CN.4/541 (2004); G. Gaja, "Third Report of the Special Rapporteur," UN Doc. A/CN.4/553 (2005).

constitutional law. These concerns were evident, for example, in certain interactions between the German Constitutional Court and the European Court of Justice (ECJ). In *Solange I*, the German Constitutional Court was faced with a claim that a European Community (prior to establishment of the EU) enactment violated rights guaranteed by the German Constitution. Although the ECJ had previously declared that Community law was supreme over domestic law, the German court held that it nevertheless had a duty to review Community enactments for consistency with the German constitution, particularly in light of the absence fundamental rights jurisprudence to constrain Community action.[426]

In response to the Solange court's implicit suggestion that the Community internalize human rights norms, the ECJ began to review Community legislation for consistency with fundamental individual rights – despite the absence of any treaty provision defining those fundamental rights or authorizing the court to engage in this form of judicial review. We can understand this development as an example of an international regime responding to pressures for international constitutional norms that constrain the scope of international legal activity, and thus preserve spheres of state autonomy and individual rights. It is an example of constraining constitutionalization "arising from below" in the sense that in order to be able to ensure the reliability of international norms, the ECJ and later the EU was impelled to develop a doctrine of human rights at the EU level.

Similar concerns have arisen in the context of UN Security Council actions imposing sanctions on individuals and firms suspected of involvement in terrorist activities. Security Council Resolution 1267 created a committee that maintains a list of individuals and entities to which sanctions apply. The committee decides, by consensus, whether to add names to this list. However, this process was criticized for the lack of transparency and due process in listing and delisting decisions.[427] In response to these criticisms, and various legal challenges to listing decisions, the committee established guidelines

---

[426] *Internationale Handelsgesellschaft v. Einfuhr- und Vorratsstelle fur Getreide und Futtermittel (Solange I)*, Bundesverfassungsgericht [Federal Constitutional Court] May 29, 1974, 37 BVerfG 271 (1974) (F.R.G.). See also, *In Re Application of Wunsche Handelsgesellschaft (Solange II)* Bundesverfassungsgericht [Federal Constitutional Court] 73 BVerfGE 339 (1987) (F.R.G.).

[427] See Bardo Fassbender, "Targeted Sanctions and Due Process" (Mar. 20, 2006) (study commissioned by the UN Office of Legal Affairs). Retrieved from http://untreaty.un.org/ola/media/info_from_lc/Fassbender_study.pdf; Council of Europe, "The European Convention on Human Rights, Due Process and UN Security Council Counter-Terrorism Sanctions" (Feb. 6, 2006) (prepared by Iain Cameron). Retrieved from http://www.coe.int/t/dlapil/cahdi/Texts_&_Documents/Docs%202006/I.%20Cameron%20Report%2006.pdf.

that set forth new standards for listing decisions, including a requirement for more detailed information about entities to be listed. However, domestic laws implementing committee decisions continue to be challenged as violating fundamental rights, including the right to a fair hearing, respect for property, and effective judicial review. We can understand these challenges as part of larger efforts to seek constraining constitutional-type norms to impose legal constraints on Security Council action in this area.

One of these challenges arose in the *Kadi* case.[428] In that case, the ECJ found that it may exercise jurisdiction to review measures adopted by the EU to give effect to resolutions of the UN Security Council imposing sanctions in respect of terrorist financing. The ECJ determined that the asset freeze applied to the claimants' accounts, although required by the Security Council resolution, violated their fundamental rights under EU law.

Finally, there is a third category of norms that seems to merit inclusion in international constitutional law. This third category consists of international legal norms that arise in response to domestic constitutional deficiencies, particularly where the deficiency either arises from or is exacerbated by increased globalization. I refer to this third category as supplemental constitutionalization.[429]

Supplemental constitutionalization is different from enabling and constraining constitutionalization, and responds to a particular type of constitutional subsidiarity. Constitutional subsidiarity implies that under some changes in technological or social circumstances, the vertical level at which it is appropriate to provide certain constitutional rules may change. Supplemental constitutionalization responds to gaps in the domestic-law constitutional framework that are created or accentuated by globalization. These gaps may take the form of failure to apply constitutional rules to circumstances that are difficult to distinguish from those to which domestic constitutional rules ordinarily apply but that are outside the reach of domestic constitutional rules, conflicts between the constitutional rules of different states, or the possibility of unstable or inefficient competition between constitutional rules of different states.

One response to these phenomena is to agree on rules determining the scope of application of different states' constitutional rules – we might call these "choice of constitutional-law rules."[430] An alternative response to these phenomena is to harmonize constitutional law rules, or to establish constitutional law rules at the international level. Both types of supplemental

---

[428] Case C-402/05, *Kadi v. Council*, [2008] ECR I-0000.
[429] For an alternative approach, *see* Peters, *supra* note 226.
[430] Elsewhere, I refer to these as "tertiary rules." *See* Joel P. Trachtman, "The Constitutions of the WTO," 17 *Eur. J. Int'l L.* 623 (2006).

constitutionalization response, as they act on domestic legal systems, rather than regulating the international legal system, may be understood in terms of ordinary international law. However, as this phenomenon is creating a body of global constitutional law, it is appropriate to consider supplemental constitutionalization in connection with international constitutionalization.

As previously discussed, certain U.S. actions in the war on terror, including the extraordinary rendition of suspected terrorists to states accused of committing torture and the commission of human-rights abuses against terrorist suspects by U.S. agents at sites outside the United States, may provoke pressure for international constitutional norms in these circumstances. Thus, international constitutionalization may arise: (i) to enable or regularize the processes for the making of ordinary international law, under circumstances where more efficient production of law seems desirable (enabling constitutionalization); (ii) to constrain the production of ordinary international law, preserving a sphere of autonomy for the state or other actors (constraining constitutionalization); or (iii) to supplement domestic constitutional protections (supplemental constitutionalization).

## B) CONSTITUTIONAL ECONOMICS

Why engage in constitutionalization? Why have enabling, constraining, or supplemental constitutionalization? Constitutional economics brings a positive analytical perspective to these questions. Constitutional economics, a branch of new institutional economics, is a social-scientific heir to functionalism, insofar as it studies how particular constitutional settlements address particular cooperation problems.

Under this approach, constitutions are simply instruments of human interaction: mechanisms by which to share authority in order to facilitate the establishment of rules. In Buchanan's phrase, they are instruments to facilitate gains from trade – not from trade in the conventional sense, but transactions in authority. In a transaction cost or strategic model, constitutions are assumed to be designed to overcome transaction costs or strategic barriers to Pareto superior outcomes. Once this is accepted, it follows that constitutional rules are not natural law; instead, they are political settlements designed to maximize the achievement of individual citizens' preferences. Enabling constitutionalization, constraining constitutionalization, and supplemental constitutionalization can all be understood in these terms.

Thus, from this perspective, if there were no potential value to be obtained from cooperation, constitutions would be unimportant, and would not exist. Where gains may be made, as argued throughout this book, constitutionalization may be appropriate – constitutionalization will establish additional constitutional mechanisms at the international legal level. In this sense, demand for international law leads to the development of a constitution for global government.

Constitutional economics assumes that constitutions exist to resolve transaction costs and strategic problems that would otherwise prevent the achievement of efficient exchanges of authority. Where there is value to be obtained by agreement, constitutions may be used to facilitate the realization of this value by reducing transaction costs and strategic costs, such as the problem of states holding out or defecting from their commitments.

Much of the political science literature has been skeptical of the possibility for cooperative international constitutional solutions.[431] Garrett argues that "[I]n situations in which there are numerous potential solutions to collective action problems that cannot easily be distinguished in terms of their consequences for aggregate welfare – and the [EU] internal market is one – the 'new economics of organization' lexicon conceals the fundamental political issue of bargaining over institutional design."[432]

Brennan and Buchanan respond to this criticism by explaining that bargaining over institutional design is cooperative in nature, and that the aggregate increased value will provide incentives for agreement.[433] They compare such constitutional bargaining with "ordinary politics." First, they agree that in ordinary politics "the Pareto-optimal set would be exceedingly large."[434] They continue as follows: "[T]his prospect is dramatically modified, however, when the choice alternatives are not those of ordinary politics but are, instead, rules or institutions within which patterns of outcomes are generated by various nonunanimous decision-making procedures."[435]

The indirectness and broadly reciprocal nature of the distributional consequences of constitutional bargaining erect a Harsanyian veil of uncertainty that provides incentives for agreement on efficient institutions. This veil of uncertainty is limited because those who negotiate constitutions can predict some of the distributive consequences of constitutional-type bargains. This

---

[431] See Stephen D. Krasner, "Global Communications and National Power: Life on the Pareto Frontier," 43 World Pol. 336, 340 (1991) ("The problem is not how to get to the Pareto frontier, but which point along it will be chosen"); Geoffrey Garrett, "International Cooperation and Institutional Choice: The European Community's Internal Market," 46 Int'l Org. 533, 541 (1992).

[432] Garrett, supra note 431, at 541.

[433] Geoffrey Brennan & James M. Buchanan, The Reason of Rules: Constitutional Political Economy 28–32 (1985). See also James M. Buchanan, "The Domain of Constitutional Economics," 1 Const. Pol. Econ. 1 (1990).

[434] Id., at 29.    [435] Brennan & Buchanan, supra note 433, at 29.

argument suggests that bargaining problems can be overcome in connection with the decision to form an international organization, which can then make decisions in ordinary-politics terms.

Constitutional economics allows us to place a number of features associated with constitutionalization into an overall context, and show the relation among them. Importantly, this type of constitutional economics is not predicated on or even related to *economic constitutionalism*, the belief that liberalism is threatened by the state and must be blocked through constitutional means, including international law that plays a constitutional function in the domestic system.

Constitutional economics, similar to economics in general, is agnostic as to the types of preferences that will be articulated, or the way that individuals will value each preference. It assumes only that each individual has a utility function and enters society in order to maximize his or her preferences. Although the utility function is by no means limited to the material, constitutional economics does not accept preemptive values such as human rights, environmental protection, or wealth maximization. It would accept that some of these preferences are valued more greatly than others, or that it makes sense to make some of these preferences preemptive, for strategic or transaction-costs reasons. For example, it may understand core human rights as preferences that are so highly valued they are rarely trumped by other values.

Some scholars who study international constitutionalization suggest that legitimacy is a better metric by which to assess constitutional structures than the normative individualist focus on individual preferences of constitutional economics. However, normative individualism sees even the concept of legitimacy through a preference metric. Legitimacy, if it is to be understood in rational terms, is no more than the satisfaction of preferences or, again in constitutional economic terms, the acceptance of reduced satisfaction of preferences pursuant to a structure that was agreed ex ante because of the anticipation of maximization of preferences. This is the Harsanyian and Rawlsian concept of stochastic symmetry. In other words, legitimacy is no more than the acceptance ex post of the results of a mechanism that was designed and accepted, ex ante, to maximize aggregate preferences. "In Constitutional Economics, rules are assumed to be legitimate if rational individuals seeking to maximize utility (can) unanimously agree to them."[436]

---

[436] Anne van Aaken, "Deliberative Institutional Economics, or Does Homo Oeconomicus Argue? A Proposal for Combining New Institutional Economics with Discourse Theory," in *Deliberation and Decision: Economics, Constitutional Theory, and Deliberative Democracy* 3. 7 (Anne van Aaken, Christian List, & Christoph Luetge, eds., 2004).

I might add that each of us labors under bounded rationality, and so legitimacy may also include the extent to which we are made aware that our preferences are maximized in the way I have described. This is the public relations, or marketing, function that is so important to legitimacy in practice.

Constitutional economics can be understood as a commitment, theory, methodology, and policy orientation. As a commitment, it is predicated on normative individualism, holding that institutional arrangements are to be established in order to maximize individual welfare in the eyes of the individual. As a theory, it postulates that citizens in a constitutional moment will agree on a constitution that maximizes their collective welfare. As a methodology, it derives hypotheses on the basis of this theory, and tests them empirically. As a policy orientation, it advises that the task of framers of constitutions, and of analysts, is to engage in comparative institutional analysis[437] – even if the reference is historical or hypothetical – in order to determine which institutional features will maximize the net achievement of preferences.

In our context, the policy question asked by constitutional economics is which international constitutional features will maximize the net achievement of global individual preferences. We might begin by comparing the status quo with postulated alternative international-constitutional structures. Interestingly, in the international-constitutional setting, we do not have multiple global systems existing at once, to be used to structure a comparison. So, any comparative method will be on the basis of historical experience, cross-functional comparison (as, for example, between the WTO and the ILO), or hypothetical alternatives.[438]

Constitutional economics recognizes the possibility of constitutional moments. A constitutional moment in the Buchanan and Tullock[439] sense is a historical moment at which a Harsanyian veil of uncertainty allows individuals, or in our case states, to agree on constitutional change although they are uncertain of the possible future implications. Constitutional moments generally result from a shift in the concerns, or perception of concerns, of constituents – an exogenous shock that disturbs a constitutional equilibrium.

Furthermore, a constitution may produce its own demand: once established, by reducing transaction costs and strategic costs of international arrangements, constitutions would be expected to make attractive a host of arrangements that

---

[437] Neil Komesar, *Imperfect Alternatives* (1995); Joel P. Trachtman, "The Theory of the Firm and the Theory of the International Economic Organization: Toward Comparative Institutional Analysis," 17 *Northw. J. Int'l L. & Bus.* 470 (1997).

[438] *See* Trachtman, *supra* note 27.

[439] *See* James M. Buchanan & Gordon Tullock, *The Calculus of Consent, Logical Foundations of Constitutional Democracy* (1962).

were otherwise unattractive. There may be a path-dependency characteristic to constitutional development, with tipping points that result in lumpy movement or punctuated equilibria. Thus, for example, once a centralized legislative and parliamentary feature are established for one purpose, it may make it easier to use them for other purposes.

Of course, the existing international legal constitution provides that collective decisions are made by unanimity of states – the somewhat contestable consent rule. (Customary international law is not predicated on unanimity, per se.) The consent rule has certain important characteristics. Some would say that it is perfectly democratic (at least among states, as opposed to individuals), insofar as new rules cannot be made unless all consent. On the other hand, it is just as easily understood as broadly undemocratic, allowing the tyranny of the minority to reign, insofar as the smallest minority can block collective action. The rising importance of global collective goods shows the strategic inadequacy of the consent rule. Of course, under formal requirements of unanimity, informal coercion or logrolling can reduce the inhibitive effect of unanimity.

So, assuming that a state is behaving like an individual in determining whether to move from a rule of unanimity, we would expect the state to calculate its position as follows. The state would maximize its expected utility by a cost-benefit analysis, on the basis of its understanding of the probabilities that it would get what it wants from future decision making. Of course, depending on the issue, it may want action or it may want inaction (eliding the choices in between). If the state could specify a rule of unanimity for the decisions where it prefers inaction, and a rule of the easiest possible approval in areas where it prefers action, this would be its ideal outcome. However, it is not possible to predict all the issues that may arise, and all the consequences of each issue, with great accuracy. This is fortunate, because under a veil of uncertainty, it becomes possible for states to reach agreement, whereas under certainty they would experience a greater likelihood that negotiations would break down over the division of the gains.

## C) THE MECHANISMS OF CONSTITUTIONALIZATION

In this section, I attempt to develop a taxonomy of the types of measures that can be used to carry out the enabling, constraining, and supplemental functions. The core functions performed, and the core metrics of evaluation, will continue to be the extent of enabling, constraint, and supplementation resulting from each measure.

My goal here is to set forth an analytic scheme that can provide both a vocabulary and a conceptual apparatus for the identification, classification, evaluation, and comparison of different constitutional features and orders. "The group of ideas, institutions and practices gathered under the terminological umbrella of the [terms constitution, constitutionalism and constitutionalization] may bear 'family resemblances' to each other without necessarily sharing any single quality or small group of qualities as their common essence."[440]

I use the following list of constitutional mechanisms. For each mechanism described, I attempt to explain its potential role in enabling, constraining, and supplemental constitutionalization.

*Creation of governance institutions and allocation of governance authority in a horizontal context.* Constitutions create institutions and mechanisms for governance, and allocate authority among these bodies. Governance mechanisms are typically constructed with divided power, and this type of rule determines the allocation of authority among, for example, legislatures, executives, and judiciaries (horizontal separation of powers). Horizontal separation of powers is often designed to reflect comparative institutional strengths, as well as to reflect political divisions, including the vertical division between the center and the periphery. That is, some organs in a horizontal federal structure may be designed to represent certain constituencies, such as subnational units. In the international context, horizontal allocations of authority may combine elements of enabling constitutionalization and constraining constitutionalization. That is, they may be part of a grant of power to an international organization, with requirements that may constrain the free exercise of that power.

*Allocation of governance authority in a vertical context.* In entities that are federal or have some measure of devolution, constitutions often establish the relationship between more and less centralized components of governance (vertical federalism). This can include not only clear allocations of authority according to specific rules, but also standards to be applied by courts in determining allocation of authority in specific instances. As with horizontal allocations of authority, vertical allocations in the international context typically involve elements of both enabling and constraining constitutionalism – grants of authority to international organizations, with specified limitations and procedural constraints.

*Supremacy.* Constitutional norms are ordinarily hierarchically superior to ordinary law, which is made through constitutionally approved processes. Thus, in the event of a conflict, a constitutional norm will prevail over an inconsistent ordinary-law norm. In the international constitutional context, supremacy serves as a form of constraining constitutionalization, constraining

---

[440] Thomas C. Grey, "Constitutionalism: An Analytic Framework," in *Constitutionalism, Nomos* XX 189 (J. Pennock & J. Chapman, eds., 1979).

the scope of ordinary international law. (The fact that international law is supreme vis-à-vis domestic law, at least within the international legal system, gives international law a constitutional-type role at the domestic level, but this type of international law is ordinary law at the international level.) Supremacy of certain types of rules, such as fundamental rights, may be motivated in part by supplemental constitutionalization. In the international setting, the main feature of jus cogens is supremacy over ordinary international law.

*Stability.* Constitutional norms are often entrenched in a way that ordinary norms are not. That is, it is more difficult to change a constitutional norm than to change ordinary law. As a result, constitutional norms are protected against temporary shifts in political power and enjoy a stability that ordinary law lacks. Stability in this sense is a critical component of fundamental rights, and also of broad settlements regarding the structure of society and governance. The relative stability of constitutional norms compared to ordinary law serves, such as supremacy, as a form of constraining constitutionalization, constraining the development of certain forms of ordinary law.

*Fundamental Rights.* Modern constitutions typically purport to enshrine and protect fundamental human rights. The exact content and scope of these rights is subject to debate and varies widely across different constitutions. Some constitutions focus largely, if not entirely, on political and civil rights; others might protect social, cultural, or economic rights. As noted, fundamental rights at the international level serve as a form of constraining constitutionalization as well as a form of supplemental constitutionalization.

*Review.* Modern constitutions typically provide for one or more mechanisms designed to test the legal compatibility of laws and other acts of governance with the entrenched norms or fundamental rights expressed in the constitution. This activity might be understood as a component of horizontal separation of powers, but it serves a broader purpose. A review mechanism can serve as the guardian or arbiter of constitutional settlements, making them enforceable where they might otherwise not be. By authoritatively determining whether particular acts are consistent with constitutional norms, on the basis of a prior delegation of authority to do so, this type of review may solve information problems and thereby create a more stable political equilibrium. Supremacy is a precondition for this type of review, and review may have different effects depending on the degree of invocability, the remedies, and the other structural features of review. Review can have constraining effects, where it limits the power of certain bodies. In addition, review can play an important role in supplemental constitutionalization, where review applies at the international level constitutional values or concerns that would ordinarily be applied at the national level, pursuant to domestic constitutional constraints. Again, review at the central level of member state or component legislation, as in WTO review of member-state measures, seems to be a mechanism for enforcement of ordinary international law, so is not on its face part of international constitutionalization. On the other hand, to the extent that review entails a measure of judicial legislation, the grant of review power is a type of enabling constitutionalization.

*Accountability/democracy.* We assume that constitutions, similar to other law, have as their purpose the achievement of individual or collective goals. In order to ensure faithful execution of constituent wishes, and to determine whether satisfactory progress toward the goals is being achieved, constitutions typically include mechanisms designed to provide some form of accountability to constituents. These accountability mechanisms are often, but not exclusively, justified by some version of democratic theory. Importantly, the commitment to democratic governance is qualified by the fundamental rights and stability functions referenced: constitutions serve, in part, as devices to establish precommitments that limit or channel the domain of democratic politics. In the international-constitutionalization setting, accountability may play a constraining-constitutionalization role by limiting the ability of international entities to act where they lack sufficient democratic credentials. On the other hand, accountability may play a supplemental-constitutionalization role, by adding accountability to the international governance process under circumstances where that process is taking on greater responsibilities vis-à-vis member states.

Any particular constitutional order might exhibit these mechanisms in greater or lesser degrees. Indeed, we would expect that any particular constitutional order would have a unique desirable combination of enabling, constraining, and supplemental constitutionalization.

As we examine international legal structures, it is useful to ask to what extent these structures fulfill the enabling, constraining, and supplemental functions, and how they use the mechanisms listed to do so. With this analytical template, we will be able to evaluate the degree and character of constitutionalization within any international regime. We will also be able to begin to develop a qualitative measure of the degree of fulfillment of the enabling, constraining, and supplemental functions; future research may begin to align different degrees of fulfillment with other characteristics.

Of course, constitutions are dynamic, historically and socially contingent settlements, which respond over time and space to varying needs. They may serve different functions, or serve them in different ways, depending on particular social needs. These social needs not only differ in different societies, but at different times in the same society. They are moving targets. In fact, this is one of the attractive design functions of constitutions: they mediate between stability and change. So again, gaps or variations in emphasis are not necessarily susceptible to easy normative response. In fact, some would say that this dynamic feature is a critical part, if not of a constitution, then of a constitutive process in a society. This dynamic and perhaps civic republican aspect of a constitution might be included in a list of constitutional functions or characteristics.

Hence, any attempt to categorize constitutional functions or mechanisms is prone to underinclusiveness, overinclusiveness, and overlap. For example, some would argue that freedom of commerce is constitutional.[441] Indeed, it is protected in a number of constitutional documents, but freedom of commerce can also be protected by ordinary law. One way of including freedom of commerce as constitutional under our framework would be to define it as, to some extent, a fundamental right. In this sense, freedom of international commerce may be understood in terms of supplemental constitutionalization: given globalization, purely domestic freedom of commerce becomes too limited, and must be expanded to cover a broader sphere.

Finally, the mechanisms identified, which are drawn largely from domestic experience, cannot be simply or unambiguously transposed to the international plane. Indeed, the international domain poses a distinct set of practical, analytic, and normative challenges, and that difficult problems of translation unavoidably accompany any effort to apply normatively rich and deeply contested concepts found in domestic constitutional law to the international domain.[442] For this reason, some claim that domestic constitutional settlements may simply be inapposite to international relations and that efforts to analyze international constitutional orders that are rooted in domestic constitutional experience is a category mistake.

### D) DOMESTIC AND INTERNATIONAL CONSTITUTIONALIZATION AND DEMOCRATIC LEGITIMACY

Perhaps the greatest distinction between domestic and international political orders – and the greatest problem of translation – may be in connection with

---

[441] Ernst-Ulrich Petersmann has explored the constitutional dimensions of a fundamental right to trade in a number of writings. See Ernst-Ulrich Petersmann, "Multilevel Trade Governance in the WTO Requires Multilevel Constitutionalism," in *Constitutionalism, Multilevel Trade Governance and Social Regulation* (Christian Joerges & Ernst-Ulrich Petersmann, eds., 2006); Ernst-Ulrich Petersmann, "Justice in International Economic Law? From International Law among States to International Integration Law and Constitutional Law," 1 *Global Community YB Int'l L. & Jurisp.* 105 (2006); Ernst-Ulrich Petersmann, "From Member-Driven Governance to Constitutionally Limited Multi-level Trade Governance," in *The WTO at Ten: The Contribution of the Dispute Settlement System* 86 (G. Sacerdoti et al., eds. 2006).

[442] See Neil Walker, "Postnational Constitutionalism and the Problem of Translation," in *European Constitutionalism Beyond the State* 27 (Joseph Weiler & Marlene Wind, eds., 2004); J. H. H. Weiler, *The Constitution of Europe* (1999).

democratic legitimacy. Given the possibility that international legal norms may be more isolated from the democratic legitimation practices that we see on the domestic plane, many politicians, activists, and scholars have decried the democratic deficit said to be found in various international legal orders. As constitutional norms are presumably both hierarchically superior to and more entrenched than ordinary international legal norms, we might expect the relationship between democracy and international constitutionalization to be even more problematic.

On the other hand, to the extent that international constitutional law acts as a constraint on the domain and effect of ordinary international law, it may be that international constitutional law can ameliorate ordinary international law's democracy deficit. Whether international constitutional norms would in fact do so depends, in part, on the relations between and relative strength and quality of those dimensions of constitutionalization that enable and those that constrain ordinary international law. For example, whereas domestic constitutions may be understood in some contexts to constrain democracy, and ordinary international law may also be understood this way, international constitutional norms and processes that either constrain ordinary international law or require its democratic legitimation, may be seen as enhancing democratic legitimacy overall.

## E) CONSTITUTIONAL COORDINATION AND FRAGMENTATION

An evaluative matrix also permits consideration of whether some international regimes provide the constitutional functions or mechanisms that are needed in other parts of the international system. For example, does the WTO need its own fundamental-rights function, or can it rely on the protection of fundamental rights elsewhere in the system? Under globalization, international law has developed in regional and functional pockets – the law of diplomatic relations, human rights, norms on the use of force – all in the context of a set of background norms such as *pacta sunt servanda*, the rules of state responsibility, and so forth. This highly decentralized and nonhierarchical system makes coordination in the constitutional sense somewhat uncertain.

An analysis of constitutionalization at the international level might start from the premise that international law's various functional regimes are part of a larger system of general international law, such that gaps and incoherencies are addressed by implicit rules of hierarchy or conflict of laws. There is some doctrinal support for this perspective; international tribunals as diverse as the European Court of Human Rights and the WTO's Appellate Body have emphasized the ways in which specialized international legal regimes are embedded within the larger system of public international law.[443] Moreover, this sense of international law's systemic reach finds support in various international legal contexts.[444] From this perspective, constitutionalization can provide a desirable mechanism that can harmonize or coordinate the various components of the international legal system – that can respond to fragmentation.

As discussed in Chapter 10, the future is likely to bring an increase in the density of international law, and consequently an increase in collisions between different sources of authority. Constitutions, in the Hart sense of secondary rules, can allocate authority among different sources of authority, so we might expect the future to bring an increase in the demand for this type of constitutionalization. As discussed in Chapter 10, fragmentation – the phenomenon of diverse functional sources of international law and diverse tribunals applying international law – is not necessarily a problem. There are components of fragmentation that must be understandable as benevolent functional pluralism. On the other hand, there may be fragmentation that results from inadequate integration of different functional goals. Although globalization is an integrated phenomenon, with complementarities and spillovers, most legal instruments have been developed in single-issue contexts.

To the extent that we understand fragmentation as an issue arising from the growing number of sites at which international law is produced, secondary rules – constitutional rules – that address the relationship among the different types of international law become valuable. From this perspective, the risks of normative conflict are a product of international law's highly decentralized

---

[443] *Bankovic v. Belgium & others*, App. No. 52207/99, 2001-XII E. Ct. H.R. 351 (41 I.L.M. 517) (The European Court of Human Rights:

> [...]recall[ed] that the principles underlying the Convention cannot be interpreted and applied in a vacuum. The Court must also take into account any relevant rules of international law when examining questions concerning its jurisdiction and, consequently, determine State responsibility in conformity with the governing principles of international law, although it must remain mindful of the Convention's special character as a human rights treaty. The Convention should be interpreted as far as possible in harmony with other principles of international law of which it forms part;

Appellate Body Report, *United States – Standards of Reformulated and Conventional Gasoline* 3 WT/DS2/AB/R (May 20, 1996) (the WTO agreements "should not be read in clinical isolation from public international law").

[444] An ILC Study Group suggested as much. *See* International Law Commission, "Fragmentation of International Law. Problems caused by the Diversification and Expansion of International law: Report of the Study Group of the International Law Commission," 65–101 A/CN4/L.682 (April 13, 2006) (Finalized by Martti Koskenniemi); International Law Commission "Fragmentation of international law: difficulties arising from the diversification and expansion of international law: Report of the Study Group of the International Law Commission," 7–25 A/CN.4/L.702 (July 18, 2006).

processes for the creation and interpretation of legal norms. International legal norms often develop in specialized functional regimes, such as trade, human rights, environment, or international criminal law. Each of the functionally differentiated areas of law has its own treaties, principles, and institutions. However, the values and interests advanced by any one regime are not necessarily consistent with those advanced by other specialized regimes. In practice, specialized lawmaking, institution building, and dispute resolution in any particular field tends to occur in relative ignorance of developments in adjoining fields, risking conflicting jurisprudence, inconsistent judgments, and outcomes that fail to take sufficient account of the range of relevant values.

On the other hand, the claim that constitutionalization can bring order to an otherwise highly fragmented legal order is highly controversial. Some claim that this argument presupposes a broad global agreement around core values that simply does not exist. Others view efforts to understand constitutionalization along these lines as thinly veiled political efforts by one specialized legal order – or more precisely, by specific international actors – to claim normative priority for one set of international legal norms over alternative norms. Indeed, some have gone so far as to characterize the quest for legal unity through constitutional norms as "a hegemonic project."[445] Others would argue that the search for ways to mediate between different values is simply a recognition – common in the domestic sphere – of the need to make trade-offs between different values.

Moreover, with constitutional pluralism comes the question of how different constitutional orders relate to one another, as well as the possibility of *constitutional confrontations*. These confrontations can be largely horizontal, as when Libya in effect asked the ICJ to declare a Security Council resolution to be ultra vires in the *Lockerbie* dispute,[446] or they can have a vertical component, as in the German constitutional court's *Solange* opinions, the ICJ and US Supreme Court opinions in the Vienna Convention on Consular Relations cases,[447] and the Court of First Instance's and Advocate General's opinions in

---

[445] Martti Koskenniemi, "Global Legal Pluralism: Multiple Regimes and Multiple Modes of Thought," 5 (March 5, 2005). Retrieved from http://www.helsinki.fi/eci/Publications/Koskenniemi/MKPluralism-Harvard-05d%5B1%5D.pdf.

[446] Case Concerning Questions of Interpretation and Application of the 1971 Montreal Convention Arising from the Aerial Incident at Lockerbie (*Libya v. U.S.*), 1992 ICJ Rep. 114 (April 14).

[447] *See, e.g., Medellin v. Texas*, 554 U.S. 759 (2008) (refusing to order stay of execution); *Medellin v. Texas*, 552 U.S. 491 (2008) (ICJ orders are not directly enforceable as domestic law in state courts in United States); Request for Interpretation of the Judgment of March 31, 2004, in the Case Concerning Avena and Other Mexican Nationals (*Mexico v. U.S.*), 2009 ICJ 3 (March 31) (ICJ issues provisional measures ordering United States to take all measures necessary to ensure the Medellin is not executed pending judgment in this action); Case Concerning Avena

*Yusuf* and *Kadi*. These confrontations may be mediated by a variety of mechanisms, including rules of dualism, subsidiarity, or passive virtues of courts. One of the most important functions that international constitutionalization can play is to provide mechanisms addressing how different constitutions relate to one another, and how they can be coordinated.

The constitutional issue here is one of allocation of subject matter, or jurisdictional authority among functional entities. The rules that make this allocation are termed by Hart "secondary rules," to distinguish them from ordinary laws, which are termed "primary rules." In our context, relating the UN, UNEP, WTO, the World Intellectual Property Organization, ILO, the United Nations Conference on Trade and Development, and so forth, to one another can be understood as relating different constitutional structures to one another. Hence, we might call the rules that would allocate authority among these entities *tertiary rules*. These tertiary rules allocate authority among constitutions: among state constitutions, between state constitutions and international-organization constitutions, and among international-organization constitutions. It should be noted at the outset that the structure of the international legal system itself might be understood as the one true constitutional structure, with all of these functional entities, and states, being mere substructures. However, the residual authority in this system is not clearly allocated, unlike, for example, the U.S. federal structure in which the central government seems under current historical circumstances to be the residual authority.

Thus, we operate in an era of uncertainty as to the residual authority among international organizations, or different functional sources of international law. However, this uncertainty is not necessarily inefficient. If conflicts between these rules were not sufficiently frequent and important, we would not expect states to expend the negotiation resources to establish either specific rules or more general standards by which to resolve these conflicts. The establishment of these rules would be an important component of both enabling constitutionalization and constraining constitutionalization, as it would enable and constrain the legislative authority of different functional entities in the international legal system.

Another facet of constitutionalization addresses the extent to which broad social values are integrated with one another, and more specifically, the way in which market concerns are integrated with nonmarket concerns. It is striking that both the United States and EU began with emphases on commercial relations, and developed broader capacities over time. It is also striking that

and Other Mexican Nationals (*Mexico v. U.S.*), 2004 ICJ 12 (March 31) (United States violated Vienna Convention and must give review and reconsideration to named Mexican nationals).

each domestic government has the institutional capacity to deal with interfunctional trade-offs.

It is in this sense that constitutionalization is concerned with capacities; here, the capacity to integrate diverse values. Functional subsidiarity counsels against aggregating all multilateral power to a single organization, such as the UN or the WTO, although increasing functional linkages makes some kinds of intersectoral coherence useful.[448]

Interfunctional constitutionalization can thus be understood in terms of constitutional economics. Interfunctional constitutions facilitate intersectoral trade-offs among different categories of preferences. In terms of the theory of the firm, they bring within a single institution the different categories of preferences that otherwise would intersect in the market of the general international legal system. This theoretical perspective provides a ready understanding that there will be some functional areas that should be addressed together within a single international organization, and others that will be better addressed separately.[449]

## F) GLOBALIZATION

The WTO provides a good illustration of the relationship between globalization and constitutionalization. For a number of years, the WTO has served as a lightning rod for criticism of globalization, and many concerns regarding globalization are expressed in terms of the adequacy of the structure and function of the WTO, both its process and results. This identification of globalization with the WTO seems correct, insofar as the WTO is an instrument of globalization, where globalization is defined as increasing international economic integration. Of course, the WTO is not the only instrument of globalization, and it even limits international economic integration in important ways, so a more nuanced perspective must examine the WTO within a broader context.

WTO secretariat personnel and others seek to deflect this type of criticism by pointing out that the WTO is a "member organization." This argument, building in part on realist international-relations theory, points out that the WTO itself has no power, but is merely a conduit for the exercise of memberstate power. Therefore, the argument proceeds, it is not appropriate to blame the WTO for either sins of omission or commission, because it is no more

---

[448] *See* Joel P. Trachtman, "Transcending 'Trade and...' – an Institutional Perspective," 96 *Am. J. Int'l L.* 77 (2002); Robert L. Howse & Kalypso Nicolaides, "Enhancing WTO Legitimacy: Constitutionalization or Global Subsidiarity," 16 *Governance* 73 (2003) (for a reference to the same concept as "horizontal subsidiarity").

[449] For arguments regarding the scope of issues that might be addressed within the WTO, *see* Andrew T. Guzman, "Global Governance and the WTO," 45 *Harv. Int'l L. J.* 303 (2004).

than a form for member-state action. This argument never provided great protection from criticism, largely because, even conceding its force, it leaves the possibility to criticize a type of member-state action in the form of WTO action or inaction. Moreover, this argument proves too much, for if the WTO were merely a conduit for member-state action, there would be no need to cloak member-state action in the WTO.

However, increasing economic integration both makes increasing disciplines on national regulatory autonomy useful and exposes lacunae in the international regulatory structure. Thus, as the ability to generate new international legal rules to discipline national regulation or fill lacunae becomes important, globalization gives rise to calls for enabling international constitutionalization in order to facilitate legislation of welfare-improving restrictions on protectionist or other inefficient domestic regulation. The enabling constitutionalization could be in the form of facilitation of legislation to make more specific rules, or in the form of implicit delegation to dispute settlement to complete state-contingent contracts, as discussed in Chapter 8. Enabling international constitutionalization at the WTO that facilitates legislation would mean the end of the WTO as a member organization in which each member (in formal terms) retains veto power.

To the extent that the WTO becomes an actor itself – albeit accountable to its member states as a group – it will engage responsibility for its acts. It would be analogous to a national legislature, in the sense that, although composed of individual representatives of different subgroups of people, it would be seen to act as a corporate entity, at the same time also remaining decomposable into its separate representatives.

For some of the reasons suggested in Chapter 9, there are rising demands for enabling international constitutionalization, not just to restrain protectionism but also to complement restraints on protectionism. At the same time, there are rising concerns regarding the accuracy and accountability of efforts to increase disciplines on national regulatory autonomy, as well as concerns regarding the ability of these efforts to encompass the full scope of public policy desiderata, giving rise to calls for constraining international constitutionalization.

Constraining international constitutionalization might take the form of restrictions on the scope of lawmaking at the international level, either in terms of subject matter or in terms of procedural limitations. Subject-matter limitations might take the form of requirements for supermajorities (relative to legislation on other subject matters), or carved-out national rights that are, in effect, inalienable, or at least unalienated.[450]

---

[450] See Mueller, *supra* note 198. Mueller explains that the difference between a rule of unanimity and a right is that a right cuts off wasteful negotiation and lobbying to reach unanimous

Finally, the lacunae exposed by globalization give rise to calls for supplemental constitutionalization, in some cases in the context of the WTO.[451] With greater economic integration comes the possibility of greater regulatory arbitrage, and increasing pressure on domestic regulatory preferences.

However, the WTO is but one component of a variegated and increasingly dense tapestry of global governance. So, it would be wrong to examine the WTO separately from the institutional context in which it exists. Furthermore, although it is possible that acts of enabling constitutionalization, constraining constitutionalization, and supplemental constitutionalization may best take place within the organizational confines of the WTO, it is equally plausible that they would best take place in other parts of the international legal system. Here, there are two critical questions. The first is a question of a type of horizontal and vertical constitutional subsidiarity – where should the constitutional function best be addressed? The second is that of coherence – how do the different constitutional functions fit together?

## G) UNBALANCED DEMAND FOR INTERNATIONAL LAW

The demand for additional international law is the driving force behind enabling international constitutionalization. This demand for additional international law can arise from the demand for liberalization (which in turn is caused by other social forces, including changes in technology, structure of production, and economic understanding), but the production of law to enhance liberalization has two types of knock-on effects: (i) a resulting demand for other types of international law; and (ii) where the initial liberalization measures take the form of negative integration, a resulting demand for positive integration. We see both of these types of knock-on effects in the history of the EU.

One of the factors giving rise to criticism of the WTO is a possible imbalance in the production of different types of international law. This occurs for three reasons.

> *First*, business interests are often able to lobby in a concentrated and effective way for government action that provides them with benefits. So it is not surprising that some types of liberalization measures – such as reductions of barriers to trade and disciplines on national regulatory measures that restrict trade – would achieve greater saliency in national politics, and consequently in international politics, than other types of measures. It is also
>
> agreement, where it is possible to decide in advance that such negotiation and lobbying will be fruitless.

[451] *See* Peters, *supra* note 226.

worth noting that business interests also lobby against liberalization, but the overall tendency since the 1940s has been toward liberalization. Moreover, the increasingly nuanced rules of liberalization that result entail the production of increasing volumes of international law, and of international legal institutions. This production of international-trade law has demonstration effects: showing environmentalists, human-rights activists, and other constituencies that it is possible to establish new international law addressing their concerns. Perhaps most importantly, the establishment of more binding dispute settlement at the WTO than existed prior to 1994 has suggested that more binding dispute settlement and international law may be possible in these other areas. Indeed, the move toward more binding dispute settlement at the WTO has upset a preexisting equilibrium of bindingness in international law, causing reexamination of the binding nature of other areas of law.

*Second*, liberalization itself gives rise to recognition of lacunae in the substantive or jurisdictional coverage of national regulation, or the possibility of adverse regulatory arbitrage. Environmental, human rights, tax, competition, and other types of regulation are thus challenged by liberalization, and relevant constituencies seek responsive redress. Increasing liberalization gives rise to increasing demands for regulatory harmonization, or regulatory rules of prescriptive jurisdiction. Some of these demands are on the basis of a perception of regulatory competition that is accentuated by liberalization.

*Third*, as discussed, liberalization has distributive effects that make it necessary, in order for liberalization to be sustained, to effect remedial regulation.

Thus, the demand for liberalization sets off a cascade of demands for the production of other international law. The demand for both liberalization and other international law may more easily be satisfied with greater enabling international constitutionalization. As noted, the establishment of enabling international constitutionalization creates a demand for nuanced controls in the form of constraining international constitutionalization. This cascade might appear as depicted in Figure 11–1.

One method of discipline on national regulatory measures is the type of negative-integration provision that establishes a legal standard – enforced and articulated through adjudication – prohibiting certain types of national measures that may create excessive barriers to trade. The most common type of negative-integration standard, as discussed in Chapter 9, is national–treatment-type nondiscrimination. In a sense, these rules against protectionism are specialized rules of dynamic subsidiarity. They contingently remove power from the state under a specified range of contingencies. Interestingly, these rules may be understood as serving a constraining constitutionalization role at the

# International Legal Constitutionalization

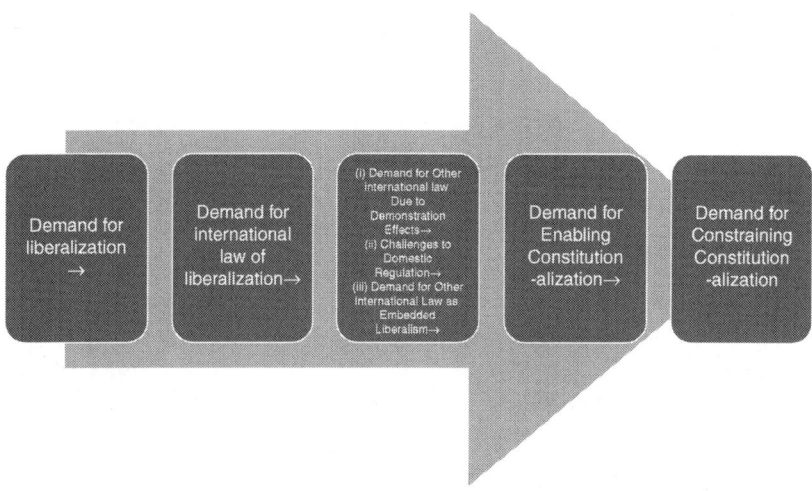

Figure 11-1. The Flow from Liberalization to Constitutionalization

domestic level: they constrain the production of ordinary law. At the international level, however, they are ordinary international law. On the other hand, to the extent that international judges are authorized – explicitly or implicitly – to interpret or craft these rules of negative integration, the authorization may be understood as a kind of enabling constitutionalization.

These types of adjudicative standards used in negative integration compete with legislative solutions to the same problems. Legislative solutions – known in this context as positive integration – might develop regimes of harmonization or recognition, or blended regimes of harmonization and recognition, as in the EU essential-harmonization program. These legislative solutions could enjoy greater political support than judicial decisions addressing the same issues.

It is in this regard that negative-integration devices – such as those in the WTO – that may be used to strike down domestic regulatory regimes may create demand for positive integration devices, such as those associated with majority voting. Deregulation at the national level through negative integration may create demand for reregulation at the central level through majority voting-based legislative capacity. This results in demand for enabling constitutionalization in terms of legislative capacity. Majority voting among states might give rise to demands for greater democratic accountability, a kind of countervailing constraining constitutionalization. Pascal Lamy has called for a WTO parliamentary consultative assembly for this reason.[452]

---

[452] Pascal Lamy, "What Are the Options After Seattle?" speech to the European Parliament, Brussels, January 25, 2000. *See also* Gregory Shaffer, "Parliamentary Oversight of International

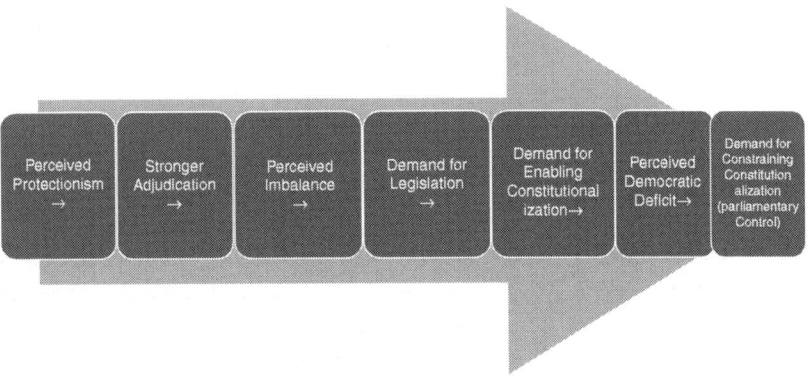

Figure 11–2. Institutional Evolution of Constitutionalization

So the causal chain here might appear as depicted in Figure 11–2.

This conjectural causal chain shows a link between adjudication and legislation. In this model, the power of adjudicative negative integration gives rise to a need for the check of legislative capacity for positive integration. The possibility of centralized legislation gives rise to the need for centralized democratic accountability. This diagram elides much nuance, but it is intended to provide a suggestion of how the commencement of economic integration may set off a cascade of governance demands along a predictable path.

Thus, we began to see a model of the relationship between the demand for law to effect liberalization, other international law, and international constitutional law. There is also an interesting relationship between enabling constitutionalization and constraining constitutionalization. Enabling constitutionalization and constraining constitutionalization are two sides of the same coin. As a sculptor adds clay with one tool and cuts it away with another, so enabling constitutionalization adds to the powers of the international legal system, whereas constraining constitutionalization refines the grant of powers and artfully, and often conditionally, cuts back on it.

## H) LEGISLATION

In the international legal system today, the default system for making law is by consent. The consent principle is often carried forward into decision

Rule-Making: The Political, Normative and Practical Contexts," 7 (3) *J. Int'l. Econ. L.* 629 (2004); Richard Falk & Andrew Strauss, "On the Creation of a Global Peoples Assembly: Legitimacy and the Power of Popular Sovereignty," 36 *Stan. J. Int'l L.* 191 (2000); Robert L. Howse, "How to Begin to Think About the Democratic Deficit at the WTO," in *International Economic Governance and Non-Economic Concerns: New Challenges for the International Legal Order* 79 (Stephan Griller, ed. 2003).

making within international organizations. Thus, for example, WTO decision making is effected by consensus, despite provisions of the WTO Charter that permit decision making by majority. Furthermore, most significant decisions, aside from dispute settlement, are effected through treaty amendment, which requires individual state consent. If we ignore the differences between a requirement of consensus (no objection) and a requirement of unanimity (express assent), these methods are consistent with the general system of treaty making and amendment in international law. These methods are also consistent with the pre-Single European Act (1987) method for legislation in the European Community: unanimity, or at least no objection, was required for legislation. Interestingly, in both the European Community prior to 1987 and in the WTO today, formal provisions for majority voting are ignored in favor of rules of unanimity.

I have suggested that there may be a kind of dynamic imbalance, or cascade, leading from strong dispute settlement to greater capacity for legislation: from one type of enabling constitutionalization to another. There is a dynamic relationship between enabling constitutionalization of the judicial type and the legislative type. Strong dispute settlement at the international level might not immediately be recognized as enabling international constitutionalization. However, to the extent that strong international dispute settlement is understood as contributing to the capacity to make law at the international level, its establishment must be understood as a type of enabling international constitutionalization.

Thus, in 1995, at the inception of the WTO, including its Dispute Settlement Understanding, the global community engaged in a type of enabling international constitutionalization. In fact, in functional terms (as opposed to formal terms), the WTO exhibits no other significant features of enabling international constitutionalization. That is, its main transnational (as opposed to intergovernmental) feature is dispute settlement.

Consensus- or unanimity-based decision making presents a significant formal limitation. By "limitation" I do not mean to convey a negative judgment: it may be that this limitation is normatively attractive in particular contexts. The limitation is that unanimity – especially in a multilateral context – makes legislation exceedingly difficult. In formal terms, any legislative measure must present benefits to each state: there is no room to achieve legislative transactions that are potential Pareto efficient but that harm one state – even a small state – even mildly. Thus, much welfare is left on the table. This formal limitation thus cries out to be overcome. In fact, we might say that a formal unanimity-based system involves no enabling international constitutionalization at all: all decisions are still dependent on each member's determination.⁴⁵³ There are formal and informal methods by which to overcome this limitation. The formal method is to write or amend international organization treaties to provide for majority voting. The informal method is to engage in logrolling-type transactions, or package deals that, on a net basis, benefit all parties. In a sense, enabling constitutionalization may be understood simply as a particularly broad package deal.

Interestingly, as suggested, the requirement of consent or unanimity-based decision making cannot be defended by a reference to democracy. It can only be defended by such a reference to the extent that the national desire is negative or defensive – to the extent that the goal is to defeat legislation that may be adverse, in contrast with a goal to pass legislation that is beneficial. This can easily be seen where a single state has the capacity to block decisions that are desired by the overwhelming majority of states.⁴⁵⁴ This cannot be explained in terms of democracy.

Furthermore, for a similar reason, the requirement of consent or unanimity-based decision making cannot be defended by a reference to rights, or national autonomy. We might begin by saying that a decision rule of unanimity in international law protects national autonomy, just as a supermajority or unanimity rule in municipal legislation protects individual autonomy. However, again, this is seen purely from a defensive standpoint, where autonomy means being left alone, and does not include the ability to influence the behavior of others. For, assuming for a moment that a state has equal interests in avoiding constraints on its behavior and procuring constraints on other states' behavior, then any voting rule should be equally attractive to any other voting rule. What you lose in legislation constraining others you gain in autonomy, and vice-versa. However, if there is a surplus to be gained from making a certain amount of international law, a constitutional arrangement that results in a less-than-optimal amount of international law is undesirable.

Of course, where you expect to be in the minority more often – where you expect the costs of lost autonomy to exceed the benefits of constraints on others – that reduced capacity to legislate becomes attractive. Under these circumstances, a rule of unanimity or supermajority rule would be desirable.

---

⁴⁵³ On the other hand, if we take a step farther back, we might understand the rule of pacta sunt servanda as a type of enabling international constitutionalization.

⁴⁵⁴ A good example is the 2008 rejection by Ireland of the proposed Treaty of Lisbon, establishing a constitutional structure for the EU. In response, German interior Minister Wolfgang Schäuble made the following statement: "Of course we have to take the Irish referendum seriously, but a few million Irish cannot decide on behalf of 495 million Europeans." Stephen Castle and Judy Dempsey, "Rejection of Treaty Hints at Split in EU," *Int'l Herald Trib.* 1 June 16, 2008.

However, it may be even more desirable for other states to compensate you in advance for your willingness to accept an arrangement that is otherwise efficient.

This perspective explains constitutional moments. A constitutional moment would occur when an exogenous shock changes constituent perceptions of the value of legislation. Constituents would be expected to engage in enabling constitutionalization when the anticipated value of constraint on others rises in relation to the anticipated cost of lost autonomy. Changes in technology, or increasing globalization, might raise the value of constraint.

However, assuming that logrolling, package deals, linkage, side payments, or vote buying are possible without transaction costs, we would expect the efficient level of constraint and autonomy to emerge under any voting rule, just as an efficient allocation of property rights would arise in domestic society under zero transaction costs. So the choice of a voting rule must be on the basis of differential transaction costs. How is this transaction–cost-based explanation consistent with the idea that constitutional moments arise from changes in the value of legislation – from transaction benefits? Constituents would examine the combination of transaction benefits and costs: an increase in transaction benefits would justify greater transaction costs; a decrease in transaction costs would enable the achievement of transaction benefits that were otherwise out of reach. Changes in transaction benefits result from changing technology, preferences, social structures, or other factors, which are not likely to be immediately malleable through purposive action. On the other hand, the transaction-cost component of the equation may be addressed through purposive action, in the form of enabling constitutionalization, assuming that changes in voting rules have effects on transaction costs.

Therefore, in theory, whereas enhanced dispute settlement may increase the possibility that enhanced legislative capacity at the WTO would be desirable, much depends on the question of whether sufficient impetus in the form of transaction gains or costs would motivate states to move toward some form of voting. This type of shift seems to have taken place in the 1980s in the EU.[455]

Interestingly, a move toward enabling international constitutionalization in the form of enhanced legislative capacity would demand a move toward constraining international constitutionalization. In this case, constraining international constitutionalization might take the form of restrictions on the subject matter of legislative capacity exercised at the WTO, as well as human-rights limitations on the types of measures that could be legislated.

---

[455] See Trachtman, supra note 50.

I) ACCOUNTABILITY AND THE DEMOCRACY DEFICIT

As previously suggested, accountability is a subtle concept, as is the idea of a democracy deficit. The subtlety arises from the conundrum of positive legislative capacity versus negative (or blocking) legislative capacity. The principle is that democracy in the sense of majority rule is not necessarily enhanced by supermajority provisions – or by other devices that constrain international governmental action – because these devices prevent the majority from achieving its goal. This issue is at the core of most claims of "American unilateralism" – many of these are claims that the United States fails to join a multilateral treaty, such as the Kyoto Protocol or the Rome Statute of the International Criminal Court, thereby defeating the will of the majority.

Furthermore, once we think of democracy in terms of accountability, the international setting and possibility of externalities adds an interesting wrinkle. Under externalities that are addressed by international law, the international law makes the restricted state accountable to foreign persons who are affected by the restricted state's actions. Thus, reducing the scope of international law only shifts control away from affected persons to less affected persons: a reduction of accountability. So, the so-called democracy deficit often alleged to be caused by international law might be understood as simply erroneous, at least insofar as the international law is well-designed to give affected persons control over policy. On the other hand, it is certainly possible that international legal commitments are used by national regimes in order to defeat domestic democratic accountability. So no generalized conclusions can be reached regarding the relationship between the growth of international law and government and the overall accountability of government.

In addition, it is necessary to link any international organization's constitution to its member states' constitutions. To the extent that the international organization is truly a member organization – an international as opposed to transnational organization – perhaps the democracy-deficit critique is misguided, and the real question is one of member-state democracy. Thus, under circumstances of decision making by unanimity, direct accountability at the international level would not serve as constraining international constitutionalization, as there is little capacity at the international level to constrain. It might be understood as a type of supplemental constitutionalization: addressing an accountability issue that arises with globalization. The accountability issue under these circumstances of decision making by consensus must be that the national government is not sufficiently accountable at home, in connection with the commitments it accepts within the international-organization forum. Alternatively, if the concern is that even under a rule of unanimity, some member states lack sufficient influence in the international organization, perhaps the democracy deficit would be addressed through empowerment of those states, rather than the addition of parliamentary control at the international-organization level.

However, under circumstances of decision making by majority, arrangements for direct accountability may be understood differently, as a type of constraining constitutionalization. As constraining constitutionalization, accountability measures would ensure that decision making is accountable to constituents. Constituents desire procedures that ensure their voices are heard, especially under majority voting, where they have accepted their preferences may not hold sway.

In this context also, under majority voting, concern for fundamental rights serves as a form of constraining international constitutionalization, specifying areas into which international legislation may not infringe. Thus, if majority voting were implemented at the WTO, it would seem appropriate to also implement a set of human-rights constraints on the decisions taken by majority vote. A similar process took place in the EU, where the *Solange* decisions gave rise to the establishment of an EU human-rights capacity.

J) DISPUTE SETTLEMENT, SUPREMACY, AND DIRECT EFFECT

There is an important quasi-legislative role for dispute settlement to play at the international level. Often, this role is one of elaboration and application of general standards set by legislatures. This is in opposition to more specific rules, as discussed in Chapter 9.

Often, in connection with EU legal affairs, supremacy and direct effect are noted as features of constitutionalization. Indeed, these features – along with judicial review – are seen as the central features of constitutionalization, or at least of judicial constitutionalization. However, these features of EU law must be understood primarily as constitutionalization at the domestic level: they enabled EU law to have constitution-like power at the domestic level in the EU context. They act to restrict the scope of ordinary law at the domestic level, and thus play a quasi-constitutional role at that level. The same would be true in the case of supremacy and direct effect of any other international law. Interestingly, of course, international law is already supreme over municipal law within the international legal system (of course, the same was true of the Treaty of Rome). However, it is within the domestic legal system that this supremacy, and effect, is contested. So, in connection with supremacy and direct effect, the interesting international aspect is the source of the domestic constitutional rule: whether it is a matter of domestic law or international law.

The main point, however, is that supremacy and direct effect are generally only constitutional in the domestic legal system, and not in the international legal system.

Before we move on, concluding that the discussion of supremacy and direct effect as international constitutional issues is merely a category mistake, we must note that there is another, more subtle, effect that can be understood in terms of international constitutionalization. Under the prevailing horizontal structure of the international legal system – with only limited mandatory adjudication, and where even such adjudication as exists cannot generally form the basis for strong enforcement – international law often lacks the compliance force of municipal law. However, direct effect allows the international legal system, and such international law as is directly effective, to take advantage of the strong compliance force provided by the municipal legal system. In this sense, direct effect is a component of enabling international constitutionalization: it provides legislative capacity to the international system by lending the relevant international law greater force than it would otherwise have. Supremacy within the municipal setting plays a similar role.

## K) REDISTRIBUTION

The work of John Rawls fits well into the constitutional-economics tradition.[456] His veil of ignorance can be understood as a means to simplify negotiations of constitutional principles by putting the particular distributive consequences in the background. He uses this mechanism to speculate on the principles that would be agreed. One of the principles relevant here is the *difference principle*, which holds that economic inequality can only be justified to the extent that it redounds to the benefit of the poorest. To the extent that trade liberalization may cause increased economic inequality, it would appear appropriate to develop a redistributive mechanism in order to ensure that an appropriate portion of the benefits from free trade are redistributed to the poor.

This constitutional principle could be converted into positive constitutional law through negotiations. Constitutional reforms may be a necessary part of a redistributive settlement in the international legal system. These constitutional reforms may include a modification of decision making that would provide more power to the poor, or the establishment of rights that effect redistribution to the poor.

Similarly, the embedded-liberalism concept of Karl Polanyi and John Ruggie may also be understood within the constitutional-economics tradition.

---

[456] *See* Mueller, *supra* note 198.

Under this concept, mechanisms for redistribution through regulation are a price to be paid to those who would otherwise lose from liberalization, in order to ensure the continuity of the benefits of liberalization. To avoid disruption of this global society, by demarches in trade, economic catastrophes or violent upheavals in member states, or terrorism, it is morally and politically necessary to develop mechanisms to enhance the position of the poor.[457]

## L) AN INTERNATIONAL DEMOS?

Is it necessary to have a demos in order to have a constitution, and does the WTO have one? Joseph Weiler points out that the EU itself lacks a constitutional demos, and so is not rooted in a central federal-type power.[458] Existing international organizations, such as the UN or the WTO, have much less of a constitutional demos. Claims of existence of a demos are on the basis of a type of cultural or ethnic affinity that motivates loyalty to a social structure. Indeed, a shared history – with its attendant values, concerns, and camaraderie – may be understood in institutional economics terms itself, and may indeed shape behavior. These informal institutions may be seen as complements or substitutes for formal constitutional structures, depending on the circumstances.

Although constitutional economics tends to highlight formal institutions – and would not ordinarily be demos dependent – it is open to the possibility that cultural or ethnic factors may enter its analysis, either as informal institutions or as preferences of two types. First, we may prefer a society composed of our compatriots in a cultural or ethnic sense. Second, we may have a greater preference for altruism vis-à-vis our cultural or ethnic compatriots than vis-à-vis others.

Constitutional economics is allied with the concept of constitutional patriotism – it highlights not the exogenous cultural or ethnic causes of constitutional loyalty, but the structural and contextual reasons why a constitution allows the greater satisfaction of individual preferences. However, constitutional economics recognizes the place of shared experience and characteristics, in terms of informal institutions and preferences.

So, the lack of an international demos today does not stand in the way of the existence of international constitutional law. It does, however, suggest that

---

[457] Trachtman, *supra* note 400.
[458] Joseph H. H. Weiler, "Federalism and Constitutionalism: Europe's Sonderweg," *in The Federal Vision: Legitimacy and Levels of Governance in the US and the EU* (Kalypso Nicolaidis & Robert Howse, eds., 2001); *See also* Jurgen Habermas, "Why Europe Needs a Constitution" 11 *New Left Review* (2001). Retrieved from http://www.newleftreview.org/A2343.

constitutional law at the international level would be different – in terms of the informal complements and preferences for solidarity – from a typical image of a national constitution.

## M) CONCLUSION: THE LEVEL OF ANALYSIS PROBLEM

This discussion shows that the international legal system indeed has a constitution, with enabling, constraining, and supplemental features. A constitutional matrix is a useful tool of taxonomy, but it cannot answer the question – at any particular level – of what constitutional features are needed. Rather, it is constitutional economics that provides the answer to this question. Constitutional economics examines the existing structure for decision making and evaluates the existing structure in comparison to other potential structures as a device for producing legal rules. It recognizes that it may be costly to fail to produce legal rules that could benefit citizens, and that it may also be costly to produce legal rules that harm citizens. So constitutional economics assumes that states, in the international-constitutionalization process, use enabling constitutionalization, constraining constitutionalization, and supplemental constitutionalization to establish the types of constitutions that are optimal. Optimal constitutions are those that maximize the benefits of production of international law, net of transaction costs.

Of course, there is a public-choice critique of this optimistic picture: the establishment of constitutional rules is an exercise of power, and constitutional discourse may constrain the good and enable the bad. This is the human condition, and it applies to all law. However, men and women have found it good to depart anarchy and establish constitutional rules in many contexts.

The most difficult work will be at the margins – at the places where different constitutions engage one another. These places will require delicate management. Delicate management does not necessarily require formal, specific, legal rules; in fact, it seldom does in the most important areas. Rather, it is not unusual to find these marginal areas ruled by comity in the form of mutual deference, by muddy rules that give rise to negotiations in specific cases, by threats, and by conflict. This is true even in the domestic setting. For example, there are many areas in U.S. constitutional law of give and take, uncertainty, and conflict. If such murkiness were simply wrong, or inefficient, would it not have been addressed by now?

Where rules, or standards, are developed in order to mediate between the constitutions of different international organizations, or between the constitutions of international organizations and those of states, we might understand these as tertiary rules. Constitutional economics can provide a perspective and

# International Legal Constitutionalization

set of tools that can be brought to bear on whether tertiary rules are needed, and what their structure should be. For example, the perspective of constitutional economics would endorse a rule of constitutional subsidiarity, allocating authority at the constitutional level that may address the relevant issue most efficiently. Furthermore, a kind of interfunctional rule of constitutional subsidiarity, allocating authority to the international organization best able to address the relevant issue, is also consistent with constitutional economics.

Earlier parts of this book have shown that there will be increasing demand for international law in a number of areas, on the basis of existing and future conditions. Globalization will increase demand for supplemental constitutionalization. More importantly, the functional demand for increasing international law will result in increasing demand for enabling constitutionalization. Increasing demand for enabling constitutionalization will bring with it demand for constraining constitutionalization. It is not a contradiction to say that as the international legal system becomes more powerful, it will require greater constraint. In other words, as the international legal system looks more like a government, it will require greater limitations.

## 12   Conclusion: Functionalism Revisited

> The European Community movement is a possible precursor of a future universal integration of mankind, but meanwhile it must be regarded as a distinct type of evolution in international law and relations.[459]
>
> Europe will not be made all at once, or according to a single plan. It will be built through concrete achievements which first create a de facto solidarity.[460]

This book has analyzed a number of different present and future dimensions of the potential utility of international law. Each dimension is important and highly variable, and so it would be impossible to assemble the components into a comprehensive and detailed specification of the requirements for international law. In the broadest terms, however, this book has shown reasons to expect increasing demand for international law in a number of areas, but not in all areas. Thus, we can expect increasing density of international law.

The demand for increasing density of international law will arise organically, through the demands of individuals on their states for better government addressing issues that cross borders. The demand for more international law in particular areas will give rise to demand for greater capacity to legislate international law. The border between national politics and international politics will grow increasingly indistinct.

This increasing density will give rise to increasing natural and created relationships between different areas of international law. In order to manage optimally incomplete international legal rules, including optimally incomplete specification of how different international legal rules will interact with one another, there will be increasing demand for adjudicative capacity in international law.

[459] Friedmann, *supra* note 1, at 19.
[460] Robert Schuman, "The Schumann Declaration" (May 9, 1950).

There will also be increasing demand for mechanisms to enforce some existing and new rules of international law more reliably. This will include mechanisms for surveillance, but will also include stronger mechanisms for coercive enforcement. These mechanisms for coercion need not be military, but will be designed to transcend narrow self-enforcing contracts through stronger punishment of violation.

These institutions of legislation, adjudication, and enforcement, as they develop organically – functionally – will seem increasingly governmental. It may be, as the functionalists predicted, that the growth of these governmental institutions, and the growth of their responsibilities, will increasingly induce individuals to see these international governmental institutions as important in their lives. This type of development has been observed, on a smaller scale, in connection with the growing governmentality of the federal government of the United States or the EU.

## A) INCREASING DENSITY, COMPLEXITY, FRAGMENTATION, AND SYNERGY IN INTERNATIONAL LAW

Although it has only addressed a few of the fields of international law, this book has shown an increasing need for international law of greater variety, complexity, and power. Conditions today exhibit this need, but a look at the medium-to-long horizon shows an even greater need, as well as a capability, for establishing greater international law. This is a look at the future, but a realistic one that seeks to take a hard look at imminent social needs. The most realistic, and practical, response is to plan and establish structures that can increase global welfare in light of these conditions.

Chapters 5–9 develop a vocabulary of increasing variety and complexity with which to discuss international-cooperation problems: externalities, jurisdiction, reciprocity, asymmetry, coordination problems, prisoner's dilemmas, chicken games, public goods, aggregation technologies, and state-contingent contracting. Whereas there are certainly some common structures of cooperation opportunities, each area – indeed each commitment – will have a different set of parameters, invoking a different institutional response. Although I have tried to highlight and concretize different parts of this vocabulary in each chapter, each international-cooperation issue displays elements of each of these concepts. For example, international public health includes significant externalities and public goods. The public-goods problems vary within international public health, involving different aggregation technologies. There are linkage issues with migration, intellectual-property protection, and so forth.

The structure of international legal rules and organizations will often be dictated by the type of cooperation problem the rules or organizations are intended to address. It is important to note that each international law setting is likely to have a different profile. So the type of international law and organization that results will differ for each rule. Furthermore, each state is likely to enter the international law market with different needs and demands. Parameters include the magnitude of externality, the degree of asymmetry between states, the extent of excludability, the extent of non-rivalry in consumption, and the aggregation technology for public goods. Once we have answers to these questions, the next step is to identify the likely payoffs and evaluate the likely incentives of states. This can often be done using existing game theory models, such as the prisoner's dilemma. If we see that likely behavior will differ from the most efficient behavior, there may be a role for international law to modify the payoffs, either through explicit penalties, or by linking behavior in this game to behavior in other games.

So, each international cooperation issue has a complex, multifaceted structure. Moreover, once a particular cooperation issue is linked with another, whether within or without the same subject heading, it becomes a blend that displays a different profile with different emphases among these elements. The future of international society bodes only an increase in the quantity and complexity of international cooperation issues, and therefore will require an increase in the density, variety, and complexity of international legal responses.

Existing law does not always seem to match existing conditions because laws are generally self-conscious responses, on the basis of analysis and ideas, to observed social conditions. Our observation is always of the past. We drive by looking in the rearview mirror. Therefore, law can often be expected to lag social change. The resulting conservatism might be understood in behavioral terms as a product of an availability bias: until we actually observe the problem, we are not motivated to act. Even once we observe a problem, the fundamental bias of government is conservative. This conservatism is sometimes pragmatic, avoiding solutions to problems before they arise and therefore waiting until problems arise before devising responses. However, conservatism can also be erroneous.

Despite our reference to the past, as a practical matter, all law (except ex post facto law) addresses the future: law is intended to modify or at least respond to behavior in the future, and therefore always makes assumptions about future conditions. However, most law seems to be made with the near future in mind. Of course, from a practical standpoint, it is not useful to think far into the future, because it is too difficult to know how our decisions today will affect our position in a far-off future. More troubling, our tendency is to take inadequate account of the position of future generations: we are selfish vis-à-vis our heirs.

This book predicts the intensification of the international law of cooperation in a number of areas and for a number of reasons. The causes are bottom-up, related to expected social change as described in Chapter 4 and elsewhere herein. The demand for international law arises from externalities, public goods, and economies of scale, but it is true – as Coase first pointed out – that not every externality is an occasion for law, so states must perform a cost-benefit analysis – including transaction costs and strategic barriers – to determine whether cooperation is useful and formal law is the appropriate mechanism for cooperation. In each of the substantive areas I have examined, there are clear instances of significant externalities, public goods, and economies of scale. These are significant enough that it seems likely that international cooperation would be beneficial.

This book examines particular areas in which cooperation seems to have some utility, evaluates some relevant future trends that may bear on the utility and possibility of cooperation, and suggests how international law may respond to consequent demand for cooperation. This is a bottom-up approach, but in order to move up, we also need to look at the entire picture. The demand for international law in a variety of areas has implications for the supply of and demand for international law in other areas. The whole is definitely different from the sum of its parts, and likely to be greater. The increasing density of international law will provide economies of scale and scope, and will increase the enforceability of international law, making it more useful. This results in further density.

## B) INTERNATIONAL LAW AND DOMESTIC LAW

The approach taken in this book is social-scientific, and methodologically individualist. How does the individual exert influence in international law? The basis for international law is generally to be found in domestic politics, where – especially under increasing democratization – the individual expresses his preferences through the domestic political system. The individual still largely expresses preferences in the international political and legal system through the agency of his national government. However, we must examine domestic politics to determine how international law is made and enforced.

The understanding of the state as agent or trustee of the people is antimonarchic, and democratic. It seems increasingly reasonable, and common, to view states this way. Governments do not govern, but serve. Within this democratic model, individuals and groups will advocate policies that promote their own preferences. With globalization and the increasing global impact of all sorts of policies heretofore seen as domestic, these preferences will include action or inaction by other states, or by the citizens of other states. Citizens in domestic politics will have preferences regarding international law. Moreover, the possibility of international agreements not only provides the possibility for greater welfare, but also the possibility for political coalitions that could not exist if the international arena did not exist. The possibility of international agreement can be seen as a shock to otherwise-existing domestic political equilibria.

Although we do not have a continuous transnational political system, international law provides a mechanism that can link domestic lobbies transnationally. Indeed, by virtue of the expansion of the scope of the possibilities for Pareto improving political transactions, the international extension of the scope of domestic politics, where it occurs, would generally be expected to increase domestic welfare.

Thus, the scope of domestic politics is extended by the capability of entering into international agreements. How else can we expect to engage in discourse regarding international externalities and public goods? International law and international organizations are the formal mechanisms for dealing with governmental issues that extend beyond the state.

As technology, demography, globalization, and democracy grow, they tend to increase the scope and magnitude of international externalities and public goods. All of the social trends that make it necessary to increase the scope and density of international law at the same time make the formal bounds of the state insufficient to efficiently govern important matters.

Thus, the availability of international law as a general tool is important to each government, and for this reason, each government will have at least some interest in supporting the international legal system. Indeed, there is a networkexternality effect with respect to international legal compliance. As international law becomes more extensive and intensive, and more important to the delivery of government services, the interest of government in maintaining the international legal system will increase. So, as international law grows, it grows stronger. Furthermore, as it grows stronger it will be more useful for a wider range of tasks, causing the scope of international law to become more extensive. Formation and compliance with international law is dependent on the identification and negotiation of efficient transnational political linkages. Therefore, as explained in Chapter 3, international law is the link between domestic political systems, allowing the creation of ad hoc international political systems through international legal contracting.

With increasing density and complexity of international law, and international organization, we will see the functional growth of an international

# Conclusion

political system. This is the prediction of functionalism, on the basis of cooperation needs that already exist and that will arise in the future. This international political system is shaped by functional needs. It will not be designed as a system from the top down, but will be designed organically and gradually by social need.

## C) ASYMMETRY AND ENFORCEMENT

Furthermore, our need is not just for more of the same. We need a variety of international legal structures, varying with the parameters of the cooperation issue. International law will vary in its enforceability, but under circumstances of strong asymmetry, with strong incentives for defection, cooperation can only be supported by strong enforcement measures.

The international law scene is characterized by asymmetry in virtually every field. So, it is often necessary to make side payments of various kinds, or to link different types of commitments, in order to reach agreement. This asymmetry also must often be addressed in connection with enforcement: states that are unconcerned with a particular issue are also likely to be unconcerned with respect to retaliation, or reversion to a Nash equilibrium of no international legal rule, with respect to that same issue.

In the longer run, development will result in greater homogenization of wealth, and greater symmetry. Along with greater symmetry will come greater opportunities for cooperation. However, in the medium-term, characterized by great asymmetry, there will be greater need for international law that can overcome asset specificity to allow inter-temporal exchange of commitments. For example, consideration provided early by wealthy states in exchange for consideration provided later by current poor states.

Therefore, the medium-term future of international law will require increasing capacity for side payments and linkage. Inter-functional linkage is critical to making and enforcing international law. Explicit linkage may become less important to enforcement of an international legal rule, by virtue of implicit linkage of any particular rule of international law to all other areas of international law.

Some of the world's most difficult problems, such as global warming and the relative values of currencies, will require rather long-term contracting, with states making substantial concessions in early years in expectation of reciprocity much later. This extremely high level of asset specificity will put great pressure on the reliability of international law. States will only enter into the needed long-term contracts if they are enforceable.

This type of long–term-contracting capability, and strong enforceability, will be required by particular types of cooperation problems that have great amounts at stake over extended periods. The economists' perspective, demanding that all law be self-enforcing in the short-term, is ignorant of the networked power of law. More importantly, it assumes international law to be impotent to address long-term, highly asset-specific, and asymmetric cooperation problems. Domestic law has the capability of doing so, and as we identify the need to do so in the international setting, international law can be similarly empowered. The international legal system needs a way to facilitate inter-temporal exchanges of commitments, so that efficient inter-temporal bargains may be struck.

It may be difficult to imagine how international law could be made powerful enough to address highly asset-specific cooperation problems, without establishing first a central sovereign with a global monopoly on the use of force. However, as the international legal system becomes more dense, and more valuable to each state, the system itself becomes increasingly valuable, making each state increasingly reluctant to forego it. Consider the motivation of states to comply with their obligations under EU law.

In addition, more specific instruments of coercion short of a monopoly on force may be explored. For example, a system of monetary sanctions could be sufficient: it depends on the degree of asset specificity, and the magnitude of the monetary sanctions. How could monetary sanctions be enforced? They might be enforced by establishing a system of advance deposits, to be disbursed on the occurrence of specified events, similar to a letter of credit or escrow account. A softer system might remove certain international rights, such as the right to a vote at the UN, or to use the facilities of the IMF or international legal-dispute settlement, until a state makes the required payment.

### D) IS THE FUTURE OF INTERNATIONAL LAW SOFT?

I distinguish between informal cooperation and soft law on the one hand, and formal law on the other hand. Informal cooperation and soft law may arise from the international law of coexistence – from informal diplomatic transactions in the spot market – but are increasingly facilitated by transnational networks and other non-state actors. Soft law can be workable where there are not significant enforcement issues, as in cases in which the international issue has the characteristics of a coordination game. Soft law can also be workable where there are significant enforcement issues, but where the conditions for a self-enforcing contract are met. In these cases, the soft law is merely a way of conveying information regarding a focal-point equilibrium.

However, there will be important international issues that entail significant enforcement problems in which no self-enforcing contract can be established.

Under these circumstances, international law that links performance on one matter to performance on other matters, and that can provide remedies that overcome significant asymmetry or asset specificity, is necessary. By asset specificity, I simply mean that one state's performance may take place or become locked in before the other state's reciprocation, leaving the first state vulnerable to defection. Especially where agreements involve significant temporal lags, such as in the area of carbon reduction and monetary restraint, asset specificity may be very great indeed. Formal law carries with it a critical link to the rest of the formal law system that can enhance compliance significantly, and – less importantly – formal law can be designed to include formal penalties for violation.

Thus, where you have a truly self-enforcing agreement, informal cooperation or soft law are enough. However, economists who assert that all international law must be self-enforcing are declining to accept these unique features of formal law, which are the opposite of self-enforcing. Linkage to other areas of international law makes it possible that the narrow area of law will not be self-enforcing, drawing its enforcement power from the broader system, which may well be self-enforcing.

Thus, soft law has its place in promoting coordination, and even cooperation in some circumstances. However, the limitation of the domain of soft law is simply its softness. Although it may have social effects by forming a focal point, or by engaging community sanctions or approval of retaliation, it will often have less compelling power than hard law. For the more difficult range of cooperation problems, and especially those where there is significant asset specificity, hard law will be useful.

## E) LEGISLATION, ADJUDICATION, CONSTITUTIONALIZATION AND GOVERNMENTALITY

As the need for international cooperation becomes more extensive and intensive, and as the demand for international law increases, additional international legal mechanisms will be required. These mechanisms will be desirable to make it easier to make international law, and to impose needed constraints on the production of international law. These are constitutional mechanisms. Mechanisms will also be needed to complete incomplete contracts, where it is inefficient to seek to specify in advance how different tradeoffs between policies will be made.

As the demand grows for international law, facilitating constitutionalization will be necessary to allow for easier lawmaking. Facilitating constitutionalization is also a kind of very broad reciprocity under a Harsanyian veil of uncertainty: states are willing reciprocally to accept lawmaking structures where they are uncertain regarding the distributive impact of the structures. That is, where states can see broadly that new lawmaking structures are beneficial, and where the distribution of the benefits is uncertain enough for each state to feel that it has a fair chance to share appropriately in the benefits, it is possible to make a constitutional agreement in the facilitating constitutionalization vein.

With facilitating constitutionalization comes a need for constraining constitutionalization: it is not contradictory to say that new powers require new limits. With increasing globalization, supplemental constitutionalization will also become more important. Constitutionalization as a response to fragmentation will also grow in importance, because of the growth of international law, and the consequent congestion in international law. This type of constitutionalization may help provide coherence to a fragmented field.

This book represents an exercise in speculation about the future of international law. It adopts a functionalist approach. It does not adopt a top-down approach, suggesting that there should be a certain quantum of international law, or a certain type of global government. As to global government, I rather mildly observe that, on the basis of our cooperation needs going forward, the institutions we will require will increasingly look like government. When you consider the scope and magnitude of the international cooperation problems we face and will face, and the institutions that we use to solve similar problems within the domestic context, this hardly seems provocative, or even contentious.

I further speculate that the sum of this will be something that can usefully be called "government," bringing to bear all of our concerns and knowledge about institutional design of government. This is true in the mild sense that government is the name we give to the things we decide to do together, but there is more to it than that. The intensity and breadth of our legal cooperation will grow, over time, to resemble more a federal government than a series of contractual treaties.

## F) FUNCTIONALISM AND WAR

I describe this book's approach as functionalist in order to refer to the work of Mitrany, Haas, and their intellectual heirs, but I could just as accurately avoid that term, and describe the approach as social scientific or economic, or as constitutional economic, because the functionalism I adopt is fully subsumed within a social-scientific tradition. Indeed, I argue in Chapter 1 that functionalism and neo-functionalism made some modestly wrong turns, departing from what can be justified in social-scientific terms, but that after correcting for those mistakes functionalism can be well understood in social-scientific or economic terms.

This adapted approach has accurately predicted the growth of the EU, and the same type of dynamic applies to global society, mutatis mutandis. Despite recent reversals on the monetary front, the EU has found it useful to cooperate in a range of additional areas, using majority voting and centralized mandatory adjudication. It looks like government. Robert Schuman and Jean Monnet promoted the early European Community with more than an economic welfare goal in mind: they hoped to eliminate the possibility of war between France and Germany. So far, so good. Although writing in the late spring of 2012 it is uncertain whether the monetary union project will be abandoned or greater fiscal cooperation will be implemented in order to improve the stability and utility of monetary union, there is little doubt that the other features of the EU are stable.

Most futurist proposals about international law, since at least Kant's 1795 *Perpetual Peace*, have as their goals the end of war. They predict a movement toward the end of war, and suggest rules or institutions that will put an end to war. No one can predict what institutions the future will bring, or whether or when they will put an end to war. For this reason, I have avoided addressing this issue. The cooperation issues addressed in this book do not point toward an organically arising determination to establish a global monopoly on the use of force.

However, we can point to a long historical trend of ever-greater social units, where war within the greater social unit seems to become less likely. Indeed, there are social-scientific reasons for this, in terms of growing feelings of solidarity, understanding, networks of interrelation among national governments, integration of production and growing commerce with the attendant growth in the expected costs of war, and roles of international organizations such as the UN, WTO, or IMF in serving to manage and resolve international disputes. This, too, provides support to the functionalist vision. Most speculatively, and idealistically, "Mitrany argued that the successful growth of functional international organizations, fulfilling many of the welfare responsibilities previously reserved to the state, would create positive incentives for states to maintain the peace."[461] What is the source of these incentives? What is the mechanism by which functionalism causes peace?

Mitrany's argument that the successful functional organization of services will reduce the use of force between participants is on the basis of an appreciation of enlightened self-interest. If state authorities come increasingly to rely

---

[461] Mark F. Imber, "Re-Reading Mitrany: A Pragmatic Assessment of Sovereignty," 10 *Rev. Int'l Stud.* 103, 106 (1984).

on the technical and welfare services of international functional organizations in order to satisfy the aspirations of their citizens, then each government will become vulnerable to the dislocation of those services, insofar as it wishes to fulfill domestic political objectives.[462] So Mitrany's argument regarding peace is also on the basis of a social-scientific, cost-benefit analysis perspective: functional integration increases the costs of war. Lost opportunities owing to war for cooperation are real costs. Of course, additional mechanisms may be important, too. Economic integration provides opportunities for specialization, which can enhance welfare significantly. Greater specialization results in greater interdependence. These forces will also reduce incentives for war.

Is this argument borne out empirically? In the historical evolution of everbroader social units, we see examples of a seeming decline of armed conflict between internal constituent units. Athens no longer wars with Sparta, and Florence no longer wars with Milan. If we observe the growth of the United States, or of the EU, we might see in their suppression of internal warfare evidence for Mitrany's proposition. However, there are possible counterexamples in the United States and other civil wars, in the violent breakup of federal states such as Yugoslavia, and in the domestic ethnic violence of Rwanda, the Congo, or Somalia. On the other hand, a more refined study might show how these examples fit into a broader, more nuanced model. However, that more refined study is not available yet.

So it is difficult to speculate about a future in which war has been eliminated. It is likely that international law specifically restricting the use of force will soon be required finally to confess its impotence to eliminate war,[463] although this body of international law may make some marginal or even significant contribution to this outcome by increasing the costs and reducing the benefits of going to war.

Rather, social change, to some extent facilitated by other types of international law – the intensification of the international law of cooperation predicted by this book – will be the more reliable instrument of the elimination of international war. Again, the functionalist vision seems more appropriate than the deus ex machina vision of an international law that, if only we could formulate the right rules and build the right institutions, could eliminate war. The international law of cooperation, not rules against the use of force, will have the greater effect on reducing the use of force.

---

[462] *Id.* at 111.
[463] *See* Michael Glennon, *The Fog of Law: Pragmatism, Security, and International Law* (2010).

# Index

accountability, 4, 5, 6, 48, 71, 76, 77, 81, 83, 147, 167, 255, 267, 274, 277, 278, 282, 283
acculturation, 128, 137, 139, 141
Africa, 70, 76, 77, 79, 106
Allison, Graham, 41, 42
altruism, 125
American Society of International Law, 51, 56, 57, 58, 62
anarchy, 35, 90, 286
Arab Spring, 5, 92, 141
asset specificity, 20, 37, 38, 39, 40, 62, 77, 293, 294, 295
asymmetry, 2, 20, 25, 36, 40, 76, 77, 96, 98, 110, 114, 116, 119, 120, 122, 144, 145, 149, 150, 151, 152, 162, 163, 166, 167, 178, 193, 208, 209, 245, 289, 290, 293, 294, 295
availability bias, 67, 125, 126, 290

Barrett, Scott, 156, 158, 159, 166
Basle Committee on Bank Supervision, 31, 182, 187
Basle Committee on Banking Supervision, 250
BATNA, 47

capital regulation, 180, 182
chicken game, 113, 160
China, 12, 70, 71, 74, 75, 76, 78, 79, 174, 175
climate change, 20, 81, 149, 153, 155, 156, 161, 162, 163, 166
club good, 28, 29, 100, 151
Coase, Ronald, 26, 36, 37, 45, 91, 101, 149, 249, 251, 291
collective action problem, 28, 55, 83, 92, 101, 103, 111, 112, 121, 145, 211
collision. *See* fragmentation

common pool resources, 28
comparative impairment, 240
compliance, 10, 20, 24, 33, 34, 35, 37, 39, 40, 44, 46, 47, 48, 50, 51, 52, 53, 54, 55, 56, 57, 58, 59, 60, 61, 62, 63, 64, 65, 71, 82, 111, 113, 119, 120, 121, 127, 128, 130, 131, 134, 137, 138, 139, 140, 141, 143, 144, 156, 157, 159, 161, 165, 166, 167, 176, 189, 192, 217, 230, 238, 242, 246, 247, 248, 284, 292, 295
constitutional economics, 13, 16, 254, 256, 262, 263, 273, 284, 285, 286, 287
constitutional patriotism, 254, 285
constitutionalization, 2
  constraining, 255, 256, 257, 258, 259, 260, 265, 266, 267, 272, 275, 276, 277, 278, 283, 286, 287, 296
  enabling, 255, 256, 257, 260, 265, 267, 272, 274, 275, 277, 278, 279, 280, 281, 286, 287
  supplemental, 255, 259, 260, 265, 266, 267, 268, 275, 282, 286, 287, 296
constructivism, 17, 23, 31, 58, 136
Convention Against Torture, 129, 131, 132, 134, 138
coordination game, 37, 166, 294
customary international law, 54, 55, 148, 189, 226, 232, 235
cyberspace, 3, 19, 20, 85, 86, 88, 89, 90, 91, 92, 93, 94, 95, 96, 97, 98, 103, 104, 105, 107, 109, 110, 111, 112, 116
cyberterrorism, 96, 97, 98, 99, 100, 101, 102, 103, 104, 105, 106, 109, 110, 111, 112, 113, 114, 115, 116, 117

Dai, Xinyuan, 52, 53
democracy, 7
democracy deficit, 147, 269, 282, 283

299

democratization, 1, 4, 68, 70, 71, 76, 81, 83, 119, 141, 291
demography, 77–80
deposit insurance, 179, 185
development, 74–77
disease, 27, 147, 149, 150, 151, 152
dispute resolution, 14, 38, 39, 74, 237, 241, 271
Doha Round, 72

economies of scale, 3, 10, 21, 24, 25, 26, 27, 28, 40, 69, 170, 171, 190, 222, 228, 230, 242, 249, 291
Eichengreen, Barry, 184, 191
embedded liberalism, 10, 246, 284
environmental protection, 20, 35, 68, 76, 111, 144, 146, 162, 163, 166, 167, 217, 218, 224, 244, 262
Euro, 72
European Union, 11, 13, 14, 18, 30, 31, 94, 121, 125, 144, 183, 189, 219, 250, 256, 272, 275, 280, 281, 283, 285, 289, 294, 297, 298
externalities, 1, 3, 4, 14, 18, 20, 24, 25, 26, 27, 28, 29, 30, 33, 40, 45, 56, 66, 68, 73, 82, 92, 94, 98, 100, 103, 104, 106, 107, 109, 111, 113, 118, 120, 123, 124, 125, 126, 130, 141, 146, 147, 148, 149, 151, 152, 167, 168, 169, 170, 172, 173, 174, 177, 181, 184, 187, 193, 196, 197, 198, 200, 202, 203, 204, 206, 207, 213, 214, 221, 225, 227, 230, 250, 282, 289, 290, 291, 292

financial crisis, 27, 65, 69, 72, 168, 170, 171, 173, 174, 178, 180, 181, 182, 185
forum shopping, 217, 224, 230
fragmentation, 2, 9, 17, 20, 146, 149, 150, 166, 172, 180, 191, 217, 219, 221, 222, 223, 224, 225, 226, 227, 228, 229, 230, 231, 232, 237, 238, 244, 251, 270, 296
Framework Convention on Climate Change, 154
  Kyoto Protocol, 149, 153, 154, 155, 162, 165, 282
Frank, Barney, 7
free rider. *See* public goods
Friedmann, Wolfgang, 1, 3, 11, 18, 22, 118, 226
functionalism, 13–18, 42, 56, 65, 73, 260, 288, 289, 293, 296, 297

Generalized System of Preferences, 133
Glass-Steagall, 175, 184

global government, 9, 11
globalization, 69–74
Goodman, Ryan, 99, 136, 137, 140
Gourevitch, Peter, 44
governance, 8, 14, 31, 38, 74, 90, 91, 92, 94, 103, 107, 108, 116, 129, 173, 180, 184, 186, 222, 250, 265, 266, 267, 275, 278
Grossman, Gene, 48, 49, 50, 51, 52, 55, 60, 202, 203, 205
Guzman, Andrew, 32, 33, 131

Haas, Ernst, 14, 74
Hadfield, Gillian, 34
Hafner-Burton, Emilie, 131, 132, 133, 139, 140
harmonization, 30, 82, 150, 172, 176, 180, 181, 182, 183, 185, 189, 200, 201, 202, 276, 277
Harsanyi, John, 261, 262, 263, 295
Hathaway, Oona, 128, 129, 140
Helpman, Elhanan, 48, 49, 50, 51, 52, 55, 60, 205
Hollyer, James, 131, 132
Horn, Henrik, 198, 199, 200, 201, 204, 244
human rights, 135, 136
human rights treaties, 119, 121, 123, 124, 126, 127, 128, 129, 130, 131, 133, 134, 136, 137, 138, 139, 140, 143, 144, 145

incomplete contract, 20, 33, 39, 200
incomplete contracts, 6, 38, 106, 190, 194, 200–201, 214, 215, 224, 226, 230, 244, 295
India, 12, 70, 71, 75, 76, 78, 79, 174
intellectual property, 3, 10, 19, 20, 27, 57, 77, 92, 123, 146, 150, 193, 201, 202, 203, 204, 213, 215, 245, 289
International Convention on Civil and Political Rights, 140
international economic integration, 18, 246, 249, 273
international government, 8–10, 13
International Monetary Fund, 174, 176, 187, 239, 249, 294, 297
international organization, 1, 11, 16, 17, 36, 37, 39, 42, 91, 93, 97, 98, 107, 109, 190, 191, 193, 221, 250, 251, 262, 265, 272, 273, 280, 282, 283, 287, 292
international organizations, 12, 13, 16, 17, 25, 29, 36, 41, 83, 88, 90, 191, 221, 222, 223, 227, 228, 229, 231, 239, 249, 250, 253, 265, 272, 279, 285, 286, 292, 297
isomorphism, 18, 137

# Index

Jinks, Derek, 136, 137
Johnston, Jason Scott, 243, 244
jurisdiction, 10, 25, 29, 38, 87, 88, 89, 90, 93, 94, 97, 98, 99, 104, 105, 106, 107, 108, 109, 169, 171, 172, 180, 184, 187, 223, 231, 237, 239, 247, 248, 250, 251, 259, 270, 276, 289
*jus cogens*, 225, 238, 256, 266
*jus gentium*, 12

Kant, Immanuel, 297
Kaplow, Louis, 242, 243

leakage, 73, 161, 162, 163, 164, 165, 167, 182, 191, 217
legitimacy, 57, 86, 131, 139, 249, 262, 263, 269
liberal theory, 42, 62
liberalization, 10, 35, 50, 55, 73, 122, 163, 175, 177, 183, 193, 195, 196, 197, 205, 207, 208, 209, 210, 211, 212, 213, 216, 217, 245, 246, 248, 275, 276, 278, 284, 285
linkage, 2, 20, 33, 46, 61, 141, 143, 154, 161, 166, 211, 212, 216, 220, 244, 245, 246, 247, 281, 289, 293
lobbies, 47, 48, 49, 50, 51, 52, 53, 55, 56, 58, 59, 60, 62, 63, 64, 142, 292
lock in, 63, 72, 134, 145

macroeconomic management, 40, 173, 174, 183, 191
market power, 194, 195, 196, 201, 203, 204, 205, 206, 209, 215
Mavroidis, Petros, 202
Meyer, Timothy, 32
migration, 3, 14, 19, 20, 68, 70, 71, 72, 79, 80, 141, 146, 147, 205, 206, 207, 208, 209, 210, 211, 212, 213, 215, 245, 289
Mitrany, David, 13, 15, 16, 17, 41, 42, 94, 296, 297, 298
Mo, Jongryn, 46, 47
Moe, Terry, 7, 15
monitoring, 27, 36, 37, 52, 53, 81, 82, 95, 98, 103, 113, 129, 141, 147, 171, 174, 178, 190, 191, 253, 289
Monnet, Jean, 94, 297
Moravcsik, Andrew, 42, 133
Mueller, Dennis, 125, 134, 141
multilateralism, 43, 63, 89
mutual recognition, 31, 183, 197, 198

Nash equilibrium, 37, 109, 114, 158, 160, 293

national treatment, 26, 169, 172, 197, 198, 199, 200, 201, 202, 215, 216, 276
neo-functionalism, 14, 15, 17, 296
network externalities, 19, 28, 40, 94, 104
new institutional economics, 13, 15, 16, 20, 254, 256, 260
North American Free Trade Agreement, 238

obsolescing bargains, 51
ozone, 149, 152, 153, 154, 155, 156, 157

Pareto efficiency, 36, 50, 51, 61, 64, 85, 119, 163, 212, 260, 261, 279, 292
path dependence, 18, 94, 116, 249
Posner, Eric, 143
price theory, 13, 16, 20, 132
prisoner's dilemma, 37, 54, 61, 62, 109, 112, 113, 156, 157, 158, 195, 196, 207, 209, 247, 290
proportionality, 172, 198, 199, 200, 201, 202, 216
public choice, 7, 8, 17, 23, 24, 46, 48, 57, 193, 194, 195, 196, 207, 212, 213, 241, 243, 286
  Heckscher-Ohlin, 208
public goods, 1, 4, 7, 8, 20, 25, 28, 29, 30, 33, 40, 54, 66, 68, 73, 76, 80, 82, 83, 91, 92, 100, 101, 103, 110, 111, 113, 118, 120, 126, 143, 144, 146, 149, 151, 152, 153, 154, 155, 156, 158, 160, 162, 163, 165, 167, 168, 170, 182, 187, 192, 193, 203, 204, 207, 220, 233, 289, 290, 291, 292
  weakest link, 29, 113, 151
public health, international, 18, 20, 144, 146, 150, 152, 289
Putnam, Robert, 43, 44, 45, 46

Rajan, Raghuram, 214
Rawls, John, 284
reciprocity, 7, 10, 26, 29, 35, 54, 55, 59, 60, 62, 63, 121, 122, 128, 129, 130, 139, 141, 142, 143, 170, 189, 208, 212, 215, 289, 293, 295
redistribution, 7, 8, 246, 284, 285
regulatory arbitrage. *See* regulatory competition
regulatory competition, 20, 25, 27, 29, 30, 31, 94, 108, 109, 123, 162, 171, 172, 177, 179, 181, 182, 185, 192, 222, 227, 250, 275, 276
reputation, 33, 62, 63, 121, 128, 129, 130, 131, 139
retaliation, 10, 34, 36, 39, 54, 55, 59, 60, 63, 116, 121, 128, 129, 130, 139, 143, 190, 230, 247, 293, 295
Risse, Thomas, 136

Rodrik, Dani, 5, 6, 175
Rosendorff, Peter, 131
Ruggie, John, 246, 284
rules versus standards, 244

Sandler, Todd, 144, 151, 153, 156
Schuman, Robert, 94, 297
second image, 44
secretariat, 27, 36, 253, 273
security, 95
self-enforcing contracts, 2, 31, 35, 36, 62, 163, 164, 166, 167, 248, 289, 294, 295
Sen, Amartya, 18
side payments, 141, 163, 164, 210, 211, 212, 246, 281, 293
Sikkink, Katherine, 136
Simmons, Beth, 121, 122, 124, 130, 132, 133, 134, 137, 138, 139, 143
soft law, 8, 29, 32, 33, 40, 77, 154, 182, 189, 294, 295
sovereignty, 5, 6, 10, 16, 18, 86, 87, 93, 105, 118, 128, 256, 257
Spagnolo, Giancarlo, 247
Spence, Michael, 73, 164, 174
spillover, 13, 14, 56, 74, 174
stag hunt game, 109, 112, 113, 156
Stiglitz, Joseph, 171
structural subordination, 237
stuxnet, 95
subsidiarity, 4, 6, 11, 17, 21, 24, 25, 39, 43, 83, 87, 90, 97, 100, 101, 107, 168, 194, 220, 221, 222, 223, 240, 257, 259, 272, 273, 275, 276
  constitutional, 287
  horizontal, 221
synergies, 16, 17, 21, 191, 220, 222, 227, 228

tariffs, 149, 194, 195, 196, 197, 198, 203, 204, 211, 245
technology, 80–82
territoriality, 87, 106
terrorists, 96, 136, 260
Tiebout, Charles, 29, 30, 108, 172
transaction costs, 13, 16, 26, 35, 36, 38, 82, 84, 86, 91, 92, 93, 103, 106, 107, 109, 149, 178, 196, 212, 229, 256, 260, 261, 262, 263, 281, 286, 291
two-level game, 45

United Nations, 76, 224, 249, 250, 258
  Security Council, 123, 250, 256, 258, 259, 271
United Nations Environmental Program, 224, 225, 239, 249, 272

Vienna Convention on the Law of Treaties, 224, 229, 232, 234, 236

war. *See* security
Weiler, Joseph, 285
Weingast, Barry, 34, 35, 248
Westphalian, 18, 68
Williamson, Oliver, 37, 38
World Health Organization, 150, 151, 239
World Trade Organization, 27, 31, 150, 151, 166, 175, 183, 191, 195, 196, 200, 204, 218, 219, 224, 225, 229, 232, 233, 234, 235, 236, 237, 238, 239, 246, 249, 250, 263, 266, 269, 272, 273, 274, 275, 276, 277, 279, 281, 283, 285, 297
  GATS, 26, 211, 213

Zingales, Luigi, 214

Made in the USA
Middletown, DE
23 November 2018